Cultural Competency
for **Public Administrators**

Cultural Competency
for **Public Administrators**

Editors **Kristen A. Norman-Major** and Susan T. Gooden

Routledge
Taylor & Francis Group

LONDON AND NEW YORK

First published 2012 by M.E. Sharpe

Published 2015 by Routledge
2 Park Square, Milton Park, Abingdon, Oxon OX14 4RN
711 Third Avenue, New York, NY 10017, USA

Routledge is an imprint of the Taylor & Francis Group, an informa business

Library of Congress Cataloging-in-Publication Data

Cultural competency for public administrators / edited by Kristen A. Norman-Major and
Susan T. Gooden.
   p. cm.
Includes bibliographical references and index.
ISBN 978-0-7656-2676-9 (hardcover : alk. paper)—ISBN 978-0-7656-2677-6 (pbk. : alk. paper)
1. Public administration—Social aspects—United States. 2. Executive ability—United States.
I. Norman-Major, Kristen A. II. Gooden, Susan.

JK421.C8 2012
353.70973—dc23   2011030532

ISBN 13: 9780765626776 (pbk)
ISBN 13: 9780765626769 (hbk)

Contents

v

Foreword

NORMA M. RICCUCCI

The cultural landscape of the United States has changed dramatically in the past several decades. As a field, public administration has sought not only to better understand these changes, but also to better manage the social changes within organizations to improve their overall effectiveness. During this epochal period in the nation's history, managing diversity became the order of the day. As the demography of the United States became increasingly diverse, so, too, did public organizations, through, for example, affirmative action efforts as well as a considerable body of case law upholding the legality and constitutionality of affirmative action programs throughout the country. Governments responded, albeit slowly, to the demographic changes in organizations by developing programs and policies to better manage their workforces. A solid body of research on diversity issues as well as social equity was generated by academics and practitioners of public administration, and certainly, diversity management programs remain an important tool for healthy organizations.

However, today there is recognition that the efficacy of government requires cultural competency. That is to say, the effective delivery of public services necessitates a workforce that is capable of interacting with a culturally variegated society. This critically informative book greatly moves the field forward toward achieving that important goal. As the editors astutely point out, in order "for public administrators to carry out their mission of serving the public, or community as a whole, they must have the skills to meet the diverse needs of all members of the population. Such skills are commonly referred to as cultural competency."

The framework of cultural competency is much more inclusive than traditional diversity programs. Cultural competency not only cuts across the lines of race, gender, and ethnicity, but also encompasses, for example, religion, sexual and gender orientation, language, ability, education, class, and income levels. While the significance of this issue seems axiomatic, the topic of cultural competency has received very little scholarly attention in the field of public administration. It is only the health care and social work professions that have called for the creation of culturally competent organizations and personnel. This seminal book, which includes chapters from preeminent scholars, moves the field of public administration in the right direction to ensure that cultural competencies are reflected in official policies and practices across all domains of public service.

The field of public administration is historically rooted in the managerial values of efficiency and effectiveness. Yet how can a field whose raison d'être is the provision of public services not have cultural competence as its architectural foundation? As this nation continues to grow more culturally diverse, the value of cultural competency, both in practice and pedagogy, grows exponentially, as this book makes clear. Thus the readers of this book will be exposed to new and innovative ideas that will develop their skill sets as students and practitioners of public administration and, ultimately, improve the delivery of public services. The various readings in this pioneering book will also help to establish a framework for future studies and research in the field. Overall, the book makes this imperative message resoundingly clear: cultural competence is the sine qua non of effective and efficient governance.

Cultural Competency
for **Public Administrators**

Cultural Competency and Public Administration

KRISTEN A. NORMAN-MAJOR
AND SUSAN T. GOODEN

Cultural competency is a characteristic of good government. It promotes effective delivery of services to a comprehensive and inclusive public. Governmental organizations are "indispensible to a secure and civilized life" (Goodsell 2004, 11). As the essays in this edited volume illuminate, cultural competency is fundamental to good government. It is not enough for our bureaucratic institutions to offer effective and accessible services to a few; it is our responsibility to offer these services to all. Is offering culturally competent services easy or convenient? Of course not. But neither ease nor convenience outweighs the core responsibilities of public administration. Our U.S. Postal Service delivers mail daily to all residences, which is neither easy nor convenient. However, it is fundamental to an inclusive and comprehensive mail delivery system.

Administrative mastery is a hallmark of good government (Mead 2004, 215) and is a public service value of American public administration. In defining public administration, it is important to look at both words—*public* and *administration*. Definitions of *public* consistently include language similar to the following:

- of, pertaining to, or affecting a population or a *community as a whole*
- done, made, or acting, for the *community as a whole*
- open to *all persons*
- pertaining or devoted to the welfare or well being *of the community*
- the people constituting a community, state, or nation. (Dictionary.com 2011)

Definitions of *administer* and *administration* include verbs such as *manage, supervise*, and *perform*. Public administration is both action-oriented and results-driven. Thus, by definition, in carrying out their work public administrators must serve all members of the community, not just selected parts, small groups, or particular individuals. The reality of this service to the whole is the need to recognize the diverse makeup of the population and the differing needs of the communities served. While the United States has a long history of including people from many cultures, races, income levels, religions, education levels, and abilities, the public sector has not always recognized the differing needs of communities and instead tried to get the population to fit into programs designed as one-size-fits-all. This lack of recognition of cultural differences often leads to development and implementation of ineffective, inefficient, and inequitable public services. Instead of serving the community as a whole or being open to all persons, programs and policies that lack recognition of cultural difference often leave part of the public out of public service.

Fundamentally, culturally competent public administration includes a "respect for, and understanding of diverse ethnic and cultural groups, their histories, traditions and value systems in the provision and delivery of services" (Bush 2000, 177). Within public administration, cultural competency has an important relationship to the implementation of representative bureaucracy, which calls upon governmental agencies to operate as representative political institutions of the public at large. As Bailey correctly notes, "to achieve active representation, more government employees will need to become culturally competent when carrying out their responsibilities" (Bailey 2005, 173).

WHAT THE UNITED STATES REALLY LOOKS LIKE

While some attention has been paid to the need to recognize difference, traditionally discussions of diversity have focused on issues of race, ethnicity, or gender. However, if the public sector is to serve the community as whole, public administrators must recognize that differences go much deeper than these three categories. Not only has the population of the United States become more diverse in terms of race, ethnicity, and country of origin, with growing "minority" populations in many areas, but also there is an increasing recognition of the need to pay attention to other differences that have always existed but have not always been recognized in the development and implementation of public policies. Slowly, the public sector is recognizing the need to move away from a dominant one-size-fits-all model of administration toward one that takes differing cultures, demographics, and perspectives into consideration. The chapters in this book are designed to further that process by examining an array of diversity areas.

RACE AND ETHNICITY

The U.S. Census Bureau estimates that in 2009 the U.S. population consisted of 307,006,550 people. The breakdown of this total by race and ethnicity is estimated as follows (U.S. Census Bureau 2010):

White, non-Hispanic	65.1%
Hispanic or Latino	15.8%
Black	12.9%
Asian	4.9%
American Indian/Alaskan Native	1.0%
Native Hawaiian/Pacific Islander	0.2%
Two or more races	1.7%

While the groups traditionally considered to be minorities in the United States still make up less than 50 percent of the population, their percentages are growing. Between 2000 and 2009, the black population increased by 11 percent, American Indian by 18.3 percent, Asian by 32.3 percent, Native Hawaiian by 25 percent, and Hispanic by 37.1 percent (U.S. Census Bureau 2011).

In looking at these figures, it is important to understand how the Census Bureau defines race and ethnicity. According to the instructions for the 2010 census,

> the racial categories included in the census form generally reflect a social definition of race recognized in this country, and are not an attempt to define race biologically, anthropologically or genetically. In addition, it is recognized that the categories of the race item include racial and national origin or sociocultural groups. People may choose to report more than one race to indicate their racial mixture, such as "American Indian and White." People who identify their origin as Hispanic, Latino or Spanish may be of any race. (U.S. Census Bureau 2009, 4)

Thus, for Census Bureau purposes, census data often blur the lines between race and ethnicity. Also important to consider is that ethnicity or country of origin is not separated out in the broad categories. That is, Asians include Chinese, Japanese, Korean, Indians, Vietnamese, Filipinos, and several other groups that have origins in the Far East, Southeast Asia, or the Indian subcontinent. Hispanics and Latinos include people with heritage in Mexico, Central America, South America, and Spain. Blacks include African Americans, Africans, and Haitians, and whites include those of European, Middle Eastern, and North African descent (U.S. Census Bureau 2010). Thus, the broad categories used in the census include people who may come from the regions defined by each category but also who may have very different cultures and ethnic backgrounds.

GENDER

According to 2009 figures from the U.S. Census Bureau, the United States is almost evenly split between males and females with a 50.7 percent female population (U.S. Census Bureau 2010). These figures assume a simple male/female gender distinction and do not account for transgender or other individuals who may not identify as simply male or female. Identification of gender, whether male, female, or other, is important in many areas of public administration, including labor and antidiscrimination laws and delivery of public health and social services.

AGE

The age distribution of a population is important for the public sector in determining program needs, predicting the tax base, and looking at workforce development issues. According to 2009 data, 6.9 percent of the U.S. population is under five years old, 24.3 percent is under eighteen, and 12.9 percent is over sixty-five (U.S. Census Bureau 2010). These differences are particularly important in looking at dependency ratios, meaning the relationship between people ages fourteen to sixty-five who make up the labor force and those under fourteen and over sixty-five who are often dependent on programs funded through income taxes collected from those in the workforce.

Of particular concern to policy makers and the shape of public services in the United States is the aging of the baby boom population. While those over sixty-five years of age currently constitute about 13 percent of the population, it is predicted that this number will increase to 19 percent by 2030. As the population ages, the demands made upon government will change, with more pressure put on the budgets of programs that support the elderly, such as Social Security and Medicare.

Ability

Approximately 51 million people or 18 percent of the population are considered to have a disability, including 12 percent who are classified as severely disabled. Some 11 percent of children between the ages of six and fourteen and 72 percent of people eighty and older are considered disabled (Disabled in Action n.d.). Disabilities—conditions that prevent individuals from carrying out varying tasks—include vision and hearing impairments, cognitive limitations, mental or emotional illness that severely interferes with daily activities, and ambulatory limitations such as use of a wheelchair, cane, crutches, or walker. Many individuals with both nonsevere and severe disabilities are employed. Census data from 2002 reported that 56 percent of people between twenty-one and sixty-four who have some type of disability had worked in the last year (Disabled in Action n.d.). The Americans with Disabilities Act of 1990 guarantees equal access and opportunities for those with disabilities on several fronts, including government services.

Religion

While the majority of the American population identifying itself as part of a religious tradition identifies as Christian, the numbers in other faiths are rising and the percentage of those identifying as Protestant may soon fall below 50 percent (Pew Forum 2008). According to a survey of 35,000 adults in the United States conducted by the Pew Forum on Religion and Public Life, 78.4 percent identified as Christian, with 51.3 percent as Protestant, 23.9 percent as Catholic, 1.7 percent as Mormon, and the remainder as Jehovah's Witness, Orthodox, or other Christian. In the same survey, 4.7 percent of the population identified with other religions, including Judaism, Buddhism, Islam, Hinduism, and Unitarianism, while 16.1 percent of the population was unaffiliated, including atheists and agnostics and those identifying as nothing in particular (Pew Forum 2008).

Despite the separation of church and state, religion affects the provision of public services. Debates regarding religion and public policy range from the inclusion of prayer in schools to provision of footbaths in public buildings for Muslim citizens to cleanse in before prayer. Issues also arise related to respect for religious preferences in the provision of public health services or food provided in public hospitals or schools that meets various religious practices. As these examples illustrate, public administrators are regularly faced with the development and implementation of policies that take religious preference and practice into account.

EDUCATION LEVEL

According to census data estimates, 80.4 percent of people over twenty-five are high school graduates and 24.4 percent have a bachelor's degree or higher (U.S. Census Bureau 2010). Often discussions of education focus on educational achievement gaps between white students and students of color. These differences are clearly illustrated by statistics on high school graduation and dropout rates. In 2009, 87.1 percent of whites, 84.1 percent of blacks, 88.2 percent of Asian and Pacific Islanders, and 66.9 percent of Hispanics had graduated from high school. In contrast, in 2008, 8.8 percent of white students, 12 percent of black students, and 22.3 percent of Hispanic students dropped out of high school. The highest dropout rate was for Hispanic males at 24.3 percent (U.S. Census Bureau 2011). Similar differences across race and ethnicity can be found in the data on college graduates. As of 2009, 29.9 percent of whites, 19.3 percent of blacks, 52.3 percent of Asians and Pacific Islanders, and 13.2 percent of Hispanics held a bachelor's or higher degree (U.S. Census Bureau 2011).

INCOME AND CLASS

Education level has a direct impact on income, and income in the United States is highly reflective of the education achievement data. In 2008 the median family income in the United States was $61,521 and 13.2 percent of the population lived below the poverty level, which was defined as $22,025 for a family of four (U.S. Census Bureau 2011). Median family income broken down by race and ethnicity is as follows:

Whites	$65,000
Blacks	$39,879
Asian	$75,578
Hispanic	$40,466

While 13.2 percent of the total population lived below the poverty level in 2008, the distribution across the races varied greatly, with 11.8 percent of whites, 24.7 percent of blacks, 11.8 percent of Asians, and 23.2 percent of Hispanics living below the poverty level (U.S. Census Bureau 2011).

As another measure, 2006 U.S. per capita income was $36,714. However, this ranged from a low of $9,140 in Loup County, Nebraska, to $110,292 in New York County, New York (Miller n.d.). Metropolitan areas tend to have much higher per capita incomes than nonmetro areas (Miller n.d.).

SEXUAL ORIENTATION

Currently, the U.S. Census does not specifically gather information on sexual orientation. What is found is gleaned from the census tracking of households where unmarried couples are counted. Based on the number of couples marking both members of the same sex, the Williams Institute at the UCLA School of Law estimates that in 2005 there were 8.8 million gay, lesbian, and bisexual people, both single and coupled, living in the United States (Romero et al. 2007). With a total U.S. population of approximately 300 million, 8.8 million constitutes about 3 percent. These figures are likely underestimates given both the lack of surveys asking about sexual orientation and continued fear and stigma that may prevent honest responses to such questions.

THE NEED FOR CULTURAL COMPETENCY

The diversity described by the previous demographics means that for public administrators to carry out their mission of serving the public, or community as a whole, they must have the skills to meet the diverse needs of all members of the population. Such skills are commonly referred to as cultural competency. The recognition of the need to develop cultural competency originated in the fields of health care and social work and has more recently made its way into discussions of public administration. Most work on cultural competency is found in literature on social work, health care, and K–12 education. However, the increasing awareness of the need to incorporate cultural competency into public administration was the main factor driving work on this book.

While there are several definitions of cultural competency circulating in the literature, for this work we asked authors to focus on the definition created by Terry Cross during his work at Portland State University with the Northwest Indian Child Welfare Institute. According to Cross, "cultural competence is a set of congruent behaviors, attitudes and policies that come together in a system, agency or professional and enable that system, agency or professional to work effectively in cross-cultural situations" (1988, 1). Cross goes on to explain his use of both *culture* and *competence*:

> The word culture is used because it implies the integrated pattern of human behavior that includes thought, communication, actions, customs, beliefs, values and institutions of a racial, ethnic, religious or social group. The word competence is used because it implies having the capacity to function effectively. (1)

Cross admits that fully achieving cultural competence may be idealistic and thus argues that agencies and individuals should see it as a goal to pursue that always includes room for growth, even at the highest level of competence. According to Cross's model, cultural competence develops along a continuum, with the first level being cultural destructiveness. This is the negative end of the continuum; behaviors at this end include cultural genocide and dehumanization of minority groups. The second step on the continuum is cultural incapacity. At this level agencies do not actively work to destroy a culture but do not have the capacity to serve minority members of the community. The third step, cultural blindness, is considered the midpoint of the continuum. At this point agencies tend to assume that all clients can fit into the culture of the majority and that the dominant culture's approaches to service are universally applicable.

At the fourth step in Cross's continuum, cultural precompetence, agencies and individuals begin to recognize "weaknesses in serving minorities" and attempt "to improve some aspect of their services to a specific population" (3). Basic cultural competence is the second-to-last stage in Cross's continuum. At this point agencies and individuals accept and respect difference and pay attention to the dynamics of difference in adapting service models to fit the needs of the populations served. Finally, advanced cultural competence is defined by Cross as the point where agencies and individuals hold culture in high esteem and work to "add to the knowledge base of culturally competent practice by conducting research, developing new therapeutic approaches based on culture and publishing and disseminating the results of demonstration projects" (3).

This model sets the stage for the work in this book, with authors examining how agencies and individuals move along the cultural competency continuum, what cultural competence looks like in action, and how we can prepare public administrators to incorporate cultural competency into policy development and implementation.

CULTURAL COMPETENCY, DIVERSITY, AND SOCIAL EQUITY

Along with asking them to focus on the definition of cultural competency developed by Cross, we also asked authors for this volume to focus on cultural competency as a concept distinguished from diversity and social equity. These three terms, *diversity*, *social equity*, and *cultural competency*, are often linked in the public administration literature and are sometimes used to refer to very similar things. While the three are clearly related, they refer to different aspects of serving traditionally underrepresented groups.

Discussions of diversity focus on the demographics of the population nationally as well as locally and within organizations. Understanding the diverse nature of the population sets the stage for discussions of representative bureaucracy, discrimination, civil rights, affirmative action, and civic engagement. Knowing the demographics of the public and communities to be served highlights the diverse needs of groups and can lead to work on cultural competency, but dealing with issues of diversity in and of themselves does not necessarily mean development of culturally competent policies and services.

George Frederickson (2010) and other public administration scholars have championed social equity as a core value of public administration since the first Minnowbrook conference in 1968.[1] Definitions of social equity vary from simple fairness and justice in the implementation of policy to leveling the playing field by providing extra support and services through targeted programs to groups that are traditionally underrepresented or suffer discrimination (Frederickson 2010; Svara and Brunet 2004). While cultural competency can play an important role in bringing equity to public services, it does not in and of itself solve issues of social inequity. While an important factor in building social equity, cultural competence is a distinct concept in the larger goal of bringing social equity to public administration.

In this book, the authors often note the relationship between diversity, social equity, and cultural competence because they are related and often interdependent.

However, the focus here is on moving public servants and agencies along the cultural competency continuum.

THE CHALLENGES OF CULTURAL COMPETENCY IN THE PUBLIC SECTOR

In trying to move public services along the cultural competency continuum, it is important to also recognize constraints that the public sector potentially faces. The demographic information presented earlier highlights the diverse range of people that constitute the American public. While the goal is to increase cultural competence in public services to this wide range of people, we must also consider limits brought on by budget constraints and competing goals, values, demands, and interests. Many questions are likely to arise: How many languages can be served? How much translation can we afford and which languages do we choose? How much accommodation is reasonable and affordable? Where does meeting the needs of one group potentially impinge on the rights of others? How do we balance varying ethics and cultural practices with the safety and well-being of community members? These questions are not always easy to answer, but they are critical to discussion of cultural competency and the role that the public sector plays in providing for our communities.

LAYOUT OF THE BOOK

PART I. CULTURALLY COMPETENT AGENCIES, POLICIES, AND PUBLIC SERVANTS

In the first section of the book the authors examine the qualities of culturally competent agencies, policies, and public servants. In Chapter 2, Mitchell F. Rice and Audrey L. Mathews—two of the pioneers in work on cultural competency in public administration—argue that it is time to solidify the inclusion of cultural competence in the practice of public administration, moving from ideas to firm theoretical frameworks and practices. Agencies that use the lens of cultural competency, they argue, improve the quality and delivery of programs and services to an increasingly diverse population. According to Rice and Mathews, a key factor in the development of this new culturally competent public service professional is the inclusion of education around needed cultural competency skills in the curriculum of public administration programs at the undergraduate and graduate level.

In Chapter 3, Shelly L. Peffer asks whether statutes that mandate cultural competency make a difference in ensuring the delivery of programs and services in a culturally competent manner. Peffer examines several statutory mandates in the areas of health, developmental disabilities, public education, family and child welfare, police and criminal justice, vulnerable individuals, and Native Americans. After looking at several examples of programs with such mandates, Peffer concludes that while statutory requirements help, they do not in and of themselves guarantee that programs will meet the cultural needs of the communities they serve since a key factor in the delivery of such programs is employee buy-in, which may be, Peffer argues, better gained if not forced.

The international aspects of cultural competency are highlighted in Chapter 4. Here, Chima Imoh examines the need for cultural competency when public servants are working abroad. Using the framework of a cultural dynamics orientation, he considers the cultural practices of various countries and the skills, awareness, and knowledge that public servants must possess in order to function effectively in them. The lessons conveyed in Imoh's analysis will be helpful not only to public servants serving abroad but also to domestically based public servants who find themselves, in the era of increased globalization, increasingly interacting with the international community.

In the final chapter of this section, Heather Wyatt-Nichol and Lorenda A. Naylor consider the role that human resources practices in federal agencies play in facilitating cultural competency. As federal employees work with an increasingly diverse population, both within their agencies and in their work with clients, human resources departments, they argue, are key in helping to develop cultural competency for workers and agencies. Wyatt-Nichol and Naylor examine factors such as the development of knowledge, skills, and abilities (KSA) requirements for job positions, the contents of performance appraisals, training programs, strategic plans, and capital plans to measure agencies' commitment to developing and supporting cultural competency.

PART II. CULTURAL COMPETENCY IN ACTION

The second section of this book is designed to consider cultural competency in relation to specific groups or policy areas. To begin the section, DeLysa Burnier uses the story of Frances Perkins (the first woman to serve as a cabinet secretary in the United States) to set the stage for a discussion of gender and cultural competency. Burnier argues that gender competency goes beyond simply having women in the workplace to considering the values, knowledge, and experiences women bring to the context of public service. In order to truly develop cultural competence, according to Burnier, it is also important to examine gender from the perspective of how it intersects with other factors such as race, ethnicity, class, and sexual orientation. Burnier concludes that in order to move forward on gender competency in public administration, the field must be serious in including these issues in training, teaching, and scholarship.

In Chapter 7, Abraham David Benavides reflects upon cultural competency in Hispanic communities. As the largest and fastest growing minority population in the United States, Hispanics are a vital part of the U.S. economy and of the communities in which they live. One challenge is that there is great diversity even within Hispanic communities, so programs and services that are designed to be culturally competent cannot be assumed to work equally with all Hispanic communities. Cultural competence in public services for the Hispanic community goes beyond simply providing information in Spanish. After looking at several specific examples of culturally competent programs and services, Benavides concludes that it is important to consider the specific needs of the local community in areas such as education, health, and community services and not rely on a "one size fits all" approach to policy and programs in Hispanic communities.

Continuing on the theme of building culturally competent public services related to traditionally underrepresented groups, in Chapter 8 Diane-Michele Prindeville and

Carrie D. La Tour examine efforts to increase cultural competency in the relationship between the State of New Mexico and tribal governments in the region. Using a case study of specific efforts to develop a cultural competency training program for state employees working with tribal governments, Prindeville and La Tour highlight the importance of paying attention to cultural difference, even in the process of developing such training. Key to the process in this case was the building and maintenance of trusting relationships among the parties involved. The deep history of U.S.–Native American relations and the governmental structures on both sides brings a complex context to the development of cultural competency when working together.

In Chapter 9, Wallace Swan, Mark French, and Kristen A. Norman-Major examine cultural competency around sexual orientation and the treatment of the gay, lesbian, bisexual, and transgender (GLBT) population. As several jurisdictions continue to grapple with civil rights issues around marriage, families, employment, and education for GLBT members of society, it has become increasingly challenging for public administrators to keep track of policies across jurisdictions. Swan, French, and Norman-Major consider the numerous ways the public sector interacts with the GLBT population and what that potentially means in developing cultural competence related to sexual orientation in delivery of services in areas such as employment, education, health care, and criminal justice.

Developing cultural competence in the development and delivery of public services to disabled populations is the focus of Parthenia Dinora's work in Chapter 10. Dinora examines two key factors in public service delivery to disabled persons: the Americans with Disabilities Act (ADA) and the concept of self-determination. While the ADA provides requirements for inclusion of persons with disabilities, public servants must also consider cultural factors that could affect the types of services desired by the disabled. This is where the concept of self-determination comes in as a key component in culturally competent delivery of services. Dinora highlights issues and resources that can help public administrators more carefully develop cultural competency in serving the disabled public.

In Chapter 11, RaJade M. Berry-James looks at the standards, practices, and measures of cultural competency in the health-care field. Health care was one of the first fields to recognize the need to incorporate cultural competency into delivery of services. Work in this field has served to inform work in many others, including public administration. Here, Berry-James considers the skills, knowledge, and abilities needed in the provision of culturally competent health care and the role of the National Culturally and Linguistically Appropriate Services (CLAS) standards in building cultural competency in the practice of public health and health care in general.

In the final chapter in Part II, Frances L. Edwards highlights the importance of cultural competency in the provision of emergency preparedness and disaster relief programs and services. The basis for Edwards's work is the argument that there is no point in "doing good badly." That is, ill-planned and culturally incompetent service in disasters and emergencies is virtually the same as providing no help at all. Using several real-life examples pulled from her experience in the emergency management field, Edwards reflects on the issues that must be considered in ensuring a culturally competent response in times of crisis.

PART III. EDUCATING FOR CULTURAL COMPETENCE

The third section of this book focuses on educating for cultural competence. Chapters in this section examine general and specific ways to incorporate cultural competency into the classroom when teaching and training current and future public servants. To start things off, Nadia Rubaii and Crystal Calarusse look at the evolution of including cultural competence in the accreditation standards of the National Association of Schools of Public Affairs and Administration (NASPAA), the accrediting body for professional education in public affairs. The content of NASPAA standards plays a considerable role in determining the curriculum in public administration programs at the master's level. Rubaii and Calarusse consider what the NASPAA standards for cultural competency mean for both accredited and nonaccredited programs, the role they play in promoting content around cultural competency, and the lessons to be learned from the process for all programs in public administration.

In Chapter 14, Pamela H. Lewis, Allen N. Lewis, and Felecia D. Williams examine what it means to incorporate cultural competency into public administration programs from several aspects. The authors discuss the role of missions, governance, recruitment and retention policies, professional development, and curriculum in promoting cultural competency at all levels in public administration education. They also offer several tools to help in the process of building cultural competency into departments and programs, including tools for conducting self-evaluations, which Lewis, Lewis, and Williams argue are key in building toward cultural competence.

The incorporation of cultural competency into everyday research is the focus of Susan T. Gooden's work in Chapter 15. Here Gooden considers what it means to bring consideration of culture into research beyond the obvious inclusion of traditionally underrepresented groups in research design, data gathering, and survey samples. Besides these things, Gooden argues, we must consider the cultural biases that might influence interpretation of results and the standards that are used to set the norm. According to Gooden, conducting an assessment of the cultural biases of the researchers is key in building cultural competency into everyday research.

In Chapter 16, Mario Rivera, Richard Greggory Johnson III, and Glenda Kodaseet take on the question of whether cultural competency can be taught. Comparing their classroom experiences at two very different universities, Rivera and Johnson consider what works and what does not in engaging students around issues of cultural competence. From their differing experiences they conclude that common important factors include understanding self-identity and using discourse and discussion in a safe space to unpack issues around cultural competence. Kodaseet's experience in teaching a case study related to Native cultures serves to illustrate what practices can lead to successful classroom experiences.

Building on the question of whether cultural competence can be taught, in Chapter 17 James Francisco Bonilla, Leah Ann Lindeman, and Naomi Rae Taylor consider techniques that promote development of skills and knowledge related to cultural competency as well as ways of measuring student learning. Several lessons learned by the authors in teaching a course in cultural competence and managerial leadership set a framework for promising practices, including using a multiperspective approach, starting with self, and creating the right climate. The authors conclude that while improvement in cultural competency skills is possible, there is no one right way to measure this progress and that learning is an ongoing and likely life-long process.

The final chapter in this section argues that in order to ensure that cultural competence is ingrained in the practice of public administration, training programs, particularly at the master's level, must incorporate cultural competency across the entire curriculum. Here, coeditor Kristen A. Norman-Major argues that student learning around cultural competence cannot be left to the chance that students take the right electives but must be a key part of learning in every course. Norman-Major argues that there are three main steps in building cultural competency into the master's in public administration (MPA) curriculum: establishing learning outcomes, building a framework, and creating specific course activities and assignments. The chapter concludes with examples of classroom activities and assignments that bring cultural competence into typical core courses in the MPA curriculum.

PART IV. CONCLUSIONS

The final two chapters in this book take the opportunity to step back and reflect on the role of cultural competency in public administration, the challenges that it faces, and the work left to be done. In Chapter 19, Samuel L. Brown considers the challenges that exist for cultural competency in public administration. After critiquing Cross's definition of cultural competency, Brown uses the case of Daniel Hauser—a thirteen-year-old diagnosed with Hodgkin's disease whose family refused recommended treatments on the basis of a conflict with their religious beliefs—to ask which cultural traits and traditions are deserving of consideration. That is, how do we decide between competing cultural values? Finally, Brown considers the shortfalls in cultural competency in correcting for past discrimination. While it might improve circumstances for some groups, argues Brown, cultural competency is not the magic bullet that provides an end to all discrimination.

In the final chapter of the book, we as coeditors provide our analysis of cultural competency in public administration, arguing that while as a field we are on the right track, the work is far from done. Today, cultural competency in public administration is valued as a part of the discipline, it is an important consideration in accreditation of master's programs, and some public services, particularly related to life and death issues, have made great progress in culturally competent practices. On the other hand, there is still much work to be done, including catching up to fields such as social work and public health that have made much more progress in the practice of cultural competency. We also raise concern that the traditional focus on race and ethnicity and on gender (1) does not recognize the true complexities within these categories and (2) excludes several other areas, such as sexual orientation, that need to be included in creating culturally competent public services. Finally, a fragmented education and training process that includes little accountability limits our ability to ensure that public administrators have the skill and knowledge necessary to bring the practice of cultural competence into their daily work.

Similar to our argument in the conclusion, this volume, we hope, will further the practice of cultural competency in public administration. The chapters here are designed to provide insights that will help practitioners, students, and educators alike in their work around cultural competency in public administration. Despite the depth of knowledge and variety of insights provided by the authors, however, this book is only the beginning. Learning related to cultural competency is a lifelong process for which this volume is hopefully a strong launching pad.

ACKNOWLEDGMENTS

This edited volume is the result of the efforts of many—each contributing author, our editors, our publisher, and our reviewers. We thank the contributors for developing their scholarship and for trusting our vision of the volume. Thanks also to Monica Behney, an MPA graduate student at Virginia Commonwealth University, for her invaluable assistance in editing, formatting, proofreading, and keeping track of individual author correspondence and status of manuscripts. Thanks to Harry Briggs at M.E. Sharpe for shepherding this book from its early stages to final completion. Thanks to Elizabeth Parker, Henrietta Toth, and Laurie Lieb at M.E. Sharpe for excellent editing. As editors, we also thank each other for a consistently collegial experience. Most importantly, thanks to our families, Tom, Marissa, Elijah, Basil, and Caper, for their unequivocal love and support.

NOTE

1. Held every twenty years since 1968, the Minnowbrook Conference is one of the most significant academic conferences in public administration. As described by Kim, O'Leary, Van Slyke, Frederickson, and Lambright (2010, 1), Minnowbrook Conferences "are the cicadas of public administration: appearing every twenty years and having an impact on the landscape. The gatherings represent an extraordinary assembly of intellectual talent, past and present, new and seasoned. They are intended as an opportunity to take stock of where the field is, where the field is going, and where the field needs to go."

REFERENCES

Bailey, Margo. 2005. Cultural competency in the practice of public administration. In *Diversity and Public Administration: Theory, Issues and Perspectives*, ed. M.F. Rice, 171–188. Armonk, NY: M.E. Sharpe.

Bush, Carol T. 2000. Cultural competence: Implications of the surgeon general's report on mental health. *Journal of Child and Adolescent Psychiatric Nursing* 13(4): 177–178.

Cross, Terry L. 1988. Services to minority populations: Cultural competence continuum. *Focal Point: A Publication of the Research and Training Center on Family Support and Children's Mental Health* 3(1): 1–4.

Dictionary.com. 2011. Public. http://dictionary.reference.com/browse/public.

Disabled in Action of Metropolitan New York. n.d. Facts about disability in the U.S. population. www.disabledinaction.org/census_stats.html.

Frederickson, H. George. 2010. *Social Equity and Public Administration: Origins, Developments, and Applications*. Armonk, NY: M.E. Sharpe.

Goodsell, Charles T. 2004. *The Case for Bureaucracy: A Public Administration Polemic*, 4th ed. Washington, DC: CQ Press.

Kim, Soonhee, Rosemary O'Leary, David M. Van Slyke, H. George Frederickson, and W. Henry Lambright. 2010. The legacy of Minnowbrook, in *The Future of Public Administration Around the World: The Minnowbrook Perspective*, ed. Rosemary O'Leary, David M. VanSlyke, and Soonhee Kim, Washington, DC: Georgetown University Press.

Mead, Lawrence M. 2004. *Government Matters: Welfare Reform in Wisconsin.* Princeton: Princeton University Press.

Miller, Kathleen. n.d. Data brief: County per capita income. Rural Policy Research Institute Brief. www.rupri.org/Forms/DataBrief_PCI.pdf.

Pew Forum on Religion and Public Life. 2008. U.S. religious landscape survey, report 1: Religion affiliation. http://religions.pewforum.org/reports#.

Romero, Adam P., et al. 2007. Census snapshot: United States. Williams Institute at the UCLA School of Law.

Svara, James H., and James R. Brunet. 2004. Filling the skeletal pillar: Addressing social equity in introductory courses in public administration. *Journal of Public Affairs Education* 10(2): 99–110.

U.S. Census Bureau. 2009. 2010 census constituent FAQs. http://2010.census.gov/partners/pdf/ConstituentFAQ.pdf.

———. 2010. State & County QuickFacts. http://quickfacts.census.gov/qfd/states/00000.html.

———. 2011. The 2011 Statistical Abstract: Population. www.census.gov/compendia/statab/cats/population.html.

Part I

Culturally Competent Agencies, Policies, and Public Servants

A New Kind of Public Service Professional

Possessing Cultural Competency Awareness, Knowledge, and Skills

MITCHELL F. RICE AND
AUDREY L. MATHEWS

Demographic changes in the United States can be largely attributed to growth in the Hispanic/Latino, Asian, and other minority populations (see U.S. Census Bureau 2000, 2005a, 2005b). These demographic changes are impacting American society in many ways. Ongoing research, initiated in the late 1980s and 1990s, documented the effects of demographic changes in workplaces (see, e.g., Johnston and Parker 1987; Morrison and Glinow 1990). More recent research is raising questions about demographic changes and the delivery of public programs and public services (Rice 2008, 2010). Presently, due to demographic changes, there is a much different mix of individuals—consumers, customers, clients, and workers—in communities all across the United States than there was two decades ago. Now an encounter between individuals, clients, constituents, or service recipients and the professionals of public service agencies are often exchanges involving different cultural backgrounds, beliefs, practices, and languages (Rice 2010). This is to say that public agency service delivery professionals are typically from one culture and the service recipients or clients are from or closely connected to or strongly influenced by another culture. These demographic changes provided a vision and agenda for the workplace diversity movement initiated by scholars such as Taylor Cox and Stacey Blake (1991) and Roosevelt Thomas (1991).

Research indicates that organizations that manage diversity well show a reduction in workforce turnover, an increase in productivity, an edge in attracting talented women and minorities, and public agencies providing more effective programs and service delivery (Mathews 2010). In spite of recessions, collapses, and reductions in the size and operations of major organizations and public agencies and their workforces, the impact of the demographic changes are continuing. The resulting effects and affects for the organizations and public agencies that manage diversity well are creative problem solving, innovation, and improvements in the organizations' abilities to adapt to other inevitable forces of change. The bottom line for these organizations and public agencies is the successful and effective implementation and delivery of programs and services to communities of underserved clients and/or clients with different cultural backgrounds, beliefs, practices, and languages.

It appears that organizations that have effectively used the framework and lenses of cultural competency to manage the demographic changes of clients with their organizations have improved the quality and delivery of programs and services to constituents and clients. There are numerous successful examples in both the business and public sectors, such as Hewlett Packard, Ford Motor Company, Harvard Pilgrim Healthcare, and IBM from the business sector and the City of Laredo, Texas; Salinas, California Police Department; the U.S. Department of Defense and the Center for the Advanced Study of Language; the City of Phoenix, Arizona and the Seattle, Washington Police Department from the public sector (see Rice 2008). These organizations thus fortify by example the answer to the question whether public organizations can become culturally competent (Cox and Blake 1991; Mathews 2010; Rice 2010; and Thomas 1991). The common thread certifying that these multicultural/cultural organizations are culturally competent is a diversity management orientation built on the strengths and perspectives of beliefs that individuals from different cultures can make positive contributions to the organization or public agency. The objective is to establish culturally appropriate internal and external program and service delivery strategies and approaches. The cultural competency theoretical framework's underpinnings include elements from many theories or permutations-amalgamations, definitive properties, relationship differentials, knowledge derivatives, and applied practice outcomes and effects.

This chapter discusses the importance of moving diversity management's use of cultural competency in the delivery of public programs and public agency services from the conceptual and unconnected to a legitimate theoretical framework and model. The chapter also discusses the need for a focus on cultural competency in public administration higher education programs. The chapter continues by stressing why cultural competency in public administration higher education programs is relevant to the authors' contention that calls for a new kind of public agency service delivery professional. Specifically, this chapter calls for a new kind of public agency service professional who possesses explicit cultural competency awareness, knowledge, and skills to work with racial/ethnic and cultural/linguistic groups in public administration and in the public agency service delivery process. The chapter concludes by noting the need for a cultural competency model that would integrate and transform cultural awareness and cultural knowledge about individuals and groups into culturally specific skills, practices, standards, and policies to increase the quality and effectiveness of public agency services and programs.

A NEW CULTURAL COMPETENCY BEHAVIOR IN THE PRACTICE OF PUBLIC ADMINISTRATION

As prescribed by Strauss and Corbin (1990), theoretical sampling and testing of existing literature and models are used to buttress and expand on the theoretical modeling of cultural competency for public administration and public agency service delivery. The theory building initiated by Bailey (2005), continued by Rice (2010), and reexamined by Mathews (2010) sets the foundation for this chapter. To reiterate, according to Mathews in "Diversity Management and Cultural Competency" (2010), as the workplace diversity movement's framework and lenses moved into the last decade of the twentieth century, the focus of the movement was expanded by the notions of multiculturalism and core cultural competencies. The theoretical framework for this emerging model's foundation has its origin in organization culture and behavior research conducted by social and behavioral scientists and applied practices in both the private sector and in the social sciences (Mathews 1999, 2002). Rice (2010) examined and addressed the central issues and questions for public administration researchers and scholars, and a summary of that discussion is presented herein. Cultural competency in public programs and public agency service delivery has arrived at *cultural proficiency* when the agency, its professionals, and staffs understand and effectively respond to the challenge and opportunity posed by the presence of sociocultural diversity in a defined social system. Rice (2008, 24–26) proffers that organizations have an obligation to modify their administration service delivery strategies and approaches to encompass a development process that leads to cultural proficiency. Modifications such as recruitment and communication represent "surface structure" or "first cut" changes" (see Kumpfer et al. 2002, 242).

One of the first steps to take in moving toward cultural competency in a public agency or public program is to make public services programming and public services delivery visible and accessible by translating program materials and providing the program in the primary client's language—sometimes known as a *translated* program (see Cheng Gorman 1996; Cheng Gorman and Balter 1997). This would include translating a public agency's program and service delivery literature into the language of the target population to increase awareness that services are available. Also, awareness and visibility are increased by modifying recruitment strategies, such as placing radio ads on the Spanish radio stations or in Spanish or other specific language newspapers. Except for the different language, the translated program remains essentially unchanged from the original program that was not culturally modified. Although language translation is an important modification, translated materials alone are not sufficient to make a public agency program culturally competent and culturally effective (Cheng Gorman 1996; Cheng Gorman and Balter 1997).

Cultural competency also involves a public agency's operation ridding itself of cultural discomforts or cultural discontinuities (Uttal 2006). For example, attendance and participation in a health education workshop are more effective if culturally relevant activities, terms, and lessons that are meaningful to the participants are used. Without these adaptations, the workshop may fail to convey the knowledge it is trying to impart. Cultural discomforts created by strange examples will also undermine the retention of participants and even possibly culturally offend participants. Some programs that serve racial ethnic populations are beginning to acknowledge that their effectiveness may also depend on taking a more familistic approach, such as bringing the whole family into a workshop or to a counseling session (Malley-Morrison and Hines 2004). Other programs have found it effective to recruit and retain Latino couples in a parent education program, instead of inviting only one individual parent (usually the mother) to participate (see Powell 1995). These types of adaptations are reflective of the changes necessary to provide culturally adapted programs that are going to work for a culturally different population.

Yet cultural adaptations in public agency services delivery and programming may still not go far enough. Cheng Gorman (1996) distinguishes between culturally adapted programs and those that are culturally specific. In culturally adapted programs, the examples that are used in a workshop are transformed or modified to respect the target culture's behaviors and practices. For example, activities that require a lot of writing would be replaced with oral exercises in a workshop for people from an orally expressive culture. Activities that require handholding would be removed from a workshop for individuals who are members of a low-touch culture. The key aspect of a culturally adapted program is that these changes leave the original points of a workshop or program intact but take into account the participants' cultural style of learning. In culturally specific programs, the transformations go beyond adding culturally adapted components to public service programming. Unlike the culturally adapted program, a public program or public agency that is culturally specific will integrate the target group's values, attitudes, and beliefs (Cheng Gorman 1996). This change requires that the assumptions of the overall workshop, program, and/or agency are critically examined and its philosophy is altered to reflect the value systems and worldview of the target population. For example, in a culture that does not verbally express self-emotions, the expectation for people to talk about themselves is dropped. A parenting program might use a familistic approach rather than the more commonly accepted child-centered approach used in the United States (see Kumpfer et al. 2002). Mock (2001) and Boyd-Franklin (2001) are in agreement that among ethnic families a family focused strategy is preferred rather than a youth-only focused prevention strategy because of the cultural emphasis on the "we" family identity as opposed to "I" self-identity. Culturally specific programs are designed with the purpose of facilitating success within a specific group's culture and are formatted to be culturally relevant.

ADDING CULTURAL COMPETENCY IN PUBLIC ADMINISTRATION HIGHER EDUCATION PROGRAMS

Even in the face of mounting evidence, some public administration researchers, administrators and managers, and other social services experts continue to question why public administration education and human resources training communities should inculcate the organizational cultural strategy, managing cultural diversity and applied use of cultural competency with clients and citizens, into public administration's curriculum and public organizations' human resources workforce training (see, e.g., Dean 2001; Dolan and Rosenbloom 2003; Stafford 1999; and Taylor-Brown, Garcia, and Kingson 2001). While others advocate that contemporary public administration education must provide coursework and learning focusing on cultural competency, public organizations need to become more culturally competent and the provision of culturally appropriate services is a worthwhile goal (see, e.g., Agars and Kottle

2004; Bailey 2005; Mathews 2010; and Rice 2007, 2008, 2010). Operationally, within an organization, cultural competency is achieved by integrating and transforming knowledge about individuals and groups into specific practices, standards, policies, and attitudes applied in appropriate cultural settings to increase the quality of services, thereby producing better outcomes (Davis 1997). The idea of cultural competency is an explicit acknowledgement that a one-size-fits-all public agency service delivery process cannot meet the needs of an increasingly diverse U.S. population. This means learning new patterns of behavior and applying them in appropriate situations (National Association of Social Workers 2001).

Before the new public agency service delivery professionals can appropriately step into their roles in the organization, public administration communities—both in practice and in education—need to reinvent themselves in order to produce a new public agency service delivery professional who is well grounded in cultural competency. This reinvention is necessary because evidence points to poorly working or failed community-oriented programs in housing, education, and health care. One area that stands out in these poorly working or failed programs and services is public administration's inability to embrace cultural competency and recognize the significance of understanding the cultural context in which any direct public service encounter occurs (Applewhite 1998). Other areas that support the need for a new kind of public agency service delivery professional are the following:

- the deficient and often inaccurate and inadequate public services and programs provided to minority populations (Geron 2002);
- public agencies' administration, services, and programs' lack of relevancy to the minority populations who really need them (Boyle and Springer 2001); and
- public program and public agency service delivery professionals who are not prepared to deliver relevant programs and services due to a lack of awareness and skills in cultural competency (Suzuki, McRae, and Short 2001).

It is also important that this new kind of public agency service delivery professional reinvention takes place through public administration education. According to Rice (2006, 91–92), "the teaching of cultural competency in university based public administration education programs and core curricula must be required. Second, steps must be taken to get public agencies to implement cultural competency programs, strategies, and practices in service delivery."

However, as Susan White's survey findings of twenty top MPA programs reveal, "Fewer than half of the top ranked MPA programs exposed students to core courses that relate to any aspect of diversity" (2004, 120). When courses in diversity are offered, they are elective and not required; *thus the student is self-selecting to receive formal cultural competency or diversity training* (120; emphasis added). In a much larger study conducted by Wyatt-Nichol and Antwi-Boasiako (2008), online survey invitations were distributed to 246 MPA/MPP (Master of Public Policy) program directors, 92 of whom responded, resulting in a 38 percent response rate. Interestingly, every respondent indicated that it was important (78 percent very important, 22 percent somewhat important) for graduate programs to promote awareness of cultural diversity issues. Yet course offerings on diversity have been somewhat limited. Rice (2004, 153–154) notes that "the teaching of social equity and diversity must be included in curricular and coursework in public administration education . . . to be more relevant to contemporary students and a concentrated effort must be made to provide students with a racially and ethnically diverse faculty." Yet a racially and ethnically diverse public administration faculty may be very difficult to achieve. Survey findings from thirteen directors of public administration programs in California acknowledged that a lack of diverse faculty has a bearing on the scarcity of focus on the topics of social equity, diversity, and cultural competency in public administration education (Farmbry 2005).

Further exacerbating the problem of little or no focus on diversity and cultural competency, the major textbooks in the field of public administration provide little or no coverage on cultural competency—except for the Rice text (2010), this text, and another text by Espiridion Borrego and Richard Greggory Johnson III (2011)—or equity measures (Svara and Brunet 2004). The evidence of poorly working or failed programs, lack of minority faculty, self-selection of formal cultural competency or diversity training, and lack of major textbooks that explore and promote cultural competency contributes to Bailey's (2005) contention that culturally competent organizations must have culturally competent employees who possess cultural competency awareness, knowledge, and skills. Overall, public administration's higher education community is failing public sector and nonprofit organizations, because it does not impart the nuances of cultural competency to students in both teaching and training, leading to poorly working, failed, or inappropriate programs and the lack of organizational support systems to implement culturally appropriate and culturally responsive programs and services. In the words of Forrer, Kee, and Gabriel (2007, 265), "schools of public administration and policy are unduly relying on conventional [traditional] core curricula, crowding out more contemporary curricula that would better serve students as future public managers or policy analysts." This would include crowding out contemporary curricula focusing on diversity, cultural competency and multiculturalism in the study of public administration and in the delivery of public services and programs.

DEVELOPING CULTURALLY COMPETENT PUBLIC AGENCY SERVICE DELIVERY PROFESSIONALS

As U.S. society becomes more demographically diverse, more culturally competent professionals will be needed in public administration and public agency service delivery. Cultural competency is the ability of public agency service delivery professionals to integrate into their theoretical and technical approach to assessment and intervention relevant human diversity factors that are important to the process and successful outcome of the service or program (Fuertes and Ponterotto 2003). Figure 2.1 illustrates the important elements of the cultural competency cycle. The elements shown must occur in order to develop a culturally competent professional and/or a culturally competent public agency. The key elements of the cultural competency cycle are (1) learning about other cultures; (2) becoming aware and knowledgeable

Figure 2.1 **The Cultural Competency Cycle**

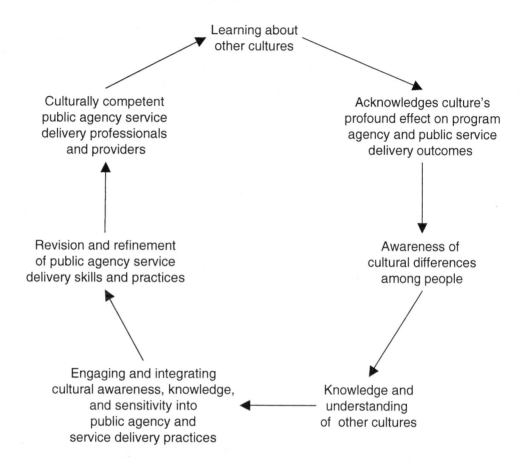

of cultural differences and their effect and impact on program agency and public service delivery outcomes; (3) engaging and integrating cultural awareness, cultural knowledge, and cultural sensitivity into public agency service delivery practices; and (4) thereby leading to culturally competent public agency service delivery professionals and providers. Cultural competency operates at the individual, professional level in the application of specific awareness, knowledge, and skills in the context of public agency service delivery encounters and at the institutional level in the promotion of organizational practices to meet the needs of diverse populations.

Table 2.1 shows the attributes of a culturally competent public agency service delivery professional. Cultural competency consists of three distinctive areas focusing on cultural awareness, cultural knowledge, and cultural skills (Sue et al. 1998) that enable a system, agency, or professional to work effectively in cross-cultural settings and to deliver public services and public programs to diverse constituents and communities. These three distinctive areas must take place in this order. In other words, cultural awareness leads to cultural knowledge, and cultural knowledge contributes to the acquisition of cultural skills.

Table 2.1

Attributes of Culturally Competent Public Agency Service Delivery Professionals

Cultural awareness	Cultural knowledge	Cultural skills
A belief that differences are valuable and that learning about others who are culturally different is necessary and rewarding.	Knowledge of diverse cultures and groups.	Ability to identify and openly discuss cultural differences and issues.
A willingness to take risks and see them as necessary and important for personal and professional growth.	Knowledge about how change occurs in values and behaviors of individuals from other cultures.	Ability to assess the impact of cultural differences on communication and to effectively communicate across those differences.
A strong commitment to justice, social change, and social equity.	Knowledge about the ways that cultural differences affect verbal and nonverbal communication.	Ability to empathize and genuinely connect with individuals who are different from themselves.
A belief in the value and significance of their own cultural heritage and worldview as a starting place for understanding others who are culturally different from them.	Knowledge about other cultures' views about gender, class, race, ethnicity, language, nationality, sexual orientation, age, religion or spirituality, and disability.	Ability to incorporate new learning and prior learning in new situations.
A willingness to examine, challenge, and change their own values, worldview, assumptions, and biases.	Knowledge about culturally appropriate resources and how to make culturally appropriate referrals.	Ability to gain the trust and respect of individuals who are culturally different from themselves.
An openness to change and a belief that change is necessary and positive.	Knowledge about the nature of institutional power in other cultures.	Ability to accurately assess their own multicultural skills, comfort level, growth, and development.
An acceptance of other worldviews and perspectives and a willingness to acknowledge that they, as individuals, do not have all the answers.	Knowledge about identity development models and the acculturation process for members of oppressed or underserved groups and their impact on individuals, groups, intergroup relations, and society.	Ability to differentiate individual differences, cultural differences, and universal similarities.
A belief that cultural differences do not have to interfere with effective communication or meaningful relationships.	Knowledge and understanding of discrimination and its impact on identity and self-esteem.	Ability to support individuals and systems that identify oppression issues in a manner that optimizes multicultural interventions.
Awareness that one's own cultural heritage and background affects one's worldview, values, and assumptions.	Knowledge about other cultures' views about education and other areas.	Ability to undertake individual, group, and institutional multicultural interventions.
Awareness of their own behavior and its impact on others.		Ability to use culture to undertake culturally sensitive and appropriate interventions.
Awareness of the interpersonal process that occurs within a multicultural dyad.		

Cultural awareness takes into account those values, attitudes, and assumptions essential to working with clients and service recipients who are culturally different from a public agency service delivery professional (Pope and Reynolds 1997; see also Campinha-Bacote 1999). Table 2.1 shows eleven aspects of cultural awareness. A highly important aspect of cultural awareness is self-awareness. Self-awareness is especially important because it involves self-evaluation and reflection about one's views of a particular culture in the form of stereotypes, biases, or culturally based assumptions (Pope and Reynolds 1997). Stated another way, self-awareness stresses understanding our own individual personal beliefs and attitudes as well as how we are the products of our own cultural conditioning. Further, understanding cultural awareness also takes into account a willingness to consider various worldviews, perspectives, and cultural differences.

Cultural knowledge consists of understanding the worldviews of various cultural groups and possessing knowledgeable professional expertise relevant to persons in other cultures. Public agency service delivery professionals must gather information about cultural groups that they are working with and learn in what ways cultural constructs influence how these groups respond to the helping process. Specifically, knowledge about cultures presumes the following specific competencies:

1. knowledge about the histories of cultures other than one's own;
2. knowledge about the role of education, money, values, attitudes, and behaviors in other cultures;
3. knowledge about the language and slang of another culture;
4. knowledge about the resources available for teaching and learning in other cultures;
5. knowledge about how each individual's own culture is perceived by members of other cultures;
6. knowledge about identity development models and the acculturation process for members of oppressed or underserved groups and their impact on individuals, groups, intergroup relations, and society;
7. knowledge about how helping services are delivered in other cultures;
8. knowledge about the ways cultural differences affect verbal and nonverbal communications;
9. knowledge about how change occurs for values and behaviors in individuals who are members of other cultures; and
10. knowledge about other cultures' views about gender, class, race and ethnicity, language, nationality, sexual orientation, age, religion or spirituality, and disability (see Table 2.1).

Cultural skills consist of those attributes that allow public service agency delivery professionals to effectively apply cultural awareness and cultural knowledge they have learned (see Table 2.1). Not having a foundation of cultural awareness and cultural knowledge makes it difficult to possess cultural skills that allow one to decide on culturally sensitive and culturally appropriate interventions and strategies. Deciding on culturally sensitive and culturally appropriate interventions and strategies requires the ability to identify and openly discuss cultural differences and issues, to assess the impact of cultural differences on communication, to genuinely connect to individuals who are different and gain their trust and respect, and to initiate individual, group, and institutional multicultural interventions, along with other attributes and skills. Overall, culturally competent public agency service delivery professionals should be able to adjust assessments and recommendations regarding clients to the culture-specific needs of the clients. This means taking into consideration both the client's and the public agency service delivery professional's culture as well as a cultural understanding of how the service fits in the client's cultural context (see Table 2.1).

CONCLUSION

Although the concept of cultural competency is still evolving and is not yet a universally recognized scientific field, in the contemporary era it has found its way into many disciplines, such as public education, and areas of practice, such as social work and mental health. Incorporating cultural competency into the study of public administration and moving public agency service delivery professionals and public agencies toward cultural competence is an ongoing effort that requires the recognition of several activities. First, the study of public administration must acknowledge that cultural differences are important in the delivery of public agency services and programs. Second, continuous internal leadership and support are required by all members of the public agency. Third, culturally competent public administration and public agency service delivery requires the following attributes: (1) cultural appropriateness; (2) cultural accessibility; and (3) cultural acceptability. Culturally appropriate public service delivery recognizes the needs of the target population or populations and the types of services provided. Culturally accessible public agency service delivery opens the door to services for different cultural groups. This includes addressing the structural barriers that can impede cultural competency. Once these barriers are addressed, culturally acceptable services are more likely to occur in all areas of the public agency.

Fourth, public administration and public agency service delivery professionals' use of cultural competency builds on the strengths and perspectives of minority cultures beliefs, habits, behaviors, and value systems to establish public agency service delivery intervention strategies and approaches. In other words, public agency professionals work from inside the public agency and utilize the beliefs, behaviors, perspectives, and values of minority cultures to help frame and provide culturally appropriate and responsive services (U.S. DHHS 2001, 5). In this way, public agency service professionals are acknowledging the significance of culture in minority groups' problems as well as in their solutions. Fifth, acquiring cultural competency awareness, knowledge, and skills is a developmental process whereby public agencies and public service delivery professionals attain cultural awareness, cultural knowledge, and cultural skills through both training and cultural encounters with individuals from different cultural groups. This process acknowledges that cultural competence is not static and requires frequent learning, relearning, and unlearning about different cultural groups. Finally, cultural competency in public administration and among public agency service delivery professionals will require new thinking outside of traditional public administration and incorporating different, nontraditional, and nonmainstream sources and approaches as articulated in the five observations above. This new thinking recognizes that the practice of public administration has a major impact on society and, as a result, must focus on cultural competency in a contemporary, multicultural era by providing cultural competency skills to future public agency service delivery professionals. Traditional public administration operations and programs have been "generic" and heavily influenced by white, middle-class values, resulting in professional training that has stressed "the melting pot" model of American culture, resulting in few culturally specific models and programs (see Kumpfer et al. 2002, 242).

Therefore, there is a strong need for effective cultural competency modeling. This modeling must take place in both teaching and practice in accordance with and as promoted within existing federal and state legislation (Bailey 2005). The cultural competency model should integrate and transform knowledge about individuals and groups into culturally specific practices, standards, and policies to increase the quality and effectiveness of services. Further, the model should contain the basis for developing criteria, assessing needs both internal and external to the organization, and adjusting the developmental processes to reflect the sociocultural diversity in a defined social system. The model also needs to acknowledge that cultural competency does not mean acquiring an encyclopedic knowledge of the world's cultures and their specific behaviors and views about values, customs, practices, or beliefs. It does, however, require that public agency service providers and service delivery professionals understand and acknowledge the role that culture plays in the success or failure of programs and services. In the end, cultural competency has its start with the dominant culture becoming self-aware of its own customs and then showing responsiveness to and understanding of the cultural differences of others—clients, employees, or services recipients within a defined program or system.

REFERENCES

Agars, Mark, and Janet L. Kottle. 2004. Models and practice of diversity management: A historical review and presentation of a new integration theory. In *The Psychology and Management of Workplace Diversity*, ed. Margaret S. Stockdale, 55–77. Malden, MA: Blackwell.

Applewhite, Steven L. 1998. Culturally competent practice with elderly Latinos. *Journal of Gerontological Social Work* 30(1/2): 1–15.

Bailey, Margo L. 2005. Cultural competency and the practice of public administration. In *Diversity and Public Administration: Theory, Issues, and Perspectives*, ed. Mitchell F. Rice, 177–196. Armonk, NY: M.E. Sharpe.

Borrego, Espiridion, and Richard Greggory Johnson. 2011. *Cultural Competence for Public Managers: Managing Diversity in Today's World*. New York: CRC Press-Taylor Francis Group.

Boyd-Franklin, Nancy. 2001. Reaching out to larger systems. *Family Psychologist* 17(3): 1–4.

Boyle, David P., and Alyson Springer. 2001. Toward cultural competency measures for social work with specific populations. *Journal of Ethnic and Cultural Diversity in Social Work* 9(3/4): 53–77.

Campinha-Bacote, Josepha. 1999. A model and instrument for addressing cultural competence in health care. *Journal of Nursing Education* 38(5): 203–206.

Cheng Gorman, Jean. 1996. *Culturally-Sensitive Parent Education Programs for Ethnic Minorities* (PC Reports 7–96–26). New York: New York University, Psychoeducational Center.

Cheng Gorman, Jean, and Lawrence Balter. 1997. Culturally sensitive parent education: A critical review of quantitative research. *Review of Educational Research* 67(3): 339–369.

Cox, Taylor, and Stacey Blake. 1991. Managing Cultural Diversity: Implications for Organizational Competitiveness. *The Academy of Management Executive* 5 (3): 45–56.

Davis, King. 1997. *Exploring the Intersection between Cultural Competency and Managed Behavioral Health Care Policy: Implications for State and County Mental Health Agencies*. Alexandria, VA: National Technical Assistance Center for State Mental Health Planning.

Dean, Ruth G. 2001. The myth of cross-cultural competence. *Families in Society* 82(6): 623–630.

Dolan, Julie A., and David H. Rosenbloom. 2003. *Representative Bureaucracy: Classic Readings and Continuing Controversies*. Armonk, NY: M.E. Sharpe.

Farmbry, Kyle. 2005. Diversity in public administration education: A view from California. In *Diversity and Public Administration: Theory, Issues and Perspectives*, ed. Mitchell F. Rice, 87–104. Armonk, NY: M.E. Sharpe.

Forrer, John, James Edwin Kee, and Seth Gabriel. 2007. Not your father's public administration. *Journal of Public Affairs Education* 13(2): 265–280.

Fuertes, Jairo N., and Joseph G. Ponterotto. 2003. Culturally appropriate intervention strategies. In *Multicultural Counseling Competencies 2003: Association of Multicultural Counseling Competencies*, ed. Gargi Roysircar, Patricia Arredondo, Jairo N. Fuertes, Joseph G. Ponterotto, and Rebecca L. Toporek, 51–58. Alexandria, VA: Association for Multicultural Counseling and Development.

Geron, Scott M. 2002. Cultural competency: How is it measured? Does it make a difference? *Generations* 26(3): 39–45.

Johnston, William B., and Arnold H. Parker. 1987. *Workforce 2000*. Indianapolis, IN: Hudson Institute.

Kumpfer, Karol L., Rose Alvarado, Paula Smith, and Nikki Bellamy. 2002. Cultural sensitivity and adaptation in family-based prevention interventions. *Preventing Science* 3(3): 241–246.

Malley-Morrison, Kathleen, and Denise A. Hines. 2004. *Family Violence in a Cultural Perspective*. Thousand Oaks, CA: Sage.

Mathews, Audrey L. 1999. *The Sum of the Differences: Diversity and Public Organizations*. New York: McGraw-Hill.

———. 2002. The mosaic of formal and informal mentoring relationships. DPA diss., University of Southern California.

———. 2005. Cultural diversity and productivity. In *Diversity and Public Administration: Theory, Issues and Perspectives*, ed. Mitchell F. Rice, 197–229. Armonk NY: M.E. Sharpe.

———. 2010. Diversity Management and Cultural Competency. In *Diversity and Public Administration: Theory, Issues and Perspectives*, 2nd ed. Mitchell F. Rice 210–263. Armonk, NY: M.E. Sharpe

Mock, Matthew. 2001. Working with Asian American Families. *The Family Psychologist* 17(3): 5–7.

Morrison, Ann M. 1992. *The New Leaders: Guidelines on Leadership Diversity in America*. San Francisco: Jossey-Bass.

Morrison, Ann M., and Mary-Ann Von Glinow. 1990. Women and minorities in management. *American Psychologist* 45(2): 200–208.

National Association of Social Workers. 2001. Standards for Cultural Competence in Social Work Practice. www.socialworkers.org/practice/standards/NASWCulturalStandards.pdf.

Pope, Raechele L., and Amy L. Reynolds. 1997. Student affairs core competencies: Integrating multicultural awareness, knowledge, and skills. *Journal of College Student Development* 38(3): 271–281.

Powell, Douglas. 1995. Including Latino fathers in parent education and support programs. In *Understanding Latino Families: Scholarship, Policy and Practice*, ed. Ruth Zambrana, 85–106. Thousand Oaks, CA: Sage.

Rice, Mitchell F. 2004. Organizational culture, social equity, and diversity: Teaching public administration in the postmodern era. *Journal of Public Affairs Education* 10(2): 143–154.

———. 2006. Cultural competency: A missing framework in contemporary public administration and public service delivery. In *Proceedings: Taking Social Equity to the Streets*, ed. Mary Hamilton, Appendix J, 89–100. Fifth Social Equity Leadership Conference, University of Nebraska at Omaha, February 2–3.

————. 2007. Promoting cultural competency in public administration and public service delivery: utilizing self-assessment tools and performance measures. *Journal of Public Affairs Education* 13(1) Winter 2007: 41–53.

————. 2008. A primer for developing a public agency service ethos of cultural competency in public services programming and public services delivery. *Journal of Public Affairs Education* 14(1): 21–38.

————. 2010. Cultural competency, public administration, and public service delivery in an era of diversity. In *Diversity and Public Administration: Theory, Issues, and Perspectives* (2nd ed.), ed. Mitchell F. Rice, 189–209. Armonk, NY: M.E. Sharpe.

Stafford, Walter W. 1999. Bringing historically marginalized groups of color into the study of the administrative state. *Journal of Public Affairs Education* 5(4): 327–334.

Strauss, Anselm, and Juliet Corbin. 1990. *Basics of Qualitative Research: Grounded Theory Procedures and Techniques.* Newbury Park, CA: Sage.

Sue, Derald Wing., Robert T. Carter, J. Manual Casas, Nadya A. Fouad, Allen E. Ivey, Margaret Jensen, Teresa LaFromboise, Jeanne E. Manese, Joseph G. Ponterotto, and Ena Vasquez-Nutall. 1998. *Multicultural Counseling Competencies.* Thousand Oaks, CA: Sage.

Suzuki, Lisa A., Mary B. McRae, and Ellen L. Short. 2001. The facets of cultural competence: Searching outside the box. *Counseling Psychologist* 29(6): 842–849.

Svara, James, and James Brunet. 2004. Filling in the skeleton pillar: Addressing social equity in introductory courses in public administration. *Journal of Public Affairs Education* 10(2): 99–109.

Taylor-Brown, Susa, Alejandro Garcia, and Eric Kingson. 2001. Cultural competence versus cultural chauvinism: Implications for social work. *Health and Social Work* 26(3): 185–187.

Thomas, Roosevelt. 1991. *Beyond Race and Gender: Unleashing the Power of Your Total Workforce by Managing Diversity.* New York: AMACOM.

U.S. Census Bureau. 2000. *Statistical Abstract of the United States.* Washington, DC: Government Printing Office.

U.S. Census Bureau News. 2005a. Texas becomes nation's newest majority-minority state, Census Bureau announces. News release, August 11.

————. 2005b. Hispanic population passes 40 million, Census Bureau reports. News release, June 9.

U.S. Department of Health and Human Services (U.S. DHHS), Administration on Aging. 2001. *Achieving Cultural Competence: A Guidebook for Providers of Services to Older Americans and Their Families.* www.AOA.gov/prof/addive/culturally/addiv_cult.asp.

Uttal, Lynet. 2006. Organizational cultural competency: Shifting programs for Latino immigrants from a client-centered to a community-based orientation. *American Journal of Community Psychology* 38: 251–262.

White, Susan. 2004. Multicultural MPA curriculum: Are we preparing culturally competent public administrators? *Journal of Public Affairs Education* 10(2): 111–123.

Wyatt-Nichol, Heather, and Kwame Badu Antwi-Boasiako. 2008. Diversity across curriculum: Perceptions and practices. *Journal of Public Affairs Education* 14(1): 79–90.

Legally Competent Public Servants

State Statutory and Regulatory Mandated Cultural Competence Provisions

SHELLY L. PEFFER

Cultural competency is a subject that is relatively new to public administrators—both scholars and practitioners—and in the law. Although the subject has recently received attention, it is often confused with issues of diversity; conversations about cultural competency generally fall back on discussions revolving around the Civil Rights Act of 1964 and the constitutional provision of equal protection. While these and other statutory and United States and state constitutional provisions play a part in cultural competency, they miss the crux of the issue. Cultural competency is not an issue of access, or even equity; it is an issue of understanding.

Cultural competency is not merely an academic issue or the new hot button issue for public administration; real harm can result from cultural incompetence. In 1980, Dade County, Florida, passed an "English-only" ordinance (Meltzer 2007). As the American Civil Liberties Union of Florida (ACLU) (2010) noted, the ordinance barred public funding for any activities that involved the use of languages other than English, resulting in the cancellation of all multicultural events and bilingual services, ranging from directional signs in the public transportation system to medical services at the county hospital. The ACLU stated, "where basic human needs are met by bilingual or multilingual services, the consequences of their elimination could be dire." The ACLU pointed to an example of a woman in Washington who in 1987 called 911 when her baby was in respiratory distress. The 911 operator was able to coach the Salvadorian woman over the telephone in Spanish on how to administer mouth-to-mouth and cardiopulmonary resuscitation to the baby until emergency services arrived. This vital help would have been prohibited had the 911 operator been employed in Dade County, Florida. The ACLU of Florida did not want this to happen in Dade County. After many attempts to repeal the ordinance, it finally fell in 1993. However, the legacy of the ordinance has left less than positive feelings about the local government on the part of the majority of citizens—a majority that is non–English-speaking.

Although, as the repeal of the Dade County ordinance attests, there has been some progress in cultural competence in public services and the law, state and local governments still have a long way to go in order to be inclusive and understanding of the needs of all cultures represented within their jurisdictions.

On a positive note, it appears that some state governments are realizing that in order to provide competent and meaningful public services to their citizens they must take into account the culture of those citizens. In an attempt to increase cultural competency in administrative agencies, many states have begun to systemically address the issue by mandating cultural competency through statutes and regulations. The term *statutory mandate* is generically used to describe a statute that requires, and not merely permits, a course of action—it is a law.

According to administrative law scholars Aka and Deason (2009), the increase in cultural competence mandates in the delivery of public services is due to increased demand. This increased demand is due to three factors: (1) the increase in racial and ethnic diversity and the consequent demographic changes in the U.S. population; (2) economic globalization and increased interactions among cultures; and (3) international calls for increased cultural awareness (e.g., the Universal Declaration on Cultural Diversity adopted by the United Nations Educational, Scientific, and Cultural Organization) (Aka and Deason 2009).

States that lead the way in mandating cultural competence in certain public service areas include Arizona, California, and Florida (notwithstanding the Dade County issue previously mentioned). This makes sense given Aka and Deason's belief that increased cultural competency in public services is, in part, due to increased demand and changing demographics. All three states have culturally diverse populations and a large influx of immigrants that is changing the state demographic. In order to provide competent and meaningful public services to emerging demographic groups, the culture of the groups must be understood and taken into account.

This chapter will look at some of the important cultural competency mandates in the law. The focus will be on state mandates; however, where relevant, important city and federal mandates will be discussed. The chapter will analyze the mandates in procedure and substance and the effect that the mandates have on public services. Finally, the chapter will discuss whether it takes a mandate to ensure cultural competency in public services and whether having cultural competency mandates guarantees culturally competent public services.

Cultural Competence Mandates

There are seven major substantive areas where states have, in some manner, mandated cultural competency in administrative services: (1) provision of health services; (2) provision of mental health services; (3) public education; (4) family and child welfare services; (5) police and criminal justice services; (6) working with vulnerable populations; and (7) Native American affairs. Examples of mandates from each of these substantive areas will be discussed in further detail.

Provision of Health Services Mandates

Mandates in the health-care field are the most common among all areas of cultural competency mandates. States mandating some form of cultural competence in the provision of health services include Alabama, Arkansas, California, Connecticut, Florida, Illinois, Indiana, Maryland, New Jersey, New York, Oklahoma, Ohio, and Utah. States such as Arizona, Florida, Oklahoma, and Ohio also have cultural competency mandates for the provision of mental health services as well. Mandates in the provision of health services include cultural competency provisions in programs to address health care disparities, credentialing requirements for health care professionals, and cultural competency provisions in disease control programs.

An interesting example of an innovative program mandating cultural competency in provision of programs to address health-care disparities is Illinois's Culturally Competent Healthcare Demonstration Program (2010). In this statute, the state acknowledges that "research demonstrates that racial and ethnic minorities generally receive healthcare that is of lesser quality than the majority of the population and have poorer health outcomes on a number of measures." In an effort to combat these disparities, the Illinois Health Improvement Plan, part of the Demonstration Program, mandates "culturally competent healthcare," defined as "the ability of the health care provider to understand and respond to the cultural and linguistic needs brought by patients to the health care encounter." The idea behind the mandate is that with a better understanding of their patients' culture, doctors can better serve the patients and provide better treatment, leading to better health outcomes for patients of all cultural backgrounds.

Another noteworthy example of a health mandate can be found in Rhode Island's Breast Cancer Act (2010). This mandate is an attempt to add a cultural competency provision to disease control efforts. In Rhode Island, breast cancer is responsible for the death of more than 200 women annually; in addition, over 22,000 women in the state currently suffer from breast cancer. In an effort to exert some control over the disease, Rhode Island passed the Breast Cancer Act, which states, in part, "The state of Rhode Island must take the lead in combating the increasingly rapid spread of breast cancer and the current lack of knowledge with respect to breast cancer's cause and cure, and effective methods of screening and treatment."

In this attempt to combat, or at least mitigate, breast cancer and its effects, the Rhode Island Department of Health is directed to provide and fund mammograms for women who qualify based on age and income, diagnostic testing to determine a diagnosis, and case management services for those with a positive diagnosis. In addition, the legislation includes "a mandate for programs of outreach, education, increased awareness, and cultural competence to the statewide community." The overriding purpose of the Breast Cancer Act is to ensure that women of all cultures and backgrounds living in Rhode Island have access to breast cancer screening and treatment and are educated in understanding the need for early detection of breast cancer.

The mission of the Rhode Island Department of Health's Women's Cancer Screening Program (WCSP) is to reduce the burden of breast and cervical cancer "among low income women with a special emphasis on reaching un/underinsured, older, medically underserved, racial, ethnic, and/or cultural minorities, including American Indians, Alaska Natives, African Americans, Hispanics/Latinos, Asian Americans, lesbians, women with disabilities, and other emergent populations . . . specifically the refugee populations" (Rhode Island Department of Health 2010). Over the course of the program, over 23,000 women have been enrolled (Rhode Island Department of Health 2010).

As noted earlier, the provision of health services is the most comprehensive area of government mandates that include cultural competency provisions. In fact, as of 2010, this is the only area where the federal government has mandated cultural competency. There are several provisions throughout the federal Public Health and Welfare Code mandating cultural competency. These provisions include cultural competency for health professionals working with diverse populations (Health Professionals Training for Diversity 2010) and cultural competency provisions in the awarding of grants concerned with minority health issues (see Agency for Health Care Research and Quality 2010; Health Information and Health Promotion 2010). Although these are general mandates, they lend support to the notion that the federal government is beginning to recognize the necessity of including cultural considerations in providing competent and comprehensive health care.

The federal government has also mandated cultural competence in the Developmental Disabilities Assistance and Bill of Rights Act of 1987. The act notes that "disability is a natural part of the human experience that does not diminish the right of individuals with developmental disabilities to live independently, to exert control and choice over their own lives, and to fully participate in and contribute to their communities through full integration and inclusion in the economic, political, social, cultural, and educational mainstream of United States society." The statute further notes that "there is a need to ensure that services, supports, and other assistance are provided in a culturally competent manner, that ensures that individuals from racial and ethnic minority backgrounds are fully included in all activities provided under this [Act]."

The purpose of the act is "to assure that individuals with developmental disabilities and their families participate in the design of and have access to needed community services, individualized supports, and other forms of assistance that promote self-determination, independence, productivity, and integration and inclusion in all facets of community life, through culturally competent programs." The act contains a policy provision that states, in part:

> It is the policy of the United States that all programs, projects, and activities receiving assistance under this [Act] shall be carried out in a manner consistent with the principles that (1) individuals with developmental disabilities, including those with the most severe developmental disabilities, are capable of self-determination, independence, productivity, and integration and inclusion in all facets of community life, but often require the provision of community services, individualized supports, and other forms of assistance; (2) individuals with developmental disabilities and their families have competencies, capabilities, and personal goals that should be recognized, supported, and encouraged, and any assistance to such individuals should be provided in an individualized manner, consistent with the unique strengths, resources, priorities, concerns, abilities, and capabilities of such individuals; (3) individuals with developmental disabilities and their families are the primary decision-makers regarding the services and supports such individuals and their families receive, including regarding choosing where the individuals live from available options, and play decisionmaking roles in policies and programs that affect the lives of such individuals and their families; (4) services, supports, and other assistance should be provided in a manner

that demonstrates respect for individual dignity, personal preferences, and cultural differences; and (5) specific efforts must be made to ensure that individuals with developmental disabilities from racial and ethnic minority backgrounds and their families enjoy increased and meaningful opportunities to access and use community services, individualized supports, and other forms of assistance available to other individuals with developmental disabilities and their families.

It is apparent that this statute has much more specificity in the need for cultural competence than the general health care provisions noted above. These provisions are largely a result of research conducted through the President's Committee for People with Intellectual Disabilities—a standing committee.

Cultural competency is an established part of modern health care both in education and in practice. Both state and federal agencies have recognized that in order to have effective health care services, cultural competency must be integrated into the practice. When governments and agencies are looking to mandate cultural competency in other areas, they often look to the health-care initiatives for guidance, practices, and procedures.

PUBLIC EDUCATION MANDATES

California, Florida, Indiana, Maryland, Minnesota, North Carolina, Oregon, Utah and Washington are among the states that mandate cultural competence in public education. These mandates generally revolve around teacher credentialing for bilingual educators and initiatives for special needs and at-risk students.

An illustration of how cultural competence is mandated in public education can be seen in the North Carolina School-Based Management and Accountability Program (2010). This legislation is especially illuminating because it is the direct result of a lawsuit filed by students alleging unequal opportunities in public education in North Carolina. In a watershed case in North Carolina, *Leandro v. State* (1997), the court held that the North Carolina Constitution recognizes that the legislative and executive branches have the duty to provide all the children of North Carolina the opportunity for a sound basic education. The litigation started primarily as a challenge to the educational funding mechanism imposed by the General Assembly that resulted in disparate funding outlays between low-wealth counties and their more affluent counterparts. With the *Leandro* decision, however, the thrust of the litigation turned from a funding issue—funding for poor counties versus funding for wealthy counties—to one requiring the analysis of the qualitative educational services provided to the respective plaintiffs.

The *Leandro* court stated that "an education that does not serve the purpose of preparing students to participate and compete in the society in which they live and work is devoid of substance and is constitutionally inadequate" (345). The court then defined sound basic education as one that provides students with at least

(1) sufficient knowledge of fundamental mathematics and physical science to enable the student to function in a complex and rapidly changing society; (2) sufficient fundamental knowledge of geography, history, and basic economic and political systems to enable the

student to make informed choices with regard to issues that affect the student personally or affect the student's community, state, and nation; (3) sufficient academic and vocational skills to enable the student to successfully engage in postsecondary education or vocational training; and (4) sufficient academic and vocational skills to enable the student to compete on an equal basis with others in formal education or gainful employment in contemporary society. (347)

Although the students prevailed in the *Leandro* case, that was not the end of the issue in North Carolina.

In *Hoke County v. State*, 358 N.C. 605 (2004), students filed an action for a declaratory judgment against the State of North Carolina and the North Carolina State Board of Education for the declaration of their educational rights. Ruling that the state had failed in its constitutional duty to provide sound basic education in rural districts, the court directed the state to remedy the deficiencies. Ultimately the case was decided and the students' motion granted in *Hoke County v. State*, 601 S.E. 2d. 199 (N.C. 2004). In the final analysis, the state was required to act to correct the deficiencies contributing to its failure to provide a constitutional educational opportunity.

In an informative bit of dicta at the end of his opinion, Judge Orr stated:

> Finally, the Court notes that the original Constitution of our state, adopted on 18 December 1776, included the specific provision "that a school or schools shall be established by the legislature, for the convenient instruction of youth" (N.C. Const. of 1776, para. 41). Some months before, William Hooper, one of North Carolina's delegates to the Continental Congress in Philadelphia, had solicited information from John Adams as to his thoughts on what should be included in a soon-to-be drafted constitution for North Carolina. Modern historians note that at the time, Adams was considered a "renowned authority on constitutionalism," and that as he contemplated the future of the country, Adams became convinced that its success rested on education, see David McCullough, John Adams, 364 (Simon & Schuster 2001). Adams, in subsequent correspondence, wrote: "[A] memorable change must be made in the system of education[,] and knowledge must become so general as to raise the lower ranks of society nearer to the higher. The education of a nation[,] instead of being confined to a few schools and universities for the instruction of the few, must become the national care and expense for the formation of the many." This Court now remands to the lower court and ultimately into the hands of the legislative and executive branches, one more installment in the 200-plus year effort to provide an education to the children of North Carolina. Today's challenges are perhaps more difficult in many ways than when Adams articulated his vision for what was then a fledgling agrarian nation. The world economy and technological advances of the twenty-first century mandate the necessity that the State step forward, boldly and decisively, to see that all children, without regard to their socioeconomic circumstances, have an educational opportunity and experience that not only meet the constitutional mandates set forth in *Leandro*, but fulfill the dreams and aspirations of the founders of our state and nation. Assuring that our children are afforded the chance to become contributing, constructive members of society is paramount. Whether the State meets this challenge remains to be determined. (*Hoke County v. State*, 358 N.C. 605 at 648–649, 2004)

The state attempted to meet the challenge with the School-Based Management and Accountability Program (2010). This program is a "Child and Family Team Initiative" that applies to elementary and secondary public education. According to the statute, "The purpose of the Initiative is to identify and coordinate appropriate community services and supports for children at risk of school failure or out-of-home placement in order to address the physical, social, legal, emotional, and developmental factors that affect academic performance." The initiative is a collaborative effort between the state's Department of Health and Human Services, the Department of Public Instruction, the State Board of Education, the Department of Juvenile Justice and Delinquency Prevention, the Administrative Office of the Courts, and other state agencies providing services for children. The agencies "share responsibility and accountability to improve outcomes for children and their families."

According to the statute, the program is based on the following principles: "one child, one team, one plan . . . individualized strengths-based care . . . [and] cultural competence." It involves teams of licensed nurses and social workers working together with children and families to provide solutions to the issues facing the children. The goal of the program is to keep children in school and to improve their performance. Taking all factors affecting the students and their families into account, the initiative attempts to provide a holistic and culturally relevant approach to student retention.

It appears that the initiative is working. According to two principals in the North Carolina school system, the program has had a positive impact on the school and the students. One principal stated:

> The . . . Team is a vital part of our school. They are involved in all aspects of attendance, discipline, academics and other problems that cause drama for at risk students. We meet almost daily on problems and the social worker is a very important part of our Student Services Management Team. Our dropout rate has gone from 42, 2 years ago, 23 last year and this year under 20. Our team really goes above and beyond for our students. We are able to get involved in almost every student problem many of which we would overlook normally because of priority until the problem gets serious. I cannot imagine not having the . . . team in our school. It has a very positive effect on our school. Our Social Worker really cares deeply for every student and never stops trying to help. (North Carolina Child and Family Leadership Council 2010)

Another principal stated:

> Our school continues to improve and the . . . program has had a direct impact on that improvement. During the past 4 years, suspensions have decreased from 215 in 2005–2006 to 53 during this past school year. Attendance has improved and the percentage of students on grade level has increased. The [team] has reached students and their families with needs that would have otherwise fallen through the crack. I don't know how we operated without them in the past. (North Carolina Child and Family Leadership Council 2010)

Cultural competency measures in public education are becoming more prevalent within state departments of education. States are beginning to recognize that in order to provide students with comprehensive effective education, both the majority and minority cultures in the community must be addressed and understood. Students are entering into a multicultural workforce, and cultural competency training should extend not only to the educators but also to the students themselves.

FAMILY AND CHILD WELFARE MANDATES

As illustrated by the North Carolina School-Based Management Program, family and child welfare issues often involve health-care services, social services, criminal justice services, and educational services. States mandating cultural competence in this area include Alabama, Arkansas, California, Connecticut, Florida, Illinois, Indiana, Maryland, Missouri, New Jersey, New York, North Carolina, Oklahoma, Ohio, Oregon, and Utah. Often when dealing with these issues, especially children's issues, states will have a comprehensive team plan to provide services to the child and/or the family and they will mandate cultural competency in that plan—that is the case with Oregon's Youth Services Wraparound Initiative (2010).

The Wraparound Initiative is a "definable team-based planning process involving a youth and the youth's family that results in a unique set of community services and service supports individualized for that youth and family to achieve a set of positive outcomes." In the context of the initiative, cultural competence means "accepting and respecting diversity and differences in a continuous process of self-assessment and reflection on one's personal and organizational perceptions of dynamic culture." The partner agencies within the initiative are mandated to ensure cultural competence in the provision of services to the youth and family through the following measures:

> (a) Implementing uniform standards to allow state and local agencies to describe the culturally appropriate services and supports available in a system of care; (b) Providing youth and families with an understandable and effective system of care services in a manner compatible with their cultural beliefs, practices, literacy skills and language; (c) Developing and implementing a process to review practices accepted by diverse communities; and (d) Identifying ways to continually improve a culturally competent system of care services and implementing a statewide system of care that reflects culturally competent practices.

According to the statute, the purpose of the Wraparound Initiative is to provide a system of care that involves a coordinated network of services, including education, child welfare, public health, primary care, pediatric care, juvenile justice, mental health treatment, substance abuse treatment, developmental disability services, and other services that "integrate care planning and management across multiple levels, that is culturally and linguistically competent, that is designed to build meaningful partnerships with families and youth in the delivery and management of services."

Another interesting family initiative is Missouri's Foster Parent's Bill of Rights (2010). The statutory Bill of Rights recognizes the importance of maintaining inherent culture in the lives of foster children. The statute states that foster parents "shall make decisions about the daily living conditions of the child, and shall be permitted to continue the practice of their own family values and routines while respecting the child's cultural heritage." Missouri foster parents are mandated to "provide care that is respectful of the child's cultural identity and needs." Recognizing that cultural competence can be learned, the state provides foster parents with "training that specifically addresses cultural needs of children, including, but not limited to, information on skin and hair care, information on any specific religious or cultural practices of the child's biological family, and referrals to community resources for ongoing education and support. This is one of the more specific competency mandates, in that it provides specific details of what the foster parents need to learn in order to achieve meaningful cultural competence.

Cultural competence mandates for family and child welfare initiatives recognize that culture is an important part of people's lives. In order to successfully intervene into family matters when the need arises, agencies must appreciate and understand the family's culture. Any attempt at a successful intervention into family issues must have a relevant and meaningful cultural component.

POLICE AND CRIMINAL JUSTICE MANDATES

In matters involving police and criminal justice policy, cultural incompetence can result in devastating harm to individuals. Many police departments have been accused of cultural insensitivity and making assumptions about people based solely on their cultural background—in other words, culturally profiling citizens in their jurisdiction. Due largely to lawsuits and clashes with various cultural groups, cities have taken the lead on mandating cultural competency training in police and criminal justice services. The training may be general in nature or it may revolve around the prevalent culture with the city.

The New York City Police Department (NYPD), which has been criticized for its cultural insensitivity, has recently begun a program called "Streetwise: Language, Culture and Police Work in New York City." The program is a training program for all new officers who have graduated from the Police Academy. According to the NYPD's website, "Streetwise helps new officers understand the important role of culture and its impact on police-community interaction. Basic language instruction helps officers improve their ability to communicate across cultures and better serve the community in which they work" (New York City Police Department 2010).

Other cities that have initiated mandates for cultural competency training for police officers include Chicago, Illinois; Hartford, Connecticut; Minneapolis, Minnesota; Yakima, Washington; Clearwater, Florida; and Houston, Texas. Since Minneapolis has one of the largest concentrations of Somali refugees in the country, many officers have learned simple Somali phrases to assist in policing (PACT 2010). Further, the Minneapolis police force has learned that using a forefinger to beckon someone is interpreted by Somalis as an obscene gesture (PACT 2010). In Yakima, Hispanics make up nearly 35 percent of the 220,000 residents and cultural competency efforts revolve around the Hispanic language and culture (PACT 2010). In practice, however, it appears that all the city of Yakima has accomplished is making information from the police department to the public available in Spanish.

Clearwater, Florida, on the other hand, has initiated a comprehensive Hispanic Outreach Program—Operation Apoyo Hispano—in its police department. Hispanic residents in Clearwater account for about 15 percent of the total population and are "an under-served population because of language barriers and cultural perceptions that keep some Hispanics from joining the mainstream" (City of Clearwater Police Department 2006). The goals of Operation Apoyo Hispano are to reach out to Hispanic residents, bridge the gap in communicating with the Spanish-speaking population, seek ways to positively resolve law enforcement issues, and increase the number of bilingual officers and staff (City of Clearwater Police Department 2006).

In 2003 the Clearwater Police Department received the Program Excellence Award from the International City/County Management Association (ICMA) for its Operation Apoyo Hispano. The award recognizes communities and their administrators for innovative and successful programs.

On the state level, Connecticut, Oregon, and Rhode Island are among the states that have mandated cultural competence in some police services. Rhode Island has made this mandate through the Select Commission on Race and Police-Community Relations Act (2010). The purpose of the commission is to assist in improving police-community relations in the state. It is charged with recommending changes that will improve relations and changes needed in "statutes, ordinances, institutional policies, procedures and practices deemed necessary to: improve law enforcement work and accountability; reduce racism; enhance the administration of justice; and affect reconciliation between diverse segments of the . . . community." Finally, it is the duty of the commission to recommend policies and procedures regarding the level and quality of diversity training and cultural competency.

As immigrant populations in the United States increase, police departments are going to face more challenges with regard to policing in multicultural jurisdictions. As of early 2010, there have been few, if any successful lawsuits brought against police departments alleging cultural incompetency. Most lawsuits against law enforcement where culture is an issue are argued on the basis of civil rights or constitutional rights. Police departments, however, are beginning to recognize that in order to avoid some of these suits and to improve community policing, cultural competence initiatives in police training and community relations can have a significant, and positive, impact on both the police force and the community as a whole.

SERVICES FOR VULNERABLE INDIVIDUALS MANDATES

One could argue that every state mandate previously mentioned could be placed in the category of services for vulnerable individuals, since they all deal with individuals who are from minority cultures and are, indeed, vulnerable. However, Indiana has a specific, and significant, mandate for its services for vulnerable populations. The Indiana mandate is charged to the Board for the Coordination of Programs Serving Vulnerable Individuals (2010). According to the statute, the board has the following duties:

> (1) Oversee the implementation of the recommendations made by the Commission of Disproportionality in Youth Services, including the ongoing review and evaluation of . . . programs, practices, and procedures; (2) Suggest policy, program, and legislative changes related to services provided to members of a vulnerable population to accomplish the following: (a) enhance the quality of and access to services with positive outcomes for vulnerable populations; [and] (b) reduce disproportionality of young persons of color in youth services by changing or eliminating policies that contribute to poor outcomes for persons of color;

(3) Oversee and coordinate the review, evaluation and development of consistent statewide standards for the use of risk and needs assessment tools that are culturally sensitive and promote objectivity in decision making at service delivery points in the system serving members of a vulnerable population; . . . [(4)] Work collaboratively within and across state and local agencies and programs to achieve statewide standards for mandatory, ongoing cultural competency training and professional practice standards for government employees, school personnel, service providers, and professionals in systems serving members of vulnerable populations; . . . [and (5)] Work collaboratively within and across state and local agencies to identify existing and to recommend new early intervention and prevention programming services for members of a vulnerable population.

The statute mandates that intervention and prevention programming is "sensitive to race and should include culturally sensitive, evidence based programming."

The Indiana statute is wide-ranging in its applicability to state agencies. Vulnerable populations include persons receiving services from the Department of Child Services, through the criminal justice or juvenile justice system, and from the Department of Workforce Development, and at-risk students or exceptional students as defined by the Department of Education. The definition of vulnerable individuals also includes young persons of color and any "other individuals recognized by the Board as members of a vulnerable population."

Although there is only one major state mandate dealing with vulnerable populations, this is a substantive area where cultural competency can make a great difference in the services provided. An understanding of the culture of the individual needing services could lead to more comprehensive and effective services. When these types of services are offered in a culture-neutral manner—if there is such a thing—they are often meaningless to the citizens and any benefit of the services or programs is lost or greatly diminished.

Native American Affairs Mandates

The final important substantive area where states mandate cultural competence is Native American affairs. New Mexico has several cultural competency mandates in its State-Tribal Collaboration Act (2009). The statute mandates that every state agency develops and implements a policy that "(1) promotes effective communication and collaboration between the state agency and Indian nations, tribes, or pueblos; (2) promotes positive government-to-government relations between the state and Indian nations, tribes, or pueblos; and (3) promotes cultural competency in providing effective services to American Indians or Alaska Natives." Further, the state agencies are mandated to "make reasonable efforts to collaborate with Indian Nations, tribes, or pueblos in the development and implementation of policies, agreements and programs of the state agency that directly affect American Indians or Alaska Natives."

In furtherance of this mandate, the New Mexico Tribal-State Judicial Consortium and the New Mexico Supreme Court's Court Improvement Project Task Force have provided a "Resource for Judges, Attorneys, Social Workers, Child Advocates, and Others Who Work with Children and Families" (2005, hereafter referenced as Judicial Consortium). In addition to providing assistance in complying with state mandates, the guide also provides assistance in complying with the federal Indian Child Welfare Act of 1978 (25 U.S.C. § 1902 [2010]). The guide notes that prior to the passage of the act, "Indian children were removed from their homes and placed in foster and adoptive placements, including institutional placements, at rates far higher than non-Indian children. Adoption rates for Indian children were eight times higher than for non-Indians, and 90 percent of adoptions were in non-Indian homes" (Judicial Consortium 2005). The 1978 act was an attempt to rectify this situation and to keep Native American families together and Native cultures viable.

The guide explains that "Native Americans in New Mexico live in 19 Pueblos, two Apache Tribes, and the Navajo Nation, as well as off-reservation throughout the state. . . . Overall, Native Americans represent nearly 10 percent of [the] population" (Judicial Consortium 2005). The guide further explains that each Native American group in New Mexico is sovereign and self-governing and differs from the others in language, government, judicial structure, custom, and tradition. Hence, it is difficult to generalize among groups, and those working with Native American populations must learn and understand the culture of the particular group they are serving.

Like previous mandates, New Mexico has recognized that in order to provide effective services, culture must be taken into account. Further, New Mexico has gone the extra step to include Native Americans in the decision-making process for matters affecting the tribes. Any attempt to be inclusive of the population and to understand the implications of policy decisions on minority cultures must necessarily include those in the minority culture in order to ensure cultural competency in public policy.

THE EFFECT OF STATUTORY AND REGULATORY MANDATES: LAWS, MORALS, AND ETHICS

Regarding the issue of cultural competency mandates, two questions come to the fore: (1) Does it take a mandate to ensure cultural competency in public services? and (2) Does having cultural competency mandates guarantee culturally competent public services? The answer, as with a great many public law issues, revolves around the distinction between law and morals or ethics.

Law can be defined as the "norms formally promulgated by a political authority that are enforceable and . . . enforced through a legal process based on adjudication" (Hazard 1995, 448). In the simplest terms, laws are societal norms that are written and expressed as generalizations. The fact that laws are "written" implies that the norms they are based upon have "a relative constancy of meaning throughout the jurisdiction and across time" (449). One of the major flaws in the law, as discussed by Hazard, is that rules of law "may lack semantic intelligibility" (449). In other words, the law is often not easily accessible or understandable. As a society, we do not learn and understand our obligations as citizens by reading the law. We do not learn to be culturally competent public servants through a cultural competence mandate. Laws, and their inherent faults as guides to behavior, give way to the concepts of morals and ethics.

Morals refer to the ideas of right and wrong that guide individuals in their daily lives. As Hazard explains, "The term 'morals' comes from the Latin word *mores*, a term that signifies usage in a community. More precisely the term can mean folkways imbued with an ethical significance. The reference to folkways reminds us that a person's morals inevitably reflect specific culture. Each of us is born into a culture that has its own specific folkways in which we become indoctrinated (451).

It is important to note the relevancy of culture in this definition. Morals do not occur in a vacuum—they are culturally relevant. Morals, however, do not necessarily imply a cultural or societal duty to others. Morals are personal and provide a framework for how individuals choose to live their lives. Moral philosophers such as Socrates, Plato, Aristotle, Hume, and Kant all recognize the subjective and personal nature of morals. When others do not hold the same moral standards, individuals often feel a sense of alienation from the rest of society.

Because of the singular nature of morals, "subjective moral standards cannot be publicly expounded like legal rules, nor can they be objectively administered [in the manner of] legal rules" (Hazard 1995, 452). Although we often say that someone has a moral duty to do something, this is not entirely accurate. The subjective and personal nature of morals keeps them from having a larger societal duty attached. Morals then leads us to ethics. Ethics may be viewed as the bridge between law and morals.

Ethics are norms that are shared by a group "on a basis of mutual and usually reciprocal recognition" (Hazard 1995, 453). As Hazard explains: "The term 'ethics' comes to us from the Greek *ethikos*, a word which signified a custom or usage. Thus, the term refers to a norm having the characteristic of being understood in a community. For a norm to have become understood in a community implies that the norm somehow was made manifest within the community" (454). It further implies that a norm is derived from past practice and has a history within a relevant community or culture. For instance, one can identify a public service ethic that exists in a particular community; those in the community are aware of the history of the ethic.

There is an interaction between laws, morals, and ethics. As Hazard explains:

> In a given community at a specific time, there is a continuous interaction among the various types of norms signified by the terms law, morals, and ethics. We all know that some laws are taken very seriously and generally observed, such as the law of homicide even in our troubled country. We know that other laws are not taken as seriously, such as the speed limit on the interstate and much of the building codes. However, those who disobey the speeding laws or the building codes do not consider themselves oblivious to community norms. Rather, they believe that the community in practice recognizes that some ethical norm has "trumped" the legal norm. Most drivers would say, for example, that driving over the posted speed limit is only technically wrongful. But they would also say that driving 85 miles an hour violates the ethics of driving. Moreover, they would say that driving at 85 is a violation that justifies an arrest and speeding ticket, whereas they would say that a ticket for driving 60 miles an hour represents an excess of governmental authority. A similar interaction occurs in virtually all situations where the discrepancy is substantial between what the law ordains and what people actually do. It is impossible for people other than psychopaths to proceed in life without being mindful of the ethical norms prevailing in their community. . . . Members of a community are in position to change the relationship between law and ethics. Obviously, this is the position of members of a modern legislature whose business includes deciding whether emergent ethical notions should be transformed into law. (456)

When people fail to fulfill their ethical duties to the community of their own volition, that ethic is often codified into law. It is the difference between "should" and "have to."

Community ethics, and ultimately laws, change when people's individual morals begin to change and new practices become the norm in the community or culture. "The flow of normative change is from subjective morality to an ethic shared by a group, eventually perhaps into expression as law" (Hazard 1995, 457).

So, back to the two questions posed earlier: (1) Does it take a mandate to ensure cultural competency in public services? and (2) Does having cultural competency mandates guarantee culturally competent public services? If individuals have the moral inclination and communities have the ethical duty to include cultural competence in their lives and work, then a statutory mandate is unnecessary. If the public administration community—agencies and administrators—have a cultural competency ethic in their practice, then they will take actions that are culturally competent without having to have a mandate that requires such action. However, as James Madison (1788) famously wrote in *The Federalist* No. 51, "If men were angels, no government would be necessary." The same could be said for laws. Whether cultural competency is too new an idea in public administration and has not yet been fully integrated into administrative education, or whether administrators simply do not believe that cultural competence is necessary, thus far cultural competence has not been an overriding ethic of administrative practice. Hence, it may not take a mandate to ensure cultural competency in administrative practice; however, mandates may encourage consistency in providing culturally competent public services and may have the effect of changing the administrative ethic so that where mandates do not require cultural competency, administrators, nonetheless, practice cultural competency.

Having a mandate, however, does not ensure that administrators will act in a culturally competent manner. A cultural competency mandate does not ensure culturally competent administrative practice any more than a speed limit law ensures that drivers follow the speed limit. Voluntary action is generally preferable to mandated action. This is the idea of the "buy-in." When individuals buy into a policy or practice, they are likely to follow that practice. However, when individuals are forced, or mandated, to follow a policy or practice, they may feel resentful of that practice and either disregard the practice or follow it only in name and not in spirit.

In order to consistently, comprehensively, and effectively provide culturally competent public services, administrators and agencies must cultivate a cultural competence ethic. It is only when the administrative community recognizes the necessity of cultural competency in administrative practice that true culturally competency in the provision of public services will be achieved.

REFERENCES

Agency for Health Care Research and Quality. 2010. Establishment and General Duties. U.S. Code 42 §299a-1.

Aka, Phillip C., and Lucinda M. Deason. 2009. Culturally competent public services and English-only laws. *Howard Law Journal* 53 (Fall): 53, 64–66.

American Civil Liberties Union (ACLU) of Florida. 2010. English-only. http://aclufl.org/take_action/download_resources/info_papers/6.cfm.

Board for the Coordination of Programs Serving Vulnerable Individuals (Indiana). 2010. Burns Ind. Code Ann. §4–23–30.2–11.

Breast Cancer Act (Rhode Island). 2010. R.I. Gen. Laws §23–12.7.2.

City of Clearwater Police Department. 2006. Hispanic outreach. www.clearwaterpolice.org/hispanic/index.asp.

Civil Rights Act of 1964. 1964. Public Law 88–352. U.S. Statutes at Large 78 (1964), 241.

Culturally Competent Healthcare Demonstration Program (Illinois). 2010. 20 ILCS 2310/2310–216.

Developmental Disabilities Assistance and Bill of Rights. 2010. Program for Individuals with Developmental Disabilities, General Provisions, U.S. Code 42 (2010), §15001.

Foster Parent's Bill of Rights (Missouri). 2010. Missouri Revised Statutes §210.566.

Hazard, Geoffrey C., Jr. 1995. Laws, morals and ethics. *Southern Illinois Law Journal* 19: 447.

Health Information and Health Promotion. 2010. U.S. Code 42 §300u-6.

Health Professionals Training for Diversity. 2010. U.S. Code 42 §293.

Hoke County v. State. 2004. 358 N.C. 605.

Hoke County v. State (N.C.). 2004. 601 S.E. 2d. 199.

Indian Child Welfare Act of 1978. 1978. 25 U.S.C. §1902 (2010).

Leandro v. State. 1997. 346 N.C. 336.

Madison, James. 1788. *The Federalist* No. 51. *Independent Journal*, February 6. www.constitution.org/fed/federa51.htm.

Meltzer, Matt. 2007. The Dade County English-only ordinance. Miami Beach 411, July 16. www.miamibeach411.com/news/index.php?/news/comments/english-only-ordinance/.

New Mexico Tribal-State Judicial Consortium and The New Mexico Supreme Court's Court Improvement Project Task Force. 2005. Preserving Native American families in New Mexico: A resource for judges, attorneys, social workers, child advocates, and others who work with children and families. New Mexico Administrative Office of the Courts.

New York City Police Department. 2010. Community affairs: Training programs—Training for police officers. www.nyc.gov/html/nypd/html/community_affairs/training_programs.shtml.

North Carolina Child and Family Leadership Council. 2010. January 2010 report to the governor. www.ncdhhs.gov/childandfamilyteams/publications/January-2010-CFST-Legislative-Report.pdf.

PACT. 2010. Hartford takes another crack at cultural-sensitivity training. *Law Enforcement News*, December 2004. www.pacttraining.com/who_we_are/articles_on_pact/len_cult_comp.

Rhode Island Department of Health. 2010. Women's cancer screening program. www.health.ri.gov/programs/womenscancerscreening.

School-Based Management and Accountability Program (North Carolina). 2010. N.C. Gen. Stat. §115C-105.20.

Select Commission on Race and Police-Community Relations Act (Rhode Island). 2010. R.I. Gen. Laws §42–137–5.

State-Tribal Collaboration Act (New Mexico). 2009. N.M. Stat. Ann. §11–18–3.

U.S. Constitution. 1868. Amendment 14—equal protection.

Vulnerable Populations Defined (Indiana). 2010. Burns Ind. Code Ann. §4–23–30.2–11.

Youth Services Wraparound Initiative (Oregon). 2010. ORS §418.975.

Cultural Competence When Serving Abroad

CHIMA IMOH

The importance of cultures and nationalities lies in the knowledge that individual identities derive from them and thinking is partly conditioned by them. The culture of an individual therefore has an impact on workplace behaviors, expectations, and tendencies. The global integration and interaction in governance and shared international problems involve different cultures, thereby creating high levels of cultural diversity in workplaces, in interactions, and around negotiation tables. This cultural diversity can lead to a unique set of challenges as the individuals from different cultures interact. Substantial numbers of staff members of such public organizations as the United States Agency for International Development (USAID) and state department offices operate in multiple regions, each with distinct cultures and subcultures. The importance of understanding the ethical values of these different cultures is appreciable because whereas most organizations and professions have codified sets of ethical rules, cultures do not.

Some major cultural constraints face public organizations and government departments that operate overseas. These constraints arise from the unfamiliar factors and problems that are associated with the international environments and value systems. The first constraint is the cultural diversity of the international environments and the effects such have on the ways people work in and manage organizations and departments. The second constraint is the ethical issues related to dealing with different values and ethical standards. Public officials serving abroad usually face problems of adjustment to new environments. Some even lack the proper motivation for a foreign assignment, whereas some experience huge cultural shock. The problems posed by these cultural differences are reduced by the awareness of the differences in cultural values and beliefs, verbal and nonverbal communication patterns, and approaches to decision making and conflict resolution (Grosse 2002, 34). Moreover, possessing a favorable disposition toward learning about other cultures helps in the establishment of rapport among interacting parties in international settings.

Hence, the improper management of the cultural diversities that exist in foreign assignments and organizations can lead to miscommunication that could disrupt workplace cohesion. However, granted that the diversity inherent in multicultural organizations presents some problems, some obvious advantages also arise from them. For example, culturally diverse workplaces can enhance creativity, lead to better decision-making processes, and result in effectiveness and higher productivity. A monocultural workplace does not enjoy the benefit of diverse opinions, a multitalented worker pool, and multiple propensities for creativity. Cultural diversity also prevents one-way thinking (groupthink) by which group members are culturally pressured to agree with mainstream thinking. Sound cross-cultural competence is of immense importance to successful foreign assignment or management. Therefore, it is critical to employ, train, develop, and retain officials who not only have technical expertise but also possess cross-cultural competences, knowledge, and experiences. This chapter examines the cultural issues involved in serving abroad and makes recommendations to help public organizations and government departments achieve the desired goal of improved management by public officials who serve abroad.

THE CULTURAL DYNAMICS OF SOCIETIES

The existence and importance of the relationships between cultural systems and organizational practices are worth appreciating. These cultural systems can permeate all levels of public organizations, and those engaged in cross-national relationships and interactions need to be concerned with these cross-cultural issues (Hofstede 1983, 75). In studying the cultural orientation of societies, the Dutch scholar Geert Hofstede analyzed cultural dimensions on the basis of power distance, individualism, collectivism, masculinity, femininity, and uncertainty avoidance (Daft 1995; Ronen and Shenkar 1985). In simple terms, these respectively mean the analysis of how people accept social inequality (power distance), the bonds between the individual and his or her societal groups (individualism versus collectivism), the extent to which the individual embraces the competitive masculine orientation or the nurturing feminine traits (masculinity versus femininity), and the extent to which people strive to control their situations (uncertainty avoidance). Hofstede explained the cultural tendency of the various nationalities through these dimensions. The concepts of individualism/collectivism and power distance are most relevant here (Figure 4.1).

The concept of individualism reflects the value of loosely knit social relationships in which individuals are expected to take care of themselves, whereas collectivism reflects a preference for closer social networks in which individuals tend to look after one another (Kemmelmeier et al. 2003). The concept of collectivism also emphasizes the interdependence between the self and one's group or community (Oyserman, Coon, and Kemmelmeier 2002, 5). Hence, collectivists place high value on collective goals, guided by group norms and authority figures (Lu 2006, 437).

While uncertainty avoidance is the tolerance or acceptance of ambiguity, risk, or chance factors (Daft 1995), power distance reflects the level at which people are comfortable with inequalities in the wielding of power among institutions and people (Kemmelmeier et al. 2003). Power distance is also a construct that refers to the degree to which relationships between individuals in a society are hierarchical (Hofstede 1985, 352). In such low power distance societies as the United States, subordinates and superiors perceive and treat each other as colleagues who have equal rights, with

Figure 4.1
Hofstede's Cultural Dimensions

Individualism Versus Collectivism
Individualism implies such societies as the United States that have high degrees of freedom where individuals are expected to look after their own interests. In individualistic cultures, the individual is assumed to be self-motivated and self-actualized, with self-interest defining relationships. The need of the individual is valued over collective, or group, needs. This dimension of culture emphasizes the protection of self-image and freedom from imposition. On the other hand, collectivism (otherwise called low individualism) applies to societies in which individuals expect others in the groups to which they belong to protect their interests, and in exchange the individuals incline toward group loyalty. This collectivism emphasizes in-group solidarity, loyalty, and interdependence among individuals.

Masculinity Versus Femininity
Masculine cultures place high value on assertiveness, independence, task orientation, and self-achievement, whereas feminine cultures value cooperation, relationship, empathy for the less fortunate, moderation, and preference for relationships. Masculinity is the male-oriented inclination to assertiveness and competition. Such societies as the United States, high in masculinity, emphasize assertiveness, acquisition of money, and material goods, while deemphasizing concern for others. However, the most masculine countries are Japan and the Latin American countries. On the other hand, femininity (also called low masculinity) emphasizes relationships, concern for others, and quality of life. The most feminine countries are Sweden, Denmark, Norway, Finland, and The Netherlands. Notably, labeling countries that emphasize cooperation, moderation, and empathy for the less fortunate as feminine is an apt example of the stereotyping that usually leads to gender bias in workplaces.

Power Distance
Power distance implies the degree to which status, wealth, or power differences are acceptable to a society. In low power distance societies, individuals strive for power equalization and justice. The low power distance Anglo-American, Nordic, and Germanic cultures place more emphasis on competence than on seniority. High power distance societies are status-conscious, respecting age and seniority, bestowing outward importance on protocol, formality, and hierarchy. Very high power distance societies, such as Saudi Arabia, Nigeria, and the Philippines, accept and support large imbalances in power, status, and wealth; much respect is shown for those in authority; and titles, ranks, and status are revered. In such low power distance societies as Norway and Denmark, inequalities are minimized.

Uncertainty Avoidance
Uncertainty avoidance refers to the degree of tolerance a society has for surprises. This dimension also refers to the degree to which individuals in the society feel uncomfortable in risky, uncertain, or unpredictable situations and the degree to which the society favors conformity or is tolerant of deviant ideas. In such high uncertainty avoidance societies as Iran, China, Mexico, and Italy, people feel threatened by uncertainty and show little tolerance for deviation. In low uncertainty avoidance societies as the United States, the Nordic countries, and the United Kingdom, people are reasonably tolerant of different behaviors and opinions, do not feel threatened by such differences, and are also willing to accept personal risk.

Source: Lewicki, Barry, and Saunders (2009), as adapted from Hofstede (1983).

the subordinates expecting to have inputs in the decisions or actions affecting them (Harrison et al. 1994). The leadership styles in such societies are often participatory. By contrast, in such high power distance societies as the Arab, Asian, and African countries, superiors expect to lead and make decisions. The leadership styles in such societies are predominantly autocratic or paternalistic.

Based on the cultural dimensions developed by Hofstede (1983, 78–85), Simcha Ronen and Oded Shenkar (1985, 444–445) added the works of other scholars to create clusters of countries of similar cultures, as follows:

1. Such countries as the United States, Canada, Australia, the United Kingdom, South Africa, New Zealand, and Ireland are high in individualism, high in masculinity, moderate in power distance, and low in uncertainty avoidance.
2. The Germanic countries like Switzerland, Germany, and Austria are moderate in individualism, masculinity, and uncertainty avoidance, and low in power distance.
3. The Nordic countries—Sweden, Denmark, Norway, Finland, and The Netherlands—are moderate in individualism and uncertainty avoidance, and are low in masculinity and power distance.
4. The Near Eastern countries—Greece, Iran, and Turkey—are low in individualism moderate in masculinity, and high in power distance and uncertainty avoidance.
5. The Arab cluster that includes such countries as Saudi Arabia, United Arab Emirates, Bahrain, Kuwait, Oman, and Abu-Dhabi is low in individualism, moderate in masculinity and uncertainty avoidance, and high in power distance.
6. The Far Eastern countries—the Philippines, Hong Kong, Malaysia, Singapore, Taiwan, Indonesia, South Vietnam, and Thailand—are low in individualism, moderate in masculinity and uncertainty avoidance, and high in power distance.
7. Latin American countries such as Argentina, Venezuela, Chile, Mexico, Peru, and Colombia are low in individualism and high in masculinity, power distance, and uncertainty avoidance.
8. Latin European countries such as France, Belgium, Italy, Spain, and Portugal are moderate in individualism and high in masculinity, power distance, and uncertainty avoidance.
9. Brazil, India, Israel, and Japan did not fit into any classification of the clusters. Ronen and Shenkar (1985, 452) indicate that economic development and technological advancement of these countries have created an override on the cultural tendencies of their geographical groupings.

Except for Hofstede (1983), none of the other studies classified African countries. However, Hofstede (78–85) defined the African clusters as follows:

1. Arabic African countries such as Egypt and Libya share the same dimensions with the Arab countries—low individualism, moderate masculinity and uncertainty avoidance, and high power distance.

2. West African countries such as Nigeria, Ghana, and Sierra Leone are low in individualism, high in power distance, and moderate in uncertainty avoidance and masculinity.
3. East African countries such as Kenya, Ethiopia, and Zambia are low in individualism, high in power distance, and moderate in uncertainty avoidance and masculinity.

THE IMPACT OF CULTURE IN FOREIGN SETTINGS

Though the interrelationships between organizations are hinged on operational matters, more attention and resources are needed to increase understanding of the cultural differences between the employees in multicultural work environments (Bird and Osland 2006), thus surpassing cultural differences and promoting interactions between cultures. Understanding different cultures helps to create strategies for communicating and negotiating with people from such cultures. Understanding the ethical values of these different cultures would likely create the required synergies in cross-cultural interactions. However, creating synergies in these interactions becomes more challenging when the national cultural distance is large. National cultural distance is the degree to which the cultural norms in a country are different from those in another country (Lu 2006, 437). These cultural differences exist in varying magnitudes and can range across values, norms, and ethics. Difficulties interacting across cultures exist because in every distinct culture, beliefs, attitudes, and norms differ and are often unconsciously practiced (Bird and Osland 2006). The larger the national distances between the countries of the interacting individuals, the more challenging the culturally influenced issues become.

As earlier noted, Hofstede analyzed the cultural orientation of human systems by using four parameters: power distance, individualism, uncertainty avoidance, and masculinity. The tendencies of any human system as defined by these cultural dimensions have profound influences on personal and organizational practices. For instance, the strict adherence to and acceptance of planning as an imperative organizational practice is related to the uncertainty avoidance dimension of culture (Triandis 1995). Human systems with high uncertainty avoidance culture usually insist on proper and detailed planning, whereas systems with low uncertainty avoidance orientation usually operate on an ad-hoc basis.

In like manner, systems with high masculine orientation operate with an aggressive and achievement-driven organizational and supervisory style. For example, a culture of emphasis on achievement, assertiveness, and material success may be appropriate for the United States. However, this tendency could create some measure of concern for many other international environments. Often it brings resentment and becomes counterproductive. Also, systems with individualistic orientation are usually quick in making decisions without detailed analysis. On the other hand, decision making in systems with collectivist orientation is usually slow but more detailed in analysis. Given these differences, diversity, if properly managed, especially in task-oriented assignments, creates such advantages as creativity, innovative ideas, and minimal groupthink.

Cultural Attitudes

For people serving abroad, the most important aspects of multicultural relationships are their effects on attitudes and communication. The culture of a society affects the values, ethics, attitudes, and assumptions of the individual. This cultural orientation also guides the individual's values, work ethics, and morality. However, basic differences exist in ethics and values of different societies. Collectivist societies such as Saudi Arabia show much respect for authorities, titles, birth, and religious status. The Saudis also attach much importance to status and rank; culturally, it is important never to criticize or berate anyone in public. In contrast, such individualistic societies as the United States are achievement societies in which rewards and honor come with personal achievement. The power distance in these societies is low and hence, not much importance is attached to status and rank.

The style and mode of communication also carry some cultural underpinnings. Among the Arabs, Africans, and Asians, a great deal of indirect and nonverbal communication takes place. In contrast, in the United States the style of communication is concise, direct, and explicit.

In societies with collectivist cultures, relationships play visible roles in all aspects of life, and government affairs are transacted mostly on a personal basis. That is, employment, career advancement, and organizational transactions are usually based on personal relationship. In these societies, even official interactions are friendship-based, and most often, official assistance is rendered on the basis of personal relationships. Opportunities for economic advancement also revolve around the government and its agencies and are usually dispensed through personal relationships. Paternalism is a very common leadership style in collectivist cultures—the boss is involved in such personal celebrations as weddings, children's welfare and graduation, and bereavements. The indication here is that the administrator should expect a certain level of nepotism and favoritism, especially in employment.

Communication Styles

Communication is probably one of the most relevant tools for managing a multicultural organization. Every management function involves some form of direct or indirect transmission of messages (Kreitner and Kinicki 2002). The creation of effective communication sustains organizations (Denhardt and Denhardt 2002). However, cultural diversity usually presents unique challenges when people from diverse cultural backgrounds attempt to communicate effectively (Goa and Ting-Toomey 1998). This diversity comes with the risks of misunderstanding that may hamper the collaboration between the concerned individuals and may adversely affect the outcomes of operations (Bouncken 2004, 240).

The cultural orientation of the individual also impacts on the style of transmitting messages. For instance, low-context cultures tend to communicate by as explicit and detailed means as possible. Hence, communication in the low-context Western culture is typically direct and explicit (Brett, Behfar, and Kern 2006). This contrasts with high-context cultures, in which the true meanings of communicative actions are usually hidden in the manner in which the message is conveyed or in some other nonverbal clues. For these high-context cultures, communications are implicit and indirect. For example, Chinese is a high-context culture that leaves a considerable part of a message unsaid, leaving the interpretation of the missing information to the other party (Laroche and Toffoli 2002, 507). The Chinese therefore tend to avoid stating their intentions directly and expressing their emotions overtly (507). Because of these differences, communication between people of different contextual backgrounds may suffer from misunderstandings because it either conveys too much or too little information (Bouncken 2004, 244).

The public service environment in the United States has essentially become multinational and multicultural, leading to a growing need for effective communication. This internationalization of the workforce therefore requires that public administrators become conscious of the communications procedures and conventions of foreign cultures, especially those relevant to their duties and functions. The need to make communication more effective by involving cultural awareness, sensitivity, and understanding has increased (Dou and Clark 1999).

However, effective communication in international settings depends on the ability to construct common-sense communication (Bird and Osland 2006). Each culture has its own distinct manner of exchanging messages (verbal and nonverbal). Therefore, ensuring the success of a foreign posting would require a deep understanding of cultural differences. By understanding the models of different cultures, public administrators can create strategies for dealing and negotiating with different cultures (Cuthertson 2003). Otherwise, if the operations of multicultural teams become hindered by poor communications, the long-term goals of the organization or department could be jeopardized.

CULTURAL COMPETENCE WHEN SERVING ABROAD

The main cultural variables that affect one's ability to function effectively abroad are communication, perception, and cultural barriers (Hodgetts, Luthans, and Doh 2005). Communication is the process of transferring meanings from sender to receiver (Hodgetts, Luthans, and Doh 2005). Miscommunication therefore occurs when messages are not received or not correctly decoded. The various issues that can cause miscommunication include the differing styles of communication, trouble with accents, and language fluency (Brett, Behfar, and Kern 2006).

When any individual understands the working language differently, tasks become impaired. The administrator should therefore bear in mind that vocabulary and language style may be a source of many incidents of miscommunication (Tokarek 2006). Likewise, harboring negative perceptions of a cultural group could also be unhealthy because it can lead to disrespectful treatment of others. The challenge is to search for new ways to create understanding of the different interacting value systems as well as improving communication by minimizing the gap of misunderstanding of the interacting cultural systems (Dou and Clark 1999).

Administrators and employees can avoid problems caused by miscommunication by taking the following proactive steps.

Steps to Cultural Competence

Choose the Appropriate Channels of Communication

In most societies, the urgency and importance of a message determines its channel of communication. An effective public administrator should know the channel appropriate for each particular situation. For instance, persons of Arab descent are more likely to recognize the importance of decisions or the urgency of announcements when they receive such face-to-face (Tokarek 2006).

Ensure Clarity of Language

When communicating in a multicultural environment, public administrators should ensure that both the spoken and written languages are clear and concise. The advice is not only to be clear but also ensure that verbal as well as nonverbal communications are reliable and consistent (Taylor 2006). Wholesome administrative management requires the same clarity of communication (Tokarek 2006).

In negotiations, an Arab would most likely understand the Western direct communication style, whereas the Westerner is unlikely to understand the indirect and implicit style of an Arab. However, by leading the way and making spoken and written language clear and concise, an Arab is likely to follow do the same.

Avoid Ethnocentrism and Be Sensitive to Cultural Differences

Public officials serving abroad should recognize the existence of cultural differences between parent and host countries and learn to accept and understand those differences. These administrators should therefore develop the knowledge and working understanding of the cultural context in which the communication takes place (Dou and Clark 1999) and accept that it may be necessary to change habits or mind-sets when communicating across cultures (Taylor 2006).

In most Arab countries, women are excluded from certain environments, are separated from men at public places, are not expected to go out in the company of males who are not their husband or relatives, and are not allowed to drive. Religious leaders justify the ban on women driving cars on the grounds that "the unsupervised movement of individual women whenever and wherever they want to go encourages sexual misconduct" (Asad 2003, 684). As Carol Frausto, a single woman and the first female commercial officer at the United States Embassy in Riyadh, Saudi Arabia, explains, because wives are often excluded from social gatherings or entertained separately, she was often the only woman at official business functions (Frausto 2000). An American's typical ethnocentric behavior might include disdain for this kind of treatment of women due to a lack of understanding of the religious and cultural underpinnings of the gender-bias in male-female relationships in Saudi Arabia.

Recognize and Deal with Miscommunication Problems Promptly

Problems emanating from cultural misconceptions and miscommunications in multicultural workplaces are often subtle. The public administrator constantly needs to be on the lookout for the telltale signs of such problems. Miscommunications in multicultural workplaces often go unnoticed, are simply ignored, or are blamed on character flaws of the communicator (Tokarek 2006). Public administrators should stay in tune with the way interpersonal relationships develop and should recognize simmering problems and step in before full-blown conflicts erupt. This skill is also important when negotiating because it gives one the ability to recognize some emotional signs that usually influence the outcomes of negotiation.

Develop Prenegotiation Relationships

Cultural undertones exist in the understanding and perception of the purpose of negotiations. From the perspective of the American society, the purpose of negotiations is essentially to arrive at and sign a binding contract. However, in the Asian, Arab, Chinese, and Japanese cultures, the major essence of negotiation is not a signed contract, but rather the creation of a relationship (Hodgetts, Luthans, and Doh 2005). The purpose of prenegotiation activities in these cultures is to establish trust. Essentially, negotiations in an international setting are about trust and mutual respect, so the orientation should focus toward long-term commitments rather than toward making a deal (Lewicki, Barry, and Saunders 2009). Personal relationships and interactions usually have positive impacts on cross-cultural negotiations. For example, in negotiations, Arabs seek to build support with bargaining partners and commence serious negotiations only after initiating personal relationships through face-to-face meetings (Hodgetts, Luthans, and Doh 2005).

Avoid Stereotyping (Understand That Subcultures Exist)

A good number of cultures have subcultures. One culture cannot therefore be a stereotype of the entire group. The cultural dynamics within most cultures are complex and are made up of different religious and ethnic groups. Citizens from countries with great cultural diversity often exhibit strong ethnic affinities to their group, and misidentifying them could bring some unexpected measures of animosity. Generalizations can be dangerous because in many ways there are greater differences within any given culture than between one culture and another (Billikopf-Encina 2000). Making quick assumptions about the cultural groups of colleagues or negotiation counterparts may undermine other meaningful efforts. For instance, the culture of the Ibos of largely Christian southern Nigeria is quite different and distinct from the culture of the mainly Muslim north. Similarly, there is no homogeneity in the values, beliefs, and behavior patterns in the so-called "Asian culture" (Lewicki, Barry, and Saunders 2009). One should therefore not jump to conclusions based on limited knowledge (Hanson and Fox 1995); when in doubt, seek clarifications.

Build Trust and Good Relationships

Another way to be an effective public administrator when serving abroad is to develop a rapport built on understanding, especially when involved in team tasks (Grosse 2002). The key to this is showing the willingness to listen to others. For effective cross-cultural communication, public administrators need to develop cultural sensitivity (Grosse 2002, 34). Moreover, outcomes are positive when public administrators show open-mindedness, respect, and patience when dealing across cultures (Grosse 2002, 30). Mistrust sometimes constitutes a barrier to mutual respect, and whenever it arises it must be overcome by creating trust and credibility.

Acquire Knowledge of the Hosts' Language and Mode of Communication

An acquisition of a rudimentary knowledge of certain aspects of a host's language and modes of communication is necessary and leads to better communication. Learning the basic language for greeting others and shopping (even when associates speak English) is quite important (Hanson and Fox 1995). An obvious or implied disrespectfulness for the hosts' modes of communications should be avoided. For instance, the Arabs show bonding and friendship through such gestures as same-sex cheek kissing and hugging. In the same way, a same-sex arm link is a nonverbal indicator of trust, friendship, and bonding. Friendly arm linking between two males in Arab, African, and Latin American cultures is a commonplace practice (Ting-Toomey 1999, 130). This, in some Western cultures, might be incorrectly interpreted as an indication of sexual orientation, and an outward show of disapproval or discomfort could cause unexpected problems. Foreign serving administrators should therefore be open-minded about accepting the new culture and avoid overt or implied criticisms of local practices and customs (Hanson and Fox 1995).

STRATEGIES FOR CULTURAL COMPETENCE TRAINING

The purpose of every training exercise is to increase the probability of attaining set goals. Training is therefore of particular importance to oversea assignments because it enhances the possibilities for tapping the full potentials of the concerned officers (Hodgetts, Luthans, and Doh 2005). Training helps the officers serving abroad understand the customs and cultures of the host countries. The topics usually covered in this cultural training are customs, social and cultural etiquette, history, politics, local suspicions, and local rivalries (Hodgetts, Luthans, and Doh 2005). An effective and competent foreign-service management becomes an imperative when one considers that the cost of an unsuccessful international assignment extends beyond the monetary expenses. An unsuccessful foreign assignment could have a negative impact on future interactions or hurt nation-to-nation relationships (Culpan and Wright 2002). The various models of cultural competency training include use of cultural assimilators, cultural integrators, workplace diversification, and in-house sensitivity.

CULTURAL ASSIMILATORS

Cultural assimilators are learning techniques, programmed to show the basic norms, customs, attitudes, and values of various countries. This cultural assimilator model has become one of the most effective approaches toward improvement in cross-cultural competence (Hodgetts, Luthans, and Doh 2005). Exposing a public administrator preparing to serve abroad to some cultural sensitivity training could be done through an assimilation program. Most of the cultural assimilators essentially require the trainee to read or observe puzzling incidents or interactions, and interpret the situation. Cultural assimilators assist in the reduction of the novelty of the host cultures, thereby reducing the potential cultural shocks associated with new foreign assignments.

CULTURAL INTEGRATORS

This model involves placing individuals who are vastly knowledgeable in the local cultures in each foreign program, operation, or location. This is the model sometimes deployed by the United States military in Afghanistan as it embeds the locals into its operations, campaigns, and rebuilding efforts. These integrators advise and guide the actions needed to ensure smooth and synchronized operations (Hodgetts, Luthans, and Doh 2005). The primary purpose of this model is to improve the effectiveness of interactions with local personnel and citizens.

WORKPLACE DIVERSIFICATION

Organizations and departments that have special interests or commitments in particular countries could use workplace recruitment of individuals from those cultures as means of enhancing cultural competence. From the outset, it is necessary to expose employees to diversity even when such officers still reside in the home country. A way to do this is to have the officers work in multicultural groups in which team members have diverse cultural backgrounds (Adler 1997). Spy agencies, nations at war, international development agencies, and law enforcement agencies use this model.

IN-HOUSE CULTURAL SENSITIVITY TRAINING

The essence of in-house competence training is to sensitize the workers about the cultures of the host countries. This is necessary because creating cultural competence in multicultural environments requires education and training (McCain 1996). The development of cultural competence through multicultural interactions in the workplace builds a better appreciation of foreign assignment experiences and skills (Dou and Clark 1999, 60). This competence training includes not only the ability to apply language skills to situations, but also the ability to make good use of communication to attain organizational goals (McCain 1996, 65). This involves exposing the officers to the culture and values of the host country. These vast cultural peculiarities could include food, manner of speech, acceptable noise levels, gender, and religious issues.

To hasten adaptability of the foreign-service officials, this in-house cultural training starts in the home country and should be continued in the host country. In addition, this training should be offered to the officer's family members because a foreign assignment is more likely to succeed if the spouse and children continue to have a positive perception of the posting.

Ethical Issues in Foreign Service

Nations operate in multiple regions, each with distinct cultures and subcultures. It is quite common for officers on foreign assignments to be born into a culture distinctively different from the one in which they work or interact. Hence, it is important to understand the ethical values of the different cultures with which they interact.

Ethics are a system of moral principles, constituting the moral compass that guides individuals in personal decision making. Ethics are about right and wrong, good and bad, benefit and harm, and they define the nature of public managers and administrators (Stoner and Freeman 1989). Ethics, simply put, involve one's rights and duties, the rules one applies in making decisions, and how one's actions affect other people (Stoner and Freeman 1989). These standards of conduct indicate how one should behave based on moral duties and virtues that constitute the ethics of the organization or society. Usually an individual has an internal set of standards, values, and principles that guide one's everyday decision making. The challenge in comprehending ethics rests on its subjectivity, its intangibility, and, to some extent, its spirituality.

Culture, which is the "standard that determines the 'rightness' of the individual's behavior in a given society" (Swaidan, Vitell, and Rawwas 2003, 176), can have effects on the ethical orientation of the individual. In fact, specific ethical or moral principles are what define a cultural group's identity. Hence, the values considered ethical by one culture may differ from those of another. Whereas some practices are acceptable in some societies, they are not in others; hence cultural differences make ethical decisions more difficult (Johnson 2007, 303).

Ethical issues tend to exist in most public decision-making processes, and ethical dilemmas arise when right or wrong are not clearly identified and each alternative has a potentially harmful ethical consequence. The issues of ethics have acquired greater importance in recent times because interactions between governments, organizations, and foreign countries have become more frequent, and primordial interests no longer govern activities and decisions. Other reasons include the increasing scope of domestic legislative enactments and the global concerns about such issues as child labor, pollution, economic exploitation, and workplace safety. Again, understanding the ethical values of different cultures helps create the required synergies in cross-cultural interactions.

On the international front, however, this difficulty in making ethical decisions is exacerbated by the marked differences in value systems and practices. It therefore becomes incumbent upon the administrator to understand these culture differences when issues of ethics and values arise. Although recent research has begun to shed some light upon these differences, there remains much uncharted territory. The moral approach to public administration requires public administrators to be cognizant of the consequences of administrative action in terms of its impact on values such as liberty, justice, and human dignity (Lan and Anders 2000). The goal is to endeavor to balance the necessity of building and sustaining those personal relationships with the need to maintain the required professional standards. A guideline in doing this is to analyze ethical issues locally while keeping an eye on their global dimensions. Thinking locally and acting globally is a strategic concept that enjoins organizations to respond to local environments and at the same time consider their global implications. These situations sometimes lead to contradictions, but the administrator should be able to navigate whatever contradictions might arise. However, such issues as bribery, environmental degradation, child labor, human rights abuses, apartheid, discrimination based on race, gender, and disabilities, and a host of other issues have been universally accepted as unethical according to United Nations declarations and should never be compromised.

CONCLUSION

Cultural relationships and differences, including values, norms, ethics, and moralities, do not only exist between nations, they also exist in varying magnitudes. Each culture has its own distinctive features, and ensuring success in foreign assignments requires deep understanding of the cultural differences. The importance of the relationship between cultural systems and the practices of public departments operating overseas is quite obvious. However, these cultural diversities can lead to unique sets of challenges as people from these different cultural backgrounds interact. Moreover, the diversities also create risks of misunderstanding, which may hamper the collaboration between interacting partners or negotiators. Miscommunication, misunderstandings, and misperceptions can impair the free flow of ideas. Therefore, an effective public official should encourage open dialogue and facilitate the understanding of cultural groups that interact.

Most countries have embassies and other agencies in multiple regions, each with distinct cultures and subcultures, which create a unique set of cross-cultural challenges. In these foreign settings, the understanding of and approaches to administrative issues such as motivation, performance evaluation, team building, and leadership also differ across cultures. Therefore, the awareness of these differences will help public officials overcome the problems posed by cultural differences.

It is clear that in the increasingly multinational relationships of today, it is critical that officials serving abroad not only have the necessary technical expertise but also possess cultural knowledge of host countries. Hence, sound management of officials in foreign assignments is of critical importance for creating and maintaining good relationships with collaborating and negotiating partners. To achieve success in foreign assignments, it is therefore important to surpass cultural differences and ethnocentrism, and promote interaction between cultures.

REFERENCES

Adler, Nancy J. 1997. *International Dimensions of Organizational Behavior.* 3rd ed. Cincinnati: South-Western College.

Asad, Talal. 2003. Boundaries and rights in Islamic law: Introduction. *Social Research* 70(3): 683–686.

Billikopf-Encina, Gregorio. 2000. Communicating Across Cultures (book). *International Journal of Conflict Management* 11(4): 378–388.

Bird, Allan, and Joyce S. Osland. 2006. Making sense of intercultural collaboration. *International Studies of Management & Organization* 35(4): 115–132.

Bouncken, Ricarda B. 2004. Cultural diversity in entrepreneurial teams: Findings of new ventures in Germany. *Creativity & Innovation Management* 3(4): 240–253.

Brett, Jeanne, Kristin Behfar, and Mary C. Kern. 2006. Managing multicultural teams. *Harvard Business Review* 84(11): 84–92.

Culpan, Oya, and Gillian H. Wright. 2002. Women abroad: Getting the best results from women managers. *International Journal of Human Resources* 13(5): 784–801.

Cuthertson, Jennifer. 2003. Business across cultures. *Business Book Review* 22: 19.

Daft, Richard L. 1995. *Understanding Management.* New York: Dryden Press.

Denhardt, Robert B., and Janet V. Denhardt. 2002. The new public service: Serving rather than steering. *Public Administration Review* 60(6): 549–560.

Dou, Wei-lin, and George W. Clark Jr. 1999. Appreciating the diversity in multicultural communication styles. *Business Forum* 24(3, 4): 54–61.

Frausto, Carol. 2000. A woman's perspective to doing business in the Kingdom of Saudi Arabia. *Westchester County Business Journal* 39(8): 22.

Goa, Ge, and Ting-Toomey, Stella. 1998. *Communicating Effectively with the Chinese.* Thousand Oaks, CA: Sage.

Grosse, Christine Uber. 2002. Managing communication within virtual intercultural teams. *Business Communication Quarterly* 65(4): 22–38.

Hanson, Jennifer, and Wanda Fox. 1995. Communicating across cultures. *Training & Development* 49(1): 56–59.

Harrison, Graeme, Jill L. McKinnon, Sarala Panchapakesan, and Mitzi Leung. 1994. The influence of culture on organizational design and planning and control in Australia and the United States compared with Singapore and Hong Kong. *Journal of International Financial Management & Accounting* 5(3): 242–261.

Hodgetts, Richard M., Fred Luthans, and Jonathan P. Doh. 2005. *International Management: Culture, Strategy, and Behavior.* 6th ed. Boston: McGraw-Hill.

Hofstede, Geert. 1983. The cultural relativity of organizational practices and theories. *Journal of International Business Studies* 14(2): 75–89.

———. 1985. The interaction between national and organizational value systems. *Journal of Management Studies* 22(4): 347–357.

Johnson, Craig E. 2007. *Meeting the Ethical Challenges of Leadership: Casting Light or Shadow.* Thousand Oaks, CA: Sage.

Kemmelmeier, Markus, Eugene Burnstein, Krum Krunov, Petia Genkova, Chie Kanagara, Mathew Hirshberg, Hans-Peter Erb, Grazyna Wieczorkowska, and Kimberly Noels. 2003. Individualism, collectivism, and authoritarianism in seven societies. *Journal of Cross-Cultural Psychology* 34(3): 304–322.

Kreitner, Robert, and Angelo Kinicki. 2002. *Organizational Behavior.* 5th ed. Boston: Irwin/McGraw-Hill.

Lan, Zhiyong, and Kathleen K. Anders. 2000. A paradigmatic view of contemporary public administration research: An empirical test. *Administration & Society* 32(2): 138–165.

Laroche, Michel, and Roy Toffoli. 2002. Cultural and language effects on Chinese bilinguals and Canadian responses to advertising. *International Journal of Advertising* 21(4): 505–524.

Lewicki, Roy J., Bruce Barry, and David M. Saunders. 2009. *Negotiations: Readings, Exercises and Cases.* 6th ed. New York: McGraw-Hill.

Lu, Lung-Tan. 2006. The relationship between cultural distance and performance in international joint ventures: A critique and ideas for further research. *International Journal of Management* 23(3): 436–445.

McCain, Barbara. 1996. Multicultural team learning: An approach towards communication. *Management Decision* 34(6): 65–68.

Oyserman, Daphna, Heather M. Coon, and Markus Kemmelmeier. 2002. Rethinking individualism and collectivism: Evaluation of theoretical assumptions and meta-analyses. *Psychological Bulletin* 128(1): 2–72.

Ronen, Simcha, and Oded Shenkar. 1985. Clustering countries on attitudinal dimensions: A review and synthesis. *Academy of Management Review* 10(3): 435–455.

Stoner, James Arthur Finch, and R. Edward Freeman. 1989. *Management*. 4th ed. Upper Saddle River, NJ: Prentice-Hall.

Swaidan, Ziad, Scott J. Vitell, and Mohammed Y.A. Rawwas. 2003. Consumer ethics: Determinants of ethical beliefs of African Americans. *Journal of Business Ethics* 46(2): 175–186.

Taylor, Shirley. 2006. Communicating across cultures. *British Journal of Administrative Management* 53: 12–13.

Ting-Toomey, Stella. 1999. *Communicating Across Cultures*. New York: Guilford Press.

Tokarek, Margaret. 2006. How to manage intercultural communication. *People Management* 12(21): 66–67.

Triandis, Harry C. 1995. *Culture and Social Behavior*. New York: McGraw-Hill.

Human Resource Management Practices That Facilitate Cultural Competence

HEATHER WYATT-NICHOL
AND LORENDA A. NAYLOR

If current demographic trends continue, the 2010 census is likely to provide evidence of an increasingly diverse society within the United States. This increases the likelihood that public servants will interact with colleagues and clientele quite different from themselves. Understanding the values and norms of target populations that an organization serves is critical for responsive public service delivery. This chapter focuses primarily on human resource management (HRM) practices that facilitate cultural competency in federal agencies.

Human resource professionals are essential in the process of developing culturally competent organizations through their roles as "employee champions, administrative experts, change agents, and strategic partners" (Bailey 2005, 192). Similarly, HRM practices can facilitate or hinder effective public service delivery in cross-cultural situations. As a result, some federal agencies have implemented HRM practices to facilitate cultural competency. For example, the requirement of "culturally and linguistically appropriate standards" among health care agencies that receive federal funds has led to the inclusion of cultural competencies in job descriptions and qualifications used in the hiring process, as well as increased training and development initiatives in health care service organizations.

Federal job descriptions might include knowledge, skills, and abilities specific to cultural competence, such as knowledge of the impact of one's cultural origins on behavior and values, the ability to communicate on behalf of the client, and acceptance of cultural differences. Federal recruitment tools might include job initiatives and outreach efforts into previously marginalized communities (geographically and socially). For example, one of the goals of the Social Security Administration is to "attract a multigenerational, multicultural workforce with the competencies needed to achieve our mission" (SSA 2008, 19). Recruitment efforts focus on ensuring a multicultural workforce. According to the Office of Personnel Management (OPM), candidates for the Senior Executive Service (SES) must demonstrate leadership competencies that include cultural awareness (OPM 2000).

Figure 5.1
Definitions of Cultural Competence

Cultural competence is the capacity of an individual or an organization and its personnel to communicate effectively and to convey information in a manner that is easily understood by and tailored for diverse audiences (USDA 2010, D1). It is a set of congruent behaviors, attitudes, and policies that come together in a system, agency, or among professionals that enables effective work in cross-cultural situations. *Culture* refers to integrated patterns of human behavior that include the language, thoughts, communications, actions, customs, beliefs, values, and institutions of racial, ethnic, religious, or social groups. *Competence* implies having the capacity to function effectively as an individual and an organization within the context of the cultural beliefs, behaviors, and needs presented by consumers and their communities (DHHS 2011).

Cultural competence can also be reinforced through training and individual performance appraisals that include measures of cultural competence. The Health Resources and Services Administration recognized the Rainbow Center for Women, Adolescents, Children and Families, in Jacksonville, Florida, for including participation in an annual cultural competence training session as part of its employee performance measures (DHHS 2001).

Our chapter explores HRM practices that have the potential to facilitate cultural competence in federal agencies. We specifically examine the degree to which diversity and cultural competency are built into

1. the hiring process through recruitment and outreach efforts, and job descriptions and qualifications
2. employee training and development
3. performance appraisals

We also assess federal agencies' strategic plans and human capital plans to determine the public commitment to diversity, multiculturalism, and cultural competency training.

RATIONALE FOR CULTURAL COMPETENCE

Developed at the individual and organizational level, cultural competency is considered to be essential for effective public service delivery. Presumably, public organizations can improve service delivery by understanding the values and norms of the target population. In addition, cultural competency provides the means to address inaccuracies in service delivery (Rice 2010).

The National Technical Assistance Center for State Mental Health Planning in collaboration with the National Association of State Mental Health Program Directors (2004) provides a rationale for cultural competence that includes quality of care, disparity reduction, risk management, linguistic competence, and fundamental social responsibility.

The movement toward cultural competence in the provision of public services is "legally and strategically driven" (Riccucci 2002). One legislative mandate is the Disadvantaged Minority Health Improvement Act of 1990 (Public Law 101–527), which requires agencies within the Department of Health and Human Services to address disparities and cultural barriers that impact health-care service delivery and access. In addition, Executive Order 13166 (August 11, 2000) issued by President Clinton requires organizations that receive federal funding to ensure access to services by individuals with limited English proficiency. As a result of the legislation and executive order, the U.S. Department of Health and Human Services mandates culturally and linguistically appropriate standards among health-care organizations that receive federal funds.

It is also worth noting that while language and culture overlap there are distinctions between the two. For example, one might learn a language without learning about the history and culture of any particular group. Triandis (1995, 12) asserts, "Culture is to society what memory is to individuals . . . it consists of ways of perceiving, thinking, and deciding that have worked in the past and have become institutionalized in standard operating procedures, customs, scripts, and unstated assumptions that guide behavior." While language proficiency contributes to cultural competence, language proficiency alone is not equivalent to cultural competence.

CULTURALLY COMPETENT ORGANIZATIONS

Culturally competent organizations are characterized as valuing diversity, engaging in self-assessment, understanding cross-cultural interactions, institutionalizing culture within organizational activities, and adapting service delivery (Cross et al. 1989). In transitioning from cultural blindness to cultural competency, the National Association of State Mental Health Program Directors (2004) highlights the importance of leadership, commitment by key staff and stakeholders, structural changes, resources, and culturally responsive services. Similarly, Riccucci (2002) notes the importance of organizational and behavioral strategies for change that are fostered through policy and practice to enhance employee skills in serving the public. Inherent in the transition to cultural competence are HRM practices that value diversity and facilitate cultural competence. HRM practices are the mechanism for communication, continuity, and rewards.

Prior to establishing specific policies to move an organization toward cultural competence, it is important to conduct individual and organizational assessments to determine the current skill levels and institutional support. An assessment is intended to address the degree to which cultural competency is reflected in the organization's strategic plan, operational policies and procedures, and day-to-day practices. Rice (2010, 196) argues that assessments are critical to cultural competency: specifically,

organizational self assessment involving both organizational leadership and staff in areas of organizational mission statements that support multiculturalism and diversity; organizational culture; outreach, hiring procedures, and hiring outcomes that reflect the engagement of individuals from undervalued and underrepresented groups; continuing staff training in cultural diversity; effective communications and appropriate languages; policy and procedural manuals that support cultural competency; and efforts to make the organization more prescriptive and more welcoming to all cultural and linguistic groups.

STRATEGIC HUMAN CAPITAL MANAGEMENT

In 1993, Congress passed the Government Performance and Results Act (GPRA, Public Law 103–62). The purpose of the act was to increase performance measurement and to "improve Federal program effectiveness and public accountability by promoting a new focus on results, service quality, and customer satisfaction." It requires all federal agencies to submit performance plans and strategic plans. According to Henry (2001, 313), public sector strategic planning "is the development, articulation, prioritization, and communication planning of significant policy goals by public organizations." Strategic plans provide key information on an organization's mission, vision, values, and future activities, which are essential in an organization's assessment of cultural competency (Rice 2010).

Human capital management systems are designed to integrate HRM practices with the strategic plan of the organization. According to Selden (2009), human capital systems have five goals: strategic workforce planning, recruitment and selection, retention, training and development, and managing and rewarding performance. At the federal level, Executive Order 13197 (Government Accountability for Merit System Principles: Workforce Information, 2001) grants authority to the Office of Personnel Management (OPM) to require HRM accountability systems among federal agencies. The Human Capital Assessment and Accountability Framework (HCAAF) was devised by OPM to provide guidance to federal agencies on how to implement human capital management systems. Elements of the HCAAF include strategic alignment, knowledge management, results-oriented performance that "promotes a diverse, high-performing workforce through the use of effective performance management systems and awards programs," talent management, and accountability (Selden 2009, 6).

METHODOLOGY

A systematic document review of the fifteen federal executive level agencies was conducted to assess the level of public commitment to diversity recruiting and hiring practices and cultural competency training. The document review consisted of the agencies' strategic plans and human capital plans, thus allowing for uniform data collection. In addition to reviewing each document, we typed in variations of the words *diverse*, *cultural*, and *training* in the online strategic plans and human capital plans of each federal agency. Agencies were categorized "yes" or "no" based on whether or not their mission and vision statements, values, and strategic goals stated in the strategic plans support "multiculturalism and diversity" (Rice 2010, 196). Multiculturalism and diversity have two dimensions: (1) workforce, and (2) public service delivery. If either of these two dimensions was discussed, the agency was coded as "yes." Next, agencies were rated "yes or no" based or whether or not their human

Table 5.1

Human Resource Management Practices That Facilitate Cultural Competence in Public Organizations

Agency	Mission statement	Vision statement	Values	Strategic goals	Human capital plan
Department of State (1789)	No	No	Yes	No	No
Treasury Department (1789)	No	No	Yes	No	Yes
Department of Defense (1789)	No	No	No	No	Yes
Department of Justice (1870)	No	No	Yes	No	Yes
Department of the Interior (1849)	Yes	No	No	Yes	Yes
Department of Agriculture (1889)	No	No	No	No	Yes
Department of Commerce (1903)	No	No	No	No	No
Department of Labor (1913)	No	N/A	N/A	N/A	No
Department of Health and Human Services (1953)	No	No	No	No	No
Department of Housing and Urban Development (1965)	No	No	N/A	Yes	Yes
Department of Transportation (1966)	No	N/A	Yes	No	Yes
Department of Energy (1977)	No	No	No	No	Yes
Department of Education (1979)	No	N/A	No	No	No
Department of Veterans Affairs (1988)	No	No	Yes	Yes	Yes
Department of Homeland Security (2002)	No	No	Yes	No	Yes

Note: N/A = not applicable.

capital plans support "staff training in cultural diversity . . . and efforts to make the organization more prescriptive and more welcoming to all cultural and linguistic groups" (Rice 2010, 196). This document review is limited in two respects. First, only information available to the general public was reviewed for this assessment. If an agency did not post a strategic plan or human capital plan on the agency's public website, then it was listed as not available. It is important to note that several federal agency websites were missing human capital plans. These include the Department of Commerce, Department of Education, Department of Health and Human Services, Department of Labor, and Department of State. The results of the document review are provided in Table 5.1.

MISSION AND VISION STATEMENT, AND STRATEGIC PLAN

Although it is widely recognized that the demographics across the country have changed and will continue to change to reflect a more diverse America, federal agency strategic plans do not reflect this transformation. Out of the fifteen federal agency strategic plans reviewed, only six agency plans mentioned the word *diversity* or implied it. These were the Department of Homeland Security (DHS), Department of Justice (DOJ), Department of the Interior (DOI), Department of State (State Dept.), Department of the Treasury, and Veterans Administration (VA). Only one of the fifteen agencies indicated that diversity, multiculturalism, or cultural competency was critical to the agency mission or vision: DOI. The DOI explicitly states its support of underrepresented populations. According to its mission statement, "The U.S. Department of the Interior protects and manages the Nation's natural resources and cultural heritage; provides scientific and other information about those resources; and honors its trust responsibilities or special commitments to American Indians, Alaska Natives, and affiliated Island Communities" (DOI n.d., 12). Five agencies mentioned diversity as part of their core values: DHS, DOJ, DOS, Treasury, and VA. The Department of Homeland Security identifies respect as one of its four core values with an emphasis on diversity. The strategic plan for DHS (2008, 3) states, "We will highly value the relationships we build with our customers, partners, stakeholders, and each other. We will honor America's liberty, democracy, and diversity."

The DOJ supports multiculturalism and diversity as a core value on both dimensions: workforce and public service delivery. Its core values include "equal justice under the law" and "respect for the worth and dignity of each human being" (DOJ n.d.-a, iii). Specifically, the DOJ strategic plan states that "we enforce these laws fairly and uniformly to ensure that all Americans receive equal protection and justice" and that "we treat each other and those we serve with fairness, dignity, and compassion. We value differences in people and ideas" (iii). The Department of Treasury identifies teamwork as a core value, which includes "respect[ing] differences in people" (2006, iii). One of the Department of the Treasury's core values is community, which includes promoting diversity (2007). A core value of the VA is professionalism, which includes a diverse workforce (VA 2010).

Only three agencies mentioned diversity in their strategic goals. The Department of Housing and Urban Development (HUD) supports diversity in its public service delivery. One of its four goals in the strategic plan is to "build inclusive sustainable communities free from discrimination" (HUD 2010, 32) and a subgoal is to "ensure open, diverse, and equitable communities" (33). In addition, one of the VA's strategic goals is to provide services to veterans with disabilities. The DOI seeks to improve education for Indian tribes (n.d., 66). In addition, the agency is committed to increasing the number of diverse candidates hired (71). The DOI definition of diversity extends beyond legally protected classes. "Dimensions of diversity include age, ethnicity, gender, physical abilities/qualities, race, sexual orientation, educational background, geographic location, income, marital status, military experience, parental status, religious beliefs, work experience, etc." (89).

TRADITIONAL HUMAN RESOURCE MANAGEMENT PRACTICES

We contend that HRM practices are essential for developing and sustaining culturally competent organizations. Traditional HRM practices used to develop and sustain cultural competency within organizations may be categorized along the personnel functions of recruitment and selection, training and development, and performance appraisal (Table 5.2).

Organizations must have an understanding of the demographic characteristics of their constituents. One might ask whether an organization serves an older population, a working-class population, a large Latino population, or some combination of characteristics. While a representative bureaucracy reflecting characteristics of the population does not automatically translate into culturally competent service delivery,

Table 5.2

Human Resource Management Practices That Facilitate Cultural Competence in Public Organizations

	Recruitment/Selection	Training/Development	Performance appraisal/ Performance measures
Department of State (1789)		"Where efficient and cost-effective, the Department, USAID, and the Foreign Service Institute (FSI) will integrate systems and coordinate strategies to improve the skill base, diversity, and performance of our workforce" (DOS Strategic Plan 2007, 39).	
Treasury Department (1789)	"Comprehensive outreach plans have the potential to dramatically increase the number and diversity of high quality applicants for positions. Initiatives focused on internal and external partnerships; applicant-friendly information, tools and processes; marketing of Treasury as an employer of choice; and entry-level programs (e.g., honors intern program) targeted towards Mission Critical Occupations (MCOs), all have the potential to reach and engage a broader talent pool. In addition, recruitment strategies and workforce planning must focus on workforce demographics and trends" (Treasury Human Capital Strategic Plan n.d., 14).		
Department of Defense (1789)	DOD initiatives to develop SES. Among the foundational principles of the initiative: 6. "SES leaders will be drawn from the best of America's diverse populations. SES leaders will represent the full spectrum of qualified, diverse talent available in the United States. The diversity of SES leaders contributes to a broader cultural awareness and fosters effective communication in the global operating environment of the Department" (Bradshaw 2007, 8).	"Informed DoD policy is needed to provide overarching guidance for 3C education, training, assessment, and institutional practices" (McDonald et al. 2008, 2).	"A near-term study should be conducted to select candidate off-the-shelf assessment tools and assess their validity within the DoD context(s). Tools that characterize the cross-cultural context, climate, competence, interactions, and performance should be considered. Outcome metrics must also be established to help link to program outcomes and establish effectiveness" (McDonald et al. 2008, 4).
Department of Justice (1870)	"In partnership with the DOJ Equal Employment Staff and the Office of Attorney Recruitment and Management, develop a comprehensive recruitment strategy to hire highly talented and diverse employees for DOJ mission-critical occupations" (DOJ Human Capital Strategic Plan, n.d.-a, 8).		

Agency			
Department of the Interior (1849)	"Having a diverse workforce is essential to providing services to the culturally and linguistically diverse populations that visit the Department's facilities and lands. Having a diverse workforce helps recruitment and retention of highly skilled employees" (DOI Strategic Human Capital Plan 2002, 11).	Student Education Employment Program: "The SEEP program offers opportunities to expand diversity recruiting and to identify candidates for skill shortage areas" (DOI Strategic Human Capital Plan 2002, 35).	
Department of Agriculture (1889)	Through one of its key strategies, the USDA plans on "identifying and modeling 'best practices' of Department-wide recruitment strategies, particularly those for diversity initiatives" (USDA Strategic Workforce Plan 2008b, 7). E. (Kika) de la Garza Fellowship Collaboration with Hispanic Servicing Institutions (HSI) National Scholars Program at Historically Black Land-Grant Universities	Agricultural Research Services "The Executive Professional Excellence and Knowledge Program (PEAK). PEAK develops a competitive pool of culturally diverse, highly qualified employees as potential, future ARS leaders. PEAK is a 24-month training and development program targeted at GS-14s and above" (USDA Strategic Workforce Plan 2008a, 35). Courses via Skillsoft catalog for Foreign Agricultural Service Competencies include: Culture and Behavior: "Diversity audits, strategies for increasing diversity awareness" (USDA/FAS 2009, n.p.). Managing cultural divides: "Develop intercultural communication skills and cross-cultural negotiation skills" (USDA/FAS 2009, n.p.).	One of five strategic human capital goals: "The Department has a diverse, results-oriented, high-performing workforce and a performance management system that differentiates between high and low levels of performance and links individual/team/unit performance to organizational goals and desired results effectively" (USDA Strategic Workforce Plan 2008b, 3).
Dept of Commerce (1903)			
Department of Labor (1913)			
Department of Health and Human Services (1953)	"Goal 1: Health Care: Improve the safety, quality, affordability and accessibility of health care, including behavioral health care and long-term care. Objective 1.4 Recruit, develop, and retain a competent health care workforce" (DHHS, n.d.)	"The Physician Cultural Competency Curriculum Modules and Culturally Competent Nursing Modules are two of the Center's most important training programs. We also created the Health Care Language Services Implementation Guide and are working on a Cultural Competency Curriculum for Disaster Preparedness and Crisis Response" (DHHS, OMH 2008, n.p.).	Useful sources for integrating cultural competence measures into performance appraisal: HRSA: Report on Measuring Cultural Competence in Health Care Delivery . . .; Comprehensive Framework and Preferred Practices for Measuring Cultural Competency . . . can serve as performance measures

(continued)

Table 5.2 *(continued)*

	Recruitment/Selection	Training/Development	Performance appraisal/ Performance measures
Department of Housing and Urban Development (1965)	"To maintain a high quality workforce, we will recruit, develop, manage and retain our diverse workforce" (HUD Strategic Human Capital Plan 2008).		
Department of Transportation (1966)			
Department of Energy (1977)	"We have developed corporate recruitment strategies to target diverse institutions; devise measures to close disparity; skill gaps will be closed; use of corporate retention strategies, career development, and training; assessment of employed improvements for applicability, efficiency, and effectiveness" (DOE Strategic Human Capital Plan 2006a, III-9).		
Department of Education (1979)			
Department of Veterans Affairs (1988)		"Perform organizational needs assessments to assess need for cultural competency training in workforce management and service delivery. Implement cultural competency training and evaluations to address identified workforce and client services needs in this area" (VA Diversity and Inclusion Strategic Plan 2009, 21).	
Department of Homeland Security (2002)	Customs and Border Patrol; Spanish Language Proficiency Test for Border Patrol Officers	Training for cultural competence includes Incident Management for First Responders of Different Cultures; The First Three to Five Seconds: Arab and Muslim Cultural Awareness for Law Enforcement; Diversity Series: Religions, Cultures, and Communities	

it does increase the likelihood of such delivery. For example, hiring a Latina who speaks Spanish increases language proficiency of the agency. Hiring individuals from humble beginnings increases the likelihood that they will be able to identify resource obstacles to service delivery (e.g., agency assumptions that citizens in need of assistance have the transportation to get to the agency or the ability to take a day off from work in the middle of the week). In addition to measuring the degree of diversity within the organization, a diversity audit (Rice 2010) should be conducted to assess the experience of various groups within the organization and to uncover hidden biases and assumptions.

Once the organization gains an understanding of its internal workforce and the target population to be served, it can conduct a needs assessment to establish training and development initiatives. The Office of Personnel Management recommends cultural audits to assess the cultural environment and identify potential obstacles (Riccucci 2002). A cultural audit may be used to "examine a public organization's values, symbols, rules, and routines, which maintain its purpose and existence to uncover counterproductive activities and barriers that may adversely impact its public service mission and service delivery process" (Rice 2010, 130).

Training needs will vary based on the purpose and location of the organization, the target population, the internal workforce, and the results produced by the cultural audit. Once training has occurred throughout the organization, performance appraisals may be used to ensure employee accountability for developing cultural competence and improving service delivery.

RECRUITMENT AND SELECTION

The framework of cultural competence extends beyond diversity management; however, it cannot occur in the absence of diversity. Human resources professionals report that important diversity management outcomes include establishing a work environment that values contributions from all members in the organization, leveraging differences for strategic advantage of the organization, and eliminating or minimizing prejudice (Society for Human Resource Management 2008). Workforce diversity is also included as a critical success factor for a "results-oriented performance culture"—one of the key elements in the OPM Human Capital Assessment and Accountability Framework (OPM 2011). Nevertheless, the Government Accountability Office (2007) reports that developing and maintaining a diverse workforce continues to be a key recruitment challenge among federal agencies. Recruitment is also among the goals of the Chief Human Capital Officers Council (CHCOC 2010): "Goal I: The Council will support OPM's strategic goals of Hiring the Best and Respecting the Workforce, by playing a critical role in the implementation of Veterans Employment, Hiring Reform, Labor-Management Relations, and Diversity." Many federal agencies mention the achievement of a high-quality workforce, including recruitment and development efforts to build and retain a diverse workforce, among the strategic goals in their human capital plans.

Organizations might assess their recruitment efforts by exploring barriers to hiring diverse staff, the degree to which advertising reaches underrepresented groups, and the extent to which diversity management and cultural competence skills are included as qualifications for various positions. Some federal agencies reach out to high schools and vocational schools to stimulate interest in science and technology, particularly among minority students. For example, NASA has developed a "grow your own" scholarship program at three Texas Air Force bases that include on-the-job training and classroom instruction in aircraft maintenance (GAO 2007). Similarly, the United States Department of Agriculture (USDA) partners with institutions of higher education with high minority enrollments, including historically black colleges and universities (HBCUs) and the Hispanic Association of Colleges and Universities, as a strategy to close skill gaps within the organization. The E. (Kika) de la Garza Fellowship program facilitates collaboration between the USDA and faculty and staff from colleges and universities that have been designated as Hispanic servicing institutions (HSI). Through the USDA's National Scholars Program, students at HBCUs pursuing degrees in agriculture or other relevant majors receive financial and in-kind assistance in exchange for working for one year at the USDA for each year of financial assistance. The agency has reported positive results from its efforts as minority representation has markedly increased over the past five years (USDA 2008b). The Department of Energy (DOE) includes a Leadership and Diversity Strategy within its strategic human capital plan to address underrepresentation. As stated within the plan, "We have developed corporate recruitment strategies to target diverse institutions; devise measures to close disparity; skill gaps will be closed; use of corporate retention strategies, career development, and training; assessment of employed improvements for applicability, efficiency, and effectiveness" (DOE 2006a, III-9). For example, the Minorities in Science and Education Consortium (MSEC) represents DOE offices, twelve additional federal agencies, and three Hispanic organizations to identify potential interns in science and engineering (DOE 2006b, III-15). Similarly, the strategic human capital plan of the Department of the Interior highlights the Student Education Employment Program (SEEP) as one initiative to recruit diverse candidates for skill shortage areas (DOI 2002). The Department of Transportation human capital strategic plan (2007, 12) highlights efforts to increase diversity through candidacy pools via the agency's Career Residency Program and the Federal Highway Administration (FHWA) Professional Development Program.

EMPLOYEE TRAINING AND DEVELOPMENT

Employee training and development are also critical to strategic workforce planning, and in recent years cultural diversity has been linked to training and development in various public sector organizations. The Government Employees Training Act (GETA; 5 U.S.C. 4101–4119) is the most comprehensive piece of legislation relevant to training and training information. This law includes providing training for the purposes of succession planning, productivity, and performance improvement. In terms of cultural competence and performance, organizational self-assessments may be used to revise job qualifications and develop appropriate training for cultural competency (Bailey 2005). For example, the Veterans Administration Diversity and Inclusion strategic plan for 2009–2013 states as one of the three major goals: "Facilitate outstanding customer service and stakeholder relations by promoting cultural competency, accountability, education, and communication" (VA 2009). To meet this goal, the agency conducts a needs assessment to determine the cultural competencies necessary for internal workforce development and effective service delivery to constituents.

In addition, candidates for the Senior Executive Service (SES) must demonstrate mastery of executive core qualifications. Cultural awareness, included among the leadership competencies, is defined as "the ability to initiate and manage cultural change within the organization to impact organizational effectiveness" (OPM 2011, 11). Key characteristics include valuing diversity, fostering cooperative environments, assessing unique needs of employees, providing developmental opportunities, and positive, constructive resolution of conflict. For example, DOD initiatives to develop SES emphasize the importance of diversity: "The diversity of SES leaders contributes to a broader cultural awareness and fosters effective communication in the global operating environment of the Department" (Bradshaw 2007, 8). Similarly, Agricultural Research Services focuses on the development of GS-14s and above through the Executive Professional Excellence and Knowledge Program to ensure diversity among future leadership of the organization (USDA 2008b, 35).

Among the requirements of culturally competent health systems, the Health Resources Services Administration (DHHS 2001) includes recruitment and training of employees who represent the demographics and reflect the values of the communities served. Centers of Excellence have been established with the objectives of eliminating provider bias in practitioner-patient relations and reducing health-care disparities among groups that have been historically marginalized. Students and faculty of health professional education programs are expected to develop diagnostic and treatment plans that consider the context of diversity and are compatible with patient beliefs (DHHS 2001). Likewise, the USDA Supplemental Nutritional Assistance Program has developed steps for cultural sensitivity in the client application process. This includes "training for frontline and eligibility staff on diversity and cultural and linguistic competence" (D25) and training on organizational policies and procedures relevant to serving clients with limited English proficiency. The USDA has also collaborated with the National Employee Development Center to establish mandatory training modules. Among the required courses is Consultation with American Indian Governments, which includes the objective of using "an understanding of cultural differences and legal and historical issues to apply a model of the consultation process to establish or enhance National Resources Conservation Service (NRCS) relations with tribal nations" (USDA n.d.-a). Similarly, courses titled Culture and Behavior and Managing Cultural Divides are offered to meet Foreign Agricultural Service competencies at the USDA (USDA 2009).

PERFORMANCE APPRAISALS

Accountability through performance measurement is useful for developing and sustaining cultural competency initiatives. The National Center for Cultural Competence checklist for organizations to move toward cultural competency includes "position descriptions and performance measures that include skill sets related to cultural competence" (NCCC n.d.). Although OPM recommends building accountability for diversity management practices through performance management systems, the applications of such practices in relation to cultural competency have not been extended across federal-level agencies. Nevertheless, cultural competency is included in performance appraisals of staff at a few organizations. For example, multicultural awareness is one of the six essential staff competencies required for Women Infants and Children (WIC) nutrition assessment at the USDA. The competency statement is written: "Understands how sociocultural issues (race, ethnicity, religion, group affiliation, socioeconomic status, and world view) affect nutrition and health practices and nutrition related health problems" (USDA n.d.-b, 2). The multicultural awareness competency requires knowledge of the target population, cultural eating patterns and family traditions, and differences in communication styles. Performance expectations include respect for different belief systems concerning medical practice, consideration of food preparation within a cultural context, and appropriate communication styles for nutrition assessment.

The Health Resources Services Administration indicates that cultural competence has also been incorporated into employee performance measures at many organizations at the local level. For example, the strategic plan of the Multnomah County Health Department requires that all managers select objectives relevant to diversity and cultural competence to be included in their annual performance review (DHHS 2001). In another example, the Rainbow Center for Women, Adolescents, Children and Families in Jacksonville, Florida, conducts cultural competence training on an annual basis; participation in the training is included in the employee performance review (DHHS 2001).

Some nonprofit organizations also include elements of cultural competency in their performance appraisal systems. One of the ongoing competencies evaluated in the annual performance appraisal for the position of administrative assistant at Chase Brexton Health-Services, Incorporated in Baltimore is "Customer Service Skills with diverse patient populations" (n.d., 5). Similarly, the Catholic Charities Center for Family Services in Baltimore includes the following criteria on its performance evaluation form for the position of community outreach specialist:

- "Promotes cultural competence by expanding knowledge of culture, cultural diversity and ethnicity within the various components of the agency." This is a core competency required of all employees.
- "Communicates effectively with colleagues and the public and uses appropriate channels of communication." This is also a core competency required of all employees.
- "Establishes and maintains professional boundaries with clients/foster parents. Possesses self-awareness of own values, biases, knowledge, skills, limitations and needs in working with them" (n.d., 1, 3).

Even in organizations that promote cultural competency practices and invest in skill development, employee performance appraisals rarely assess cultural competency. Although it might seem an arduous task to develop performance measures for cultural competency in the annual appraisal system, the process will demonstrate the organization's commitment and establish a mechanism for accountability for culturally competent service delivery. One place to start is with the results of the demographic analysis of the internal workforce and external constituents of the organization to determine the skills needed to serve the target population in comparison to the existing job descriptions.

CONCLUDING REMARKS

The consequences of not moving toward a model of cultural competency will be reflected in organizational performance, particularly in the areas of workforce planning and service delivery. As the American population increases in diversity, the likelihood also increases that public managers will interact with citizen clients who are "different" from them. The success of these interactions depends on competence—cultural and otherwise. While strategic human capital management systems are designed to integrate HRM with the strategic plan of the organization, there is evidence that cultural competence is often absent in both realms of an organization. Most federal agencies have come to embrace (or at the very least, accept) diversity in employee composition through recruitment efforts; however, developing cultural competency to serve diverse constituents is less of a concern. Even in organizations that have embraced the importance of cultural competency training, accountability through performance appraisal is lacking. How do we know if employee skill levels have improved? How do we know if service delivery has improved? Not only are cultural competency performance measures necessary for the organization, but also they are essential to assess the individual performance of frontline employees.

Despite changing population demographics, most federal agencies without a legal mandate to develop cultural competency standards have not moved toward a model of cultural competency. We argue that without a legal mandate it is unlikely that federal agencies will operate in a culturally competent way. Moreover, as revealed by the document review, uniform culturally competent training and diversity training will not be achieved without a legal mandate. Our review of strategic plans and human capital plans illustrates that training for cultural competency and diversity varies widely across federal agencies. Given the dates of these documents, it is possible that agency mission and vision statements are not updated on a regular basis. Federal agencies do not update their strategic plans or human capital plans annually. According to the Government Performance and Results Act of 1993, federal agencies are legally required to update strategic plans, which include mission statements, every five years. Given this caveat, it is possible that some federal agencies have incorporated cultural competency training plans prior to updating strategic plans. Additionally, each agency is required to file a human capital plan and then submit annual reports thereafter. In practical terms, this may mean that federal agency documents do not reflect the current provision of training. However, without a legal mandate and corresponding funding, it is unlikely that federal agencies will achieve consistent, uniform cultural competency and diversity training.

APPENDIX 5.1. ADDITIONAL RESOURCES AND PUBLICATIONS ON CULTURAL COMPETENCE

A Cultural Competency Tool Kit: Ten Grant Sites Share Lessons Learned. National Consumer Supporter Technical Assistance Center, National Mental Health Association
www.ncstac.org/content/culturalcompetency/intro.pdf

Developing and Managing Cross-Cultural Competence within the Department of Defense: Recommendations for Learning and Assessment
www.deomi.org/contribute/CulturalReadiness/documents/RACCA_WG_SG2_Workshop_Report.pdf

Development and Evaluation of a Cultural Competency Training Curriculum
www.ncbi.nlm.nih.gov/pmc/articles/PMC1555583

National Center for Culturally Responsive Institutes
www.nccrest.org/index.html

National Multicultural Institute
www.nmci.org

Research Knowledge and Policy Issues in Cultural Diversity and Education
www2.ed.gov/pubs/EdReformStudies/SysReforms/tharp1.html

U.S. Department of Health and Human Services, Office of Minority Health, Guides and Resources on Cultural Competency
http://minorityhealth.hhs.gov/templates/browse.aspx?lvl=2&lvlID=107

Wanted: Language and Cultural Competence. International City/County Management Association
http://webapps.icma.org/pm/8701/public/cover.cfm

REFERENCES

Bailey, Margo L. 2005. Cultural competency and the practice of public administration. In *Diversity and Public Administration*, ed. Mitchell F. Rice, 177–196. Armonk, NY: M.E. Sharpe.

Bradshaw, Patricia S. 2007. Developing 21st century Department of Defense Senior Executive Service leaders. Report, Thought Leader Forum, Washington, DC, April 10.

Catholic Charities Center for Family Services. n.d. Competency-based performance evaluation: Community outreach specialist. Unpublished performance evaluation form.

Chase-Brexton Health Services, Inc. n.d. Performance appraisal and competency evaluation: Administrative assistant. Unpublished performance evaluation form.

Chief Human Capital Officers Council (CHCOC). 2010. CHCO Council strategic goals for fiscal year 2010. www.chcoc.gov/stratgoals.aspx.

Cross, Terry L., Barbara J. Bazron, Karl W. Dennis, and Mareasa R. Isaacs. 1989. *Towards a Culturally Competent System of Care*, vol. 1. Washington, DC: Georgetown University Child Development Center.

Food Research and Action Center (FRAC). 2010. USDA WIC nutrition services standards: Cultural competency components checklist. Summary. http://frac.org/newsite/wp-content/uploads/2009/12/wic_cultural_competency_checklist.pdf.

Henry, Nicholas. 2001. *Public Administration and Public Affairs.* 8th ed. Upper Saddle River, NJ: Prentice Hall.

Mathews, Audrey L. 2010a. Cultural diversity and productivity. In *Diversity and Public Administration,* 2nd ed., ed. Mitchell Rice, 264–297. Armonk, NY: M.E. Sharpe.

———. 2010b. Diversity management and cultural competency. In *Diversity and Public Administration,* 2nd ed., ed. Mitchell Rice, 210–263. Armonk, NY: M.E. Sharpe.

McDonald, Daniel P., Gary McGuire, Joan Johnston, Brian Selmeski, and Allison Abbe. 2008. Developing and managing cross cultural competence within the Department of Defense: Recommendations for learning and assessment. Report, October 3. www.deomi.org/contribute/CulturalReadiness/documents/RACCA_WG_SG2_Workshop_Report.pdf.

National Center for Cultural Competence (NCCC). n.d. Checklist to facilitate the development of culturally and linguistically competent primary health care policies and structures. Excerpt from Policy Brief 1—Rationale for cultural competence in primary health care. http://nccc.georgetown.edu/documents/Policy%20Brief%201%20Checklist.pdf.

National Technical Assistance Center for State Mental Health Planning and National Association of State Mental Health Program Directors. 2004. Cultural competency: Strategies for moving knowledge into practice in state mental health systems. Report, September. www.nasmhpd.org/general_files/publications/cult%20comp.pdf.

Riccucci, Norma. 2002. *Managing Diversity in Public Sector Workforces.* Boulder, CO: Westview Press.

Rice, Mitchell F. 2010. *Diversity and Public Administration: Theories, Issues, and Perspectives.* 2nd ed. Armonk, NY: M.E. Sharpe.

Selden, Sally Coleman. 2009. *Human Capital: Tools and Strategies for the Public Sector.* Washington, DC: CQ Press.

Society for Human Resource Management. 2008. 2007 State of the workplace diversity management. Report, February. SHRM Research Department, Alexandria, Virginia.

Triandis, Harry C. 1995. A theoretical framework for the study of diversity. In *Diversity in Organizations: New Perspectives for a Changing Workplace,* ed. Martin M. Chemers, Stuart Oskamp, and Mark A. Costanzo, 11–36. Thousand Oaks, CA: Sage.

U.S. Department of Agriculture (USDA). 2006. USDA strategic plan for FY 2005–2010. June. www.ocfo.usda.gov/usdasp/sp2005/sp2005.pdf.

———. 2008a. USDA workforce planning & succession planning guidance: Farm and foreign agricultural services FY 2008–2013. April. www.apfo.usda.gov/Internet/FSA_File/wfp_succession_guidance.pdf.

———. 2008b. Strategic Workforce Plan 2008–2010. www.dm.usda.gov/USDA_Strategic_Workforce_Plan_2008-2010-III.pdf.

———. 2009. FFAS competency training & development guide. Farm Service Agency. www.fsa.usda.gov/Internet/FSA_File/competency_training_matrix.xls.

———. 2010. Cultural competency: A dash of diversity, a medley of outreach ideas. In *Putting Healthy Food Within Reach: State Outreach Toolkit.* Washington, DC: Supplemental Nutrition Assistance Program, January. www.fns.usda.gov/snap/outreach/pdfs/toolkit/2010/State/SNAP_state_Chapter03.pdf.

———. n.d.-a. Consultation with American Indian governments (000089). National Resources Conservation Service. www.nedc.nrcs.usda.gov/catalog/consultwithind.html.

———. n.d.-b. Essential staff competencies for WIC nutrition assessment. www.nal.usda.gov/wicworks/Learning_Center/VENA/VENA_AppendixD.rtf.

U.S. Department of Commerce. 2009. Strategic plan for FY 2004–FY 2009. www.osec.doc.gov/bmi/budget/strategic04-1002.htm.

————. n.d. Human capital strategic plan fiscal year (FY) 2007–2012. http://hr.commerce.gov/s/groups/public/@doc/@cfoasa/@ohrm/documents/content/dev01_006120.pdf.

U.S. Department of Defense (DOD). 2009a. Strategic management plan. July 31. http://dcmo.defense.gov/documents/2009SMP.pdf.

————. 2009b. Strategic plan for fiscal years 2010–12. Office of the Under Secretary of Defense for Personnel and Readiness, December 30. www.cpms.osd.mil/ASSETS/60522B438BD746308E0 8477E07C90F7D/FY2010-12%20PR%20Strategic%20Plan%20%28Final%20Public%20-%20 signed%29%284%20January%29.pdf/.

U.S. Department of Education. 2007. Strategic plan for fiscal years 2007–12. May. www2.ed.gov/about/reports/strat/plan2007-12/2007-plan.pdf.

U.S. Department of Energy (DOE). 2006a. DOE strategic human capital plan (FY 2006–2011). March 29. www.hss.energy.gov/deprep/ftcp/about/Strategic-Human-Capital-Plan.pdf.

————. 2006b. U.S. Department of Energy strategic plan 2006. DOE-CF0010. www.cfo.doe.gov/strategicplan/doestrategicplan.htm.

————. n.d. About DOE. www.energy.gov/about/index.htm.

U.S. Department of Health and Human Services (DHHS). 2001. Cultural competence works. Report, Health Resources and Services Administration. ftp://ftp.hrsa.gov/financeMC/cultural-competence.pdf.

————. 2008. Statement by Dr. Garth Graham, M.P.H., deputy assistant secretary for minority health OPHS on the role of OMH in eliminating health disparities. June 24. www.hhs.gov/asl/testify/2008/06/t20080624a.html.

————. n.d. Strategic plan and priorities. www.hhs.gov/secretary/about/priorities.html.

U.S. Department of Homeland Security (DHS). 2008. One team, one mission, securing our homeland: Strategic plan fiscal years 2008–2013. www.dhs.gov/xlibrary/assets/DHS_StratPlan_FINAL_spread.pdf.

U.S. Department of Housing and Urban Development (HUD). 2008. Strategic human capital management: Revised human capital plan, FY 2008–FY 2009. March. www.hud.gov/offices/adm/omap/hshcp.doc.

————. 2010. Draft FY2010–2015 strategic plan. http://portal.hud.gov/hudportal/HUD?src=/program_offices/cfo/stratplan.

U.S. Department of the Interior (DOI). 2002. Strategic human capital management plan, FY2003–2007. www.doi.gov/pfm/human_cap_plan/pdf/entire.pdf.

————. n.d. GPRA strategic plan fiscal year 2007–2012. www.doi.gov/ppp/Strategic%20Plan%20 FY07-12/strat_plan_fy2007_2012.pdf.

U.S. Department of Justice (DOJ). 2008. Working together to ensure success—Meeting the Mission: Equal employment opportunity strategic plan 2008–2012. www.justice.gov/jmd/eeos/strategicplan.pdf.

————. n.d.-a. Mission first: Linking strategy to success. Human capital strategic plan 2007–2012. www.justice.gov/jmd/ps/missionfirst.pdf.

————. n.d.-b. Fiscal years 2007–2012 strategic plan: Stewards of the American dream. www.justice.gov/jmd/mps/strategic2007-2012/.

U.S. Department of Labor (DOL). 2010. Strategic plan for fiscal years 2010–2016. www.dol.gov/dol/aboutdol/main.htm#budget.

————. 2011. Mission statement. www.dol.gov/opa/aboutdol/mission.htm.

U.S. Department of State. 2007. Transformational diplomacy: FY 2007–2012 Department of State and USAID strategic plan. May. www.state.gov/s/d/rm/rls/dosstrat/2007/.

U.S. Department of Transportation (DOT). 2006. Strategic plan, fiscal years 2006–2011. September. www.dot.gov/stratplan2011/index.htm.

————. 2007. Strategic human capital plan 2007–2011. September. http://dothr.ost.dot.gov/pdf/dot-200711strathcplan.pdf.

U.S. Department of the Treasury. 2007. Strategic plan: Fiscal years 2007–2012. www.treasury.gov/about/budget-performance/strategic-plan/Documents/strategic-plan2007-2012.pdf.

———. n.d. Human capital strategic plan for the fiscal years 2008–2013. www.treasury.gov/about/organizational-structure/offices/Mgt/Documents/Human-Capital-Strategic-Plan.pdf.

U.S. Department of Veterans Affairs (VA). 2009. Diversity and inclusion: Strategic plan for FY 2009–2013. Report, February. www.diversity.hr.va.gov/docs/strat.pdf.

———. 2010. Strategic plan FY 2006–2011. www4.va.gov/performance/.

U.S. Government Accountability Office (GAO). 2005. Diversity management: Expert-identified leading practices and agency examples. Report, January. GAO-05-90. Washington, DC.

———. 2007. Human capital: Federal workforce challenges in the 21st century. Statement of J. Christopher Mihm, March 6. GAO-07-556T. Washington, DC.

U.S. Office of Personnel Management (OPM). 2000. Building and maintaining a diverse and high quality workforce. www.opm.gov/diversity/diversity-3.htm.

———. 2011. Human Capital Assessment and Accountability Framework Resource Center. www.opm.gov/hcaaf_resource_center/resources.asp.

U.S. Social Security Administration (SSA). 2008. Key foundational elements in strategic plan FY 2008–2013. www.socialsecurity.gov/asp/KeyFoundationalElement.pdf.

Part II

Cultural Competency in Action

Developing Gender-Competent Public Administrators

DeLysa Burnier

Frances Perkins, the first woman to serve as a cabinet secretary in American government, might be surprised today to be recognized as an early example of a culturally competent public administrator. In 1933, when President Franklin Roosevelt appointed her secretary of labor, the concepts of diversity, cultural competence, and gender were not part of anyone's administrative vocabulary. However, the concept of social justice was, and her entire professional life was dedicated to making life better for the immigrant and working poor. Perkins never doubted that government could be a force of good in people's lives, and her many legislative accomplishments, such as the minimum wage, the eight-hour workday, workplace safety, unemployment insurance, and Social Security, are public policies people depend on still today.

During her nearly thirteen-year tenure at the Department of Labor, Perkins was a tireless advocate for the dispossessed. She gave voice to those who were unemployed, to those who labored for low pay in unsafe working conditions, to children forced to labor, to workers without collective bargaining rights, and to countless ordinary people who had suffered through the Great Depression. Perkins made organized labor angry because securing social and labor reform legislation mattered more to her as secretary of labor than labor organization and collective bargaining issues (Wandersee 1993). Both she and President Roosevelt believed that the government should "protect not just the organized worker, but the working class as a whole" (Wandersee 1993, 8).

As secretary of labor, Perkins worked to ensure that the Department of Labor was "dedicated to human needs," and she insisted that department members view workers not as abstractions, but as "men and women of flesh and bone" (Perkins 1934, 283). Specifically, the "winter's coat, the plumbing, the interest on the mortgage, a good diet, the baby's milk, marriage, and cultural needs, even soda waters and rides on the pony in the park must always precede generalized abstract theory in our thinking" (283). In her effort to meet those needs, Perkins brought a high level of personal energy to the department and infused it with her strong moral commitment to improving working people's lives (Martin 1976). Perkins made a point of meeting and talking to working people, preferably in their own union halls or community centers, whenever she traveled. She observed that "on their own ground they would express themselves and ask questions" (Perkins 1946, 136).

Perkins reorganized the department to be more efficient, sought competitive salaries for employees, ended political patronage appointments, and moved to merit-based hiring. Perkins avoided using her private office elevator so that she could mingle and talk with the department's employees in the main office elevator (Mohr 1979). She desegregated the new Labor Department cafeteria after discovering there were roped sections for whites and blacks (Mohr 1979). Perkins hired Lawrence Oxley to head the newly created Division of Negro Labor, where he was the first African American to hold a government executive position at Labor. He remembered her welcome and that she was glad to have him "join the family" (Colman 1993, 65). Perkins was committed to equal opportunity, as well as to merit-based hiring in the field offices of the U.S. Employment Services and for those hired to administer federal grants (Martin 1976, 355). Thomas Eliot, a key member of her legal and legislative team, recalled that she was a "good listener" and "worked with us as colleagues, never trying to dominate us" (1992, 153).

Even as she worked to be an effective culturally competent administrator, others around her remained in the grip of traditionally gendered cultural constructions. The media regularly wrote about her physical appearance and clothes in the harshest of terms, with one article noting how "surprisingly feminine" she was (Burnier 2008). The media also denigrated her professional identity as a social worker, derided Perkins for keeping her own name, and for using the correct title of "Madam Secretary." They reported that she gave herself the title and they regularly misused it by attaching it to her name or misspelling *madam* (Martin 1976, 17).

Her close professional relationship with Roosevelt was ignored by both the media and members of Congress, who preferred to represent her as a government outsider. To this day few know the key role she played in establishing Social Security. Her cabinet colleague, Harold Ickes, maintained that Perkins was voluble and long-winded during cabinet meetings and then monopolized scarce face-time with the president afterward (Burnier 2008). He fully expected her to leave after one term. Mary Anderson, chief of Labor's Women's Bureau, complained that Perkins never did enough for working women, ignoring her efforts to secure legislation that benefited men and women workers alike (1951).

Far worse was a late 1930s media and congressional whispering campaign intimating that Perkins was a Russian Jewish communist whose real name was Matilda Watski. The charge gained so much traction with the public that Perkins felt forced to issue a statement explaining "who she was." That statement did not stop the campaign and she eventually found herself facing impeachment charges in the House of Representatives. Although her name was cleared and all charges were dropped, Perkins's administrative effectiveness was compromised and the Department of Labor lost both budget and programs in the following years.

Wanting always to be remembered for her social reform work, Perkins did not discuss her gender or being a woman "first" in her memoir (1946). She did note that she was nervous about her first cabinet meeting because she did not want her "colleagues to get the impression that I was too talkative" (152). Her only other comment on gender was that "as far as Roosevelt was concerned, I was one of the team. The men in the cabinet . . . treated me as a colleague and an equal. There was no special deference . . . because I was a woman. Nor was there any suggestion of a patronizing note" (153). In the 1930s, getting through the door was a significant gender accomplishment, so it is not surprising that such minimal "equal" treatment was all Perkins expected from her male cabinet colleagues.[1]

THE CONTEMPORARY RELEVANCE OF PERKINS'S NARRATIVE

Perkins's narrative was used here to introduce the topics of cultural and gender competency for several reasons. First, her story is almost unknown among public administration scholars and students, despite her being a pioneer in care-centered public administration, humanistic leadership, and cultural competency (Burnier 2008; Newman 2004). For too long, Perkins has been part of "public administration's buried heritage," which includes Jane Addams and other settlement women reformers (Stivers 2000, 49). According to Camilla Stivers, the "settlement women" sought substantive policy reforms aimed at making people's live better. They placed caring for others, not efficiency, at the center of administration. By contrast, the "bureau men" were interested in procedural and administrative reforms aimed at making government work more efficiently. The bureau men's philosophy became the prevailing orthodoxy in public administration. Only recently has the settlement women's philosophy gained attention from public administration scholars.

Second, Perkins's narrative highlights the fact that she and other social reformers, like Addams, actively worked to make social services and settlement workers culturally competent for the working poor and immigrants in the early twentieth century. Much of the current cultural competency scholarship is focused only on the present. It ignores this early history of culturally competent administrative practice and the extent to which major social movements such as the Progressive, civil rights, and black power movements pushed government to become more responsive and equitable in the delivery of public goods and services.

Third, Perkins's narrative is important because she modeled a different kind of public administrator. Not only did her gender set her apart from most public administrators of the day, but also she eschewed the still orthodox model of the neutral public administrator. Perkins was publicly committed to social justice, and she sought to make life materially better for those living on the economic margins. New Deal policies and programs were important because they centered on the idea that "the people mattered" and that "all the political and practical forces of the community should and could be directed to making life better for ordinary people" (Perkins 1946, 167, 173). Underlying contemporary discussion of the culturally competent administrator is a similar model of the committed, rather than neutral, public administrator.

Finally, Perkins's narrative highlights the difficulties faced by administrators who are different from the traditional cultural construction of the public leader as male, white, and heterosexual, or who attempt to lead by alternative values, knowledges, and experiences. Not always, but often, their political and administrative paths are rocky and their efforts greeted with skepticism and anger. One wonders now how anyone could have believed that Perkins, a Protestant from Massachusetts who worked for years in New York state government, could also be Jewish and a Russian communist, except that some people today persist in believing that President Barack Obama was not born in Hawaii and is a Muslim. It is for these reasons that Perkins's narrative provides scholars and students alike with a "usable past" that enriches and deepens current understandings of cultural and gender competency in public organizations (Stivers 2000).

CULTURAL COMPETENCE AND PUBLIC ADMINISTRATION

Perkins's interest in social justice was sparked by the huge demographic changes the United States experienced in the late nineteenth and early twentieth centuries—changes that produced large social and economic inequalities. Similarly, contemporary scholars and practitioners have been impelled to examine cultural competence in the late twentieth and early twenty-first centuries because of the sweeping demographic changes that have occurred in the United States. As Ruth Dean notes, "We live in a multiethnic, multiracial, multiclass society" (2001, 624). Several states already have majority minority populations and several more are moving in that direction. In recognition of the role Hispanic/Latino voters played in his election to the presidency, Obama selected Hilda Solis, the first female Hispanic to serve in the cabinet, as Secretary of Labor. He also selected Sonia Sotomayor for the Supreme Court—the first Hispanic to serve on the high court. Since the mid-1990s, numerous federal laws and regulations have required culturally competent program delivery, especially in the areas of education and health care (Bailey 2010).

With some exceptions, there has been little public administration scholarly or practitioner work in the area of culture competence. According to Mitchell Rice, "The focus on cultural competency in public administration and public service delivery is evolving very slowly, so the concept has yet to be clearly accepted and understood by the community of public administration" (2010, 190). By contrast, disciplines such as social work, nursing, counseling, mental health, and health care have produced a wide array of scholarship on the topic. In 2001 social work's main professional organization, the National Association of Social Work, issued cultural competence standards centering on ethics and values, cross-cultural knowledge, cross-cultural skills, and delivery of services, among others (Gentlewarrior et al. 2008). Neither the American Society for Public Administration nor the National Association of Schools of Public Affairs and Administration has issued similar standards.

At its most basic, becoming a culturally competent organization means that "mainstream organizations need to be responsive to all segments of the population" (Chin 2000, 27). According to Jean Lau Chin, "The pivotal 1989 monograph, *Toward a Culturally Competent System of Care* [by Terry Cross, Barbara Bazron, Karl Dennis, and Mareasa Issac] defined cultural competence as a set of behaviors, attitudes, and policies that enable a system, agency, or group of professionals to work effectively in cross-cultural situations" (2000, 25–26). Writing in *Public Management*, Abraham Benavides and Julie Hernandez note that cultural competence is a "much broader concept" than equal employment opportunity, diversity training, or affirmative action and that it "begins with the dominant culture becoming self-aware of its own customs and then being responsive to and understanding of the cultural differences of other people within a system" (2007, 15). Additionally, "cultural competency converts the knowledge gained about groups and individuals into policies and procedures that result in practices that increase the quality of the services to produce better outcomes" (15). Margo Bailey states that *"Culturally competent public administration* [italics in the original] is a 'respect for, and understanding of, diverse ethnic and cultural groups, their histories, traditions, beliefs, and value systems'" (2010, 171). Translated into practice, cultural competency means that "public organizations and their employees" attempt "to effectively provide services that reflect the different cultural influences of their constituents or clients" (171).

Together, the above definitions suggest that becoming a culturally competent public organization requires a comprehensive, continuous review of an organization's external relations and activities with clients, customers, leaders, and representatives from the minority and ethnic communities it serves. Public organizations also must conduct such reviews of their internal cultures, beliefs, values, practices, policies, mission statements, performance measures, and workforce composition to make sure that they too reflect a commitment to cultural competency. Overall, "cultural competence is a continuous process of striving to provide services effectively within the client's cultural context. It is an ongoing process rather than an outcome" (Weaver 2005, 64).

Creating culturally competent public organizations directly challenges public administration's traditional commitment to the bureaucratic method of organizing, wherein the model administrator neutrally delivers public goods and services, adheres strictly to official procedures, lacks discretion in job performance, and applies rules equally to all clients or customers without regard to circumstance or situation (Rice 2010). In contrast, public organizations that embrace cultural competence will reorient their cultures toward creating a "social equity subculture," where "responsibility to those clients who require more public services than others" is emphasized, along with more "innovative public service delivery and techniques" (Rice 2010, 126). Similarly, Hilary Weaver notes that "cultural competence requires helping professionals to bring a sense of social justice . . . to their work" (2005, 2).

Mary Abrums and Carol Leppa argue that culturally competent care cannot even be provided "unless underlying issues of discrimination are examined and confronted" (2001, 270). More specifically, creating culturally competent public organizations should be viewed not simply as a practical response to the country's demographic changes, but also as a necessary normative response to its history of discriminatory and oppressive treatment of minorities, women, and ethnic groups. In fact, there is a growing public policy literature that shows how social constructions of women, minorities, and other groups are embedded in policies in ways that target groups as worthy or not worthy and deserving or not deserving of government help, which in turn shapes the types of programs, benefits, and administrative treatment individuals receive (Burnier 2006; Mettler 1998; Schneider and Ingram 2005). Once these social constructions are embedded in policy, they tend to endure and become very difficult to change.

In significant ways, then, culturally competent public administration departs from the traditional bureaucratic model of administration. By contrast, its focus on cultural inclusion, social justice, and social equity makes it much more compatible with alternative models of public administration such as care-centered (Burnier 2003), transformational (King and Zanetti 2005), and democratic (Box 2007).

BECOMING GENDER-COMPETENT

The traditional bureaucratic model of administration is wanting not only on grounds of social justice and inclusion, but also in its insistence that bureaucratic structures, values, and practices are gender-neutral. As long ago as 1984, Kathy Ferguson made a "feminist case against bureaucracy" wherein she criticized the rational-legal outlook for its exclusion of women's experiences and alternative values such as individual human development and community needs.

Several years later, Stivers argued in her benchmark book *Gender Images in Public Administration* that when public administration is viewed "through the lens of gender, its public dimensions are revealed as gendered rather than neutral" (2002, 3). Stivers documents that public administration's "images of professional expertise, management, leadership, and public virtue . . . contain dilemmas of gender" (2002, 3). These images possess "features commonly and unthinkingly associated with masculinity" that "help to keep in place or bestow political and economic privilege on the bearers of masculine qualities at the expense of those who display culturally feminine ones" (3).

Consonant with Stivers's study, Patricia Martin argues that "feminist theorists and researchers have shown that workplaces are infused with gender" and that this research calls "into question claims that gender is irrelevant in rational-technical-legal bureaucracies" (2003, 343). She concludes that "gender is pervasively practiced in bureaucratic workplaces," usually to women's disadvantage and men's advantage (Martin 2003, 343). The "gender dynamics" that are created in organizations through the practices of gender "routinely make workers, particularly women workers, feel incompetent, exhausted and/or devalued" (Martin 2006, 255).

Collectively, this scholarship demonstrates that bureaucracy is not gender-neutral, so coming to understand the multiple ways in which gender figures into bureaucratic structures, values, and practices specifically and administrative life more generally is central to developing gender-competent public administrators. Further, if public organizations are to become truly culturally competent, then gender as an analytic concept must receive deeper attention by public administration scholars, practitioners, and students, both as a stand-alone concept and one that intersects with other areas of cultural competency such as race, ethnicity, class, and sexual orientation.

UNDERSTANDING GENDER AS AN ANALYTIC CONCEPT

The term *gender* suggests "that information about women is necessarily information about men, that one implies the study of the other" (Scott 1988, 32). Further, gender is inclusive of both sexes and highlights how the two sexes exist relationally. Gender is a "constitutive element of social relationships based on the perceived differences between the sexes" (Scott 1988, 42). Cecilia Ridgeway maintains that gender "is one of our culture's two or three primary frames for organizing social relations" and as such forms a strong background frame that, while varying with context and organizational or institutional structures, "infuses gendered meanings into organizational practices" (2009, 145). Ridgeway contends that "the background gender frame is the primary mechanism by which material, organizational structures become organized by gender" and that "these organizational structures sustain widely shared cultural beliefs about gender" (153–154).

Scott extends the analytic reach of gender with her proposition that gender is "a primary way of signifying relationships of power" (1988, 42). She holds that gender and gender relations are never neutral, but instead embedded in and shaped by such larger systems of power as society, culture, economics, and politics. Gender(ed) power is not static or fixed, but rather is fluid and dynamic. Different historical moments and contexts produce and reproduce a vast array of gender power arrangements that affect how men and women come to understand themselves, each other, and the world around them.

With respect to public administration, Stivers found that "the characteristic masculinity of public administration—though far from monolithic—is systemic: It contributes to and is sustained by power relations in society at large that distribute resources on the basis of gender (though not solely on this basis) and affect people's life chances and their sense of themselves and their place in the world" (2002, 3). A gender-competent public administrator, then, must focus on the gender power relations that are produced and reproduced in the organization both internally and externally, with the aim of discovering who, if anyone, is being advantaged or disadvantaged by them and in what ways.

In sum, using gender analytically offers a deeper, more complex understanding of the concept that is at once interactional, relational, and structural and always unfolding in multiple ways.[2] Moreover, gender relations both shape and are shaped by the political, social, and economic power arrangements of a given historical moment.

UNDERSTANDING GENDER AND THE CONCEPT OF INTERSECTIONALITY

Women's Bureau chief Mary Anderson had worked at the Department of Labor for many years when Perkins arrived as secretary. Anderson reported in her 1951 memoir that at first she was "jubilant" at the news of Perkins's appointment because "at last we would have someone who really understood our problems. . . . I felt that I had a friend to whom I could go freely and confidently, but it did not turn out that way" (183). Anderson never quite explained why it "did not turn out that way," other than to note that Perkins suggested merging the Children's and Women's Bureaus as part of a reorganization plan, and the mere "memory of it made things difficult for me from then on" (184). Perkins further disappointed Anderson when Perkins had to be reminded to say in congressional testimony that the minimum wage should be equal for both men and women (148). Still another reason for Anderson's wariness with Perkins stemmed from the fact that "a good many of the representatives of organized labor did not like her . . . partly because she was a woman and partly because they thought of her as a social worker and not a real labor person" (148).

Richard Neustadt and Ernest May believe that the relationship between Perkins and Anderson failed because neither could understand the other's identity position (1986). Anderson was an unmarried Swedish immigrant with little education who went to work in her early teens as a domestic. She worked her way up to trade union leadership positions after years of garment and shoe factory work. Perkins was married, a woman from a prosperous New England family, with a master's degree from Columbia University, who chose a profession in social reform. Anderson self-identified as a working-class, trade unionist woman, while Perkins self-identified as a woman social reformer, who happened to be upper-middle-class. Despite both being working women dedicated to the cause of labor, neither could see the other for what she was because of their class differences.

Anderson's relationship with Perkins makes concrete the more abstract point that gender should not be viewed in isolation. Gender instead should be understood in relation to, or intersecting with, identity constructs such as race, ethnicity, class, and sexual orientation. Evangelina Holvino argues that intersectionality is a key concept that permits "complicating gender," which means "exploring the racialized and classed dimensions of gender in order to get to a more complete understanding of women and their situation(s)" (2006, 4). Intersectionality assumes that individual identities are plural and fluid, not additive and essential. According to Gina Samuels and Fariyal Ross-Sheriff, intersectionality "avoids essentializing a single analytical category of identity by attending to other interlocking categories" (2008, 5). Relying on a single category would prevent deep understanding because identities are both presented and experienced variously depending on the situation and context. Samuel and Ross-Sheriff maintain that intersectionality "stretche[s] our thinking about gender . . . to include the impact of context and to pay attention to interlocking oppressions and privileges across various contexts" (5).

Thus far, only a handful of public administration scholars have addressed the need for an intersectional understanding of gender (Hutchinson and Mann 2004; McGinn and Patterson 2005; Stivers 2002). Kathy McGinn and Patricia Patterson call for more scholarship that recognizes "all individuals (both women and men) as gendered beings, with multiple and intersecting sources of identity, challenge, and meaning" (2005, 940). Domonic Bearfield also urges "the field to engage in research focused on the intersection of multiple identity categories such as gender and race" (2009, 384). Continued scholarship in this area will be important and, as Bearfield notes, it must be integrated into the discipline if public administrators are to become culturally competent (2009).

Gender-competent public administrators, then, must pay attention to gender even as they recognize that gender is not the sole construct around which people develop their identities. Holvino suggests that leaders and managers should adopt a "model of simultaneity" that recognizes that race, class, ethnicity, sexual orientation, and gender are experienced "simultaneously" by individuals, rather than serially or separately. The model also views race, class, ethnicity, class, and gender as "simultaneous processes of identity, institutional, and social practice" (2010, 249). Adopting Holvino's model means recognizing how and in what ways these identity constructs both are embedded in organizational structures, procedures, and values and profoundly influence internal and external organizational interactions and relationships.

A final obligation for public administrators who seek to become gender and intersectorally competent is that they see people as individuals, not just group members, which means understanding employees, clients, and customers well enough to know how they self-identify and in what situations and contexts. Holvino refers to this as "creat[ing] a real connection" whereby the administrator learns about people's "concrete histories, identities, emotions, needs, and aspirations instead of presuming that there is a 'generalized other'" (2003, 2). The public administrator who is gender and intersectorally competent must have an "openness to learning, inquiring, and being moved by others" and should assume a "stance of inquiry" toward employees and clients or customers by taking the time to discover "how a person presents her/himself to others and how s/he takes in experiences and information from others" (2).

UNDERSTANDING GENDER AS PRACTICE

Policies and programs aimed at making public organizations compliant with equal employment opportunity laws, affirmative action, and managing diversity are necessary and important steps that help to "create the capacities for agencies to become [gender] competent" (Bailey 2010, 177). An agency cannot be gender-competent without them, but these initiatives themselves alone do not make an agency or its administrators gender-competent. Employees, clients, and customers may still experience its culture as gendered because of how gender actually is practiced by leaders, managers, and other employees throughout the organization.

Individuals put gender into practice through their actions and interactions with others (Martin 2003). According to Patricia Martin, these interactions are not easily observed or examined by others because they occur quickly and incidentally, they are as likely to be unintentional as intentional, and they may occur in front of others but not always. What makes these interactions tricky from the perspective of gender competence is that individuals, when confronted by what they said or did, are likely to deny that they were acting in gendered ways even though they were perceived as doing so by another individual (Martin 2003). From their perspective they were not intentionally acting gendered, but rather just acting as themselves in the workplace.

Martin argues that the interactions and actions that occur between men and women in the workplace produce "gender dynamics" within an organization. These dynamics emerge from how "men and women socially construct each other at work by means of a two-sided dynamic of gendering practices and practicing of gender" (2003, 343). Although these gender dynamics "significantly affect both women's and men's work experiences," Martin claims these dynamics are more likely to be culturally constructed as masculine and for that reason "they impair women workers' identities and confidence" (343). Gender as a practice refers to historical and institutional understandings that are deeply rooted in our culture and that continue to shape gender interactions and actions in the present. These practices enculturate individuals into becoming girls and boys who are able to perform in feminine and masculine ways. "Gendered practices are learned and enacted in childhood and in every major social site of social behavior over the life course, including in schools, intimate relationships, families, workplaces, houses of worship, and social movements" (352). Gender as a practice pervasively influences organizational practices, including decisions about who is viewed as suitable to hire, the division of labor, human resource policies, promotion, and leadership opportunities. It is important to acknowledge that gender practices do change and are subject to social and political pressure. For example, most organizations no longer view maternity policy as something that applies only to women. Health benefits are now extended in some organizations to same-sex partners, breaking a long-standing understanding that they were only for "spouses."

Practicing gender, as noted earlier, refers to how men and women put gender into practice. According to Martin, practicing gender "directs attention to the literal activities of gender—physical and narrative—the doing, displaying, asserting, narrating, performing, mobilizing and maneuvering" (2003, 354). How men and women practice gender at work establishes "the means by which the gender order is constituted" organizationally (354). Depending on how and in what ways gender is put into practice at work, women (and men) may feel either included or excluded, valuable or invaluable, marginal or central to the organization's work. Similarly, the practice of gender will influence how customers and clients feel about an organization. For example, are women treated with respect? Are employees careful not to make assumptions about a woman (or man's) age, marital and family status, race, religion, sexual orientation, or class status? If public organizations are to become gender-competent, then the "twin dynamics of gendering practices and practicing of gender at work must be made visible" (Martin 2003, 361). An organization's practices and how it practices gender must be subject to scrutiny. With respect to practice, this requires raising questions about stated policies, procedures, and organizational practices such as when meetings are scheduled and if training and mentoring are available to both men and women. Such scrutiny historically has been effective, causing many organizations to change their policies, procedures, and practices. In contrast, changing how gender is practiced is much more challenging because of the difficulty in making visible those "literal activities" that occur at the microlevel of the organization.

The practicing of gender happens in the moment, and it is precisely this ephemeral, transitory character that renders it hard to document, to make visible in effect, in the same way that policies, procedures, and practices can be documented and examined. Making visible how gender is practiced requires organizations to have sound policies on workplace discrimination and harassment, for example, and to train employees in how to create their own documentation of problematic ways in which they experience the practicing of gender. Such training also should equip employees, including leaders and managers, with critical self-awareness about the practicing of gender with an understanding of the need to create spaces where plural masculinities and femininities can be practiced.

Gender Competency: A Summary

Becoming a gender-competent public administrator first requires a complex, multifaceted stance toward gender that begins with embracing the assumption that public organizations are not gender-neutral. These organizational structures, values, and practices likely are culturally constructed as masculine, leaving those who identify with structures, values, and practices culturally constructed as feminine at a distinct disadvantage. Second, gender must be understood analytically as a concept with relational, interactional, and structural dimensions that are interdependent and implicate all organizational actors. Third, gender should not be viewed insularly because it intersects with other pivotal identity constructs such as race, class, ethnicity, and sexual orientation. Gender-competent public administrators must be willing, therefore, to incorporate difference broadly at the level of organizational policies, procedures, and decisions while being attentive to how individual employees, clients, and customers enact their "different" identities in the workplace and at the street level. Finally, men and women put gender into practice in the workplace through myriad actions and interactions. Gender-competent public administrators must become, in Martin's term, "reflexive" about how gender is practiced everyday in their organizations. This requires "cogitating, studying, or thinking carefully" about the practice of gender with the aim of "consider[ing] carefully" one's own actions and "their likely effect" on others prior to acting (Martin 2006, 260).

Perkins reported in her memoir, as earlier noted, that she was treated "as a colleague and an equal" by the president and other cabinet officers (1946, 153). The degree to which collegiality and equality are extended to women and men remains an important measure by which to assess whether progress toward gender competency has been made in public organizations. Perkins, however, based her assessment strictly on her formal interactions with colleagues in official cabinet meetings, which was a very narrow standard. For gender competency to be fully realized today, public organizations' policies and procedures, along with the full range of formal and informal practices, interactions, and actions must be examined critically in the present and over time. One wonders whether Perkins, if she had used this broader standard as her guide, would have still felt treated "as a colleague and an equal," especially since biographies of her show that she was subject to a range of gendered practices, interactions, and actions by the president, cabinet members, and other officials in situations other than formal cabinet meetings (Downey 2009; Martin 1976).

TEACHING GENDER COMPETENCY: PLACING CARE AT THE CENTER

With this more complex understanding of gender competency now clarified, the next task is to explain why that understanding should be an essential element of public administration teaching and its curriculum. Gender competency as conceived in this chapter should be integrated into courses across the master of public administration curriculum, including courses in leadership, organization theory, and human resource management, so that it does not become viewed as a topic specific to a particular course. Only if gender competency is taught widely will it be recognized as an essential concept that both men and women must grasp if they are to become effective public administrators.

This chapter affirms that teaching gender competency involves more than learning about representative bureaucracy, equal employment opportunity law, and affirmative action. Although these are important topics, teaching them strictly from a traditional orientation will not necessarily lead to probing the relational and interactional dimensions of gender that are integral to becoming a gender-competent administrator or challenging the assumption that bureaucracies are gender-neutral. Consequently, it is imperative that scholarship that takes a feminist or gender perspective or draws on women's organizational and leadership experiences be placed on course syllabi alongside more traditional material. Exposure to such scholarship helps build appreciation, support, and acceptance among students for a breadth of organizational structures, leadership styles, public values, and knowledge bases that go well beyond those founded exclusively on efficiency, performance, rationality, and command and control.

Because the discipline, according to Bearfield, has yet to "make a commitment to the study of gender," many professors and practitioners may be unaware that a wealth of gender scholarship consonant with the alternative understandings noted above is available (2009). An ever-expanding body of leadership scholarship that draws on multicultural and white women's experiences as leaders has emerged in public administration (Burnier 2005; Chin et al. 2007; Fletcher 2001). Women scholars have pioneered in developing a relational approach to leadership that makes the case for establishing caring relationships both inside and outside the organization. Helen Regan and Gwen Brooks describe this approach as privileging the multiple and fluid relationships and processes that a leader cultivates and manages over time in support of collaboration, caring, courage, intuition, and organizational vision (1995).

Stivers's *Bureau Men/Settlement Women* offers a counternarrative of the field's conventional narrative that centers on the work of "settlement women" such as Jane Addams (2000). Stivers argues that during the Progressive Era, settlement women's values, practices, and reform goals formed a clear "feminine alternative" to the bureau men, whose "masculine" values, practices, and reform goals continue to shape public administration today. Among the values and practices settlement women emphasized were care, connection, learning from others, and cooperative problem solving. Recently, Hindy Lauer Schachter was able to connect care discourse with performance measurement discourse by making the argument that "feminist theory with its emphasis on care offers a new face on how agencies should define substantive performance" (2008, 270).

Still another scholarly development arises from Mary Guy, Meredith Newman, and Sharon Mastracci's groundbreaking work on emotional labor (2008). Despite its importance to the smooth flow of work, enhanced organizational life, and the well-being of clients, care work and emotional labor often go unrecognized. They are treated as what some people (usually women) do because they are good at it and devalued with the fiction that such work and labor cannot be evaluated by conventional quantitative performance measures. Mastracci, Newman, and Guy define "emotional labor [as] the process of managing one's own emotions, sensing the emotions of others, and using that knowledge to govern actions on the job" (2010, 125). The authors hold that emotional labor must be taught in the public administration curriculum so that administrative practice can be better understood as "relational rather than controlling;" they believe that it is more "than a rule-governed procedure, it is also an intersubjective process" (129).

The common thread running through all this scholarship is the commitment to making visible the concept of care. Care scholarship is relatively new and is primarily produced by women scholars using gender and feminist theory as their analytic framework (Burnier 2003; McSwite 2004; Stivers 2005). Care-centered administration offers a distinct alternative to the traditional bureaucratic and market-based models of administration. The care perspective's assumptive base is relationships and relational values, which presume that the task of creating democratic relationships of mutuality and reciprocity in the public sector is as important as the efficient delivery of public goods and services. Indispensable to creating and maintaining these democratic relationships are gender-competent public administrators who adopt a care perspective and thereby are able to treat all employees, clients, and customers as colleagues and equals.

THE PRESENT MOMENT: WHY GENDER COMPETENCY?

Government at all levels and across branches today looks different from the days when Perkins was the lone woman in Roosevelt's cabinet photographs. Women serve throughout the federal government and are visible in state and local government. Presidents now routinely select more than one woman for the cabinet, and positions that historically appeared to be reserved for men, such as secretary of state, are no longer so reserved. Presidents Bill Clinton, George W. Bush, and Barack Obama each appointed women for that very position, with Bush appointing the first African American man and woman.

Since the late 1960s and 1970s there have been numerous laws, court rulings, and regulations that prevent gender discrimination in federal and state hiring and employment. Not only have employment rights been protected, but also women have been the beneficiaries of a range of laws and rules that promote family-friendly workplaces, diversity, partner benefits, and time off for family and medical issues. Overt gendered behavior, such as sexual harassment, is formally prohibited in the workplace, and all public organizations have rules and procedures in place for dealing with such behavior if it occurs. Gender stereotyping, too, of the sort Perkins faced is less of an issue today as gender consciousness among men and woman has grown.

Yet, for all the progress made, being a woman can still mean facing oppression in the workplace, and being a man still means enjoying certain advantages. Gender stereotyping, for all the present sensitivity and awareness, has not disappeared from the political and administrative arenas. Clothing, jewelry, and physical appearance remain a significant prism through which to examine women in public life. Unmarried women continue to find themselves the subject of whispering campaigns about their personal lives, while married women find themselves explaining domestic arrangements and family choices.

In the National Performance Review reports, the signature federal government reform initiative of the 1990s, it was men in government who were represented as the "reinvention doers, whereas women [were] mostly reinvention helpers" (Burnier 2006, 867). Gender stereotypes also were evident in the discussions of welfare policy and Social Security. Even contemporary graduate students rely on stereotypes for white and multicultural men and women. Richard Johnson and Espiridion Borrego found that graduate students viewed women across class and multicultural identities in negative stereotypic terms, leading the researchers to conclude "that gender should be part of cultural competencies" (2009, 214).

Equal gender representation in the federal public service remains problematic. Norma Riccucci surveyed the federal public service to determine whether workforce equity progress was made. Using the years 1984–2004 as her baseline, Riccucci found that "women overall increased their employment by 4.2 percent" (2009, 375). Diverse women were part of this gain while white women's numbers declined by 0.2 percent. The Senior Executive Service (SES) "became more diverse during the period examined, particularly in terms of gender" (376). Riccucci concluded that "white women achieved the largest increase in employment in the SES," but overall the "SES has achieved relatively little racial or ethnic diversity over the last 20 years or so" (376).

Not only does a glass ceiling still persist in the federal service, but also so do glass walls continue to confine women and people of color. As of 2004, women were concentrated in "agencies within the Departments of Education, Health and Human Services, Housing and Urban Development, and Treasury, whereas men held posts in such agencies as the Departments of Transportation, Defense, and Homeland Security" (Riccucci 2009, 378). Pay equity issues continue for women as well.

Despite years of equal employment and other diversity initiatives, progress in social equity generally and in making the upper levels of the federal workforce more gender diverse has been slow, especially for multicultural women. Riccucci suggests that "educating the public workforce more broadly on issues surrounding race and gender is paramount" (2009, 379). She also notes that more training is needed, along with a commitment to social equity as part of achieving an organization's overall mission. Pessimistic about all these efforts to change the federal workforce, Riccucci quotes Stivers's equally skeptical observation: "the structural nature of public administration's masculine bias means that equal opportunity strategies for advancing women's careers in public service, important as they are as a means of simple justice, cannot be counted on in and of themselves to change public administration affairs" (380). In light of this present moment, which is poised on the divide between the promise of progress and the prospect of regression, public administration must begin taking seriously the broad concept of gender competency in training, teaching, and scholarship.

Notes

Written in memory of my mother, Barbara Burnier, and my doctoral adviser and mentor, Dr. Frederick M. Wirt, both of whom were models of gender competence.

1. Frances Perkins was born in 1880 in Boston, Massachusetts, and grew up in Worcester, Massachusetts, in a prosperous family dedicated to education. Perkins graduated from Mount Holyoke in 1902 and a few years later headed west to Lake Forest, Illinois, to teach at a private school. Her years at Mount Holyoke had kindled her lifelong interest in social justice and improving industrial working conditions for the poor, and not surprisingly she began to volunteer at Hull House and Chicago Commons during her school vacations. Realizing that social work was her true vocation, she moved to

Philadelphia to become executive secretary for an organization focused on the experiences of arriving immigrant and Southern women.

She earned her master's degree from Columbia University in 1910 and then became executive secretary of the New York Consumers' League, an affiliate of the National Consumers' League founded by social reformer Florence Kelley. Kelley was much admired in the social and industrial reform movement and especially by Perkins. Kelley was a professional mentor and lifelong inspiration for Perkins. In 1911 Perkins witnessed the terrible Triangle Shirtwaist fire and in the fire's aftermath was appointed to the New York State Factory Investigating Committee charged with improving working conditions in factories throughout the state. While serving on this committee she became friends with Al Smith, and when he was elected governor in 1918 he appointed Perkins to the Industrial Commission of the New York State Department of Labor. She served as chair of the Industrial Board from 1926 to 1928.

When Franklin Roosevelt was elected governor in 1928 he appointed Perkins head of the New York State Department of Labor. The two became close working colleagues and friends, and she made a public name for herself when she challenged the veracity of the Hoover administration's unemployment statistics. When Roosevelt was elected president in 1932 he invited her to join his administration, and she served as secretary of labor from 1933 until 1945. President Harry Truman appointed her to the Civil Service Commission, where she remained until Dwight Eisenhower's election in 1952. After leaving the federal government, she began a twelve-year academic career that took her first to the Labor Industrial Relations Institute at the University of Illinois at Urbana-Champaign and then to Cornell University's School of Industrial and Labor Relations. She was married to Paul Wilson and had one daughter (Pasachoff 1999). She died in 1965.

2. For other perspectives on gender, see Judith Butler's *Gender Trouble* (1990), wherein she argues that gender is performative, as well as Janet Hutchison and Hollie Mann (2004), who argue for a multigendered perspective. These scholars draw on poststructural, postmodern feminist, and queer theories in their formulations of gender. For yet another view on gender, see Catherine Connell, who examines the workplace experiences of transgendered individuals in order to argue that the interactional view of "doing gender" should be undone and reformulated as "doing transgender" (2010).

REFERENCES

Abrums, Mary, and Carol Leppa. 2001. Beyond cultural competence: Teaching about race, gender, class, and sexual orientation. *Journal of Nursing Education* 40: 270–275.

Anderson, Mary. 1951. *Women at Work*. Minneapolis: University of Minnesota Press.

Bailey, Margo. 2010. Cultural competency and the practice of public administration. In *Diversity and Public Administration: Theory, Issues, and Perspectives*, ed. Mitchell F. Rice, 171–188. Armonk, NY: M.E. Sharpe.

Bearfield, Domonic. 2009. Equity at the intersection: Public administration and the study of gender. *Public Administration Review* 69: 383–386.

Benavides, Abraham, and Julie Hernandez. 2007. Serving diverse communities: Cultural competency. *Public Management* (July): 14–18.

Box, Richard. 2007. *Democracy and Public Administration*. Armonk, NY: M.E. Sharpe.

Burnier, DeLysa. 2003. Other voices/other rooms: Towards a care-centered public administration. *Administrative Theory & Praxis* 44: 365–372.

———. 2005. Public leaders are gendered: Making gender visible in public affairs leadership education. *Journal of Public Affairs Education* 11: 181–192.

———. 2006. Masculine markets and feminine care: A gender analysis of the national performance review. *Public Administration Review* 66: 861–872.

———. 2008. Frances Perkins' disappearance from American public administration: A genealogy of marginalization. *Administrative Theory & Praxis* 30: 398–423.

Butler, Judith. 1990. *Gender Trouble: Feminism and the Subversion of Identity*. New York: Routledge.

Chin, Jean Lau. 2000. Culturally competent health care. *Public Health Reports* 115: 25–33.

Chin, Jean Lau, Bernice Lott, Joy Rice, and Janis Sanchez-Hucles. 2007. *Women and Leadership: Transforming Visions and Diverse Voices*. Malden, MA: Blackwell.

Colman, Penny. 1993. *A Woman Unafraid: The Achievement of Frances Perkins*. New York: Atheneum Press.

Connell, Catherine. 2010. Doing, undoing, or redoing gender? Learning from the workplace experiences of transpeople. *Gender & Society* 24: 31–55.

Dean, Ruth. 2001. The myth of cross-cultural competence. *Families in Society* 82: 623–630.

Downey, Kirstin. 2009. *The Woman Behind the New Deal*. New York: Doubleday.

Eliot, Thomas. 1992. *Recollection of the New Deal: When the People Mattered*. Boston: Northeastern University Press.

Ferguson, Kathy. 1984. *The Feminist Case Against Bureaucracy*. Philadelphia: Temple University Press.

Fletcher, Joyce. 2001. *Disappearing Acts: Gender, Power, and Relational Practice at Work*. Cambridge: MIT Press.

Gentlewarrior, Sabrina, Anna Martin-Jearld, Alyson Skok, and Katelyn Sweetser. 2008. Culturally competent social work: Listening to diverse people. *Affilia: Journal of Women and Social Work* 23: 210–222.

Guy, Mary, Meredith Newman, and Sharon Mastracci. 2008. *Emotional Labor: Putting the Service in Public Service*. Armonk, NY: M.E. Sharpe.

Holvino, Evangelina. 2003. CGO Insights No. 17: Working across differences: Diversity practices for organizational change. April: 1–4. Boston: Center for Gender in Organizations, Simmons School of Management.

———. 2006. CGO Insights No. 24: Tired of choosing: Working with the simultaneity of race, gender, and class in organizations. March: 1–4. Boston: Center for Gender in Organizations, Simmons School of Management.

———. 2010. Intersections: The simultaneity of race, gender and class in organization studies. *Gender, Work and Organization* 17: 248–277.

Hutchison, Janet, and Hollie Mann. 2004. Feminist praxis: Administering for a multicultural, multi-gendered public. *Administrative Theory & Praxis* 26: 79–95.

Johnson, Richard, and Espiridion Borrego. 2009. Public administration and the increased need for cultural competence in the twenty-first century. *Administrative Theory & Praxis* 31: 206–220.

King, Cheryl, and Lisa Zanetti. 2005. *Transformational Public Service: Portraits of Theory in Practice*. Armonk, NY: M.E. Sharpe.

Martin, George. 1976. *Madam Secretary Frances Perkins*. Boston: Houghton Mifflin.

Martin, Patricia. 2003. "Said and done" versus "saying and doing": Gendering practices, practicing gender at work. *Gender & Society* 17: 342–366.

———. 2006. Practicing gender at work: Further thoughts on reflexivity. *Gender, Work and Organization* 13: 254–276.

Mastracci, Sharon, Meredith Newman, and Mary Guy. 2010. Emotional labor: Why and how to teach it. *Journal of Public Affairs Education* 16: 123–141.

McGinn, Kathy, and Patricia Patterson. 2005. A long way toward what? Sex, gender, feminism and the study of public administration. *Public Administration Review* 28: 929–942.

McSwite, O.C. 2004. Creating reality through administrative practice: A psychoanalytic reading of Camilla Stivers' *Bureau Men, Settlement Women*. *Administration & Society* 36: 406–426.

Mettler, Suzanne. 1998. *Gender and Federalism in New Deal Policy*. Ithaca, NY: Cornell University Press.

Mohr, Lillian. 1979. *Frances Perkins: "That Woman in FDR's Cabinet."* Great Barrington, MA: North River Press.

Neustadt, Richard, and Ernest May. 1986. *Thinking in Time: The Uses of History for Decision-Makers*. New York: Free Press.

Newman, Meredith. 2004. Madam Secretary Frances Perkins. In *Outstanding Women in Public Administration*, ed. Claire Felbinger and Wendy Haynes, 83–102. Armonk, NY: M.E. Sharpe.

Pasachoff, Naomi. 1999. *Frances Perkins: Champion of the New Deal*. New York: Oxford University Press.

Perkins, Frances. 1934. *People at Work*. New York: John Day.

———. 1946. *The Roosevelt I Know*. New York: Viking.

Regan, Helen, and Gwen Brooks. 1995. *Out of Women's Experience: Creating Relational Leadership*. Thousand Oaks, CA: Corwin Press.

Riccucci, Norma. 2009. The pursuit of social equity in the federal government: A road less traveled? *Public Administration Review* 69: 373–382.

Rice, Mitchell F. 2010. Cultural competency, public administration, and public service in an era of diversity. In *Diversity and Public Administration: Theory, Issues, and Perspectives*, ed. Mitchell F. Rice, 189–209. Armonk, NY: M.E. Sharpe.

Ridgeway, Cecilia. 2009. Framed before we know it: How gender shapes social relations. *Gender & Society* 23: 145–160.

Samuels, Gina, and Fariyal Ross-Sheriff. 2008. Identity, oppression, and power: Feminisms and intersectionality theory. *Affilia: Journal of Women and Social Work* 23: 5–9.

Schachter, Hindy Lauer. 2008. Feminist theory and the political dimension of performance measurement. *Public Performance and Management Review* 32: 263–274.

Schneider, Anne, and Helen Ingram. 2005. *Deserving and Entitled: Social Construction and Public Policy*. Albany: State University of New York Press.

Scott, Joan. 1988. *Gender and the Politics of History*. New York: Columbia University Press.

Stivers, Camilla. 2000. *Bureau Men/Settlement Women: Constructing Public Administration in the Progressive Era*. Lawrence: University Press of Kansas.

———. 2002. *Gender Images in Public Administration: Legitimacy and the Administrative State*. Thousand Oaks, CA: Sage.

———. 2005. A place like home: Care and action in public administration. *American Review of Public Administration* 35: 26–41.

Wandersee, Winifred. 1993. I'd rather pass a law than organize a union. *Labor History* 34 (1): 5–32.

Weaver, Hilary. 2005. *Explorations in Cultural Competence*. Belmont, CA: Thomson Brooks/Cole.

Cultural Competency in Hispanic Communities

ABRAHAM DAVID BENAVIDES

Ethnic and racial diversity continue to be on the rise in the United States. The 2010 U.S. Census will no doubt show once again that the United States is the most diverse nation in the world. Individuals from every nation in the world count the United States as their home country. As the extent of the diversity continues to expand, various organizations, including state and local governments, will need to ensure that their institutions are capable of communicating with, providing services to, and representing an increasingly diverse and linguistically different population. As the previous chapters have shown, the task at hand is not easy. However, becoming culturally competent will be the key to successful management as we move forward in the twenty-first century.

News events related to immigration specifically and Hispanic issues generally have propelled an interest in this topic to the front page of the newspaper and to the council chambers of local and state governments. Some cities and states have taken issue with unauthorized workers in the United States, for instance, and have crafted fragmented city ordinances or confusing state laws to combat the issue. From sanctuary cities on the one hand to enforcement cities on the other and neutral cities uncomfortably in the middle, the range of inconsistent policies is bound to continue and to increase. The inaction on the part of the federal government is also cause for concern both for cities and states and for the Hispanic community.

The following chapter focuses on the growing Hispanic population in the United States and the importance of becoming culturally competent with this dynamic group of people. The first section will set the framework by showing the growth and the political and economic impact that Hispanics are experiencing. Next, cultural competency will be explored and its direct implications for the Hispanic community will be analyzed. Finally, the chapter will present some concrete examples of what can be accomplished by states and local municipalities with respect to the Hispanic community and cultural competency.

HISPANIC OR LATINO?

The Hispanic community has a long and varied history in the United States. A number of Hispanics can trace their lineage to seventeenth- and eighteenth-century Texas,

New Mexico, Arizona, or California—states that used to be part of Mexico until the Mexican War. Others can claim a legacy directly back to Spain on the European continent. More recently, many Hispanics have immigrated legally to the United States from North, Central, and South America, while others are unauthorized to be in the United States. This latter group has received most of the public and political attention, which has distorted a rational, comprehensive understanding of the larger Hispanic community. To understand a large, diverse group of people within a larger society, it is beneficial to have a basic understanding of how their identity was officially created within government. The Congress of the United States through the Voting Rights Act of 1965 as amended required the director of the U.S. Census Bureau to collect information on race and Hispanic origin for purposes of bilingual election determinations. The 1970 U.S. Census provided, for the first time, a glimpse of the nation's growing diversity because it included an option for respondents to claim Spanish origin on the long form of the U.S. Census. According to Gibson and Jung (2002) of the Population Division of the U.S. Census Bureau, "The history of census data on Hispanic origin (which is identified as an ethnic origin rather than as a race in federal statistics) is quite different from the history of census data on race. While there were various indicators of portions of the Hispanic origin population, including data on mother tongue, data on the population with Spanish surname, and the designation of Mexican as a race in the 1930 census, the first attempt to identify the entire Hispanic origin population was in 1970" (1).

The public policy implications for a growing and changing population necessitated more accuracy in reporting. Public administrators during the Nixon administration adopted the term *Hispanic* in 1973 when they divided the nation's population into five distinct groups—American Indian or Alaskan Native, Asian or Pacific Islander, Black, Hispanic, and White. By 1976 the U.S. Congress passed Public Law 94–311, Statistics Relating to Social, Health, and Economic Conditions of Americans of Spanish Origin or Descent. The reason for this law, which mandated collection and analysis of specific information for Americans of Spanish origin and descent, was fivefold. First, Congress realized the significant growth in the number of Americans who "identify themselves as being of Spanish-speaking background and trace their origin or descent from Mexico, Puerto Rico, Cuba, Central and South America, and other Spanish-speaking countries." Second, it was well known that Americans of Spanish origins have made "significant contributions to enrich American society and have served their Nation well in time of war and peace." Third, the resolution noted the racial, economic, and political discrimination that was focused on this group and that their basic opportunities, as American citizens, were being denied them. Fourth, "improved evaluation of the economic and social status of Americans of Spanish origin or descent would assist State and Federal Governments and private organizations in the accurate determination of their urgent and special needs." And finally the law, in and of itself, provided a type of needs assessment that was necessary to justify and provide funds to assist the group. The law directed a number of federal departments to "collect and publish regularly, statistics which indicate the social, health, and economic condition of Americans of Spanish origin or descent" (U.S. Code 2010).

During this same period, a number of federal agencies formed an ad hoc committee that "developed terms and definitions for the collection of a broad range of racial and ethnic data by Federal agencies on a compatible and non-duplicative basis" (U.S. OMB 1994). The result was Directive 15 from the Office of Management and Budget. These categories and definitions for Hispanics and non-Hispanics became effective in May 1977 (and were amended in 1997) for all compliance and record keeping in all federal agencies. Thus the word *Hispanic* was defined (for classification purposes) as "a person of Mexican, Puerto Rican, Cuban, Central or South American or other Spanish culture or origin, regardless of race." The label *Hispanic* was first used in an official national capacity to designate individuals of Spanish origin during the 1980 U.S. Census. During the 2000 U.S. Census, the word *Latino* was included for the first time because of its common use and because it had been previously adopted during the Clinton administration in 1997. The selection for this item on the 2000 U.S. Census was Spanish/Hispanic/Latino. The census also provided four subgroup responses: Mexican, Mexican American, Chicano; Puerto Rican, Cuban, and Other. Over 35 million individuals identified themselves as Hispanic or Latino on the 2000 U.S. Census (U.S. Census Bureau 2000). Hispanic and/or Latino(a) Americans are Americans with ancestors in any number of countries. In this chapter I use the term *Hispanic* rather than *Latino(a)*. It is a professional and personal preference. These interchangeable terms are used to describe Spanish-surnamed people and/or individuals whose ethnic culture primarily descends from North, Central, and South America (including the Caribbean). Passel and Taylor (2009) of the Pew Hispanic Center indicate that

> the labels are not universally embraced by the community that has been labeled. A 2006 survey by the Pew Hispanic Center found that 48 percent of Latino adults generally describe themselves by their country of origin first; 26 percent generally use the terms Latino or Hispanic first; and 24 percent generally call themselves American on first reference. As for a preference between "Hispanic" and "Latino," a 2008 Center survey found that 36 percent of respondents prefer the term "Hispanic," 21 percent prefer the term "Latino" and the rest have no preference.

To complicate matters, the U.S. Census notes that Hispanics can be of any race and are many distinct nationalities (Hobbs and Stoops 2002). Neither term, however, completely captures the diversity that exists among these peoples. To understand the Hispanic community, therefore, it is essential to comprehend that the labels and terms used to categorize this group of people all fall well short of a succinct description and definition of who Hispanics and Latinos really are. Nevertheless, for me the term *Hispanic* is all-inclusive because it appears to include a broader range of individuals who consider themselves to be of this particular origin.

DEMOGRAPHICS AND ECONOMIC IMPACT

During the last few years there has been a rise in the foreign-born populations in the United States. From budding immigrant populations in South Carolina, Oregon, and Arkansas to continued growth in California, Florida, and Texas, Hispanics make up an increasing share of the population, according to the U.S. Census. The Hispanic

Table 7.1

U.S. Hispanic Population Projections Through 2050

Source of data and year	Hispanic population (in millions)	Percent Hispanic of the total population
U.S. Census		
1970	9.6	4.7
1980	14.6	6.4
1990	22.4	9.0
2000	35.3	12.5
Projections		
2010	47.8	15.5
2020	59.7	17.8
2030	73.0	20.1
2040	87.7	22.3
2050	102.6	24.4

Source: Adapted from U.S. Census Bureau, 1970, 1980, 1990, and 2000 Decennial Censuses; Population Projections, July 1, 2010 to July 1, 2050.

population is the largest minority group in the country (about 50.5 million), growing faster than any other group; it currently constitutes about 16.3 percent of the U.S. population (U.S. Census 2011). It is expected that the population will continue to grow and could reach nearly 60 million by 2020 and compose about 18 percent of the U.S. population (see Table 7.1). Sixteen states (Arizona, California, Colorado, Florida, Georgia, Illinois, Massachusetts, Nevada, New Jersey, New Mexico, New York, North Carolina, Pennsylvania, Texas, Virginia, and Washington) have at least half a million Hispanic residents, and Hispanics are the largest minority group in twenty states (Arizona, California, Colorado, Connecticut, Florida, Idaho, Iowa, Kansas, Massachusetts, Nebraska, Nevada, New Hampshire, New Jersey, New Mexico, Oregon, Rhode Island, Texas, Utah, Washington, and Wyoming) (U.S. Census Bureau 2009). It is interesting to note that only the country of Mexico (population 110 million) has more Hispanics than the United States.

According to the Pew Hispanic Research Center, the ten largest Hispanic population groups by country of origin in the United States are Mexican, Puerto Rican, Cuban, Salvadoran, Dominican, Guatemalan, Colombian, Honduran, Ecuadorian, and Peruvian. Their respective populations are found in Table 7.2.

The United States is composed of Hispanics from all Latin American countries, including the Caribbean, and Spain. The cultural legacy of this group is part of the collective tapestry that forms the U.S. culture. A common misconception of a number of public administrators is that all Hispanics are the same regardless of country of origin. This belief is unreliable and can lead to the implementation of policies that are inappropriate for the intended group. For instance, most Hispanics in California and Texas have a close relationship with the country of Mexico. The proximity of Mexico to the United States and the large Hispanic population in these states have allowed for an increased understanding of the Mexican culture. The birthday piñata and Cinco de Mayo celebrations are not uncommon in a number of families and

Table 7.2

Hispanics in the United States by Country of Origin

Country of origin	Population
Mexican	30,746,000
Puerto Rican	4,151,000
Cuban	1,621,000
Salvadoran	1,560,000
Dominican	1,334,000
Guatemalan	986,000
Colombian	882,000
Honduran	608,000
Ecuadorian	591,000
Peruvian	519,000

Source: Pew Hispanic Center.

communities in the United States. However, a Cinco de Mayo celebration in Florida, whose Hispanics are mostly from Cuba, or in New York, whose Hispanics are predominantly Puerto Rican, would be unusual. Hispanics from New Mexico have close ties to both Mexico and Spain, and Hispanics in Washington, DC, originate mainly from Central and South America. The consequence inherent in labeling large groups of people with diverse backgrounds within categories is often the loss of significant details that enrich particular cultures.

Although the cultures in the various countries from which Hispanics come vary greatly, the Spanish language and common history contribute to a convergence. The verbal manifestations of culture are found in most languages, for culture and language are fundamentally interconnected. J.R. Gladstone (1969) suggested that "language is at once an outcome or result of the culture as a whole and also a vehicle by which the other facets of the culture are shaped and communicated" (114). The fact that most Hispanics speak or understand Spanish or have a connection to this language gives them a shared communality, despite their various accents and regional modes and idioms of speech. Similarly, a mutual historical connection to either traditional indigenous cultures or a spirit of independence from Spain has given many Hispanic cultures of America a spirit of unity. The close connections with Latin America in general and with Mexico specifically have made Hispanic culture as a whole well entrenched in American society.

Furthermore, the Hispanic population is growing faster than the non-Hispanic populations. The implications of this growth impact not only culture but politics as well. It is projected that six of the eight states that are expected to gain seats in the House of Representatives, thanks to the 2010 Census count, will receive them because of the growth in the Hispanic population. Only Utah and Georgia will gain their new seats without Hispanic growth (America's Voice 2010). While the Hispanic community as a whole is not very active politically, the foundation is being laid for this group to have enormous political impact in the future. Recent political events have shown that Hispanics are beginning to flex their political muscle. For instance, Judge Sonia Sotomayor was confirmed a member of the Supreme Court in 2009

Table 7.3

Hispanic Buying Power

Largest Hispanic markets	Dollars (in billions)
California	253
Texas	175
Florida	101
New York	76
Illinois	43
New Jersey	37
Arizona	31
Colorado	21
New Mexico	18
Georgia	15

Source: Humphreys (2009).

and Susana Martinez is the first female Hispanic governor of New Mexico; Hilda L. Solis is secretary of the U.S. Department of Labor, Ken Salazar is secretary of the U.S. Department of Interior; Bill Richardson (former governor of New Mexico) ran for president in 2008, Alberto Gonzales was U.S. Attorney General in 2005, and a number of other Hispanic Americans have held cabinet-level positions. Currently there are two Hispanic senators and twenty-five Hispanic members of the House of Representatives.

Another area in which Hispanics are having significant impact is the economy. In 2008, Hispanic buying power reached $951 billion, or 8.9 percent of the total in the United States. According to Humphreys (2009), "Buying power, also referred to as disposable income, is the total personal income available for spending on goods and services after taxes" (1). A 2009 study by the Selig Center for Economic Growth at the University of Georgia found that Hispanic households in Texas contributed more than $175 billion to the state's economy; the center expects Hispanic buying power to increase to $252 billion by 2013 (Humphreys 2009). Although Hispanics are found in every state, many are concentrated in states in the southwest. Therefore their buying power has the biggest impact in these states (see Table 7.3).

Hispanics constitute the fastest growing segment of the U.S. labor force. As Humphreys (2009) notes:

> From May 2000 through May 2009, the number of jobs held by Hispanics increased by 25.2 percent—nearly four million jobs—which is impressive compared to the minuscule 0.7 percent (109,000 jobs) and 1.1 percent (1.26 million jobs) gains realized by African Americans and whites, respectively. But, even though the number of jobs held by Hispanics is up by nearly 4 million from where it stood at the beginning of the decade, the recession is hitting Hispanics very hard. (10)

The 2010 unemployment rate in the United States was 9.7 percent according to the Bureau of Labor Statistics in the Department of Labor. The Hispanic unemployment rate stood at 12.4 percent. This gap has fluctuated over the years but most recently it has become smaller. Nevertheless, the recent recession has caused hardship in the Hispanic community. Hispanics make up about 15 percent of the U.S. labor force, yet by late 2010 they accounted for 20 percent of the unemployed. The housing crash and the economic unrest, intensified by the recession, played a big role in the loss of jobs in the construction and service sectors. Nevertheless, some states with small but growing Hispanic populations have had some success. Recently the Idaho Department of Labor reported that Hispanic buying power in that state grew ten times faster than that of the non-Hispanic majority. "The buying power of Idaho's Hispanic population rose 3.1 percent in 2009 to $2.5 billion. Last year was the sixth straight year Idaho Hispanics have fared better than Hispanics nationwide" (2010, 3).

As predicted by demographers, our communities are changing. Cities that were expected to increase in minority and immigrant populations have done so. Therefore the challenge now is to diversify managerial skills in government to serve all people. Ethnic, racial, and cultural differences exist in all aspects of society, but nowhere are they more clearly evident than in our local communities. Local government officials are learning to adapt to culturally and linguistically different populations. Many local governments have been proactive in their response to the needs of these communities while others are still seeking for ways to proceed. Experience has shown that success-ful governments are responsive to citizens. Thus most city officials make an effort to know their people and respond to their needs. As communities change, governments will need to continually modify their service delivery patterns and practices in order to be supportive of the groups within their city limits. A number of these adjustments are made in managerial practices and others by either adding to or adjusting existing programs (Benavides and Hernandez 2007).

CULTURAL COMPETENCY

To better serve a people, it is important to understand them culturally and linguisti-cally. Public administration has been influenced by concepts such as social equity, affirmative action, representative democracy, equal opportunity, managing diversity, cultural diversity, multiculturalism, equity and diversity, and a diverse workforce, to name a few. Cultural competency is in this line of concepts that pack meaning and are intended to promote the social welfare of all people in society. However, one of the differences between the terms above and cultural competency rests in the focus on outcomes. The concepts above prompt the public administrator to act affirmatively, representatively, or with equality when dealing with groups of people or managing individuals with different backgrounds. Cultural competency, on the other hand, is the process of understanding those we serve to the point of managing and adapting services to meet the needs of the people. These efforts to provide equitable outcomes for all of society rest not only in the actions on the part of the public administrator but in a true understanding of how public services can better the lives of those being served. Therefore a public administrator will not only act on behalf of individuals or groups in the traditional sense, but will make an effort to understand culturally who is being represented. Lack of awareness about cultural differences can cause difficulties in both the delivery of services and a misunderstanding concerning the public services that should be delivered. Social equity, representative democracy, and equal opportunity, for instance, have a noticeable place in the literature of public administration. However, cultural competency goes beyond this literature to inform the public administrator of the necessity to be culturally competent in the delivery of services.

The United States is a nation of immigrants that has always welcomed new peoples within its borders. A major strength of this nation has always been the ability to value diversity and accept and respect differences. These differences include thoughts, ways of communication, values, traditions, celebrations, religions, and sports. It is true that immigrants must make an effort to learn the laws and customs of this country. However, in the transition as individuals and groups assimilate, acculturate, and become contributing members of the society; governments must make an effort to facilitate this development. This process of understanding the new members of our society and the willingness and ability of a system to value the importance of culture in the delivery of services to all segments of the population is called cultural competency. In essence, cultural competency is defined as "a set of congruent behaviors, attitudes, and policies that come together in a system, agency, or among professionals and enables that system, agency, or those professionals to work effectively in cross-cultural situations" (Cross et al. 1989; Isaacs and Benjamin 1991). In other words, city employees can make an effort to learn patterns of behavior for a particular group and respond to those behaviors in a culturally appropriate manner. For instance, city employees can make an effort to understand customs, beliefs, and values. Furthermore, they can develop the capacity to function, act, or react to particular groups that will most often lead to improved service delivery. Operationally defined, cultural competence "is the integration and transformation of knowledge about individuals and groups of people into specific standards, policies, practices, and attitudes used in appropriate cultural settings to increase the quality of services, thereby producing better outcomes" (Davis 1997, 18).

Bailey (2005) argues that "in practice, culturally competent public administration emphasizes the capacity of public organizations and their employees to effectively provide services that reflect the different cultural influences of their constituents or clients" (177). Her argument suggests that representative bureaucracy has been "the primary lens through which public administration has examined the impact of diversity upon public sector organizations" (192). Bailey notes that culturally competent practices have been adopted in a number of disciplines, including social work, education, psychiatric services, and health care. Rice and White (2005) suggest that the time has come to "shift from looking at hiring numbers (affirmative action) and assimilation to focusing on valuing difference (multiculturalism and managing diversity in public organizations" (230).

SERVING DIVERSE COMMUNITIES: MANIFESTATIONS OF CULTURAL COMPETENCY

The International Hispanic Network (IHN) is a nonprofit organization composed of mainly Hispanic government officials, executives, and public managers in local governments. Its primary mission is to improve the management of communities with ever-increasing Hispanic populations. In 2005 IHN commissioned a study on municipal best practices for the Hispanic community (Benavides 2005, 2008; Benavides and Hernandez 2007; Hernandez, Brown, and Tien 2007). The survey was sent to all cities with Hispanic populations over 12 percent and to all Hispanic city managers. It highlighted the efforts being made by a number of communities with respect to cultural competency. The results clearly showed that "cultural competency converts the knowledge gained about groups and individuals into policies and procedures that result in practices that increase the quality of the services to produce better outcomes" (Benavides and Hernandez 2007, 15). In other words, culturally competent local governments can better serve their citizens. The best practice examples in the survey also "provided an initial glimpse into how cities are implementing various programs to serve the Hispanic community. In general, the results of the best practice study show that some cities are taking steps to serve their communities. A number of cities have made extraordinary efforts to put in place services that have assisted in the transition of new immigrants" (Benavides 2008, 75). Additionally, it was found that

> civic engagement of diverse communities has involved the traditions of second and third generation Hispanics and has provided meaningful services to all Hispanics. Thus collaborating and seeking participation from Hispanics that have been in the United States for years, has helped cities customize programs that help new Hispanic immigrants as well as those that have been in this country for decades. (Benavides 2008, 74–75)

The local government programs highlighted in the IHN survey included community relations officers to bridge the gap between residents and, for instance, the police department, full-fledged community centers with a variety of services, Hispanic advisory councils, interpretation of city council meetings into Spanish, language skills programs, and a Hispanic heritage month. These examples illustrated how different cities are making an effort to more fully understand how the principles of cultural competency can have a positive effect on service delivery. These examples demonstrate the ingenuity on the part of some local governments to reach out and fully represent all members in their communities. In government, as in other disciplines, cultural competency emerged as an inward desire of administrators who genuinely wanted to serve the public. This desire informed their capacity to understand new residents and provide appropriate services. The following sections present a number of programs that have been ongoing in a number of cities.

HISPANIC ADVISORY COUNCILS AND COMMITTEES

One essential cultural competence skill that cities must acquire is the ability of their law enforcement officers to communicate with residents. In many Latin American countries, it is customary for a driver, when stopped by a police officer, to get out of the vehicle and walk back to where the police officer is located. Here in the United States, the practice is just the opposite: the driver must remain in the vehicle until instructed otherwise. In Seattle, Washington, the police department, understanding this cultural and problematic difference, created a video in both English and Spanish that instructed both police officers and residents concerning the practice here in the United States. It was created under the direction of the Latino Advisory Council and the Seattle Police Department (Benavides 2008; see Figure 7.1). Similarly, the city of Newport News, Virginia, established the Hispanic Advisory Committee (HAC) to the City Manager in 2008. The formation of this committee was founded upon earlier efforts by the police department to gain trust and a working relationship with the Hispanic community. A number of Hispanic residents were not reporting crime-related incidents because of a lack of trust in the police department. In Latin America, many police officers are corrupt and there is a general lack of trust in their ability to execute their duty. This lack of trust, which came with the new immigrants to the United States, was a cultural barrier that the Newport News police department did not create, but had to understand and overcome. Kirstyn Barr, the community relations and communication specialist in the office of the city manager, noted, "Through outreach initiatives and education, trust levels began to increase and positive relationships were developing. As a result, crime rates in areas where many of the city's Hispanic community members resided began to drop" (2010, 3). The success of these initiatives lead to the creation of HAC, which has an expanded focus to include public safety, health, human services, libraries, and education. The mission statement of this organization is to "function as a liaison between city administration and the Hispanic community and to advise and make recommendations to the City Manager on current and future issues, needs, programs and services as they relate to the Hispanic community and to ultimately improve the quality of life for all residents of the city." According to the group's charter, the goals of the Hispanic Advisory Committee are to

- create and improve communication links between the residents and city government
- evaluate existing city services, identify needs, and improve access
- develop partnership and trust between city government and the Hispanic community, and
- promote and support Hispanic culture in the city of Newport News

Since the creation of HAC its members have cooperated with and advised the city on the cultural particulars of Hispanics in their city, assisted city staff with various outreach programs, and facilitated learning opportunities for the community. The committee has also made "numerous recommendations to city staff on ways to improve communication with community members with limited English proficiency and fostered trust between the city and the Hispanic community by identifying ways to resolve barriers to city programs and services that may exist for residents" (Barr 2010, 3).

Other cities have similar arrangements. For instance, Clearwater, Florida, started a Police Minority Relations Committee that in turn has started a program called Operation Apoyo Hispano. According to its report, the program is intended to "reach out to our Hispanic neighbors, bridge the gap in communicating with our Spanish speaking population, seek ways to positively resolve law enforcement issues, and increase the number of bilingual police officers and staff" (Clearwater Police Department 2005).

Figure 7.1
Seattle Latino Advisory Council and Community Liaison

The Advisory Council was organized to meet with the police for the purpose of bridging the communication gap between the police department and the Hispanic community. The advisory council discusses concerns, issues, recommendations, needs, perspectives, and insights from the Latino communities. The purpose of the group is to provide input and feedback directly to the department. Additionally, the organization has a Latino liaison officer, a full-time position that reports to the deputy chief. The goals of the program are to build relationships between the Seattle Police Department and the Hispanic community. This program has been instrumental in showing the need for community social service programs that focus on gang prevention and intervention and recovery services. Four specific partnerships were created that led to significant outcomes. First, the council members worked on making the South Park boxing gym a police activities league. They were able to provide the boxing gym with over $20,000 worth of boxing equipment, which increased youth interaction with police officers. Second, the council started several youth/police activities in order to reduce violence. It started soccer and basketball events with the local community centers and partnered with Allstate to put on a Life Choices and Law Workshops. Third, the council organized an international exchange with the Peruvian National Police to create training for officers. This has created a better understanding of cultural issues and provided training in specialized units, such as antiterrorism, antidrug, and education units. The council has also become the host for graduation training with the Peruvian National Police. Fourth, the Seattle Police Department has a liaison assigned to the thirty-seven consulates in the state of Washington. The liaison assists with any possible issues of crime or arrival of dignitaries into the Seattle area. The liaison works closely with the Mexican and Peruvian Consulates since there is a high population of immigrant communities from these countries. Additionally, the council has organized a "National Night Out Against Crime" in various parks in the city and provided a sample video that looks at the Hispanic community and issues of concern involving experiences and perceptions between Hispanics and law enforcement. A significant result of these initiatives has been a reduction in Hispanic youth-related crime.

Source: Benavides (2005).

A final example is that of Lebanon, Pennsylvania. The committee in this town holds prescheduled monthly meetings. The meetings are opened to the public and agendas and minutes are provided. Topics related to understanding and communications are covered in the meetings. The mayor's office is responsible for giving information to the press. The goal is to promote communication, education, understanding, and respect for one another (Benavides 2005). These examples clearly demonstrate an effort by the participants to engage the community not only on a superficial level, but also at a depth that significantly promotes harmony and positive exchanges.

Hispanic/Latino Cultural Centers

The degree of participation, involvement, and commitment associated with various levels of engagement must be determined by the community. Hispanic cultural centers are large undertakings with the purpose of establishing a permanent and central location where Hispanic residents can address some of their basic needs. Activities and services at these locations include, but are not limited to English and Spanish classes, computer training, immigration and naturalization courses, first aid and finance classes, child care, budgeting and counseling courses, sports, recreation, rooms to rent for meetings, parties, fiestas, cultural events such as art and musical presentations, and guest speakers. In some communities these organizations are run by and supported with tax dollars from the local government. In others, they are nonprofit organizations that are funded by various means, including grants from the local community and, most often, United Way–type organizations. These nonprofit Hispanic cultural centers are all over the United States in large and small cities, including Grand Rapids, Michigan (Hispanic Community Center), Joliet, Illinois (Spanish Community Center), Seattle, Washington (Centro Cultural Hispano Americano), Dudley, North Carolina (The Hispanic Community Development Center), Nampa, Idaho (Hispanic Cultural Center of Idaho), and Austin, Texas (Mexican American Cultural Center). Although these nonprofit Hispanic cultural centers have been quite successful, so have those run by local municipalities. These include those in Miami-Dade County, Florida (Department of Cultural Affairs), Santa Clarita, California (Newhall Community Center), Alexandria, Virginia (Hispanic Orientation and Education Program), Newark, New Jersey (La Casa de Don Pedro), Los Angeles, California (Department of Cultural Affairs), and Dallas, Texas (Latino Cultural Center), which is operated by the city's office of cultural affairs and supports a number of recreational, educational, and cultural activities.

In Newark, New Jersey, La Casa de Don Pedro Inc. is a nonprofit, community-based organization geared to provide for the well-being of low- and moderate-income families by helping them in financial poverty and fostering self-sufficiency. Although a nonprofit, the majority of its funding comes from the city and county. La Casa offers more than twenty-two programs, including counseling, child care, education, job training, job placement, energy conservation, youth and family counseling, cultural enrichment programs, and community development. The goal of the program is to assist minorities by providing empowering tools for low- and moderate-income families to break the cycle of poverty.

A final example of a Hispanic/Latino cultural center is that of Santa Clarita, California. It is called the Newhall Community Center and it provides Hispanic youth and families with a wide range of activities, including tutoring, boxing, Ballet Folklórico, English as a second language (ESL), art, sports, and adult classes. The Hispanic community participated in the development and design of the new center, which opened in 2006. The goals of the program are to serve, support, and respond to the needs of the Hispanic community. This is accomplished in part by providing recreational and educational opportunities for low-income, high-risk youth. The results have been that attendance at the center has more than doubled since 1998, programs have increased over 60 percent, and crime and gang involvement in surrounding neighborhoods has diminished. Families feel more empowered to get involved with the city and young people have improved their grades in school. A number of young participants have obtained jobs and become role models for other youth.

Figure 7.2
Elgin, Illinois, Hispanic Outreach Program

City administrators created the Hispanic Outreach Program to meet the need for understanding because of the explosive growth in the Hispanic community and accompanying cultural and language barriers. The program was designed to ensure the Hispanic community was engaged in and a real partner with city administration in securing services and addressing policies. The program seeks to ensure Hispanics have a voice on city matters that affect them. The city created Hispanic outreach positions for both the police and other departments in the city. The goals of the program are as follows:

1. Be a member of all Hispanic organizations in the city and be an active member of the most important ones.
2. Stay in close contact with recognized Hispanic leaders via office meetings, coffees, lunches, and dinners.
3. Be actively involved in and help plan all Hispanic events in the city. Specifically, the city can help with sponsorships, permits, and development plans.
4. A constant and honest evaluation of both the outreach position, those the city serves, and a willingness to adjust to changing circumstances.

In evaluating the program, the city found that the following elements made the program successful:

1. Face-to-face contact has always been the most successful. Being personable is the key.
2. Positive public exposure. The Hispanic community has to connect a name with a face.
3. Refuse to fall victim to ethnocentricity. For instance, irrespective of the outreach worker's ethnicity, the Hispanic community must be convinced the worker is working for the best interest of ALL Hispanics in the community.
4. Do what you say and say what you mean. City representatives must have credibility, respect, and be extremely communicative.

The results have been positive. The Hispanic community has been talking about the city's efforts and Elgin is viewed as the city that can help. The city has received written thank-you letters, awards, and other honors. Additionally, city staff has been asked to serve on local community and nonprofit boards. Because of the success with the Hispanic community, the city has also started a Laotian outreach program because of the high number of Laotians that have settled in Elgin.

Source: Benavides (2005).

HISPANIC CELEBRATION EVENTS

Another culturally competent activity that is popular in a number of cities is having or sponsoring cultural festivals. For instance, the city of Mesquite, Nevada, provides an annual ethnic celebration with food, music, and games celebrating different cultures. The majority of the events highlight the Hispanic culture due to the large Hispanic

---

Figure 7.3
Hispanic Heritage Month in Chandler, Arizona

The city has created a program that produces a series of events to commemorate National Hispanic Heritage Month. These events include a poster contest, a mariachi festival, folclórico dance workshops, a Hispanic heritage photo exhibit, a garibaldi night (a mariachi variety show), a Hispanic book fair, an educational forum, and a college night at a local community college. The goals of the program are to create awareness in the community of the many contributions that Hispanics make in the city. Elements that have made the celebration of National Hispanic Heritage Month successful in Chandler are the many partnerships that are established to accomplish this enormous task. The planning committee consists of city staff members, students and faculty from the local community college, members of the Hispanic community, and members of the Chandler Coalition for Civil and Human Rights. In addition, the committee partners with numerous local businesses and the media to offset the costs of producing all the events and making them free to the public. Chandler's Hispanic Heritage celebration has enjoyed tremendous success, attracting thousands of people throughout the month to the various events. In addition, it has received tremendous positive coverage in both the English and Spanish media.

Source: Benavides (2005).

---

population in the city. Nevertheless, the events foster respect and understanding in the community toward all ethnic groups and cultures. These festivals are reasonable in terms of their organization and development and offer an opportunity for a city to begin a gradual outreach to the Hispanic community.

The success of jazz festivals, symphony pops concerts in the park, balloon fests, and other events unique to various cities rests on the fact that they are composed of three elements. First, they have a signature event that draws on the uniqueness of the town or highlights a business sector that merits promotion. Second, there is an economic development component that drives revenues and, despite the investment from the city, allows for a break-even point or generates revenues. Related to this effort is the positive environment created that makes the city an attractive and livable place. Finally, a key distinguishing factor is the partnerships and cooperation that are created between the city, nonprofit organizations, businesses, and community organizations. Just as these events tend to be effective and popular, Hispanic festival events can also follow this model and be successful. The city of Tempe, Arizona, has experienced some success in following this particular model. The Tempe Tardeada is the City of Tempe's Hispanic Heritage Festival (a *tardeada* is a social dance that is traditionally held on Sunday afternoons). This event has completed seven very successful years, and each year the attendance has surpassed that of the previous year. The festival attempts to reenact the early days of the Hispanic settlers by inviting the community to share in traditional music, dance, and food. One key focus of this celebration is the educational feature. The Tempe Historical Museum partners with the planning committee to share the history and contributions of Tempe's early Hispanic settlers. The goals of the program are to identify and recognize the Hispanic roots of Tempe and educate the community with a celebration of the Hispanic culture. The program has been successful because the Diversity Office of the city partners with the Tardeada Advisory Board to plan the event. The Tardeada Advisory Board is a group of individuals who represent the Hispanic community and give insights into the culture. The board members bring to the table their life experiences and cultural knowledge, as well their passion for sharing their heritage. The result is that the advisory board and the Hispanic population in Tempe can share their legacy and educate the community on the contributions of their ancestors. The inclusion of the various community partners in the planning of this event has been an integral part of its success. The community not only gets educated and informed, but also gets to share in a celebration that includes eight continuous hours of Hispanic dance, music, arts and crafts, and food.

CULTURAL COMPETENCE PRACTICES

A number of cities in the United States have chosen to take an assortment of other actions with respect to their Hispanic communities. All of these practices, programs, and services are an attempt to bridge the cultural competence gap and better understand and serve all individuals in their communities. Table 7.4 shows a list of these activities, ranging from practices that would require a light investment to those that demand moderate resources to finally those that would necessitate a heavy investment on the part of the local government. These practices result in the promotion of cultural competency to varying degrees. Practices in the light investment category encourage recognition that the Hispanic community is present and should be represented. Activities include initial outreach programs and the translation of resources and brochures into Spanish to help the Hispanic community better understand the local government. The programs in the moderate investment grouping endorse activities that are more responsive to the community and promote a more in-depth understanding. Festivals, grants, advisory councils, and other practices are geared to lay the foundation for appropriate service delivery. By engaging the community at this level, public officials will gain a better understanding of what the community needs. The final category demands a heavy investment by the city and is evidenced by significant cooperation and developed partnerships. These relationships foster growth and not only help ensure suitable funding levels for targeted services but provide a base for sustainable service delivery.

A few examples of these programs are included here to illustrate their variety and practicality. For instance, the city of Bell Gardens, California, offers an academic no-interest loan to college-bound students to pay for tuition and fees. Students are required to fill out an application and be city residents. Approximately $5,000 worth of student loans is offered every year. Students need to pay back the loan and give the city ten hours of community service for each $1,000 received. The goal of the program is to offer college-bound students in the community a chance to receive a higher education. A desired outcome of the program is that more residents will be educated, which is a key to bringing more success to the community as a whole.

The city of Douglas, Arizona, offers a summer reading program for students in

Table 7.4

Cultural Competency and the Hispanic Community

Level of investment	Examples of cultural competency practices	How investment promotes cultural competency
Light Investment	Equal Employment Opportunity Employer Business cards, utility bills, community resource guide, and other brochures provided in both English and Spanish Summer reading program for Hispanic youth Special town hall meeting once a year conducted in Spanish City manager PR—manager meets with Hispanic community to describe services Diversity training workshops	Recognition that the Hispanic community is present and should be represented Legal compliance Acknowledgement of language as a barrier to effective communication
Moderate Investment	Grants to Hispanic organizations for after-school character-building activities, English classes or English as a second language (ESL) classes, day labor site program Festivals, Cinco de Mayo, ethnic celebrations, Hispanic Heritage Month Translation and interpretation services for council meetings Community advisory councils to obtain community input Mentorship program for potential Hispanic supervisors and managers Soccer league established to reach community and provide information	Responsive government engages community and provides activities to promote understanding
Heavy Investment	Spanish classes for employees (conversational, intermediate, advanced) Hispanic community relations officer Hispanic outreach programs such as community policing Police community aid—informs community about law enforcement practices and the judicial system; recruits Hispanics for city boards Hispanic/Latino community center—fully developed center that provides a wide range of community services and promotes partnerships	Cooperation and partnerships to foster growth and appropriate service delivery

grades one through five. The library staff focuses on all students whose reading skills are below average; about 85 percent of the participants are Hispanic. The staff works with 20 to 30 children for thirty days and between 150 and 175 students each summer. Children from Agua Prieta, Sonora, Mexico are also invited to attend. Because children count the pages they read and are not required to read at a certain level, they can read just for fun. This is the best thing they can do to improve their reading skills. The city also organizes a math tutoring effort that is a partnership between Cochise College, the work-study student program, and the local school district. The results have been that city staff has assisted local elementary schools with increasing student reading and math skills.

As one reads the variety of practices and activities that have been implemented at various cultural competency investment levels, it becomes quite obvious that not all localities can incorporate many of the ideas presented here. In the 2005 IHN survey of municipal best practices for the Hispanic community, it was found that only 24 percent of the cities surveyed had undergone a needs assessment to evaluate the needs of their Hispanic community (Benavides 2005). Conducting a needs assessment is critical in addressing future service delivery needs, and more local governments should adopt this strategy. These tools are more than quick fixes for situational crises driven by controversy. A needs assessment should be seen as an approach that will enhance service delivery. Benavides (2005) notes that "needs assessments are helpful ways to explore what is being done, what can be done, and identifying gaps in service delivery" (8). He goes on to say that "cities will need to do more to obtain a clear understanding of the Hispanic population's needs and barriers to city services" (8). These instruments have also been called cultural surveys, community needs assessment surveys, general needs assessment questionnaires, and other such similar names. Needs assessments are a systematic way of identifying strengths and weaknesses and are essential if cultural competency is to be achieved. It would be unwise at best for a city to unilaterally decide to have a "fiesta" without first determining if this is the real need of the Hispanic population in the community. Perhaps the actual need is a soccer field, or English classes, or assistance in accessing local government services. If a city is in doubt about what do to, yet wants to act, city officials should ask the Hispanic community. A basic tenet of cultural competency is understanding and this cannot take place without first obtaining essential information and knowledge about a community. As Roger Kaufman and Fenwich English (1979) noted, "If we are to change, it makes sense to correctly identify what should be changed; armed with this information, we are better able to know what interventions to select to bring about the required change" (8). There are many ways to conduct needs assessments, including general community surveys, focus groups, interviews, key person survey or "expert" testimony, current population surveys, statistics on social indicators, city records, and simply talking and listening to the community (Posavac and Carey 1992; Rossi and Freeman 1993).

During the needs assessment phase conducted by Santa Clarita, California, the city staff found out exactly what the Hispanic community needed. The responses to their inquiries were specific and varied. The residents requested regular programs for children and teens; more code enforcement in the neighborhoods; a Hispanic deputy that they could talk to and who would listen to them; a new park in the neighborhood; a new community center; curbs, gutters, and sidewalks in the neighborhoods; dental care for their children and dental education in the schools; more covered bus shelters; and more bulk trash pick-up (Pulskamp 2005). The city complied with every request, including a $10 million community center.

In Dalton, Georgia, a needs assessment led to a workforce housing initiative program. The city created a position in cooperation with The National Council of La Raza, the largest national Latino civil rights organization, and the University of Georgia to educate Spanish-speaking citizens about the home-buying process and how to acquire better-quality housing. The goal was to provide education, improve

---

Figure 7.4
Reno, Nevada, Diversity Language Skills Program

The purpose of the Reno Diversity Language Skills Program is to provide instruction in practical Spanish and improve the language skills of city employees. It is available to any interested city employee by tapping the multilingual Spanish skills of city employees who have been certified at one of three levels of proficiency. The city established a partnership with Truckee Meadows Community College and International Professional Development Services (IPDS), a local business whose primary emphasis is Spanish language skills training and development. Employees who have been certified operate as cofacilitators to assist in Spanish language instruction under the guidance of IPDS. Only those employees who have been certified as having an advanced proficiency in Spanish are able to do translation work for written materials. One of the elements that have made the program successful is the participating employees' commitment to expanding the city's ability to meet the needs of the Spanish-speaking residents. They view this ability as one of the many components that make up excellence in customer service. Employees willing to learn, certified employees willing to give of their time to promote learning, and a commitment from the city's management team to provide an opportunity for their staff to participate in these biweekly workshops has led to success. The result has been that eighteen employees have been certified by the local community college, with four current employees certified at the advanced level. Of this number, eight employees have served as cofacilitators of the program since its inception in 2003. A total of forty-eight classes have been offered with an average of twelve to fifteen employees in attendance over the same period. The funding for the conversational Spanish classes and the certification fees originate from the city's training and development budget.

Source: Benavides (2005).

---

living standards, and move people to homeownership of single-family homes. The program has improved living conditions for many families and given them hope for a better life. A positive outcome has been that the city is becoming recognized as a trusted partner in the Hispanic community.

Finally, an innovative and essential program was created to address a serious problem in Tucson, Arizona. An emergency shelter called Casa Amparo/Brewster Center was established to help Hispanic women and their children escape domestic violence. The emergency facility provides a bilingual crisis line and safe shelter to victims of domestic violence 24 hours a day, 365 days a year. Casa Amparo provides culturally sensitive shelter services, including safety planning, domestic violence education, legal advocacy, child advocacy, support groups, immigration assistance, and information and referrals. Survivors and their children can stay in the shelter for up to 120 days. All staff is bilingual (Spanish/English) and individuals are encouraged to become self-sufficient and plan for their future. The continuum of services provided in the clients' primary language and in a culturally competent manner has been a key to their success. The Brewster Center also offers transitional and permanent housing options with bilingual support services at its Wings of Freedom housing complex. The goal of the program is to provide Hispanic women and their children experiencing domestic violence with a safe, nurturing environment that honors their culture. Casa Amparo was the first shelter in Arizona to focus on bilingual Spanish/English and culturally competent services for the Hispanic population. A related program called Sin Violencia ¡Ganaremos!/Brewster Center ("without violence we can win") is situated on the south side of Tucson in the heart of Tucson's Hispanic/Latino community. It is a walk-in center for survivors of domestic violence and their children. It is different from the Casa Amparo program in that it is not a shelter. All staff speak fluent Spanish and focus on the provision of culturally relevant services.

CONCLUSION

The Hispanic population will continue to increase in numbers during the next few decades. The 2010 census clearly shows that the growth in states that typically were not home to large Hispanic populations now have a significant Hispanic presence. The growth in these emerging Hispanic states will continue to bring challenges and opportunities for understanding. Currently the emerging Hispanic states are Arkansas, Iowa, Kansas, Minnesota, Nebraska, Oklahoma, Tennessee, Utah, and Wisconsin. Operationally defined, an emerging Hispanic state had an increase of 200 percent in the Hispanic population during the 2000 Census (U.S. Census Bureau 2000). The new and established Hispanic states have also seen a growth in the Hispanic population, and many of these states will become majority minority states in the coming years. According to the U.S. Census Bureau, an established Hispanic state has traditionally had a significant Hispanic population and includes the following states: Arizona, California, Colorado, Illinois, New Jersey, New Mexico, New York, and Pennsylvania. The new Hispanic states which now have a significant Hispanic population are Florida, Georgia, Massachusetts, Nevada, North Carolina, Oregon, South Carolina, and Washington (U.S. Census Bureau 2000).

The apparent reality for the near future is that the constituency base for many of our cities is changing. This change will necessitate action. Local governments will need to choose how to respond to these changes in terms of service delivery. Cultural competency is one technique or method that can help local administrators in their duty to provide services. In essence, cultural competency provides a framework for understanding and the tools necessary to effectively comprehend the community. For instance, because the city of Santa Barbara, California, was culturally sensitive to its diverse population, it decided to have its city council meetings simultaneously interpreted into Spanish. Residents can listen to what is being said in real time in English or Spanish. Both are rebroadcast on a city TV channel. Earphones are provided at the city council meetings so anyone whose first language is Spanish can plug them in and hear the interpretation of what is being said. The goal is to allow those whose first language is Spanish the same access to government and to city council deliberations. The results have been a general satisfaction in the Spanish-speaking community. Additionally, there is a degree of satisfaction for the English-speaking residents who wish to celebrate their history and the roots of the city, since the first fifty years of the city's business were conducted in Spanish.

The examples presented here are mere suggestions of the thousands of possible service delivery responses that each locality can devise. As needs assessments are conducted, most local governments will realize that the services requested by the Hispanic community are not too dissimilar from those of the general population—good roads, schools, parks, and other traditional local government services. Exercising cultural competency will help local government managers gain a better understanding of the people they serve. A lack of understanding is no excuse for neglect.

REFERENCES

America's Voice. 2010. The new constituents: How Latino population growth will shape congressional apportionment after the 2010 Census. Executive Summary, October. http://amvoice.3cdn.net/f47fea7d54228b1871_5ym6id8ie.pdf.

Bailey, Margo. 2005. Cultural competency and the practice of public administration. In *Diversity and Public Administration: Theory, Issues, and Perspectives*, ed. Mitchell F. Rice, 177–196. Armonk, NY: M.E. Sharpe.

Barr, Kirstyn. 2010. Providing meaningful access: An assessment of service provision to LEP persons. Report of the City of Newport News Hispanic Advisory Committee to the City Manager. www.nngov.com/city-manager/hispanic/hac_assessment.

Benavides, Abraham David. 2005. Municipal best practices for the Hispanic community survey. A professional report written for the International City Management Association International Hispanic Network, Addendum 2006.

———. 2008. Municipal best practices: How local governments are responding to a growing Hispanic community. *Journal of Public Management and Social Policy* 14(1): 59–78.

Benavides, Abraham David, and Julie C.T. Hernandez. 2007. Serving diverse communities: Cultural competency. *Public Management Magazine* 89(6): 14–18.

City of Newport News (Virginia). 2011. Hispanic Advisory Committee to the City Manager. www.nngov.com/city-manager/hispanic/charter.

Clearwater Police Department (Florida). 2005. Hispanic Outreach/Operation Apoyo Hispano. www.clearwaterpolice.org/hispanic/index.asp.

Cross, Terry L., Barbara J. Bazron, Keith Dennis, and Mareasa R. Isaacs. 1989. *Towards a Culturally Competent System of Care*, vol. 1. Washington, DC: Georgetown University Child Development Center, CASSP Technical Assistance Center.

Davis, K. 1997. Exploring the intersection between cultural competency and managed behavioral health care policy: Implications for state and county mental health agencies. Alexandria, VA: National Technical Assistance Center for State Mental Health Planning.

Gibson, Campbell, and Kay Jung. 2002. Historical census statistics on population totals by race, 1790 to 1990, and by Hispanic origin, 1970 to 1990, for the United States, regions, divisions, and states. Working Paper Series No. 56, September. Population Division, U.S. Census Bureau. www.census.gov/population/www/documentation/twps0056/twps0056.html#intro.

Gladstone, J.R. 1969. Language and culture. *ELT Journal* 23(2): 114–117.

Hernandez, Julie C.T., John C. Brown, and Christine C. Tien. 2007. Serving diverse communities: Best practices. *Public Management Magazine* 89(5): 12–17.

Hobbs, Frank, and Nicole Stoops. 2002. *Demographic Trends in the 20th Century*. Census 2000 Special Reports, November. U.S. Census Bureau. www.census.gov/prod/2002pubs/censr-4.pdf.

Humphreys, Jeffrey M. 2009. The multicultural economy 2009. *Georgia Business and Economic Conditions* 69(3): 1–16.

Idaho Department of Labor. 2010. Buying power 2009: Hispanic influence rises. Report. http://labor.idaho.gov/publications/hispanicbuyingpower2009.pdf.

Isaacs, Mareasa, and Marva P. Benjamin. 1991. *Towards a Culturally Competent System of Care*, vol. 2. Washington, DC: Georgetown University Child Development Center, CASSP Technical Assistance Center.

Kaufman, Roger, and Fenwick English. 1979. *Needs Assessment: Concept and Application*. Englewood Cliffs, NJ: Education Technologies.

Passel, Jeffrey, and Paul Taylor. 2009. Is Sotomayor the Court's first Hispanic? Pew Hispanic Center, May 28. http://pewresearch.org/pubs/1238/sotomayor-supreme-court-first-hispanic.

Posavac, Emil J., and Raymond G. Carey. 1992. *Program Evaluation: Methods and Case Studies*. 4th ed. Englewood Cliffs, NJ: Prentice Hall.

Pulskamp, Ken. 2005. Serving communities with Latino populations. Presentation given at the International City/County Managers Association, Minneapolis, Minnesota.

Rice, Mitchell F., and Harvey L. White, eds. 2005. *Diversity and Public Administration: Theory, Issues, and Perspectives*. Armonk, NY: M.E. Sharpe.

Rossi, Peter H., and Howard E. Freeman. 1993. *Evaluation: A Systematic Approach*. 5th ed. Newbury Park, CA: Sage.

U.S. Census Bureau. 2000. United States Census 2000. www.census.gov/main/www/cen2000.html.

———. 2006. Hispanics in the United States. PowerPoint presentation. www.census.gov/population/www/socdemo/hispanic/files/Internet_Hispanic_in_US_2006.pdf.

———. 2009. Hispanic Americans by the numbers. Infoplease. www.infoplease.com/spot/hhmcensus1.html.

———. 2011. Overview of race and Hispanic origin: 2010. 2010 Census Briefs, March. www.census.gov/prod/cen2010/briefs/c2010br-02.pdf.

U.S. Code. 2010. Title 15: Commerce and trade. Statistics relating to social, health, and economic conditions of Americans of Spanish origin or descent. U.S.C. §1516a. http://vlex.com/vid/social-americans-spanish-origin-descent-19233226.

U.S. Department of Labor (DOL). 2011. Table A-3. Employment status of the Hispanic or Latino population by sex and age. News release, Bureau of Labor Statistics, May 6. www.bls.gov/news.release/empsit.t03.htm.

U.S. Office of Management and Budget (OMB). 1977. Directive 15. www.learner.org/workshops/primarysources/census/docs/office.html.

———. 1994. Standards for classification of federal data on race and ethnicity. *Federal Register*, June 9. www.whitehouse.gov/omb/fedreg_notice_15.

———. 1997. Revisions to the standards for the classification of federal data on race and ethnicity. *Federal Register* Notice, October 30. www.whitehouse.gov/omb/fedreg_1997standards.

Cultural Diplomacy

Collaboration Between Tribal and State Governments

DIANE-MICHELE PRINDEVILLE
AND CARRIE D. LA TOUR

> Even if you're not a member of the dominant culture, you have to know it to get by. To be successful, you have to know it really well. But they, the members of the dominant culture, they don't have to know anything about anybody else's world to get by. All they have to do is just be.
>
> —Anonymous

Whether discussing diversity programs or cultural competency training in public organizations, the need for such measures is invariably challenged based on the underlying belief that racial and ethnic prejudice has been eradicated and that, at any rate, "We don't discriminate here." As a result, it is nearly always useful to begin this type of discussion with a brief refresher about the U.S. government's domestic policy and practices, especially involving the long and complicated relationship between the U.S. government and the sovereign nations indigenous to North America. Historically, federal Indian policy, implemented largely through the Bureau of Indian Affairs (BIA), has promoted assimilation of indigenous peoples into the dominant Anglo (European American) culture with the objective of eliminating Native cultures from the United States. Examples include the forcible placement of Indian children in BIA boarding schools and the termination by Congress of indigenous nations.

Cultural conflict and the impact of other such assimilationist policies have had devastating effects on the spiritual, emotional, mental, and physical well being of Native Americans since First Contact. Policy makers assumed that cultural genocide would result in the total absorption of Native American peoples into mainstream America and that their languages and traditions would all but vanish, as has occurred with most immigrant populations. This, however, has not been the case. Although they have certainly declined in numbers due to war, disease, and genocidal practices, more than 560 Indian nations and over 200 federally "unrecognized" tribes constitute a dynamic and thriving Native America.

As sovereign nations, Native American tribes experience a unique government-to-government relationship with the United States. The Doctrine of Tribal Sovereignty recognizes that "each Tribe begins its relationship with the federal government as a sovereign power, recognized as such in treaty and legislation" (Cohen 1942, 122). Although pueblos and reservations are located within states' borders, their status as sovereign nations means that states do not have jurisdiction over them, yet states seldom understand or respect this. In fact, the U.S. Supreme Court established the precedent that state laws have no authority in Indian country without the express consent of Congress (*Worcester v. Georgia* 1832). Deloria and Lytle note that "Indian Tribes exercise in some respects more governing powers than local non-Indian municipalities and in other respects more important powers than states themselves" (1984, 14). Nevertheless, tribal-state relations have often been marred by conflict and resentment due to misperceptions and mistrust. In an effort to both reverse the direction of policy and to mitigate the damage caused by the federal government's efforts at forced assimilation, New Mexico tribal leaders, in collaboration with the governor's office and key state legislators, have enacted legislation to ensure a mutually satisfying and productive future for tribal/state relations.

New Mexico is home to twenty-two pueblos, Indian nations, and tribes that are constitutionally recognized as sovereign entities. The Pueblo peoples, whose ancestors first settled the region, were residing in the Southwest as far back as 10,000 B.C. (Sando 1992; Woodbury 1979). According to U.S. census estimates for 2010 persons identifying as American Indian and Alaska Native compose 11.4 percent of the state's population (U.S. Census Bureau 2010). Despite their relatively small number, their influence and that of the Diné (Navajo) and Apache peoples is significant and visible in the arts, architecture, religious practices, agriculture, and cuisine of New Mexico. By developing successfully their economic base, several of these Native nations have in recent years grown tribal revenues, services, and employment and educational opportunities for enrolled members.

These gains have translated to increased influence in local and state politics with Native candidates winning seats on school boards, county commissions, and the state legislature. Despite their impact and participation in all facets of life in New Mexico, however, few non-Indians know or understand much about the state's indigenous residents. In fact, not only misconceptions about "reservation life" but also ugly stereotypes of Native people persist. The state's pueblo and tribal governments increasingly demand political responsiveness, equal access to public services, and a genuine role in intergovernmental affairs. Their leaders recognize the need to educate non-Indian officials and public service providers about the state's pueblos and tribes. Indeed, as scholars note, "Practitioners' attitudes—the knowledge and beliefs about the populations they serve that they bring to each interaction—can affect the efficacy of services, especially when these attitudes include biases against cultural groups or misunderstandings of behavioral manifestations of cultural values" (Mistry, Jacobs, and Jacobs 2009, 489).

This chapter examines in detail the collaboration among the New Mexico Indian Affairs Department (IAD), tribal leaders, the Indian Law Program, and the New Mexico State Personnel Office (SPO) to develop and implement for State of New

Mexico employees a training program in cultural competency. Note that the BIA is not a partner in this collaboration. In fact, the BIA has lost much of the influence it once held over tribal governments and Native peoples. As federal Indian policy has evolved and greater autonomy is granted to Indian nations, the BIA is viewed by tribes more as a nuisance that must be dealt with than as a resource or source of support. The BIA's patronizing and historically punitive relationship with indigenous peoples precludes the possibility of Native nations developing trusting relationships with this federal agency. It is likely that the idea of creating collaborative cultural competency training for BIA employees would be perceived by tribal leaders as "too little, too late." On the other hand, the State of New Mexico does not suffer from as tragic a history relative to its dealings with the pueblos and Indian tribes within its borders. Moreover, in recent years, New Mexico's governors have sought to improve relations between Santa Fe and the state's tribal leaders. This case illustrates the value of building and maintaining trusting relationships among organizations and leaders who recognize, acknowledge, and respect each others' cultural differences with the goal of working for the common good: in this instance, improving the delivery of state programs and services to Native populations in New Mexico.

LITERATURE REVIEW

In 1975 the State of Oregon established the Legislative Commission on Indian Services. Its purpose is to advise the legislative and executive branches on ways to improve communication and coordination with tribes while increasing cooperation and minimizing disputes. The commission provides information and

> offers strategy and advice to state agencies, Tribes, legislators, the Governor's office, organizations and the public on ways to maximize positive interactions and to develop partnerships. The key is to have a way to learn enough about each other to know when partnerships are feasible. . . . The State continues to realize there is much to be gained *for all of Oregon's citizens* by acknowledging and supporting tribal sovereignty. (Legislative Commission on Indian Services 2004; emphasis in original)

In 2001, at the request of the commission, the legislature overwhelmingly passed Senate Bill 770 requiring that Oregon state agencies consider tribal governments when developing policies and implementing programs affecting tribes' interests (Legislative Commission on Indian Services 2004). The law includes three provisions: (1) an annual summit meeting of the governor, tribal leaders, and state and tribal staff who work together; (2) at minimum, annual training on tribal sovereignty, legal rights of tribal members, and issues of concern to tribes for managers of state departments and others who work closely with tribes; and (3) an annual report by each state agency to the governor and to the Legislative Commission on Indian Services summarizing its activities with tribes (Legislative Commission on Indian Services 2004). As we will see, Oregon's State Tribal Government-to-Government Law (2009) provides the model for New Mexico's State-Tribal Collaboration Act (2009).

As the demographic composition of the United States becomes increasingly diverse in all respects (e.g., age, race, ethnicity, sexuality, religion, country of origin), the field of public administration must better prepare its graduates to serve our multicultural society by developing cultural competencies among all racial and ethnic groups (Johnson and Borrego 2009). Achieving such competencies involves an educational process whereby organizations and individuals acquire "cultural awareness . . . cultural knowledge . . . and cultural skills" through training and interactions with people from other cultures (Rice 2007a, 632). The "practice of cultural competency stresses effectively operating in different cultural contexts and providing services that reflect the different cultural influences of constituents or clients" (Rice 2007b, 42). Bailey suggests that a way of evaluating culturally responsive organizations is to determine whether they value diversity; can identify and assess critically their cultural biases; are aware of how cultural differences shape relationships; incorporate cultural knowledge into their operations; and adjust service delivery to meet constituents' particular needs (2005).

Also referred to as cultural sensitivity, cultural awareness, and cultural responsiveness, cultural competency is an ongoing process that is aided by education. In their empirical study, which challenges the effectiveness of cultural competency, Mistry, Jacobs, and Jacobs (2009) propose an alternate concept that they call "cultural attentiveness." Rather than identifying best practices or principles for interacting with culturally diverse groups, these authors suggest taking an approach of "deliberate and careful thought about cultural issues" (502). Olsen, Bhattacharya, and Scharf agree that cultural competency is not a particular set of knowledge, skills, and abilities. Instead, they see it as "a journey and a way of being" (2006, 3). Cultural competency decreases conflict and improves interactions by providing a greater understanding of another's perspective. It thereby helps to diminish bias, whether racial, gender, sexual, or religious. Increased understanding leads to feelings of empathy, which create the potential for community, unity, and egalitarianism. Through egalitarianism, public administrators promote democracy and greater participation in the governing process (Box 2007).

Common sense dictates that understanding the culture of a community served by a public program is an "essential step to improving governance and service delivery" (Brintnall 2008, 39). Rice suggests that cultural competency training enables public organizations to "build on the strengths and perspectives of minority cultures' beliefs, habits, behaviors, and value systems to establish service delivery intervention strategies and approaches" (2007b, 632). Directly involving consumers of program services in planning and decision making results in a closer working relationship between service providers and consumers and may lead to improved services, increased satisfaction of residents with service delivery, and greater communication between public employees and community members.

Facilitating communication aids in building trust and positive relationships between public service providers and citizens. This is the purpose of a recent collaboration by the New Mexico Indian Affairs Department (IAD), tribal leaders, the Indian Law Program, and the New Mexico State Personnel Office (SPO). Among several objectives, the resulting legislation, New Mexico's State-Tribal Collaboration Law, calls for the development and implementation of cultural competency training for State of New Mexico employees. The law is significant because its passage

- Testifies to the value and importance of Native nations and their peoples to the state of New Mexico
- Establishes the power and authority of Native nations to influence public policy in the state
- Should improve the provision of state services for Native Americans while increasing the professionalism of state employees
- May affect Native peoples' opinions, providing them with a more favorable view of New Mexico state government
- May lead to increased participation in New Mexico state politics if Indian people feel that their tribal sovereignty is respected and their needs as citizens are being addressed.

METHODOLOGY

This descriptive study employs various sources and methods of data collection. Specifically, our data was drawn from (1) personal interviews with key state employees, (2) participant observation of a pilot training program that we attended, (3) content analysis of state legislation and official reports, and finally, (4) news stories and journal articles covering state-tribal relations as well as cultural competency training for public administrators serving Native American clients. Francine Hatch, senior policy analyst for IAD, and Reese Fullerton, deputy director of SPO, were key in planning, organizing, and developing the pilot cultural competency training project for state employees. Because of their knowledge, role, and relative accessibility, we asked for and held face-to-face interviews with each of them in Albuquerque. The interviews, roughly one hour and thirty minutes long, were conducted using Holstein and Gubrium's strategy, the "active" interview (Holstein and Gubrium 1995). While the researcher loosely follows a previously prepared interview guide, this conversational style of interviewing is relatively natural as it allows for some dialogue back and forth between participant and researcher. The strategy encourages an informal and friendly dynamic, creating an environment more conducive to open communication than a formal scripted setting in which researchers are constrained by what they can say and how they may behave. Hatch was interviewed on April 27, 2010, and Fullerton was interviewed the next day.

To observe firsthand the cultural curriculum training for state employees, we asked Fullerton and Hatch if we might be permitted to attend the pilot training. After initial concerns about the potential chilling effect our presence might have on the willingness of other attendees to speak out, we were grateful to be allowed to attend. Observing the training firsthand was infinitely more valuable than merely reviewing the training manual, especially since we would have missed out on meeting the tribal leaders, hearing their perspectives, asking them questions, and being invited to Santa Ana Pueblo's Feast Day by their governor. By attending the pilot training, we were also able to meet the state personnel and hear their questions, their concerns, and, at the end of the day, their critiques and suggestions for the training (Berg 2009).

We were particularly interested in observing the participants and the climate at the pilot training. As researchers and professional trainers, we know that recipients of any training must be open to new ideas, ready to learn, and willing to alter their behavior for change to occur. Our participation at the pilot training would enable us to note whether state department leaders, on whom real lasting organizational change would depend, were open to and supportive of a statewide cultural competency training program. While a brief interview with a handful of state department heads might result in one set of findings, spending eight hours with thirty leaders of state agencies in question-and-answer sessions and informal discussion would give us a richer and likely more comprehensive view of their opinion and support for the proposed program. In addition, our observations of the interaction between the Indian and non-Indian participants, and between the participants and trainers, might also give us a sense of the types of relationships that existed among these leaders and their organizations. Successful implementation of a statewide cultural competency training program for state employees would doubtless require building trust among organizational leaders who recognize, acknowledge, and respect each others' cultural differences.

Discussion of the Findings

Objectives of the Training

Having served as lieutenant governor in the Pueblo of Santa Clara, Cabinet Secretary Alvin Warren, IAD, has a keen understanding of the issues that sometimes arise between Indian nations and representatives of state government. While prejudice may be far less overt today than in the past, intolerance for difference is still evidenced in attitudes and policies that press for the assimilation of diverse racial and ethnic groups into the dominant Anglo culture. Stereotypes and chauvinist views restrict opportunities for productive partnerships and otherwise successful working relationships between tribal and state governments. A more common cause of conflict, however, may be ignorance of cultural differences among racial and ethnic groups. For instance, to avoid misunderstanding or offending, interaction with traditional or elderly tribal members often requires a protocol different from the dominant culture's notions of etiquette (Kalbfleisch 2009). This illustrates the importance of cultural sensitivity to public administration. As Rice notes, "When culture is ignored or not considered . . . by a public agency, there is a very strong possibility that individuals, families and groups will not get the services or support they need, or, worse yet, they will likely receive services and assistance that is more harmful than helpful" (Rice 2007b, 50). One successful example of cultural responsiveness may be illustrated by the University of New Mexico Hospital in Albuquerque, where Navajo medicine men have worked collaboratively on staff with UNMH physicians for years, to better serve Navajo patients and their families.

To develop an effective training program in cultural sensitivity for state employees who deliver services to Native American citizens, Secretary Warren met with tribal leaders from all twenty-two pueblos, nations, and tribes in the state. Simply stated, he asked them what they wanted from such a project. While they had difficulty defining cultural competency, they agreed on three broad objectives: (1) that state officials recognize the differences among Indian nations, (2) that the training help build better tribal/state relations, and (3) that these objectives, and a mandated cultural responsiveness training for state employees, be codified. This would ensure continuation of the policy regardless of the administration in power.

Although the need for cultural awareness training has long been evident, especially given the shameful history of federal/Indian relations in this country, the possibility of implementing mandated statewide training for state government employees did not exist. In particular, the political and economic conditions were not right for passage of Senate Bill 196, the State-Tribal Collaboration Act (STCA), until 2009. By that time, Native American leaders had developed greater expertise in state politics and policy making, they had built important relationships with non-Indian leaders in federal and state government, and increased revenues from gaming and other enterprises enabled tribal governments to influence political campaigns. A movement toward social justice in the field of public administration also contributed to an environment ripe for change. The result was groundbreaking legislation, which codified the relationship among New Mexico's pueblos, Indian nations, and tribes and the state government. In brief, the STCA

> requires that all state agency managers and employees who have ongoing communication with Tribes complete a training, provided by the State Personnel Office in collaboration with IAD, on promoting effective communication and collaboration between the state agencies and Tribes, the development of positive state tribal government-to-government relations, and cultural competency in providing effective services to American Indians or Alaska Natives. (Hatch 2009)

This is also the stated purpose of the training manual. The act facilitates identification, by all parties, of issues of mutual concern and of strategies to resolve them (New Mexico Indian Affairs Department 2010, 34). It also requires each state agency to compile an annual report of programs that serve Native Americans, evaluating each state department's effectiveness and the amount of money spent on these activities (Hatch 2010).

The purpose of the mandated cultural sensitivity training is to ensure that indigenous peoples throughout the state receive quality public services with a "respect for, and understanding of, [their] diverse ethnic and cultural systems, their histories, traditions, beliefs and value systems" (Bush 2000, 177–178). Ensuring that state service providers understand the history and respect the traditions, beliefs, and values of New Mexico's Native peoples is especially important when we consider the treatment of Native Americans by government in the past. The legacy of racial and cultural genocide of indigenous nations by the United States endures, as does the resulting mistrust of government by Native Americans. This will only be overcome with time and through the interaction of Native people with non-Indian public employees who exhibit cultural awareness, sensitivity, and responsiveness. Nevertheless, creating a cultural competency training program was not a simple task.

New Mexico's tribal leaders had difficulty agreeing on a single definition of cultural competency, largely because they represent twenty-two sovereign nations ranging in size from Pojoaque Pueblo, with about 260 tribal members, to the Navajo Nation, with approximately 68,000 members (Indian Pueblo Cultural Center 2010). Each tribe has its own distinct form of governance, religious practices, culture, and traditions. While several of the twenty-two nations share one of eight indigenous languages, their dialects are sufficiently different that members of one pueblo may not easily understand members of another. While Native American people may have greater insights into each others' experience of being Indian in present-day America, their ethnicity alone does not ensure competence either in their own or another Native person's traditional tribal culture. Consider this: A Navajo baby adopted into an Anglo-American Mormon family is unlikely to understand or be sensitive to the Navajo culture unless an effort is made to teach her the customs and traditions of her people and she is able to visit her homeland. Alternately, "urban Indians," members of tribes that are not federally recognized, and Native people whose mixed tribal heritage prevents them from being enrolled with any single tribe may all have different views of Native culture. Unfortunately, diverse perceptions of Indian identity within the Native population can turn into disputes about who maintains more authentic traditions or cultural practices and who is more, or less, Indian.

Clearly, concepts such as identity and culture are both rich and complex. When examined in the ways discussed above, some may question whether cultural competency is attainable. However, as Dean notes, the process of learning, developing respect, and gaining an appreciation of other cultures and ways of being is essential to creating effective working relationships with those who are different from ourselves (2001). We believe that cultural awareness and sensitivity are critical for successful diplomacy among political entities, such as New Mexico tribes and state government. When we consider the genocide, wars, diseases, slavery, relocations, and other atrocities visited upon Native peoples by the United States and previous colonizers, we marvel at the tenacity and tremendous adaptability of indigenous cultures. Indeed, it is the ability of North America's tribes to adapt to adverse conditions that has enabled them to endure over time. To greater or lesser degrees, their cultures have adapted as well. Keeping in mind the diversity of New Mexico's twenty-two tribes, state employees completing cultural sensitivity training should recognize the differences among the Indian nations; develop a respect for, and understanding of, their various ethnic and cultural systems, histories, traditions, beliefs, and value systems; and work to improve tribal/state relations.

Development of the Cultural Competency Curriculum

From its inception, the goal of designing and delivering a statewide cultural competency training program for state employees was a collaboration among four entities: the Indian Affairs Department, leaders representing the twenty-two Native nations in New Mexico, the State Personnel Office, and top management from all thirty-three state agencies. The principal decision makers of the organizations responsible for ensuring the program's successful implementation had to be involved and able to influence its development and outcome. Secretary Warren made sure to meet with tribal leaders from all twenty-two nations, gathering their input (Hatch 2010), and Francine Hatch spent "hundreds of hours with state agencies to ask the right questions," inviting their partnership in the project (Fullerton 2010). Hatch (2010) confirms the existence of a productive working relationship between several of the tribes and state agencies: "The legislation is important but I think the interest and desire to work together, to collaborate and consult, was there before, anyway." To illustrate, fifty-nine tribal liaisons serving a diplomatic function have been designated within the thirty-three cabinet-level agencies; they facilitate effective communication and relationships between the tribes and the state. A collaborative approach was taken because it is the Native way of ensuring that all have a voice in decision making: cooperation and finding a mutually satisfactory outcome are stressed over one party "winning." A further advantage to a collaborative approach is that it increases the chances of support and buy-in by participants in the decision process. In fact, all state departments were in full support of Senate Bill 196 and several already have their own cultural competency training in place.

Once it was clear that all parties fully supported the idea of statewide cultural competency training for state employees, a four-step process was initiated to determine the content of pilot training, which would be "tested out" with different stakeholders. Feedback in the form of comments, suggestions, and critique would result in revisions and improvements to the final curriculum, which would then be delivered to approximately 2,200 state employees across New Mexico. Step 1 consisted of creating a working group made up of tribal leaders and managers of state agencies and staffed by the IAD and SPO. The group's objective was to identify key concepts and principles or critical information for non-Natives that should be included in the training curriculum. These included an explanation of tribal sovereignty, communicating with tribal governments, and appropriate protocol for interacting with Native peoples. This information is contained in the training manual and reproduced here as Appendixes 8.1 and 8.2, under the respective headings "Communication Protocol with Tribal Governments" and "Etiquette—Dos and Don'ts."

Step 2 involved rallying resources. Again, Hatch of IAD and Fullerton of SPO partnered to locate sources of funding for the pilot training as no monies had been earmarked by the state legislature for the mandated training. While the state should have been an obvious source of funding, by this time New Mexico, like many states, was facing large budget shortfalls that prevented the legislature from appropriating funds for any new initiatives. Nevertheless, Hatch and Fullerton were able to access a Kellogg Foundation grant, some funds from IAD's budget, and contributions from some of the New Mexico Indian nations. Corporate foundations are one of the few sources of available funding in the present economic climate.

Step 3 entailed developing and implementing the first pilot training session on May 25, 2010, for Tribal Leaders, tribal liaisons, and other state department personnel. This eight-hour test run of the training curriculum was presented to about thirty participants who were asked to complete a brief evaluation in the form of a survey following the daylong event. A four-hour version of the pilot training will be presented to New Mexico cabinet secretaries and state department executives to solicit their feedback as well. Depending on the comments provided by the different groups, a second pilot training might be required. When the training curriculum is finalized, Step 4, "Training for Trainers," will be implemented. It is expected that these trainers will then be prepared to deliver the cultural competency training to state employees across New Mexico.

While the various stakeholders had input to the content of the pilot training, Hatch, Fullerton, and Helen Padilla, an attorney and director of the Indian Law Center, had primary responsibility for the design and delivery of the pilot training on May 25, 2010. The training was held from 9 A.M. to 5 P.M. at the Institute for American Indian Arts in Santa Fe, New Mexico. Each participant was given a draft-training manual that included the following items:

- A copy of the agenda
- A map and list of all pueblos and reservations within the state
- A brief history of federal Indian policy for tribes in New Mexico
- Background information on tribes and tribal governments
- A list of Tribal languages spoken
- A list of members of the tribes' governing bodies and contact information
- Etiquette for interacting with tribal officials
- Communication protocol
- Legal foundation for cooperation and collaboration between the tribes and the state
- List of Native American intertribal organizations
- A bibliography (Indian Law Center 2010).

The pilot training began with a prayer in Keres, the language spoken by Acoma Pueblo, by former Acoma governor Ron Shutiva, who serves as tribal liaison with the New Mexico Department of Transportation. This was followed by Secretary Warren welcoming and reminding the attendees that this "is a critical evolutionary moment in the role between state and tribal governments." He added that New Mexico is a leader in "forging partnerships between state and tribal governments" and that "this is a very exciting time." Warren stressed that the finalized training will provide an educational foundation for state employees to better communicate, support tribal government, and improve cultural competency. Deputy Director Fullerton followed this line of thought, adding "We want to create a safe place . . . to give trainings where people get it in their heart, in their mind, and in their gut." Both men strongly encouraged feedback in the way of suggestions, comments, and critiques of the day's activities. Taking into account cultural differences in communication styles, participants were offered the opportunity to write their comments or questions on Post-it notes, rather than having to speak out in a group setting.

Introductions came next. The approximately thirty participants were asked to identify themselves and their affiliation. Nearly all the attendees took the time to explain their role and motivation for supporting this state-tribal partnership. The introductions themselves illustrated the different cultures represented as communication styles varied. For example, storytelling, a way of communicating through the relating of past experience or allegory, was prominent among Native participants, in contrast to a simple listing of facts more common among the Anglos present. In general, traditional or less assimilated Indians employ an indirect "communication style where information is communicated through story, example, and metaphor" (Kalbfleisch 2009, 161). Even in a professional setting, sharing a story about one's family or a personal experience might be more beneficial to building rapport than referencing one's credentials. The attendees took the time to speak, to listen, and for all to be heard. While one spoke, the others remained silent. The attendees spoke as long as they needed to. The day's agenda allotted only about half the time that the introductions actually required. This served as an important reminder to event organizers of the need to be mindful of a Native perspective of time that values the quality of human interaction rather than one that stresses keeping busy and meeting appointments.

An informal lecture on tribal sovereignty and core values followed. This was delivered by Regis Pecos, current chief of staff for the Speaker of the House of the State of New Mexico, and former governor of Cochiti Pueblo. Governor Pecos demonstrated, in the form of a time line, the relationship between the United States and Native nations since First Contact and the impact of federal Indian policy on what he termed indigenous peoples' core values. His discussion of Native American core values was central to understanding the need for policy reforms and cultural competency training at all levels of government. Core values were identified as land, language, "a way of life," family, community, governance, and environment.

Land provides a foundation for life, while teaching respect, the need for sustainability, and balance. One's very identity is tied to the land. The gift of language is the ability to communicate, the means to understand how to live and how to participate spiritually. "A way of life" refers to the blending of the community's spiritual and daily activities, which is a far different notion from Western views of organized religion. In the case of traditional theocratic pueblos, for example, there is no separation between church and state. Even some constitutionally governed pueblos incorporate religious ceremonies within their political practices. Prayer and ceremony are ways of celebrating life and giving thanks and, as such, are essential components of Native life. Family is the "place to learn about respect, community and compassion" (Pecos 2010). Family is the vehicle by which we learn about relationships. Governance is the gift of the creator, the process by which communities maintain balance in the "way of living" and appreciating all life. Governor Pecos explained that from time immemorial, tribal leaders have had a sacred responsibility to protect tribal lands and to govern tribal members. This responsibility is equivalent to the covenants we draw from our state constitution. Environment provides sustenance for life, for future generations. Each of these core values is linked and integrated, harmoniously supporting the others. Each core value has also been compromised by consistent and repeated attacks from assimilationist and other policies aimed at the eradication of Native peoples over time. As Governor Pecos explained, one of the threats facing Native peoples is the allocation by the federal and state governments of resources that sometimes compromise Native core values. To illustrate, if a Head Start program for Indian children does not incorporate their language, stories, or music but provides a curriculum reflecting only the values of the dominant education system, the program may inadvertently contribute to further destruction of tribal culture. Native leaders must be diligent to ensure that funding and programs do not compromise the future of their peoples.

Helen Padilla, director of the Indian Law Center and a cocreator of the pilot training, gave a presentation on federal Indian policy that focused on the history of intergovernmental relations and tribal sovereignty. Fundamental to understanding the limitations placed on the powers that Indian governments are able to exert, federal Indian law and policy explains the history and present relationship between Native nations and the United States. An overview of key legal cases and laws is essential to any training that seeks to educate participants about the Native perspective on the role of government and the American judicial system. A critical point made by Padilla is that, depending on the circumstances, Indian nations can use their sovereign status as a sword or as a shield. When used as a sword, sovereignty becomes a tool allowing tribes to exercise power and authority over their jurisdictions (Padilla 2010). The shield of sovereignty serves to protect tribal lands and ways of life. As LaFrance notes, it is essential to have a clear understanding of the role that tribal sovereignty and Indian self-determination play in Native American identity if one is to work effectively with Native communities (LaFrance 2004).

While this information was useful to the group, the method by which it was presented was decidedly non-Native. This irony was not lost on either of us as the instructor was a Pueblo woman trained in the law. There was limited opportunity for interaction between instructor and trainees, and questions were unwelcome. This portion of the day's training highlighted the importance of maintaining an open and interactive communication style to encourage learning. It also made us think about the origin of stereotypes and the danger of assuming that a member of a particular culture will display all the traditional characteristics of that group. When we spoke earlier with Reese Fullerton about how the trainings would be delivered, he suggested that content should be determined by Indian community leaders. However, ideally, teams comprised of Native and non-Native trainers should be employed. Understanding cultural differences in communication and social interactions is critical to acquiring cultural competency. A training team can best model appropriate behavior while providing opportunities to share real-life experiences.

The former governor of Tesuque Pueblo, Charlie Dorame, followed Padilla's presentation by facilitating an interactive discussion with pilot participants. Tribal leaders suggested to state agency personnel approaches for working effectively with tribal governments and their members. State employees were able to ask questions in a candid and safe atmosphere. Dean notes the importance of "respectful, nonjudgmental, and deeply interested questioning and the exchange of beliefs" to increasing understanding and improving communication among different cultural groups. Because culture is dynamic and therefore constantly changing, Dean does not believe that cultural competency is achievable. However, she stresses the need for involvement in the process of relationship building and striving to understand those with whom we work: it is "not that we need to agree with our clients' practices and beliefs; we need to understand them and understand the contexts and history in which they develop" (Dean 2001, 628).

This productive session offered important information on some of the differences among Indian nations, including facts about their forms of government, traditions, protocol, and what to expect when meeting with officials. For example, Governor Dorame explained that tribal leaders often will speak in their native tongue with one another while conducting business, even when outsiders are present, because that is the language with which they are most comfortable. The governor warned that visitors to pueblo and tribal governments also need to be flexible and patient. Tribal leaders are very busy and frequently must make do with limited resources; they are, after all, in a similar position to heads of state of small foreign nations. As such, they are frequently faced with pressing issues that need immediate attention. They may be late or may need to cancel an appointment, which should not be interpreted as rudeness or unwillingness to cooperate. In applying the literature to the New Mexico tribal context, state employees must be capable of functioning in environments that are culturally different from their own, especially where diplomacy is required (Rice 2007a). For example, as Governor Pecos explained, the ceremonial use of tobacco may be observed during tribal council meetings, an occurrence unlikely in non-Indian government.

The pilot training did not account for the diversity among New Mexico pueblos, Athabascan cultures (Apaches and Diné), and urban versus reservation residents. No training exercises, such as role-playing, were offered for attendees. Furthermore, no suggestions were made for state personnel to attend Indian cultural events, such as the annual feast days hosted by all pueblos, or to visit Native museums, like the very educational Indian Pueblo Cultural Center in Albuquerque. Rice suggests that acquiring cultural competency is "a developmental process whereby organizations and individuals attain cultural awareness, cultural knowledge, and cultural skills through both training and cultural encounters with individuals from different cultural groups" (Rice 2007b, 51).

COST OF THE TRAINING PROGRAM

Unfortunately, no funds were appropriated by the legislature for the training and, interestingly, we were told that no budget was developed or estimates made of what it might cost the state to design and deliver the training. We found this surprising considering that about 2,200 state employees are targeted to receive the training. The New Mexico state legislature plays a key role in establishing the legitimacy of mandatory cultural competency training for state employees; it has the authority to make this a budgetary priority so the necessary resources are provided to ensure the policy is implemented. Unfunded mandates are not received well by agencies and seldom create successful results. Creation of a budget might be premature, however, until the precise nature and makeup of the statewide training are specified and details such as its duration and frequency of delivery are known. For example, when asked whether the cultural competency training would be delivered one time only or as an ongoing process, the deputy secretary of state personnel responded that while this was as yet undecided, it was possible that an annual "refresher" course lasting from two hours to a half day might be required of state employees.

EVALUATION OF THE TRAINING PROGRAM

While it is as yet undetermined exactly how program success will be measured, evaluation of the training is an important consideration and will be addressed before the final statewide training curriculum is launched. When asked about program evaluation, the SPO deputy director suggested a possible survey of recipients of the training that might incorporate a Likert scale (Fullerton 2010). On the other hand, the State-Tribal Collaboration Act does require each state agency to compile an annual report of programs that serve Native Americans, evaluating each state department's effectiveness and the amount of money spent on these activities. It also calls for the appointment of a tribal liaison within each state department to work specifically on relevant programs and collaborations with New Mexico's pueblos and tribes. Several state agencies have been using this model for some time.

When we consider the pilot training we attended, we recognize particular aspects that contributed to its potential effectiveness. Foremost was its authenticity. The training was planned, designed, and implemented primarily by Native staffers under the direction of a coalition of Native leaders who strongly supported the need for cultural sensitivity training. This was an important opportunity for tribal governments to affect policy in a way that could improve significantly the experiences of tribal members in dealing with state employees, programs, and services. Further, the collaborative nature of the training avoided blaming or shaming non-Natives for their ignorance and for lacking cultural awareness; instead, facilitators generally encouraged learning. An atmosphere was created that allowed participants to share ideas and offer solutions to better understand and meet the needs of their Native coworkers and clients. Until the training program is closer to being finalized, however, it is too soon to say exactly how its effectiveness might be measured.

RECOMMENDATIONS

Implementing cultural competency training in state government is testimony to the shift in organizational theory from the old paradigm of delivery of services based on efficiency to a new one based on equity. Achieving equity in all aspects of public administration, such as promoting cultural competency, necessitates an investment of time and resources by elected officials and agency department heads. It also requires tribal leaders to communicate their needs and concerns and to advocate for change. Continued dialogue among these parties is essential to achieving success at all levels of government.

Making employees, both new and veteran, understand the importance of the training and how it fits into the mission of the agency is another important piece of the puzzle. Supervisors must be diligent in monitoring employees' perceptions of the training through dialogue with employees. The transition from culturally incompetent to culturally competent does not happen overnight. Our society's exposure to years of prejudice, misinformation, and misconceptions about Native peoples, as well as the difficulty in changing a deeply embedded organizational culture, takes time to reverse. Part of any cultural competency training should include a history lesson and critical examination of one's own culture. For example, a lesson in the role of the Spanish, Mexican, and U.S. governments when they each colonized the region is useful in understanding the cultures, religions, and governments of the Native peoples of New Mexico. Individuals need to understand how centuries of conquest and adaptation affect a people. Further, employees receiving the training should understand its purpose.

It is important for other state governments creating cultural competency tribal training to include a brief history of federal Indian policy for tribes in their state, a map that shows where the reservations are located, a list of the Native languages spoken, and sample tribal government organizations charts. Also, a communication protocol should be established. This is not a cookie-cutter training that can be applied across the United States. There are more than 560 Indian nations in the lower 48 states (not taking into account Alaskan villages), and each requires its own unique training protocol.

At the time of this writing, the New Mexico training program remains a work in progress. As the SPO deputy director observed, "[we] may need to do two pilots" (Fullerton 2010). He was referring to the pilot training presented to the group of tribal leaders and management-level state employees on May 25 in Santa Fe. The purpose of the "pilot" was to gather feedback from the carefully selected attendees about the speakers and the content, quality, and effectiveness of their presentations, and any other comments or suggestions those attending wished to offer. For example, the pilot included a PowerPoint presentation titled "Understanding Sovereignty Issues When Working Effectively with Tribal Governments" that lasted about two hours, including time for questions and answers. The bulk of the presentation (roughly forty-eight of fifty-five slides) dealt with federal Indian policy and intergovernmental relations, while only seven slides dealt with issues that could be clearly identified as addressing cultural sensitivity or cultural competency. Some of the participants articulated concerns that this portion of the training might be too legalistic for street-level administrators who constitute the majority of state employees targeted for this training, and that a focus on learning culturally appropriate behaviors might be more helpful in improving service delivery to Native people. At the end of the day, during the period established for "Group Feedback and Next Steps" on the agenda, an attendee noted that cultural competency had not been defined, nor had it been specifically discussed at any time during the entire day's presentations. This statement spoke volumes of the need for revisiting the training and, as the deputy director had observed, for offering a second pilot training.

We were interested in the potential for the training program to be adapted successfully for use by public sector employees working with indigenous populations in other areas of the United States or Canada, as well as those serving other ethnic and racial populations. The SPO deputy director thought this was possible: "In terms of the concept, definitely" (Fullerton 2010). New Mexico state government would be willing to share its training program. As all governments face increasing scarcity because of economic pressures, both states and tribes find that collaboration benefits them and their citizens. Many states and tribes already partner to cooperatively regulate their joint use of resources, coordinate programs, and meet the need for public services (Pevar 2002, 119). Federal agencies, which have extensive interaction with tribes, could also benefit from this training. A 2009 article states, "Federal Bureau of Investigation agents don't receive cultural awareness or language training when assigned to serve Indian reservations. [And yet,] many tribal communities don't believe non-tribal court personnel and non-tribal police are culturally sensitive" (*Indian Country Today* 2009). If federal and state agency representatives practiced cultural sensitivity while interacting with tribes, they would build trust, which enables cooperation. Building relationships on a foundation of open communication, understanding, and trust facilitates the best possible outcome when working with Indian nations. This may be accomplished through the use of tribal liaisons, as mentioned earlier.

When asked what changes they would like to see transpire as a result of the training, tribal leaders shared several aspirations. First, they hope that state employees, after participating, will understand the protocol for attending tribal council meetings by becoming familiar with the "Dos and Don'ts" offered in the training manual. Also, tribal leaders want the state of New Mexico and the tribes to build a common agenda in which all entities are willing to meet halfway. They also hope that the cultural curriculum training will encourage state agencies to take a proactive approach by offering services to Indian nations and asking how their agencies may be of assistance to Indian people.

Conclusion

This chapter examined a partnership among New Mexico tribal leaders, the state Indian Affairs Department, the state Personnel Office, and the Indian Law Program to create cultural competency training for state employees. The case illustrated the value of developing trusting relationships between organizations and leaders who respect each other's cultural differences with the goal of improving delivery of services to Native peoples across New Mexico. It also addresses tribal/state relations, an area previously unexplored by the literature.

The tribal leaders present at the pilot training see the State-Tribal Collaboration Act, and the statewide training in particular, as an important step in further improving state/tribal relations and an ideal opportunity to build fruitful relationships. Diplomacy is achieved through mutual respect and a shared desire to work together for the betterment of all New Mexico's residents. Tribal leaders hope those visiting pueblos and tribes feel comfortable enough to be themselves, to be respectful, and to be open to different views and beliefs. The pilot training highlighted the role of tribal sovereignty while stressing the need for policy that promotes tribal core values. It is our hope that training in cultural competency for public employees will be provided in other states seeking to begin the much-needed process of improving relations with Native nations across the country.

Finally, we offer a comment on the current literature on cultural competency. It does not examine tribal/state relations. This is a unique government-to-government relationship and as such cannot be compared to other interactions within or across governments. For states to effectively incorporate cultural responsiveness when working with tribes and pueblos, two principles must be established. As LaFrance notes, to initiate a respectful dialogue, states must recognize and accept tribal sovereignty and the right of Native Americans to self-determination (2004). These concepts form the core of the Native perspective; they must be acknowledged and respected by state legislators and administrative leaders. Secondly, state and federal leaders must do away with policies that promote cultural assimilation of Native peoples into the dominant culture. Forced assimilation has had devastating effects on indigenous communities throughout the world and does not necessarily equate with quality of life. When implemented, these two principles help to establish the foundation of trust and mutual respect required for diplomacy to be truly effective.

APPENDIX 8.1. COMMUNICATION PROTOCOL WITH TRIBAL GOVERNMENTS

State and tribal governments often share responsibilities for providing needed programs and services, effectively using limited resources, and addressing issues of mutual concern. The most important aspect of state/tribal communication is to understand that the tribal governments are the fundamental authority and that it is most appropriate to contact tribal leadership directly regarding services, programs, policies, concerns, and questions about a particular tribal matter.

Based on issue, the governor's office, the New Mexico Indian Affairs Department, and the tribal state liaisons within each agency may serve as a good resource and provide advice on proper communication protocol with each tribe. In general, when communicating with tribal governments, it is best to contact the tribal leadership directly.

Written correspondence should be addressed to the respective tribal governor, president, or chair, with a copy sent to the appropriate tribal director or department, as appropriate.

- *Tribal counterparts.* Many state agencies have tribal counterparts. For example, the New Mexico Health Department could work with the Pueblo of San Felipe Health and Wellness Department on health promotion and disease prevention issues. Working with tribal staff is helpful in addressing particular issues or day-to-day technical and programmatic questions. However, it is best to notify the respective tribal leader in regard to all-important issues.
- *The tracking process* should include the following steps:
  — Mail the letter of request or invitation
  — E-mail the letter of request and invitation
  — Fax the letter of request or invitation, re-fax if necessary
  — Make a phone call to follow up

In-person meeting with tribal leaders. It is best to communicate and coordinate with tribes on a government-to-government basis. For in-person meetings, it is best that the meeting coordination take place as early as possible with tribal leaders directly or through their tribal administrators or secretaries. Meeting logistics should be agreed on between the tribe and the state.

- When meeting at a tribe's invitation,
  — Be respectful of tribal protocol. Wait to be invited into the meeting space and sit in designated area.

— The tribal leader may begin the meeting with a prayer. After the prayer, wait for the tribal leader to begin the meeting with introductions.
- When meeting at the state's invitation,
    — Create a welcoming environment; shake hands and introduce yourself.
    — Include the option to begin your meeting with a prayer.
    — When the tribal leader and representatives speak, give them the courtesy of your patience and respect. Your regard of tribal government leaders and representatives is a reflection of your department and state.
    — Provide handouts when possible.
    — Offer refreshments.
    — Provide a comfortable waiting area for visitors accompanying the tribal leaders.

APPENDIX 8.2. ETIQUETTE—DOS AND DON'TS

DOS

- Learn how the community refers to itself as a group of people (i.e., the tribal name).
- Be honest and clear about your role and expectations and be willing to adapt to meet the needs of the community. Show respect by being open to other ways of thinking and behaving.
- Listen and observe more than you speak. Learn to be comfortable with silence or long pauses in conversation by observing community members' typical length of time between turns talking.
- Casual conversation is important to establish rapport, so be genuine and use self-disclosure (e.g., where you are from, general information about children or spouse, personal interests).
- Avoid jargon. A tribal community member may nod politely, but not understand what you are saying.
- It is acceptable to admit limited knowledge of Native American cultures and invite people to educate you about specific cultural protocols in their community.
- If you are visiting the home of an Indian family, you may be offered a beverage and/or food, and it is important to accept it as a sign of respect.
- Explain what you are writing when making clinical documentation or charting in the presence of the individual and family.
- During formal interviews, it may be best to offer general invitations to speak, then remain quiet, sit back, and listen. Allow people to tell their story before engaging in a specific line of questioning.
- Be open to allowing things to proceed according to the idea that "things happen when they are supposed to happen."
- Respect confidentiality and the right of the tribe to control information, data, and public information about services provided to the tribe.
- State jargon, acronyms, and standard operating procedures that are commonplace for state employees may not be familiar to tribal members. Therefore, adjust your presentation accordingly. Educate, don't patronize.

DON'TS

- Avoid stereotyping based on looks, language, dress, and other outward appearances.
- Avoid intrusive questions early in conversation.
- Do not interrupt others during conversation or interject during pauses or long silences.
- Do not stand too close to others and/or talk too loud or fast.
- Be careful not to impose your personal values, morals, or beliefs.
- Be careful about telling stories of distant Native relatives in your genealogy as an attempt to establish rapport unless you have maintained a connection with that Indian community.
- Be careful about pointing with your finger, which may be interpreted as rude behavior in many tribal communities.
- Avoid frequently looking at your watch and do not rush things.
- Avoid pressing all family members to participate in a formal interview.
- Do not touch sacred items, such as medicine bags, other ceremonial items, hair, jewelry, and other personal or cultural things.
- Do not take pictures without permission.
- *Never* use any information gained by working in the community for personal presentations, case studies, research, and so on without the expressed written consent of the tribal government.

REFERENCES

Bailey, Margo, L. 2005. Cultural competency and the practice of public administration. In *Diversity and Public Administration: Theories, Issues and Perspectives*, ed. Mitchell F. Rice, 177–196. Armonk, NY: M.E. Sharpe.

Berg, Bruce L. 2009. *Qualitative Research Methods for the Social Sciences*. Boston: Allyn & Bacon.

Box, Richard, ed. 2007. *Democracy and Public Administration*. Armonk, NY: M.E. Sharpe.

Brintnall, Michael. 2008. Preparing the public service for working in multiethnic democracies: An assessment and ideas for action. *Journal of Public Affairs Education* 14(1): 39–50.

Bush, Carol. 2000. Cultural competence: Implications of the surgeon general's report on mental health. *Journal of Child and Adolescent Psychiatric Nursing* 13(4): 177–178.

Cohen, Felix. 1942. *Handbook of Federal Indian Law*. Albuquerque: University of New Mexico Press.

Dean, Ruth Grossman. 2001. The myth of cross-cultural competence. *Families in Society* 82(6): 623–630.

Deloria, Vine, Jr., and Clifford M. Lytle. 1984. *The Nations Within: The Past and Future of American Indian Sovereignty*. Austin: University of Texas Press.

Fullerton, Reese. 2010. Deputy Director, New Mexico State Personnel Office. Personal Interview.

Hatch, Francine. 2009. The State-Tribal Collaboration Act. *I-News* (New Mexico Indian Affairs Department), January, 2. www.iad.state.nm.us/docs/inews/jan09-inews.pdf.

———. 2010. Senior Policy Analyst, New Mexico Indian Affairs Department. Personal Interview.

Holstein, James A., and Jaber F. Gubrium. 1995. *The Active Interview*. Beverly Hills, CA: Sage.

Indian Country Today. 2009. Editorial: Cultural training needed for FBI. October 30. http://64.38.12.138/News/2009/017214.asp.

Indian Law Center. 2010. State-Tribal Collaboration Act Training of State of New Mexico Employees, draft, v. 1, May 5.

Indian Pueblo Cultural Center. 2010. www.indianpueblo.org/museum/education/index.html.

Johnson, Richard Greggory, III, and Espiridion Borrego. 2009. Public administration and the increased need for cultural competencies in the twenty-first century. *Administrative Theory & Praxis* 31(2): 206–221.

Kalbfleisch, Pamela. 2009. Effective health communication in native populations in North America. *Journal of Language and Social Psychology* 28: 158–173.

LaFrance, Joan. 2004. Culturally competent evaluation in Indian country. *New Directions for Evaluation* 102: 39–50.

Legislative Commission on Indian Services. 2004. Oregon's approach to state-tribal relations. January. www.leg.state.or.us/cis/ODAIR/state_tribal_relations.pdf.

Mistry, Jayanthi, Francine Jacobs, and Leah Jacobs. 2009. Cultural relevance as program-to-community alignment. *Journal of Community Psychology* 37(4): 487–504.

New Mexico Indian Affairs Department. 2010. 2009 summit status report, New Mexico State-Tribal Leaders Summit, April. www.iad.state.nm.us/docs/stca/tribal_leaders_summit/2009/2009Summit ReportFINAL4-30-2010.pdf.

Olsen, Laurie, Jhumpa Bhattacharya, and Amy Scharf. 2006. Cultural competency: What it is and why it matters. www.californiatomorrow.org/media/ccompetecy.pdf.

Padilla, Helen B. 2010. Understanding tribal sovereignty when working with tribal governments. Indian Law Center, State-Tribal Collaboration Act Training of State of New Mexico Employees, draft v. 1:2–3.

Pecos, Regis. 2010. Tribal sovereignty and core values. Lecture presented at the State-Tribal Collaboration Act Training for State of New Mexico Employees. Santa Fe, New Mexico, May 25.

Pevar, Stephen L. 2002. *The Rights of Indians and Tribes: The Authoritative ACLU Guide to Indian and Tribal Rights.* 3rd ed. Carbondale: Southern Illinois University Press.

Rice, Mitchell F. 2007a. A post-modern cultural competency framework for public administration and public service delivery. *International Journal of Public Sector Management* 20(7): 622–637.

———. 2007b. Promoting cultural competency in public administration and public service delivery: Utilizing self-assessment tools and performance measures. *Journal of Public Affairs Education* 13(1): 41–57.

Sando, Joe. 1992. *Pueblo Nations: Eight Centuries of Pueblo Indian History.* Santa Fe, NM: Clear Light.

State-Tribal Collaboration Act. 2009. New Mexico Statutes Annotated 1978 11–18–1 through 11–18–5.

State Tribal Government-to-Government Law. 2002. Oregon Revised Statute 182.162–168. January 1, 2002.

U.S. Census Bureau. 2010. State & County QuickFacts. http://quickfacts.census.gov/qfd/states/35000. html.

Wilkinson, Charles, and American Indian Resources Institute. 2004. *Indian Tribes as Sovereign Governments.* 2nd ed. Oakland, CA: American Indian Lawyer Training Program.

Woodbury, Richard B. 1979. Prehistory: Introduction. In *Handbook of North American Indians: Southwest,* vol. 9, ed. Alfonso Ortiz, 22–30. Washington, DC: Smithsonian Institution Press.

Worcester v. Georgia. 1832. 31 U.S. 515, 557, 558, 560.

Cultural Competency Around Sexual and Gender Orientation and Identity

WALLACE SWAN, MARK FRENCH
AND KRISTEN A. NORMAN-MAJOR

WHAT IS CULTURAL COMPETENCY?

Cultural competency is the capability not only to understand one's own culture, but also to understand and respond sensitively to the differing cultures of other people. The need for cultural competency for public managers and administrators derives from the fact that the United States has evolved from one predominant (white, male, straight) culture to one that now additionally includes people from a wide range of racial, ethnic, gender, and sexual orientation groups.

Duke University in its toolkit for managers suggests:

> Cultural competence is the experiential understanding and acceptance of the beliefs, values, and ethics of others as well as the demonstrated skills necessary to work with and serve diverse individuals and groups. (Duke University n.d., 1)

According to Duke's toolkit, a culturally competent organization includes

> a defined set of values and principles, and demonstrated behaviors, attitudes and structures that enable employees and leaders to work effectively cross-culturally. Demonstrated capacity to (1) value diversity, (2) conduct self-assessment, (3) manage the dynamics of difference, (4) acquire and institutionalize cultural knowledge and (5) adapt to diversity and the cultural contexts of the communities they serve. Incorporate the above in all aspects of policy making, administration, practice, service delivery and involve systematically consumers, key stakeholders and communities. (Duke University n.d., 1)

ESTABLISHING A BASE FOR UNDERSTANDING CULTURAL COMPETENCY ISSUES FOR GAY, LESBIAN, BISEXUAL, AND TRANSGENDER PERSONS

As organizations create tools and practices to become culturally competent, they must consider the cultural differences and needs of the populations with which they work and interact. This includes working with gay, lesbian, bisexual, and transgender people (GLBT). "In 2005, there were an estimated 8.8 million gay, lesbian, and bisexual people (single and coupled) living in the U.S." (Romero et al. 2007, 1). Since the derivation of the term *homosexual* in 1886 by the German writer Richard Freiherr von Krafft-Ebing, and the beginning of the use of the term "gay" in the early 1900s, there has been an awareness of two separate and distinct orientations, but with this recognition has come a lack of societal acceptance for GLBT people. Over the last forty-plus years, since the Stonewall rebellion in 1969, American society has slowly begun to recognize and consider the acceptance of the GLBT population as equals in society. While this transformation is by no means complete, there is an increased recognition of the need to include issues related to the GLBT population in a discussion of civil rights, equality, and cultural competency. Because the public sector on occasion plays a leadership role in the expansion of civil rights, equality, and cultural competency, it is important that public administrators include the needs of the GLBT population in developing culturally competent policies and practices. As LeVay notes in his 2011 work on the science of sexual orientation,

> the scientific knowledge currently available does bolster the idea that gays and lesbians are distinct "kinds" of people who are entitled to protection from discrimination, especially by governments . . . the multitude of research studies published since 1991 have greatly strengthened the idea that biological factors play a significant role in development of sexual orientation—both in men and in women. More than that, they tend to bolster a particular type of biological theory. This is the idea that the origins of sexual orientation are to be sought in the interactions between sex hormones and the developing brain. (x–xi)

Because of cultural factors, the life of a GLBT person evolves developmentally differently from that of a non-GLBT person. GLBT people may, early in their life, begin to deal with the major developmental stages of accepting their identity, or they may repress their orientation, or they may "come out" at a much later point in their life (Coleman 1988). The development process, combined with cultural and location factors, causes very different ways in which GLBT people may interface with the public sector:

1. There is research indicating that 20 to 40 percent of homeless youth have a GLBT orientation, a percentage that is proportionately much larger than the percentage for GLBT youth in the general population (Ray 2006). For example, "Medical News Today reports that a new study in the American Journal of Public Health shows that homelessness is much more common among gay, lesbian, and bisexual teens. Their study included over 6,300 Massachusetts teens. Twenty-five percent of gay and lesbian teens were found to be homeless while only 3 percent of heterosexual teens reported being homeless" (Lavender 2011). Often this is because gay youth are kicked out of their homes by unaccepting parents. Public programs that serve homeless youth must thus be aware of this fact and be sensitive to the issues faced by GLBT youth.

2. GLBT high school and college students (and occasionally heterosexual students presumed to be gay) often face bullying and harassment from fellow students and sometimes faculty and staff as well. This bullying can lead to dire consequences, including suicide, as illustrated by the case of Tyler Clementi, who committed suicide

after his roommate used video technology to record him having sex with another man and then uploaded it onto the Internet. Faculty, administrators, and medical as well as social service staff need to be culturally competent around GLBT issues in order to create welcoming and safe school environments for GLBT students of all ages.

3. GLBT people often face discrimination in employment and promotion. For example, a 1995 study examining employment factors in one large metropolitan county found that there were no GLBT top executives in the human services agency (Swan 1995). Discrimination in hiring and promotion indicates the need for increased cultural competency in practices within public agencies and in the work of enforcing workplace antidiscrimination policies. Public administrators at all levels, but particularly executives and human resources professionals, must consider GLBT issues in creating welcoming and nondiscriminatory workplaces.

4. Hate violence is a significant factor that faces many GLBT people and that may have negative effects upon their work life and health status. The National Coalition of Anti-Violence Programs (NCAVP) 2010 report shows that in 2009 there were 2,181 victims of anti-GLBT violence during the course of 1,556 incidents resulting from actions by 1,623 offenders (4). The 2009 FBI hate crimes report, developed from a separate database, indicated that approximately half of hate crimes derived from racial bias, 20 percent resulted from religious bias, and 18 percent derived from sexual orientation bias (FBI 2010). However, another study conducted by the Southern Poverty Law Center concluded that "homosexuals are far more likely to be victims of violent hate crime than any other minority group" and that "homosexuals, or those perceived to be gay, are more than twice as likely to be attacked in a violent hate crime as Jews or blacks; more than four times as likely as Muslims; and 14 times as likely as Latinos" (Associated Press 2010, 1).

This higher level of hate violence directed toward GLBT people indicates the need for public safety officers and employees of the judicial system to be culturally competent when dealing with GLBT victims of crime.

5. The public sector will face growing demands to meet the needs of senior citizens, including GLBT seniors who are becoming more organized in their efforts to secure services. Some GLBT seniors have been out most of their lives while others have come out much later in life. Many who have faced years of employment discrimination or are unable to access retirement benefits from partners or former partners may have low incomes and limited assets (Grant 2010). Others will be dealing with health care concerns and issues of ailing and aging friends and partners who need care.

> A major challenge facing LGBT seniors nationwide . . . is the threat of discrimination and economic insecurity, as well as a lack of traditional support networks and proper healthcare. In fact, LGBT seniors who live alone are at increased risk for depression, substance abuse, unnecessary institutionalization, and premature death . . . a 1999 study found that 65 percent of gay and lesbian seniors surveyed reported living alone—nearly twice the rate of all seniors. The study also found that 90 percent of gay and lesbian seniors had no children, compared to 20 percent of all seniors . . . According to a 2005 survey, more than a quarter of LGBT baby boomers reported great concern about discrimination as they age. Less than half expressed strong confidence that healthcare professionals will treat them "with dignity and respect." LGBT seniors also face institutional discrimination. For example, Social Se-

curity survivor benefits are not paid to same-sex partners. Medicaid regulations protect the assets of a spouse when the other enters a nursing home, but this protection is not offered to same-sex couples. Tax laws and other regulations of 401k's and pensions also discriminate against same-sex partners. (Center Facts n.d.)

6. The repeal of the "Don't Ask, Don't Tell" legislation for military services in December 2010 eliminated sanctioned discrimination against GLBT citizens wanting to serve in the military. While formal barriers are being removed during 2011, it will take considerable effort and training to change the culture of the military to openly accept GLBT soldiers and remove unsanctioned discriminatory behaviors. Leaders in all branches of the military, including National Guards, will need to create culturally competent policies and practices that openly welcome GLBT service men and women.

7. As seventeen states begin to recognize marriages, civil unions, or domestic partnerships (or a combination of the three), others grapple with extending benefits to same-sex couples including hospital visitation rights for unmarried partners (now mandated for all federally funded hospitals), as well as adoption and foster-care policies for GLBT couples and individuals. Still, thirty-three other states have either sought to ban such rights for all their GLBT citizens, or have taken no position on this issue. Public officials in all localities must know state and local policies, but must increasingly deal with the effects of differing policies across government boundaries. Rights granted in one jurisdiction typically are not recognized in another. This increasing complexity of civil rights issues involving families and relationships will require the attention of civil servants at many levels.

8. A 2011 study of 6,450 "transgender and gender non-conforming study participants . . . from all 50 states, the District of Columbia, Puerto Rico, Guam and the U.S. Virgin Islands" noted that "discrimination was pervasive throughout the entire sample, yet the combination of anti-transgender bias and persistent, structural racism was particularly devastating . . . Respondents lived in extreme poverty" (Grant, Mottet, and Tanis 2011, 2). The study showed that transgender individuals were far more likely than the general population to live in poverty and to attempt suicide, often because they suffered job bias, harassment, and physical or sexual assault.

9. Mental health services are often not available for members of the GLBT community, and factors related to community acceptance result in worse mental health for mental health of GLBT people; for example, a longitudinal national survey conducted twice, most recently with the same group in 2004–2005, showed that GLBT people in states that banned GLBT marriage had worse mental health than those in states that had no such provisions (Haas 2011).

10. Recent studies by NCAVP indicate that "LBGTQ domestic violence and intimate partner violence has risen by 15 percent in the period since 2008" and ending in 2011 (Gilmore and Slavin 2011). This increase may be a result of an enhanced emphasis upon reporting activity that was not previously recorded.

The preceding paragraphs outline ten ways that the public sector interacts with the GLBT population around specific issues. Along with these is the basic human rights expectation to serve anyone who walks through the door of a public agency in a culturally competent manner, including the GLBT population. A number of efforts to ensure GLBT cultural competency are now being initiated at the federal level, including the U.S. Department of Education's "summit on bullying," the simplification of the passport process in the U.S. State Department, and efforts to eliminate barriers to adoption and foster care, among many others (Bond 2011). As the sector that occasionally leads the public in setting behavioral standards, the public sector has an increasingly vital responsibility to include sexual orientation as a component of cultural competency.

THE LEGAL CONTEXT GOVERNING CULTURAL COMPETENCY ABOUT GLBT PERSONS

As noted above, public managers need to be aware that, in contrast to most other minorities, GLBT individuals may or may not have legal protections depending upon the governmental jurisdiction for which they work or in which they live.

For instance, at the federal level, GLBT people essentially have no legal protection for marital rights as a result of the Defense of Marriage Act (1996). The General Accountability Office in its 2004 updated study of the topic found "1,138 federal statutory provisions classified to the United States Code in which marital status is a factor in determining or receiving benefits, rights, and privileges" (U.S. GAO 2004, 1). However, the rights of individual civilian federal employees are protected by Executive Order 13087, which does not allow discrimination in the federal workplace based upon sexual orientation (Lambda Legal n.d.).

At the state and local levels, there is a patchwork of laws that in some states protect GLBT people while in others do not (see Appendix 9.1 on page 159 for summary.) According to research conducted by the National Gay and Lesbian Task Force, thirteen states plus the District of Columbia do not allow discrimination based upon gender identity/expression or sexual orientation and another eight states prohibit discrimination based upon sexual orientation. Three states restrict foster care and four states ban adoption by GLBT parents. The District of Columbia and twelve states ban hate crimes based upon sexual orientation and gender identity, and eighteen states ban hate crimes based upon sexual orientation. There are fifteen states with hate crimes laws that do not prohibit hate crimes based upon either sexual orientation or gender identity, and five states that have no hate crimes laws (NGLTF 2010).

When it comes to regulating same-sex relationships, the United States has a wide variety of alternatives that all depend upon where one lives. For example, Connecticut, Iowa, Massachusetts, New Hampshire, New York, and Vermont and the District of Columbia have full marriage equality; that is, same-sex couples receive the same rights and benefits as married heterosexual couples although these rights are not universally recognized across states and jurisdictions. Only two states, New York and Maryland, recognize same-sex marriages that were performed in other states (NGLTF 2010). Same-sex couples in California, Maine, Maryland, Nevada, New Hampshire, New Jersey, Oregon, Vermont, Washington, and Wisconsin have access to domestic partnerships, while those living in Rhode Island, Hawaii, Illinois, New Hampshire, New Jersey, and Vermont may unite in "civil unions" which have some but not all of the characteristics of a marriage (NGLTF 2010).

Numerous states oppose GLBT marriages or other forms of legally recognized relationships. Thirty states have statutory prohibitions against same-sex marriage, and ten states have prohibitions against same-sex marriage in the form of constitutional amendments. There are also numerous states with even broader prohibitions against same-sex relationships such as domestic partnerships and civil unions. Seven states have broader statutes banning same-sex relationships, and nineteen states have constitutional amendments that incorporate these broader prohibitions (NGLTF 2009a–d). Major efforts are underway in a number of states (Minnesota, New Hampshire, and North Carolina, among others) to establish a constitutional ban on gay marriage. And several 2012 presidential candidates support a United States constitutional ban on gay marriage in all states.

Why Is Understanding Gay Marriage as a Legal Issue a Matter of Cultural Competency?

One key element of the legal context described above involves understanding the importance of marriage to many GLBT people. The issue of marriage equality does not encompass merely a desire by GLBT people to "get married in a church," since many already do that, or to have "societal recognition for their union," or to gain benefits, since they already have the support of most people in the GLBT community. Rather, it is an issue of social and economic inequity that has been prevalent for centuries, as amply documented by John Boswell (1994) in *Same-Sex Unions in Premodern Europe*. In contrast to the United States, currently ten countries (Argentina, Belgium, Canada, Iceland, Netherlands, Norway, Portugal, Spain, Sweden, and South Africa) provide full marriage rights to GLBT people (BBC 2010a). There are also many countries that provide civil unions, registered partnerships, or other similar arrangements that provide some but not all of the rights of marriage. These countries include Denmark, Finland, France, Germany, Israel, New Zealand, Switzerland, and the United Kingdom (Belge 2010). At issue for the GLBT population in the United States is both the lack of rights in many states and localities and the inconsistencies in rights in those jurisdictions that have adopted laws regarding same-sex relationships. As an example of the issue facing local jurisdictions, residents who live in the City of Minneapolis and twelve other Minnesota cities are allowed to register as domestic partners. This allows GLBT residents of these cities in the state to simply be on a list of the people who live together in a committed relationship; and this provides them with no rights. In addition, these partnerships may not be recognized in other jurisdictions in the state, including neighboring cities. Like GLBT people in other states without marital rights, GLBT people are precluded from an additional 515 Minnesota rights that married heterosexual couples are allowed to have such as pension benefits for surviving partners, joint filing tax breaks, and automatic hospital access to visit an ill partner. These rights are documented by a 2007 Project 515 report titled "Unequal Under the Law: 515 Ways Minnesota Laws Discriminate Against Couples and Families" (Project 515 n.d.).

According to NGLTF, a few other states (e.g., Colorado, Hawaii, Maine, and Wisconsin) offer limited benefits to same-sex couples. Even though some states grant marital rights to GLBT people, the United States does not allow them to participate in any federal benefits; for example, the ability of a partner of a member of the military to receive a deceased partner's Social Security benefits, which is one of many major economic deprivations, pursuant to the Defense of Marriage Act.

Understanding the emotional impact of having no rights as a person in a relationship is basic to understanding the real life of a GLBT person who happens to be in that status.

OBTAINING CENSUS DATA ON GLBT HOUSEHOLDS

Data on GLBT citizens is not collected in a systematic manner as is the case for other areas of cultural competency, such as race, ethnicity, gender, and disability status. Census data is important because more than $400 billion is allotted to communities and states based upon this data, and it is also used in determining boundaries of legislative and congressional districts as well as placement of public facilities such as schools, hospitals, parks, community centers, and housing developments (U.S. Census Bureau 2010). To date, census data has not included details on all GLBT individuals. However, beginning in 1990, data has been collected on same-sex couples living in the same household. This came about when the Census Bureau added an "unmarried partner" category to the census in order to collect data on couples living together. While this designation was originally directed toward heterosexual couples, data on same-sex couples was collected as well when both partners in a same-sex household indicated their sex on their forms (Gates and Ost 2004). While the data is limited, it has led to some interesting findings. For example, the 1990 census data showed that more than one in six men and almost one in fourteen women living as part of a same-sex couple had served in the military. The 2000 census showed that gay or lesbian couples lived in over 99 percent of all U.S. counties (*Curve Magazine* 2010).

While gathering data on same-sex couples is important for analysis of policies related to civil rights for same-sex couples, the lack of data on GLBT single individuals means a lack of data that could help shape policies as well as indicate discriminatory policies toward the GLBT population. For example, 2005 estimates indicated that while there were 1,553,886 gay and lesbian individuals in coupled relationships (776,943 gay and lesbian couples), in that same year one could draw the conclusion that 7,246,114 single gay, lesbian, and bisexual persons were not identified as such since the estimated number of gay, bisexual, and lesbian people in the United States at that same time was 8,800,000 (Romero et al. 2007). Recent evaluation of the 2010 census figures estimate that there are now 901,997 same sex couples in the United States (Tavernise 2011). Census data related to gender, race, and ethnicity has been important in helping to shape public policies, distribute public services and resources, and end discriminatory policies for several groups. The lack of data on GLBT single individuals as well as transgender and bisexual persons means it is difficult to include the needs of most of the GLBT population in discussions of policy and resources.

WORKFORCE DIVERSITY ISSUES RELATING TO GLBT PERSONS

From the viewpoint of the GLBT community, there are several alternative ways to view the problem of dealing with a predominantly heterosexual world that dominates

American culture. One approach is to simply say that it is impossible for those from another framework to understand the world of the person from a minority culture. This is known as the concept of "incommensurability," which suggests that people from two different cultures, in this case "gay" and "straight," simply cannot comprehend what the other culture involves. Fox and Miller note in their work:

> The point is that one does not ordinarily inhabit more than one paradigm, cannot see through the lenses of alternative paradigms. No argument developed in terms of one paradigm can be telling to those who argue in terms of an alternative one. Inhabitants of different paradigms are . . . ships passing on a moonless night without running lights. (2006, 636)

A second strategy for dealing with a predominant culture is to work endlessly to educate the people from the majority culture about the life of those in the minority culture. The first approach ensures isolation from the dominant culture, while the second approach of developing cultural competency can be exhausting for the GLBT person who is chosen to be the "token." This leads to a third, intermediate strategy, which is to ensure that the leadership of an agency sets an example by creating a new subculture and modeling acceptance of differing sexual orientations by making statements that show that people who are different are actually valued in the organization. For example, 160 GLBT appointees to key unclassified federal offices (22 of whom required U.S. Senate confirmation) were selected by the Obama administration during the first two years of its existence (Bond 2011).

From census data we know that "same-sex couples live in every state in the U.S. and constitute 1.0 percent of coupled households and 0.6 percent of all households in the country" (Romero et al. 2007, 1). Data also shows that same-sex couples live in almost every county in the nation. While we have at least some estimate of the numbers of gay and lesbian people in the United States, we do not have any estimates of the numbers of bisexual and transgender people, which would make the totals considerably higher. We can reasonably assume that GLBT people are employed in many governmental, corporate, nonprofit, and university workplaces around the country. However, the existence of federal and state laws and regulations prohibiting recognition of the rights of GLBT people is one of the major factors limiting the ability of the public service to be supportive of the rights of its GLBT public employees in many states as well as in the U.S. military, where until its repeal the "Don't Ask, Don't Tell" ban led to 3660 discharges at a cost of $193.3 million during the period from 2004 to 2009 (O'Keefe 2011).

A 2009 workplace study by the Human Rights Campaign Foundation (HRC Foundation) sampling 761 people from all possible diversity categories and all workplace sectors around the country shows that major problems make many GLBT people unwilling to divulge their sexual orientation to their parents, friends, and coworkers. The HRC Foundation study notes:

> The majority of LGBT workers (51 percent) hide their LGBT identity to most at work, the simplest indication that more work needs to be done to translate inclusive policies to an inclusive climate. A total of 23 percent are open to a few people and 28 percent are not open to anyone with whom they work . . . 22 percent are open to half or most people with whom they work. (11)

The reality is that for those who are not open about their sexual orientation, life is difficult. Again the HRC Foundation study notes

> 54 percent of LGBT employees who are not open to anyone at work report lying about their personal lives, compared to 21 percent of employees open to everyone about their LGBT identity. LGBT workers' inability to participate honestly in everyday conversations hinders trust and cohesion with their co-workers and superiors. Open LGBT employees are also less likely to feel depressed, avoid people and search for another job. (13)

Why do GLBT employees hide their orientation? According to the HRC report

> Half (51 percent) of all LGBT employees say one reason they are not open is because disclosing their sexual orientation or gender identity may make co-workers feel uncomfortable, and 39 percent do not want to risk losing connections with co-workers. Four in 10 (41 percent) say the possibility of being stereotyped is a reason for not being open. Nearly three in 10 (28 percent) decide not to be open because they feel it may be an obstacle to career advancement or development opportunities. Slightly more than one in 10 (13 percent) LGBT employees would fear for their personal safety. (15)

Clearly, working in an unwelcoming workplace can lead to several problems for GLBT employees. According to the HRC study, GLBT workers, whether open or not, reported serious issues such as having to lie about their personal lives, feeling depressed, avoiding people including clients and customers, avoiding any social events at all connected with work, feeling distracted or exhausted, and staying at home to avoid the stress of dealing with sexual orientation issues at work or searching for other jobs (HRC 2009). As a counter to this, GLBT employees reported that when they are able to "feel free to be themselves, voice their opinions and engage openly in non-work-related conversations, they feel free from discrimination and believe they are valued, accepted and part of a team" (HRC 2009, 11).

When building a culturally competent and welcoming workplace for GLBT employees, public organizations should consider and include the following factors:

1. The presence of openly GLBT employees in senior management and supervisory positions.
2. Acknowledgement of GLBT partners and families.
3. Support for the GLBT client base.
4. The presence of a policy that does not tolerate inappropriate jokes and comments.
5. Consistent enforcement of Equal Employment Opportunity policy.
6. Dealing with situations that could negatively impact GLBT employees in a proactive manner.
7. Clearly stating criteria for advancement and development.
8. Positively reacting when GLBT employees first disclose sexual orientation or gender identity (HRC 2009).

These factors are important steps in creating welcoming and culturally competent workplaces that allow GLBT employees to fully participate and bring their skills and assets to the workplace.

PROVIDING CULTURALLY COMPETENT HEALTH SERVICES TO GLBT PEOPLE

As is the case in other areas within public administration, it is reasonable to expect that organizations should provide health care services in a culturally competent manner to GLBT people. Once again, the U.S. census data indicates that there are gay and lesbian couples and/or individuals in every state and almost every county in the United States, so their health needs require a response. Often, these services are provided through public health agencies and hospitals and, as the population ages, through in-home care, assisted living facilities, and nursing homes. Social service employees providing support services will need to serve GLBT members of society. Unfortunately, culturally competent care for GLBT people is often unavailable. A number of studies, compiled in a compendium of culturally competent care guidelines for GLBT people by Seattle and King County Public Health staff, indicate the following:

> A 1998 survey of nursing students showed that 8 to 12% (depending on whether the respondent rated gay, lesbian or bisexual) despised lesbian, gay and bisexual people, 5–12% found lesbian, gay and bisexual people disgusting and 40–43% believed that lesbian, gay and bisexual people should keep their sexuality private. In a 1996 survey of 1,027 New Mexico physicians, 4.3% indicated that they would deny gay and lesbian people acceptance to medical schools and 10.1% believed that gay and lesbian physicians should be discouraged from seeking obstetrics/gynecology training. In the same study, over 20% of the general practitioners, 9.3% of family practice physicians and 4% of pediatricians reported that they would discontinue patient referrals to gay and lesbian surgeons . . . In a survey published in 1988, 84% of lesbians surveyed had experienced a general reluctance to seek health care . . . This study revealed that 96% of lesbians "anticipated situations in which it could be harmful to them if their health provider knew they were lesbian" . . . A 1981 study showed that when a patient was known to be gay, physicians tended to interpret the presenting problem in sexual terms. When the patient was not identified as homosexual, other diagnoses were more often considered. (King County 2011, 1)

In working with health care for GLBT populations, several factors need to be considered in building a model of culturally competent care. For example, intake forms and discussions with the patient often are oriented to heterosexuals, asking questions about marital status and gender as male/female. Simply including options such as "living with a domestic partner" or allowing space for transgender individuals to enter something besides "male" or "female" may create a greater feeling of comfort for GLBT persons seeking care (King County 2011). Health care providers must also consider their reactions and openness to patients who may feel less than willing to share personal and medical histories for fear of judgment or mistreatment. Questions that are open-ended and asked in a nonjudgmental manner help build a relationship of trust with GLBT patients (King County 2011).

These are only a few of the issues that can be considered in creating culturally competent health care. The Human Rights Campaign, in its work on measuring equity in how health care facilities treat GLBT patients, includes measures of cultural competency training and client services. According to the HRC:

> Cultural competence, at the provider level and at the institutional level, is increasingly becoming a key goal of education on LGBT health issues. A provider's lack of cultural competence has been shown to negatively affect not only provider-patient interaction and care-giving, but also the patient's care seeking behavior.
>
> Everyone who works in healthcare facilities should receive training on LGBT cultural competence because an individual's experience while accessing healthcare is influenced by everyone they interact with in the process. Creating a nonjudgmental and secure environment through training on LGBT-specific, basic skills and competencies will ensure patients feel welcome and relieve anxiety or confusion among employees. (2010b, 1)

K–12 EDUCATION ISSUES

On April 6, 2009, Carl Joseph Walker-Hoover, 11, of Springfield, Massachusetts, hanged himself on the second floor of his family's home. On July 9, 2010, Justin Aaberg, 15, of Anoka, Minnesota, hanged himself in his bedroom. On September 9, 2010, Billy Lucas, age 15, of Greenburg, Indiana, hanged himself in his grandmother's barn. On September 13, 2010, Cody Barker, 17, of Shiocton, Wisconsin, took his own life. On September 19, 2010, Seth Walsh, 13, of Tehachapi, California, hanged himself from a tree in his yard. On September 23, 2010, Asher Brown, 13, of Houston, Texas, shot himself in the head in his home. "Those boys did not know each other, but they did have something in common. They'd been bullied at school, and one by one, they all apparently came to the same conclusion: If you're gay or thought to be gay, life just isn't worth living" (Miller 2010, 1). These recent tragedies have sparked intense debate about the effects of antigay bullying in our schools and communities. Whatever one's social, political, and religious beliefs, we can all agree that the death of even one student is a tragedy. Our nation's public education system has a responsibility to provide a safe environment for students to learn, free of physical and mental abuse and bullying. But while federal protections address discrimination on the basis of race, color, national origin, religion, sex, and disability, federal laws do not protect lesbian, gay, bisexual, and transgender students. There have been attempts to provide protection for GLBT students at the federal level. The Safe Schools Improvement Act (H.R. 2262) was introduced in the 111th Congress on May 9, 2009, by Representative Linda Sanchez (D-CA) and has 130 cosponsors. The last action on this House bill occurred on June 4, 2009, when it was referred to the House Subcommittee on Early Childhood, Elementary, and Secondary Education, where it awaits further action. Another bill, the Student Non-Discrimination Act (H.R. 4530), was introduced in the 111th Congress on January 27, 2010, by Representative Jared Polis (D-CO) and has 127 cosponsors. The last action on this House bill occurred on February 23, 2010, when it was referred to the House Subcommittee on Higher Education, Lifelong Learning, and Competitiveness, where it, too, awaits further action. The accompanying Student Non-Discrimination Act Senate bill (S. 3390) was introduced in the 111th Congress by Senator Al Franken (D-MN) on May 20, 2010, and has thirty cosponsors. The last action on this bill occurred on May 20, 2010, when it was read twice and referred to the Senate Committee on Health, Education, Labor, and Pensions. As of this writing, all three of these important bills remain in committees of the House and Senate awaiting action in order to bring them to the entire House and Senate for a vote.

Absent federal statutes and legislation, GLBT students must rely on relevant statewide school laws and policies and/or policies and procedures approved by their local school boards. Currently, fourteen states, plus the District of Columbia, have laws that address discrimination, harassment, and/or bullying of students based on sexual orientation and gender identity. These states (with the year the law was enacted) are California (2002), Colorado (2008), District of Columbia (2001), Illinois (2010), Iowa (2007), Maine (2005), Maryland (2008), Minnesota (1993), New Hampshire (2010), New Jersey (2002), New York (2010), North Carolina (2009), Oregon (2007), Vermont (2001/2007), and Washington (2002/2009). Additionally, three other states, Connecticut (2001), Massachusetts (2002), and Wisconsin (2001), have laws that address discrimination, harassment, and/or bullying of students based on sexual orientation (HRC 2010b).

When a state is without statewide school laws, individuals must rely on local school district policies and procedures. The good news is that more school boards are recognizing the need to add sexual orientation to their harassment policies. The bad news is that the majority of school boards have not taken that action. Two recent examples illustrate the positive steps some school boards are taking. First, in November 2010, the Minnesota School Board Association (MSBA) advised school districts to expand their harassment and violence policy to specify LGBT students. According to one news report:

> The MSBA's updated harassment policy is much more specific. It prohibits any form of harassment or violence on the basis of race, color, creed, religion, national origin, sex, age, marital status, familial status, and status with regard to public assistance, sexual orientation, or disability. The MSBA is also pushing for school boards to put more pressure on school officials to intervene when they witness bullying. The proposed wording isn't new: It is from Minnesota's human rights legislation passed in 1993. The MSBA believes that strengthening a local school district policy might clarify issues for employees who are not sure what their role is. (Burnette 2010, 1)

A second example comes from Dallas, Texas, where on November 18, 2010, the Dallas school board approved an anti-bullying policy that includes protections for gay and lesbian students, the first of its kind in the state of Texas. The Dallas Independent School District began considering the policy after a recent nationwide spate of suicides by teenagers who had been bullied in school. The policy is lengthy and detailed and takes effect immediately. The climate and culture of most of our middle and secondary schools are not conducive to GLBT youth. On September 14, 2010, the Gay, Lesbian, and Straight Education Network (GLSEN) released its 2009 National School Climate Survey of 7,261 middle and high school students. The survey "found that nearly 9 out of 10 LGBT students experienced harassment at school in the past year and nearly two-thirds felt unsafe because of their sexual orientation. Nearly a third of LGBT students skipped at least one day of school in the past month because of safety concerns" (Kosciw et al. 2010, 1). These statistics indicate a great need for teachers and administrators to become more culturally competent in improving the school climate and culture for GLBT students.

Three national organizations are working to address the needs of and provide support for GLBT students: the Trevor Project, based in West Hollywood, California; the "It Gets Better" Project, based in Manhattan, borough of New York City; and the Gay, Lesbian and Straight Education Network (GLSEN), based in New York City. All three organizations are focused on reducing the number of GLBT student suicides.

The Trevor Project. "The Trevor Project is a national organization focused on crisis and suicide prevention efforts among lesbian, gay, bisexual, transgender and questioning (LGBTQ) youth" (Trevor Project 2010a, 2). It was founded by the creators of the 1994 Academy Award–winning short film, Trevor, a comedy/drama about a gay thirteen-year-old boy who, when rejected by friends because of his sexuality, makes an attempt to take his life (Trevor Project 2010a). When the film was scheduled to air in 1998, the filmmakers, concerned that some viewers might be facing the same issues as Trevor, wanted to provide information regarding available sources of support during the airing. When they found that no such supports existed, they decided to form their own. The Trevor Lifeline became the first and only nationwide, around-the-clock crisis and suicide prevention lifeline for GLBT questioning youth. Besides a suicide prevention hotline, the Trevor Project provides online support to young people through the organization's website, and guidance and resources for educators and parents (Trevor Project 2010a).

It Gets Better. It Gets Better (www.itgetsbetterproject.com) began with a YouTube video designed to bring hope to youth experiencing harassment because of sexual orientation. Founder Dan Savage wanted to find a way to let youth experiencing bullying know that it does get better. The It Gets Better Project is now a worldwide movement that includes over 5,000 user-created videos and over 15 million views (It Gets Better Project 2010). Those submitting videos include Secretary of State Hillary Clinton, Representative Nancy Pelosi, Adam Lambert, Anne Hathaway, Colin Farrell, Matthew Morrison, Joe Jonas, Ke$ha, Sarah Silverman, Tim Gunn, Ellen DeGeneres, Suze Orman, and many more, including John Berry, the first openly gay director of the Federal Office of Personnel Management (It Gets Better Project 2010). President Barack Obama, in creating a video for the It Gets Better Project on October 21, 2010, stated:

> We've got to dispel this myth that bullying is just a normal rite of passage; that it's just some inevitable part of growing up. It's not. We have an obligation to ensure that our schools are safe for all of our kids. And for every young person out there you need to know that if you're in trouble, there are caring adults who can help. (The White House 2010)

The Gay, Lesbian and Straight Education Network (GLSEN). The Gay, Lesbian and Straight Education Network (GLSEN) is a national education organization, founded in 1990, working to ensure safe schools for all students, regardless of sexual orientation and gender identity. According to its mission:

> The Gay, Lesbian & Straight Education Network strives to assure that each member of every school community is valued and respected regardless of sexual orientation or gender identity/expression.
>
> We believe that such an atmosphere engenders a positive sense of self, which is the basis of educational achievement and personal growth. Since homophobia and heterosexism undermine a healthy school climate, we work to educate teachers, students and the public at large about the damaging effects these forces have on youth and adults alike. We recognize that forces such as racism and sexism have similarly adverse impacts on communities and we support schools in seeking to redress all such inequities.
>
> GLSEN seeks to develop school climates where difference is valued for the positive contribution it makes in creating a more vibrant and diverse community. We welcome as members any and all individuals, regardless of sexual orientation, gender identity/expression or occupation, who are committed to seeing this philosophy realized in K–12 schools.
>
> (GLSEN 2011)

In response to the recent antigay bullying incidents, GLSEN launched its Safe Space Campaign in November 2010, which is designed to promote visible support for LGBT students in American middle and high schools (GLSEN 2011).

Along with the above national organizations, several professional education associations have recognized the need for their members to be more culturally competent in working with diverse students and families, including GLBT students and families. For example, the American School Counselor Association's position statements include a category titled "The Professional School Counselor and Cultural Diversity." The association believes that "effective and ethical school counselors need to possess cultural competence including self-awareness, knowledge of others' worldviews, and use of culturally sensitive skills" (ASCA 2009). The National Association of School Psychologists has a section called "Promoting Cultural Diversity and Cultural Competency" on its website, including a "Self-Assessment Checklist for Personnel Providing Services and Supports to Children and their Families" developed by Georgetown University Center for Child and Human Development. This checklist is intended to raise the awareness and sensitivity of human services personnel to the importance of cultural diversity and cultural competence, including in K–12 school systems (Goode 2009). Also, the National Education Association (NEA) provides an online Diversity Toolkit that addresses both cultural competence for educators and also sexual orientation and gender identity (NEA 2010).

As noted earlier, the Human Rights Campaign has recognized the importance of those working in the health-care field being culturally competent to the needs of GBLT individuals. As a result of this work, HRC has started to extend this cultural competency to the education field. Through its Welcoming Schools Program, HRC works to provide educators and parents with materials to empower and encourage them to create learning environments in which all students are welcome and respected. The Welcoming Schools Program works to help educators become more culturally competent and responsive to the needs of GLBT students and families (HRC 2010b).

As a base to start building cultural competence with respect to nontraditional families and GLBT students in schools, Mark French in a 2009 article in *Principal Magazine* suggests the following strategies:

> (1) Review your school and district forms for inclusivity; (2) be knowledgeable and aware of your state, district, and school policies for harassment and name-calling; (3) provide language to describe the varieties of families in your school and community; (4) welcome and include gay parents in the same way you welcome all parents into your school; and (5) consider including gay parents in units on families and addressing the accomplishments of gay individuals. (French 2009, 28)

One school district effectively helping its employees become more culturally competent to respond to the needs of GLBT students is the New York City Department of Education (NYC DOE). To create safer schools for all students, including lesbian, gay, bisexual, transgender, and questioning (LGBTQ) students, the NYC DOE launched the Respect for All initiative in 2007.

> The initiative includes efforts to notify all students, parents, and staff about district policy prohibiting student-to-student bias-based bullying, harassment, and intimidation and the related reporting procedures. The Program also mandates that each school have at least one designated staff member to whom reports about bias-based bullying, harassment, or intimidation can be made. As part of the initiative, the district also provides training for staff from each school. (Greytak and Kosciw 2010, 1)

According to Connie Cuttle, director of professional development in the Office of School and Youth Development for the New York City Department of Education, the Respect for All program is being implemented from kindergarten through grade twelve. In a 2010 evaluation of the program's first year, educators who received the Respect for All training

> demonstrated increased knowledge of appropriate terms; access to LGBTQ-related resources; awareness of how their own practices might have been harmful to LGBTQ students; empathy for LGBTQ students; belief in the importance of intervening in anti-LGBTQ remarks; communication with students and staff about LGBTQ issues; engagement in activities to create safer school for LGBTQ students; and frequency of intervention in anti-LGBTQ name-calling, bullying, and harassment. (Greytak and Kosciw 2010, v)

In addition to implementing Respect for All, the New York City Department of Education has the following language in its Citywide Standards of Discipline and Intervention Measures. Students have a right to

> be in a safe and supportive learning environment, free from discrimination, harassment, bullying, and bigotry, and to file a complaint if they feel that they are subject to this behavior; receive courtesy and respect from others regardless of actual or perceived age, race, creed,

color, gender, gender identity, gender expression, religion, national origin, citizenship/immigration status, sexual orientation, physical and/or emotional condition, disability, marital status and political beliefs. (NYC DOE 2010, 7)

Such training and standards are good examples that can be used by other districts in creating cultural competence and welcoming schools for GLBT students and their families.

Developing GLBT Cultural Competency in Higher Education

The lack of acceptance of GLBT people in the education system is not limited to the K–12 environment. As noted earlier in this chapter, the roommate of a gay man at Rutgers University made a video of his roommate, Tyler Clementi, with a male partner in bed and circulated it on the Internet. The result was that Tyler Clementi killed himself by jumping off the George Washington Bridge. This and other cases have led leaders in higher education to recognize the need to review policies and develop culturally competent policies and services for GLBT students.

One example of such policies and training is the Safe Zone Network Training program presented at Hamline University in St. Paul, Minnesota. The goals of this program are as follows:

To educate about homophobia and the realities of being GLBT. To encourage the development of healthy attitudes concerning GLBT people and to foster an appreciation for diverse sexual orientations. To develop and empower GLBT allies to take supportive stances concerning GLBT people and issues. To fight homophobia and heterosexism. To build, strengthen and sustain an inclusive living [and] . . . work environment of the university. (Hamline University Office of the Dean of Students n.d., 1)

The curriculum for this training reflects content typical of building awareness around GLBT issues on campus. Activities in the training program are designed to help participants do the following:

1. Determine cultural predispositions that lead to misunderstanding about GLBT people.
2. Learn "relevant definitions" that give precise explanations of many terms that are often confused by the lay public, for example differentiating between gender identity, gender roles, transgender persons, transsexuals, cross-dressers.
3. Review and dispel "commonly held incorrect beliefs."
4. Define homophobia and discuss differing levels of homophobic attitudes.
5. Discuss the process of "coming out" and how an ally might be helpful to a GLBT person who is making this journey.
6. Discuss how one can become an "ally"—moving from "awareness" to "knowledge/education" to "skills" and thence to "action."

7. Self-assess one's attitudes and beliefs about GLBT people, through a self-assessment survey.
8. Move one's organizational unit toward improved acceptance of GLBT people.

When this training is complete, participants may volunteer to serve as a faculty or staff member in a "Safe Zone," thus pledging to be a person who will listen nonjudgmentally to the concerns of a faculty or staff member, student or ally who is dealing with a GLBT issue (Hamline University Office of the Dean of Students n.d.). These types of training are important in the establishment of safe and welcoming campuses for GLBT students, faculty, and staff. While the Safe Zone training used at Hamline University is just one possible model, the general content is typical of cultural competency training programs across sectors and can be used as a base in creating similar programs in other schools and organizations.

DEVELOPING CULTURAL COMPETENCY IN SEXUAL ORIENTATION ISSUES IN A PUBLIC, NONPROFIT UNIVERSITY OR A BUSINESS ORGANIZATION

Training such as that provided in the Hamline University Safe Zone course could easily be adapted to a cultural competency or diversity training unit that could be presented in a public, nonprofit university or a business environment. This training approach presents the real-life issues that GLBT people face. Why do it this way? Because without educating people on the issues of the broader GLBT experience, employees may simply think that GLBT people are simply "straight" people who have a different sexual attraction, so the employees cannot figure out what the problem is and why they should become culturally competent. They suffer from "incommensurability," as discussed previously. The need for cultural competency is best explained as the assumption that some administrators, managers, supervisors, and employees may have worked with a GLBT person but generally do not have any idea about the issues that GLBT people actually face in their lives. As a result, colleagues treat them the same as other people—but without realizing that GLBT people are dramatically disadvantaged by unconscious cultural patterns of economic and social discrimination and consequent disaffiliation by non-GLBT people. The goal is thus to educate people and change the way that managers and employees approach issues of sexual orientation.

A goal when building an approach to GLBT cultural competency in any organizational environment is that one must first start at the level of the empirical facts of GLBT people's lives and their cultural experience. There are many resources that can aid in doing this, including those cited in the "References" to this chapter.

After reading materials such as those cited in the "References" (especially the HRC Foundation "Degrees of Equality . . . ," the NGLTF "Outing Age 2010 . . ." report, the GAO study on the "Defense of Marriage Act . . . ," and the NCAVP report on "Hate Violence . . .") employees might be able to make GLBT people's lives better by socially reconstructing the rules and procedures in their organizations and recognizing that the legislative position of an organization on such issues is vital in changing the environment where GLBT employees live.

Corporations have tended to be in the forefront of developing programs that ensure cultural competency for their employees. Among the Fortune 500 corporations, " the vast majority (89 percent) prohibit discrimination on the basis of sexual orientation, more than a third (43 percent) prohibit discrimination based on gender identity . . . and the majority (57 percent) provide domestic partner health insurance benefits to their employees" (HRC 2010a). Many corporations ensure cultural competency by (1) developing nondiscrimination policies, (2) providing partnership benefits, (3) ensuring that their corporate executives model positive behavior toward GLBT employees, (4) reviewing their diversity programs to ensure that GLBT diversity is included, (5) making sure that employees who are identified as "out" are included in organizational program planning that relates to sexual orientation minorities, and (6) ensuring that the organization is represented in gay pride celebrations and parades. These types of policies and activities can serve as a model for the public sector and other organizations in building cultural competence around issues of sexual orientation and making GLBT colleagues and clients feel welcome and safe.

CONCLUSION

To build cultural competency around sexual as well as gender orientation and identity in the public sector, public administrators must receive both basic cultural competency training as well as education in more complex skills that derive from the wealth of research that is now available about specialized GLBT issues such as homelessness, seniors, social mobility, interaction with bureaucracies, education, and hate crimes. As a leader in establishing expectations for how different communities are treated, the public sector needs to continue to work to build cultural competence around the needs of and services for the GLBT community. Much work remains to be done on a macro level in creating consistent civil rights policies for GLBT persons, including those related to marriage and families. In the meantime, public administrators must be aware of the challenges and issues faced by GLBT members of their communities and create policies that provide support, eliminate bias and bullying, and open doors for the GLBT community to receive needed services and fully participate in the public sector, schools, and the workplace.

NOTE

In this chapter, the acronym GLBT is usually used to refer to gay, lesbian, bisexual, and transgender individuals. These groups are also referred to as LGBT, GLBTQ (gay, lesbian, bisexual, transgendered, and queer) or LGBTQA (gay, lesbian, bisexual, transgendered, queer and allies). The authors' intention is to include all these groups in their discussion of cultural competency related to issues of sexual orientation when using the acronym GLBT.

Appendix 9.1

State Laws Related to GLBT Rights

State	Law banning discrimination based on sexual orientation[1]	Law banning foster care or adoption for same-sex parents[2,3]	Laws banning hate crimes[4]	Recognition of same-sex relationships[5]	Same-sex relationships[6]	Protection of students against discrimination, harassment, bullying[7]
Alabama	No		Hate crime law not including sexual orientation, gender identity		Statutory ban against same-sex marriage; broad prohibition of same-sex relationships by constitutional amendment	Prohibits bullying in schools but no categories of protection
Alaska	No		Hate crime law not including sexual orientation, gender identity		Broad prohibition of same-sex relationships by statute; statutory ban against same-sex marriage	Prohibits bullying in schools but no categories of protection
Arizona	No		Hate crime law including sexual orientation		Statutory ban on same-sex marriage; constitutional amendment against same-sex marriage	Prohibits bullying in schools but no categories of protection
Arkansas	No		No hate crime laws		Statutory ban on same-sex marriage; constitutional amendment against same-sex marriage; broad prohibition of same-sex relationships by constitutional amendment	Prohibits bullying in schools but no categories of protection
California	Yes, based on sexual orientation, gender identity, and/ or expression		Hate crime law including sexual orientation, gender identity	Broad recognition: domestic partnerships	Constitutional amendment against same-sex marriage	Protection of students against discrimination, harassment, bullying based on sexual orientation and gender identity

(continued)

Appendix 9.1 (continued)

State	Law banning discrimination based on sexual orientation[1]	Law banning foster care or adoption for same-sex parents[2,3]	Laws banning hate crimes[4]	Recognition of same-sex relationships[5]	Same-sex relationships[6]	Protection of students against discrimination, harassment, bullying[7]
Colorado	Yes, based on sexual orientation, gender identity, and/or expression		Hate crime law including sexual orientation, gender identity	Limited recognition: "designated beneficiaries"	Statutory ban against same-sex marriage; constitutional amendment against same-sex marriage	Protection of students against discrimination, harassment, bullying based on sexual orientation and gender identity
Connecticut	Yes, based on sexual orientation		Hate crime law including sexual orientation, gender identity	Full marriage equality		Protection of students against discrimination, harassment, bullying based on sexual orientation
Delaware	Yes, based on sexual orientation		Hate crime law including sexual orientation		Statutory ban against same-sex marriage	Prohibits bullying in schools but no categories of protection
District of Columbia	Yes, based on sexual orientation, gender identity, and/or expression		Hate crime law including sexual orientation, gender identity	Full marriage equality		Protection of students against discrimination, harassment, bullying based on sexual orientation and gender identity
Florida	No	Adoption statute (now repealed)	Hate crime law including sexual orientation		Broad statutory prohibition of same-sex relationships; broad prohibition of same-sex relationships by constitutional amendment	Prohibits bullying in schools but no categories of protection
Georgia	No		No hate crime laws		Statutory ban on same-sex marriage; broad prohibition of same-sex relationships by constitutional amendment	Prohibits bullying in schools but no categories of protection
Hawaii	Yes, based on sexual orientation, gender identity, and/or expression		Hate crime law including sexual orientation, gender identity	Civil unions	Statutory ban against same-sex marriage	Regulation or code addressing discrimination, harassment, and/or bullying

Idaho	No	Hate crime law not including sexual orientation, gender identity		Statutory ban on same-sex marriage; broad prohibition of same-sex relationships by constitutional amendment	No law
Illinois	Yes, based on sexual orientation, gender identity, and/or expression	Hate crime law including sexual orientation	Civil unions	Statutory ban against same-sex marriage	Protection of students against discrimination, harassment, bullying based on sexual orientation and gender identity
Indiana	No	No hate crime laws, but includes sexual orientation in hate crime reporting		Statutory ban against same-sex marriage	No law
Iowa	Yes, based on sexual orientation, gender identity, and/or expression	Hate crime law including sexual orientation	Full marriage equality		Protection of students against discrimination, harassment, bullying based on sexual orientation and gender identity
Kansas	No	Hate crime law including sexual orientation		Statutory ban on same-sex marriage; broad prohibition of same-sex relationships by constitutional amendment	Prohibits bullying in schools but no categories of protection
Kentucky	No	Hate crime law including sexual orientation		Statutory ban against same-sex marriage; broad prohibition of same-sex relationships by constitutional amendment	Prohibits bullying in schools but no categories of protection
Louisiana	No	Hate crime law including sexual orientation		Statutory ban against same-sex marriage; broad prohibition of same-sex relationships by constitutional amendment	Prohibits bullying in schools but no categories of protection

(continued)

Appendix 9.1 (continued)

State	Law banning discrimination based on sexual orientation[1]	Law banning foster care or adoption for same-sex parents[2,3]	Laws banning hate crimes[4]	Recognition of same-sex relationships[5]	Same-sex relationships[6]	Protection of students against discrimination, harassment, bullying[7]
Maine	Yes, based on sexual orientation, gender identity, and/or expression		Hate crime law including sexual orientation	Limited recognition: domestic partnerships	Statutory ban against same-sex marriage	Protection of students against discrimination, harassment, bullying based on sexual orientation and gender identity
Maryland	Yes, based on sexual orientation		Hate crime law including sexual orientation, gender identity	Limited recognition: domestic partnerships and recognizes same-sex marriages performed in other states		Protection of students against discrimination, harassment, bullying based on sexual orientation and gender identity
Massachusetts	Yes, based on sexual orientation		Hate crime law including sexual orientation	Full marriage equality		Protection of students against discrimination, harassment, bullying based on sexual orientation
Michigan	No	Bans adoption for same-sex couples married in other jurisdictions	No hate crime laws		Statutory ban on same-sex marriage; broad prohibition of same-sex relationships by Constitutional Amendment	No law
Minnesota	Yes, based on sexual orientation, gender identity, and/or expression		Hate crime law including sexual orientation, gender identity		Statutory ban against same-sex marriage	Protection of students against discrimination, harassment, bullying based on sexual orientation and gender identity
Mississippi	No	Bans adoption by couples of same gender	Hate crime law not including sexual orientation, gender identity		Statutory ban against same-sex marriage; constitutional amendment against same-sex marriage	Prohibits bullying in schools but no categories of protection

State					
Missouri	No		Hate crime law including sexual orientation, gender identity	Statutory ban against same-sex marriage; constitutional amendment against same-sex marriage	Prohibits bullying in schools but no categories of protection
Montana	No		Hate crime law not including sexual orientation, gender identity	Constitutional amendment against same-sex marriage; broad statutory prohibition of same-sex relationships	No law
Nebraska	No	Bans adoption and foster care for homosexuals or people unmarried and living with another adult	Hate crime law including sexual orientation		No law
Nevada	Yes, based on sexual orientation		Hate crime law including sexual orientation	Broad recognition: domestic partnerships	Prohibits bullying in schools but no categories of protection
New Hampshire	Yes, based on sexual orientation		Hate crime law including sexual orientation	Full marriage equality; broad recognition—civil union	Protection of students against discrimination, harassment, bullying based on sexual orientation and gender identity
New Jersey	Yes, based on sexual orientation, gender identity, and/ or expression		Hate crime law including sexual orientation, gender identity	Broad recognition: civil union	Protection of students against discrimination, harassment, bullying based on sexual orientation and gender identity
New Mexico	Yes, based on sexual orientation, gender identity, and/ or expression		Hate crime law including sexual orientation, gender identity		Regulation addressing discrimination, harassment, and/or bullying

(continued)

Appendix 9.1 (continued)

State	Law banning discrimination based on sexual orientation[1]	Law banning foster care or adoption for same-sex parents[2,3]	Laws banning hate crimes[4]	Recognition of same-sex relationships[5]	Same-sex relationships[6]	Protection of students against discrimination, harassment, bullying[7]
New York	Yes, based on sexual orientation		Hate crime law including sexual orientation	Grants same sex marriages; Recognizes same-sex marriages from other states		Protection of students against discrimination, harassment, bullying based on sexual orientation and gender identity
North Carolina	No		Hate crime law not including sexual orientation, gender identity		Statutory ban against same-sex marriage	Protection of students against discrimination, harassment, bullying based on sexual orientation and gender identity
North Dakota	No		Hate crime law not including sexual orientation, gender identity		Statutory ban against same-sex marriage; broad prohibition of same-sex relationships by Constitutional Amendment	No law
Ohio	No		Hate crime law not including sexual orientation, gender identity		Broad statutory prohibition of same-sex relationships; broad prohibition of same-sex relationships by constitutional amendment	Prohibits bullying in schools but no categories of protection
Oklahoma	No		Hate crime law not including sexual orientation, gender identity		Statutory ban on same-sex marriage; broad prohibition of same-sex relationships by Constitutional Amendment	Prohibits bullying in schools but no categories of protection
Oregon	Yes, based on sexual orientation, gender identity, and/or expression		Hate crime law including sexual orientation, gender identity	Broad recognition: domestic partnerships	Constitutional amendment against same-sex marriage	Protection of students against discrimination, harassment, bullying based on sexual orientation and gender identity

State			Hate crime	Civil unions	Marriage	Schools/workplace
Pennsylvania	No		Hate crime law not including sexual orientation, gender identity		Statutory ban against same-sex marriage	Regulation addressing discrimination, harassment, and/or bullying
Rhode Island	Yes, based on sexual orientation, gender identity, and/or expression		Hate crime law including sexual orientation	Civil Unions		Prohibits bullying in schools but no categories of protection
South Carolina	No		No hate crime laws		Statutory ban against same-sex marriage; broad prohibition of same-sex relationships by Constitutional Amendment	Prohibits bullying in schools but no categories of protection
South Dakota	No		Hate crime law not including sexual orientation, gender identity		Statutory ban against same-sex marriage; broad prohibition of same-sex relationships by Constitutional Amendment	No law
Tennessee	No		Hate crime law including sexual orientation		Statutory ban against same-sex marriage; constitutional amendment against same-sex marriage	Prohibits bullying in schools but no categories of protection
Texas	No		Hate crime law including sexual orientation		Statutory ban against same-sex marriage; broad statutory prohibition of same sex relationships; constitutional ban on same-sex relationships	Prohibits bullying in schools but no categories of protection
Utah	No	Bans foster care and adoptions by unmarried persons; preference of married couples over single adults	Hate crime law not including sexual orientation, gender identity		Statutory ban against gay marriage; broad statutory prohibition of same sex relationships; constitutional ban on same-sex relationships	Code of ethics addressing discrimination, harassment, and/or bullying

(continued)

Appendix 9.1 (continued)

State	Law banning discrimination based on sexual orientation[1]	Law banning foster care or adoption for same-sex parents[2,3]	Laws banning hate crimes[4]	Recognition of same-sex relationships[5]	Same-sex relationships[6]	Protection of students against discrimination, harassment, bullying[7]
Vermont	Yes, based on sexual orientation, gender identity, and/or expression		Hate crime law including sexual orientation, gender identity	Broad recognition: civil union		Protection of students against discrimination, harassment, bullying based on sexual orientation and gender identity
Virginia	No		Hate crime law not including sexual orientation, gender identity		Statutory ban against same-sex marriage; broad statutory prohibition of same sex relationships; constitutional ban on same sex relationships	Prohibits bullying in schools but no categories of protection
Washington	Yes, based on sexual orientation, gender identity, and/or expression		Hate crime law including sexual orientation, gender identity	Broad recognition: domestic partnerships	Statutory ban on same-sex marriage	Protection of students against discrimination, harassment, bullying based on sexual orientation and gender identity
West Virginia	No		Hate crime law not including sexual orientation, gender identity		Statutory ban against same-sex marriage	Prohibits bullying in schools but no categories of protection
Wisconsin	Yes, based on sexual orientation		Hate crime law including sexual orientation	Limited recognition: domestic partnerships	Broad prohibition of same-sex relationships by constitutional amendment	Protection of students against discrimination, harassment, bullying based on sexual orientation
Wyoming	No		No hate crime laws			Prohibits bullying in schools but no categories of protection

Note: Blank cells in table indicate that there are no specific laws regarding this issue in the state.
[1]NGLTF (2009d); [2]NGLTF (2011); [3]NGLTF (2009a); [4]NGLTF (2009b); [5]NGLTF (2010); [6]NGLTF (2009c); [7]HRC (2010b).

References

American School Counselor Association (ASCA). 2001. The professional school counselor and cultural diversity. http://asca2.timberlakepublishing.com/files/CulturalDiversity.pdf.

Ancis, Julie. 2008. Cultural competency at a distance: Challenges and strategies. *Journal of Counseling and Development* 76(2): 134–143.

Associated Press. 2010. FBI: Hate crime incidents, victim numbers down. Abc15.com, November 22. www.abc15.com/dpp/news/state/fbi%3A-hate-crime-incidents,-victim-numbers-down.

BBC. 2010a. Q &A: Argentina gay marriage law. July 15. www.bbc.co.uk/news/world-latin-america-10650267.

———. 2010b. Student kills himself after gay sex footage put online. September 30. www.bbc.co.uk/news/world-us-canada-11446034.

Belge, Kathy. 2010. Where can gays legally marry? About.com: Lesbian Life. http://lesbianlife.about.com/cs/wedding/a/wheremarriage.htm.

Bond, Brian. 2011. Obama administration and the LGBT community. Minneapolis: National Gay and Lesbian Task Force Conference, Minneapolis, February.

Boswell, John. 1994. *Same-Sex Unions in Premodern Europe.* New York: Villard Books.

Burnette, Daarel. 2010. Schools may add to harassment policies. Minneapolis-St. Paul *Star Tribune*, November 22. www.startribune.com/local/north/109350934.html.

Center Facts, n.d., "LGBT Seniors in the District of Columbia." www.thedccenter.org/facts_seniors.html.

Coleman, Eli. 1988. *Integrated Identity for Gay Men and Lesbians: Psychotherapeutic Approaches for Emotional Well-Being.* New York: Harrington Park Press.

Curve Magazine. 2010. Why the census matters to all GLBT Americans: An interview with Dr. Gary Gates, Williams Institute, and Che Ruddell-Tabisola, U.S. Census and Our Families Count. www.curvemag.com/Curve-Magazine/Web-Articles-2010/Why-the-Census-Matters-to-All-LGBT-Americans.

Defense of Marriage Act. 1996. Public Law 104–199. An act to define and protect the institution of marriage. http://frwebgate.access.gpo.gov/cgi-bin/getdoc.cgi?dbname=104_cong_public_laws&docid=f:publ199.104/pdf.

Duke University. n.d. Managing Diversity at Duke. Durham, NC. www.duke.edu/web/equity/resources/toolkit.html.

Federal Bureau of Investigation (FBI). 2010. FBI releases 2009 hate crime statistics. November 22. www.fbi.gov/news/pressrel/press-releases/2009hatecrimestats112210.

Fox, Charles, and Hugh Miller. 2006. Postmodern philosophy, postmodernity, and public organization theory. In *Handbook of Organization Theory and Management: The Philosophical Approach*, ed. Thomas Lynch and Peter Cruise. Boca Raton, FL: Taylor and Francis.

French, Mark. 2009. Including nontraditional families. *Principal* 89(2): 28.

Gates, Gary. 2009. Census 2010 LGBT Basics. http://escholarship.org/uc/item/86c791qg?query=census%20 2010%20lgbt%20basics.

Gates, Gary, and Jason Ost. 2004. *The Gay and Lesbian Atlas.* Washington, DC: Urban Institute Press.

Gilmore, Lisa, and Terra Slavin. 2011. National reporting and data driven advocacy: Ending anti-LGBTQ violence by the numbers. Presentation, National Gay and Lesbian Task Force Conference, "Creating Change: The National Conference on LGBT Equality," Minneapolis, MN, February 5.

GLSEN. 2011. "Our Mission." www.glsen.org/cgi-bin/iowa/all/about/history/index.html.

Goode, Tawara D. 2009. Promoting cultural diversity and cultural competency: Self-assessment checklist for personnel providing services and supports to children with disabilities and special health needs and their families. Georgetown University Center for Child & Human Development. http://nccc.georgetown.edu/documents/ChecklistCSHN.pdf.

Grant, Jaime. 2010. *Outing Age 2010: Public Policy Issues Affecting Lesbian, Gay, Bisexual and Transgender Elders.* Washington, DC: National Gay and Lesbian Task Force Policy Institute.

Grant, Jaime, Lisa Mottet, and Justin Tanis. 2011. *Injustice at Every Turn: A Report of the National Transgender Survey.* Executive Summary. Washington, DC: National Center for Transgender Equality and National Gay and Lesbian Task Force.

Greytak, Elizabeth, and Joseph Kosciw. 2010. Year one evaluation of the New York City Department of Education Respect for All Training Program. A Report from the Gay, Lesbian and Straight Education Network. New York: GLSEN. www.glsen.org/binary-data/GLSEN_ATTACHMENTS/file/000/001/1633-2.PDF.

GovTrack.us. 2010a. H.R. 2262: Safe Schools Improvement Act of 2009. www.govtrack.us/congress/bill.xpd?bill=h111-2262&tab.

———. 2010b. H.R. 4530: Student Nondiscrimination Act of 2010. www.govtrack.us/congress/bill.xpd?bill=h111-4530&tab.

———. 2010c. S. 3390: Student Nondiscrimination Act of 2010. www.govtrack.us/congress/bill.xpd?bill=s111-3390.

Haag, Matthew. 2010. Dallas ISD adopts anti-bullying policy that includes protections for gay students. *Dallas Morning News*, November 19. www.dallasnews.com/news/community-news/dallas/headlines/20101119-dallas-isd-adopts-anti-bullying-policy-that-includes-protections-for-gay-students.ece.

Haas, Anne. 2011. Paper presented at panel entitled "LGBTQ Mental Health: A Priority Issue," National Gay and Lesbian Task Force NGLTF conference, Minneapolis, MN, February 5.

Hamline University Office of the Dean of Students. n.d. Hamline University Safe Zone Network Training Handbook.

Human Rights Campaign (HRC). 2007. Welcoming schools: A new, comprehensive guide for creating LGBT-inclusive elementary schools. Washington, DC: Human Rights Campaign.

———. 2010a. LGBT equality at the Fortune 500. October 1. www.hrc.org/issues/fortune500.htm.

———. 2010b. Statewide school laws and policies. www.hrc.org/documents/school_laws.pdf.

———. 2011. LGBT cultural competence. www.hrc.org/issues/cultural-competence.htm.

Human Rights Campaign Foundation. 2009. Degrees of Equality: A National Study Examining Workplace Climate for LGBT Employees. Report. Washington, D.C.

It Gets Better Project. 2010. www.itgetsbetter.org/pages/about-it-gets-better-project.

King County. 2011. Culturally competent care for GLBT people: Recommendations for health care providers. Public Health—Seattle & King County, Seattle, Washington. www.kingcounty.gov/healthservices/health/personal/glbt/CulturalCompetency.aspx.

Kosciw, Joseph, Emily Greytak, Elizabeth Diaz, and Mark Bartkiewicz. 2010. The 2009 national school climate survey: The experiences of lesbian, gay, bisexual, and transgender youth in our nation's schools. A Report from the Gay, Lesbian and Straight Education Network. www.glsen.org/cgi-bin/iowa/all/news/record/2624.html.

Lambda Legal. n.d. The rights of LGBT public employees. www.lambdalegal.org/our-work/publications/facts-backgrounds/page-31986660.html.

Lavender, 2011. Homelessness more common among gay, bisexual teens. *Lavender*, August 11–24.

LeVay, Simon. 2011. *Gay, Straight, and the Reason Why: The Science of Sexual Orientation.* New York: Oxford University Press

Miller, Kenneth. 2010. Gay teens bullied to the point of suicide. *Ladies' Home Journal.* www.lhj.com/relationships/family/raising-kids/gay-teens-bullied-to-suicide.

National Association of School Psychologists. 2010. Promoting cultural diversity and cultural competency. www.nasponline.org/resources/culturalcompetence/checklist.aspx.

National Coalition of Anti-Violence Programs (NCAVP). 2010. Hate violence against the lesbian, gay, bisexual, transgender and queer communities in the United States in 2009. Report. www.avp.org/documents/NCAVP2009HateViolenceReportforWeb.pdf.

National Education Association (NEA). 2010. Diversity toolkit. www.nea.org/tools/18834.htm.

National Gay and Lesbian Task Force (NGLTF). 2009a. Foster care laws and regulations in the U.S. July 1. www.thetaskforce.org/reports_and_research/foster_care_regulations.

———. 2009b. Hate crimes laws map. July 14. www.thetaskforce.org/reports_and_research/hate_crimes_laws.

———. 2009c. State laws prohibiting recognition of same-sex relationships. June 30. www.thetaskforce.org/reports_and_research/marriage_map.

———. 2009d. State nondiscrimination laws in the U.S. July 1. www.thetaskforce.org/downloads/reports/issue_maps/non_discrimination_7_09_color.pdf.

———. 2010. Relationship recognition for same-sex couples in the U.S. March 17. www.esletc.com/handouts/SameSexCouplesUS2010.pdf.

———. 2011. Anti-adoption laws in the U.S. April 21. www.thetaskforce.org/downloads/reports/issue_maps/adoption_laws_04_11_color.pdf.

New York City Department of Education (NYCDOE). 2010. Citywide Standards of Discipline and Intervention Measures.

O'Keefe, Ed. 2011. "'Don't Ask, Don't Tell' Cost Military $193.3M Over Five Years." *Washington Post*, January 20. www.sldn.org/news/archives/washington-post-report-dont-ask-dont-tell-cost-military-193.3m-over-five-ye/.

Project 515. n.d. www.project515.org.

Ray, Nicholas. 2006. Lesbian, gay, bisexual and transgender youth: An epidemic of homelessness. New York: National Gay and Lesbian Task Force Policy Institute and the National Coalition for the Homeless. www.thetaskforce.org/downloads/HomelessYouth.pdf.

Romero, Adam P., Amanda K. Baumle, M.V. Lee Badgett, and Gary J. Gates. 2007. *Census Snapshot: United States*. December. Los Angeles: Williams Institute, UCLA School of Law. www3.law.ucla.edu/williamsinstitute/publications/USCensusSnapshot.pdf.

Swan, Wallace. 1995. The lavender ceiling: How it works in practice. In *Breaking the Silence: Gay, Lesbian, and Bisexual Issues in Public Administration*, ed. Wallace Swan. Washington, DC: American Society for Public Administration.

Tavernise, Sabrina. 2011. "New Numbers, and Geography, for Gay Couples." *New York Times*, August 25. www.nytimes.com/2011/08/25/us/25census.html?pagewanted=all.

The Trevor Project. 2010a. About Trevor. www.thetrevorproject.org.

———. 2010b. The Trevor Lifeguard Workshop Program. www.thetrevorproject.org/LWP.

U.S. Census Bureau. 2010. 2010 Census fact sheet for lesbian, gay, bisexual and transgender persons. March. http://2010.census.gov/partners/pdf/factSheet_General_LGBT.pdf.

U.S. General Accountability Office (GAO). 2004. Defense of Marriage Act: Update to prior report. www.gao.gov/products/GAO-04-353R.

The White House. 2010. It gets better video transcripts. Remarks of President Barack Obama. www.whitehouse.gov/it-gets-better-transcript.

The Williams Institute. n.d. Census 2010 LGBT basics. www3.law.ucla.edu/williamsinstitute/pdf/CENSUS2010LGBTBASICSv2.pdf.

Partnership for People with Disabilities

PARTHENIA DINORA

UNDERSTANDING DISABILITY IN THE CONTEXT OF CULTURE

Public agencies are responsible for acknowledging and responding to people's interests and concerns when establishing priorities, developing policies, and planning programs and services. In evaluating these interests and concerns, they must consider the voice of people with disabilities. In 2008, people with disabilities made up over 36 million or 12.1 percent of the U.S. population (Erickson, Lee, and von Schrader 2010). "Disability" represents a wide array of conditions that can impact life in minimal to extensive ways, crossing all racial, gender, educational, and socioeconomic lines.

Data from the 2009 Community Survey indicate that one-third of the U.S. population is from racially, ethnically, and culturally diverse groups; 20 percent of the population speaks a language other than English at home; one in eight Americans are foreign-born; and between 2000 and 2009, the foreign-born population increased in the United States by about 24 percent (Grieco and Trevelyan 2010). The interplay between disability and such cultural and linguistic diversity can pose challenges for public administrators. Non–disability-focused public agencies are sometimes unsure how to effectively support people with disabilities in accessing and using the agencies' core services. Consider an individual who is deaf trying to access services from the Department of Motor Vehicles or a person with an intellectual disability attempting to file an order of protection at the county courthouse. These scenarios can be further complicated when people with disabilities come from diverse racial and ethnic backgrounds and their primary language is not English.

Similarly, public agencies whose mission is to support people with disabilities are often not sure how to adequately support people who come from diverse racial and ethnic backgrounds. Often, the impact of culture on disability is underestimated.

Several policies and practices related to people with disabilities can assist public administrators in navigating these choppy waters. This chapter focuses on two such policies. The first, the Americans with Disabilities Act (ADA), is a foundational law that serves as the baseline for the integration of people with disabilities in the United States. In that the ADA specifically prohibits the discrimination or exclusion of people with disabilities by public programs, it has significant implications for public sector policy and practice.

A second area of interest to public administrators regarding disability is self-determination. Self-determination is a core value and practice in the disability field that encourages individual choice and control for people with disabilities. However, self-determination can mean different things to different people, especially those from diverse ethnic backgrounds. In the second half of the chapter, self-determination is defined and discussed within the context of diversity. Selected tools to assist public administrators in considering culture and disability are highlighted.

THE AMERICANS WITH DISABILITIES ACT

The Americans with Disabilities Act (P.L. 101–336) is comprehensive civil rights legislation adopted to prohibit discrimination against people with disabilities in the United States. The legislation, which defines disability as "a physical or mental impairment that substantially limits a major life activity," was signed into law by President George Bush on July 26, 1990, and later amended with changes effective January 1, 2009.

The ADA affords similar protections against discrimination to Americans with disabilities as the Civil Rights Act of 1964, which made discrimination based on race, religion, sex, national origin, and other characteristics illegal. It focuses on practices that subordinate people with disabilities and asserts that government must eliminate the legal, physical, economic, and social barriers that impede their full involvement in society.

Public and private businesses, state and local government agencies, private entities offering public accommodations and services, transportation, and utilities are required to comply with the law. Specifically, the ADA outlines five areas ("titles") in which persons with disabilities have legal rights: employment, public services, public accommodations, telecommunications, and other miscellaneous provisions. A summary of the five titles appears in Figure 10.1.

As noted in Figure 10.1, Title II of the ADA specifically relates to the provision of public services. While one should consult the legislation for specific language, some examples of what the ADA prohibits related to public services are highlighted in Figure 10.2. A case study of how Title II of the ADA can play out in the work of public administrators appears in Figure 10.3.

It is important to note that while the ADA is landmark legislation for preventing discrimination against people with disabilities, it is a baseline standard. Public programs and services should seek to go beyond this standard by encouraging full choice and participation for all people, including those with disabilities. One way that public administrators can accomplish this is through approaches that support self-determination.

Figure 10.1
Five Titles of the ADA

- Title I prohibits employers, including cities and towns, from discriminating against qualified job applicants and workers who have or acquire a disability. The law covers all aspects of employment, including the application process and hiring, training, compensation, advancement, and any other employment term, condition, or privilege.
- Title II prohibits state and local governments from discriminating against people with disabilities in their programs and activities. Title II also sets forth the applicable structural accessibility requirements for public entities.
- Title III prohibits private enterprises that provide public accommodations and services (e.g., hotels, restaurants, and transit systems) from denying goods, services, and programs to people based on their disabilities. Title III also sets forth the applicable structural accessibility requirements for private entities.
- Title IV makes available telecommunications devices and services for the hearing and speech impaired. These regulations spell out certain mandatory minimum standards that telephone companies must maintain to be in compliance with the ADA.
- Title V includes some miscellaneous provisions that relate to the construction and application of the ADA, including alternative dispute resolution.

Figure 10.2
Examples of ADA Prohibitions Related to Public Services

City and state entities
- may not refuse to allow a person with a disability to participate in a service, program, or activity because the person has a disability;
- must provide programs and services in an integrated setting, unless separate or different measures are necessary to ensure equal opportunity;
- must eliminate unnecessary eligibility standards or rules that deny individuals with disabilities an equal opportunity to participate in their services, programs, or activities unless "necessary" for the provisions of the service, program, or activity;
- are required to make reasonable modifications in policies, practices, and procedures that prevent equal access to individuals with disabilities, unless it necessitates a fundamental alteration in the program;
- must furnish auxiliary aids and services when necessary to ensure effective communication, unless this causes an undue burden or fundamental alteration;
- may provide special benefits, beyond those required by the regulation, to individuals with disabilities;
- may not place special charges on individuals with disabilities to cover the costs of measures necessary to ensure nondiscriminatory treatment, such as making modifications required to provide program accessibility or providing qualified interpreters; and
- must operate their programs so that, when viewed in their entirety, they are readily accessible to and usable by individuals with disabilities.

Source: U.S. Department of Justice (1993).

Figure 10.3
Americans with Disabilities Act in Public Administration

A county planning office is seeking public input on a comprehensive plan for land use. The office has scheduled a series of public meetings and presentations to promote input on the plan from a cross-section of stakeholders in the county including the citizenry and community business leaders.

Title II of the ADA requires state and local governments make their programs and services accessible to people with disabilities. This requirement extends not only to physical access at government facilities, programs, and events—but also to policy changes that governmental entities must make to ensure that all people with disabilities can take part in, and benefit from, the programs and services of State and local governments. *In addition, governmental entities must ensure effective communication – including the provision of necessary auxiliary aids and services - so that individuals with disabilities can participate in civic life.*

In order to meet the requirements of the ADA, this county office should include an accessibility statement on all notifications about the planned meetings and presentations. The statement could include the following language, *"if you are a person with a disability who requires an accommodation in order to participate in the meeting or presentation, please contact [insert contact] in advance at [insert contact information] to request accommodations."* This would allow for needed accommodations such as sign language interpreters or Braille handouts to be arranged for prior to the meetings and allow for the full participation of all interested citizens.

SELF-DETERMINATION

ORIGINS

The concept of self-determination for people with disabilities has its historical roots in the normalization, independent living, and disability rights movements of the 1960s and 1970s and the self-advocacy movement of the 1980s (Wehmeyer and Schwartz 1998). Self-determination first appeared in the disability literature in 1972, in a chapter of a book on the principle of normalization by Wolfensberger. Nirje's chapter, "The Right to Self-Determination," was a response to what he believed to be the limitations that institutional life placed on individuals with disabilities. He asserted that a person's identity is shaped through individual circumstances and experiences; thus people with disabilities should be given the opportunity for training in self-assertion, community experience, and independence so that they can have the opportunity to develop into fully realized individuals (Nirje 1972).

UNDERSTANDINGS OF SELF-DETERMINATION

Many definitions of self-determination have emerged in disability-related disciplines. In the special education and vocational rehabilitation fields, Wehmeyer (1996) describes self-determination as (1) best defined in relationship to characteristics of a person's behavior, (2) viewed as an educational outcome, and (3) achieved through lifelong learning, opportunities, and experiences (22). Others in special education and vocational rehabilitation stress that self-determination may involve, but is not synonymous with, independence and autonomy. What they consider key to the construct is that an individual determines the context and the extent to which each of the chosen "self-determined" behaviors will be manifested (Erwin and Brown 2000; Wehmeyer et al. 2003).

Doll and colleagues assert that self-determination emerges as children, youth, and adults develop and acquire skills that allow them to be more independent and deliberate. Thus, harking back to the work of Nirje, they contend that limited opportunities to practice skills necessary for self-determination at early ages can substantially constrain adolescents in the expression of self-determined behaviors (Doll et al. 1996).

In the world of adult services and supports for people with disabilities, alternate theories of self-determination have also emerged. Nerney and Shumway (1996) identify several key value-based principles in this theory. These principles are listed Figure 10.4. In this conceptualization, self-determination is not just another "program" for individuals, but instead a reform that changes the structure of supports for people with disabilities (Nerney 2005).

Therefore, self-determination in the context of supports and services for people with disabilities has two facets, a value-based facet and a functional facet (Turnbull and Turnbull 2006). The value-based definition of self-determination centers on the guiding principles of individual freedom, decision-making authority, adequate and appropriate supports for community living, and the exercising of social and civic responsibility. The functional definition of self-determination is more specific, relating to the realization of greater levels of choice and control over paid supports (Turnbull and Turnbull 2006).

SELF-DETERMINATION AND PUBLIC ADMINISTRATION

So what does self-determination mean for public administrators? Self-determination refers to the right of individuals to have full decision-making control over their own lives, including the option to seek out help if and when they need it. It involves the ability to freely participate in the political, economic, cultural, and social aspects of community life—activities that are often accessed or facilitated through public agencies. When supporting self-determination for people with disabilities, public agencies view people with disabilities, regardless of the nature of their disability, as competent, complete, and valuable members of the community. Agencies engage with people with disabilities at multiple levels, including in employment, volunteer positions, on boards and commissions, and in advisory roles. Thus, disability is not "external" to the organization or agency, but rather part of the natural diversity of the community at large. A case study of how public administrators can promote self-determination appears in Figure 10.5. It is important to note, however, that as American society becomes more and more diverse, so too is the population of people with disabilities. Public administrators must also understand and address how culture can impact self-determination for people with disabilities.

Figure 10.4
Principles of Self-Determination in Adult Services and Supports

1. Freedom: The ability of individuals with freely chosen family and/or friends to plan a life with necessary support rather than purchase a program;
2. Authority: The ability of a person with a disability (with a social support network or circle if needed) to control a certain sum of dollars in order to purchase these supports;
3. Support: The arranging of resources and personnel—both formal and informal—that will assist an individual with a disability to live a life in the community rich in community association and contribution; and
4. Responsibility: The acceptance of a valued role in a person's community through competitive employment, organizational affiliations, spiritual development, and general caring for others in the community, as well as accountability for spending public dollars in ways that are life-enhancing for persons with disabilities.

Source: Nerney and Shumway (1996).

Figure 10.5
Case Study: Promoting Self-Determination

A city arts commission is interested in highlighting the relationship between the arts and community development. It is planning a grant solicitation that focuses on the expanding role that arts organizations play in the broad cultural, social, educational, and economic areas of community life. Funds from the grant will be provided to arts and other community-based organizations to form alliances and partnerships to strengthen communities through projects that connect the arts with local issues and opportunities.

The commission could promote self-determination through its grant solicitation in a variety of ways. First, it could include community members with disabilities in the grant review process. This would emphasize that the perspective of people with disabilities within the arts community is valued and respected. Additionally, the solicitation could provide examples of alliances and partnerships that not only showcase people with disabilities as beneficiaries of community development activities, but also as driving forces behind projects that connect the arts with local issues and opportunities. For example, the solicitation could showcase a local Center for Independent Living (CIL) that hosts monthly art exhibitions featuring local artists with and without disabilities. Proceeds from these exhibitions benefit the artists, the CIL, and a local food bank. Examples such as this further reinforce the view of people with disabilities as competent, complete, and valuable members of the community.

CULTURAL FOUNDATIONS OF SELF-DETERMINATION

Self-directed approaches that emphasize personal control, individualism, self-help, and goal orientation are rooted in an Anglo-European ethnic cultural framework (Landmark and Zhang 2006; Smith and Routel 2010; Turnbull, Beegle, and Stowe 2001). However, the value placed on independently "doing" and "accomplishing" is not shared among all cultural groups. Many cultures in Asia, Africa, and Central and

Table 10.1

Collectivist and Individualist Cultural Orientations

Cultural orientation	Personal characteristics	Potential impact
Individualism	Self-expression Assertiveness Self-advocacy Self-reliance Personal control	• Communicates personal views and opinions about services • Goal-oriented • Focuses on individual talents and potential • Seeks greater participation in service decision making
Collectivism	Person is viewed primarily as part of a family unit Self-interests are secondary to interests of the family Group goals	• Family may be hesitant to seek assistance from outside sources • Individuals may be uncomfortable advocating for themselves • Self-sufficiency may not be the goal of services

Source: Adapted from Sotnik and Jezewski (2006, 24).

South America emphasize collectivism or group goals over individual goals and put great value on respect for authority, conformity, cooperation, interdependence, and avoiding interpersonal conflicts (Nevid 2009). In fact, more than 70 percent of the world's nations have been labeled as collectivist or group-oriented (Mindess 2006). As Sotnik and Jezewski (2005) point out, this worldview can have a direct influence on how one experiences and reacts to services. Some possible influences are illustrated in Table 10.1.

Potential tensions between culture and self-determination need to be better acknowledged and addressed. Fortunately, resources exist that can help public agencies and personnel better balance disability and culture, while supporting self-determination for people with disabilities.

CULTURAL COMPETENCY DEVELOPMENT OPPORTUNITIES

While multiple definitions of cultural competence exist, Cross and colleagues in 1989 offered a definition of cultural competence that established a solid foundation in human services that continues to be relevant today. In their discussion, they presented five core elements that impact an institution's or agency's ability to achieve cultural competency. These elements include the degree to which the agency (1) values diversity; (2) has the capacity for cultural self-assessment; (3) is conscious of the dynamics inherent when cultures interact; (4) has institutionalized culture knowledge; and (5) has developed adaptations to service delivery reflecting an understanding of cultural diversity.

As Helms and Richardson (1997) note, these elements can fall into three general categories: (1) an *attitudes and beliefs component* that includes an understanding of one's own cultural conditioning that affects personal beliefs, values, and attitudes; (2) a *knowledge component* that involves understanding and knowledge of the worldviews of culturally different individuals and groups; and lastly (3) a *skills component* that requires the use of culturally appropriate intervention and communication skills in working with individuals and groups.

Table 10.2

Selected Resources on Cultural Competency

Resource	Website address
General Cultural Competency	
National Center for Cultural Competence	www11.georgetown.edu/research/gucchd/nccc
Health Resources and Services Administration, "Culture, Language, and Health Literacy"	www.hrsa.gov/culturalcompetence
Centers for Disease Control, National Prevention Information Network, "Cultural Competence"	www.cdcnpin.org/scripts/population/culture.asp
Self-Assessment Tools and Information	
Cultural and Linguistic Competence Policy Assessment (National Center for Cultural Competence)	www.clcpa.info
The Role of Self-Assessment in Achieving Cultural Competence (*The Cultural Competence Exchange* 4, Fall/Winter 2001)	www11.georgetown.edu/research/gucchd/nccc/documents/selfassessment.pdf
Cultural Competency Organizational Self-Assessment (OSA) Question Bank (AIDS Education & Training Center)	www.aids-ed.org/aidsetc?page=etres-display&resource=etres-197
Understanding and Targeting Specific Population Groups	
U.S. Census Bureau	www.census.gov
The Provider's Guide to Quality and Culture (Management Sciences for Health)	http://erc.msh.org/mainpage.cfm?file=1.0.htm&module=provider&language=English
Office of Minority Heath (U.S. Department of Health & Human Services)	http://minorityhealth.hhs.gov
Culture Clues Tip Sheets (Patient and Family Education Services)	http://depts.washington.edu/pfes/CultureClues.htm
Center for International Rehabilitation Research Information and Exchange, "Cultural Competence"	http://cirrie.buffalo.edu/culture
Cultural Broker Information	
Bridging the Cultural Divide in Health Care Settings: The Essential Role of Cultural Broker Programs	http://nccc.georgetown.edu/documents/Cultural_Broker_Guide_English.pdf

In each of these three areas, several organizations and agencies offer a range of downloadable resources for understanding and improving cultural competency. Table 10.2 details several of these resources and their website addresses. These resources include items on general cultural competency, self-assessment tools and information, and sources for better understanding specific population groups. In particular the National Center for Cultural Competence at the Georgetown University Center for Child and Human Development offers tools for *self-assessment*. Tools such as "The Role of Self-Assessment in Achieving Cultural Competence" and "Cultural and Linguistic Competence Policy Assessment (CLCPA)" offer both organizations and individuals ways to systematically evaluate their attitudes and beliefs regarding culture. The Health Resources and Services Administration and the Centers for Disease control also provide general resources on cultural competency.

Gaining *new knowledge* about different cultural groups can be accomplished in a variety of ways. In this information age when comprehensive search engines can provide users with countless resources in the blink of an eye, people need to look no further than the Internet and Google to start their education. Table 10.2 offers multiple websites that provide useful information on different population groups. Of note, the U.S. Census Bureau regularly publishes data and reports on the spectrum

---

Figure 10.6
The Role of a Cultural Broker

A social service worker who supports aging adults thinks that assisted living would be the most beneficial living arrangement for an aging Japanese male who has acquired a disability through a stroke. Having little knowledge of Japanese culture, the provider seeks the input of a cultural broker in order to gain a greater understanding of how culture could impact the decision making of this individual and his family. A cultural broker has specific expertise and training on how to bridge, link, or mediate between groups or persons of differing cultural backgrounds for the purpose of reducing conflict and facilitating decision-making.

The cultural broker conducts a series of meetings with the man and his family to find out more about the influence of the Japanese culture on their lives—their values and beliefs; the roles played by individuals within the family; their views on independence; and their beliefs about caring for family members in need. Through this process, the cultural broker discovers that the client may have a difficult time adjusting to an assisted living environment because he would no longer be a part of his family's household. Traditional Asian cultures are grounded in the family. Many generations of a family may live together in the same household, and elders are highly respected. Adults in the family are expected to assume full responsibility for aging family members, and elders needing assistance are typically cared for in the family home.

Moving to an assisted living arrangement might cause feelings of abandonment in the aging adult because it is counter to his idea of family responsibility. Also, family members would feel that this type of move would be disrespectful to the elder member of their family. The culture broker communicates all this information back to the social service worker with the recommendation that a move to assisted living would have a detrimental impact on this family because it violates many of the core values of their culture.

---

of population groups living in the United States; the U.S. Department of Health and Human Services Office of Minority Heath offers comprehensive data and profiles on minority groups within the United States; the University of Washington's Medical Center's Patient and Family Education site offers Culture Clues Tip Sheets on a variety of cultural and ethnic groups; the Provider's Guide to Quality and Culture provides information on culturally competent healthcare services; and the Center for International Rehabilitation Research Information and Exchange provides an eleven-volume monograph series, including specific information on cultural perspectives of foreign-born persons in the United States.

Lastly, to enhance the *skills component*, which includes the use of culturally appropriate interventions and/or communication skills, many options and resources are available to organizations and individuals. One alternative that emphasizes skills in appropriate communication is employing the use of cultural brokers. Cultural brokering is the process of linking or acting as an advocate for persons of differing cultural backgrounds. An effective cultural broker has the knowledge, skills, and sensitivity to be aware of cultural factors that impact a person's life and has the training to act as an informed go-between (Jezewski and Sotnik 2001). An example of how a cultural broker can be employed to advance the work of public employees appears in Figure 10.6.

Various resources are available on cultural brokering. A computer-based tutorial in CD-ROM format, "Successful Outreach to Foreign-Born Consumers through Culture Brokering," available through the Center for International Rehabilitation Research Information and Exchange, provides comprehensive "how-to" information. Another useful tool, "Bridging the Cultural Divide in Health Care Settings," was developed by the National Center for Cultural Competence to provide information on planning, implementing, and sustaining cultural broker programs (see Table 10.2).

Another avenue available to assist with the skills piece of developing effective, culturally appropriate communication skills is through training. Many organizations, offer training programs that develop skills, awareness, and understanding of key diversity issues.

SUMMARY

Public agencies face a challenge in understanding and responding to the unique needs of diverse constituencies, including people with disabilities, people from immigrant communities, racial and ethnic minorities, and people who cross over several of these population groups. The ADA, which outlines how government must eliminate the legal, physical, economic, and social barriers that impede the full involvement of people with disabilities in society, can serve as a foundation for equal opportunity in accessing and using public programs and services. Approaches that encourage self-determination can take public programs to the next level, where people with disabilities are seen as equal members of society who can not only benefit from public programs and services, but also enhance them with their input and full participation. It is important to note that the disability population is as complex and diverse as the general population. Public administrators should access and use the many online resources available to them to understand their own beliefs about diversity, learn about the worldviews of others, and develop skills in communicating with different groups. This effort will enable them to reach out, understand, and plan and direct public services to meet the needs of all communities.

REFERENCES

Cross, Terry, Barbara Bazron, Karl Dennis, and Mareassa Isaacs. 1989. *Towards a Culturally Competent System of Care*, vol. 1. Washington, DC: Georgetown University Child Development Center, CASSP Technical Assistance Center.

Doll, Elizabeth, Deanna Sands, Michael Wehmeyer, and Susan Palmer. 1996. Promoting the development and acquisition of self-determined behavior. In *Self-Determination Across the Life Span: Independence and Choice for People with Disabilities*, ed. D.J. Sands and M.L. Wehmeyer, 65–90. Baltimore: Paul H. Brookes.

Erickson, William, Camile Lee, and Sarah von Schrader. 2010. *Disability Status Report: The United States*. Ithaca, NY: Cornell University Rehabilitation Research and Training Center on Disability Demographics and Statistics.

Erwin, Elizabeth, and Fredda Brown. 2000. Variables that contribute to self-determination in early childhood. *TASH Newsletter* 26(11): 8–10.

Grieco, Elizabeth, and Edward Trevelyan. 2010. Place of birth of the foreign-born population: 2009. *American Community Survey Briefs*. Washington DC: U.S. Census Bureau.

Helms, Janet, and Tina Richardson. 1997. How "multiculturalism" obscures race and culture as differential aspects of counseling competency. In *Multicultural Counseling Competencies: Assessment, Education and Training, and Supervision*, ed. D.B. Pope-Davis and H.L.K. Coleman, 60–79. Thousand Oaks, CA: Sage.

Jezewski, Mary, and Paula Sotnik. 2001. Cultural Brokering: Providing Culturally Competent Rehabilitation Services to Foreign-Born Persons. Buffalo, NY: Center for International Rehabilitation Research Information and Exchange. http://cirrie.buffalo.edu/culture/monographs/cb.php.

———. 2005. Culture and disability services (with a focus on culture and foreign-born characteristics). In *Culture and Disability: Providing Culturally Competent Services*, ed. J.H. Stone, 15–31. Thousand Oaks, CA: Sage

Landmark, Leena, and Zhang, Dalun. 2006. Parent practices in facilitating self-determination skills: The influences of culture, socioeconomic status, and children's special education status. *TASH Connections*, 32: 5–6.

Mindess, Anna. 2006. *Reading Between the Signs: Intercultural Communication for Sign Language Interpreters*. Boston: Intercultural Press, 2006.

Nerney, Tom. 2005. Self-determination after a decade. *TASH Connections* 3/4: 3–5.

Nerney, Tom, and Donald Shumway. 1996. *Beyond Managed Care: Self-Determination for Persons with Developmental Disabilities*. Concord: University of New Hampshire Press.

Nevid, Jeffery. 2009. *Psychology: Concepts and Applications*. Boston: Houghton Mifflin.

Nirje, B. 1972. The right to self-determination. In, *Normalization,* ed. W. Wolfensberger, 176–193. Toronto: National Institute on Mental Retardation.

Smith, Phil, and Christie Routel. 2010. Transition failure: The cultural bias of self-determination and the journey to adulthood for people with disabilities. *Disability Studies Quarterly* 30(1). www.dsq-sds.org/article/view/1012/1224.

Sotnik, Paula, and Mary Ann Jezewski. 2005. Culture and disability services. In *Culture and Disability: Providing Culturally Competent Services*, ed. J.H. Stone, 15–30. New York: Sage.

Turnbull, Ann, and Rutherford Turnbull. 2006. Self-determination: Is a rose by any other name still a rose? *Research and Practice for Persons with Severe Disabilities* 31(1): 1–6.

Turnbull, Rutherford, Gwen Beegle, and Matthew Stowe. 2001. The core concepts of disability policy affecting families who have children with disabilities. *Journal of Disability Policy Studies* 12(3): 133–143.

U.S. Department of Justice. 1993. *Title II Technical Assistance Manual*. Washington, DC: U.S. Department of Justice. www.ada.gov/taman2.html.

Wehmeyer, Michael. 1996. Self-determination as an educational outcome: Why is it important to children, youth and adults with disabilities? In *Self-Determination Across the Life Span: Independence and Choice for People with Disabilities*, ed. D.J. Sands and M.L. Wehmeyer, 15–34. Baltimore: Paul H. Brookes.

Wehmeyer, Michael, and M. Schwartz. 1998. The relationship between self-determination and quality of life for adults with mental retardation. *Education and Training in Mental Retardation and Developmental Disabilities*, 33 (1): 3–12.

Wehmeyer, Michael, Brian Abery, D. Mithaug, and Roger Stancliffe. 2003. *Theory in self-determination: Foundations for educational practic*e. Springfield, IL: Charles Thomas Publisher.

Cultural Competency in Health Care

Standards, Practices, and Measures

RaJade M. Berry-James

As we entered the new millennium, America's population grew by 13 percent; almost one-third of all Americans were members of a minority group; and in almost one out of every five homes, a language other than English was spoken (U.S. Census Bureau 2000). Population projections show that by the year 2050, nearly half of all Americans will be non-white (U.S. Census Bureau 2004). The richness of America's diversity requires public sector professionals to broaden their *awareness* of cultural and social differences as well as promote positive *attitudes* toward developing cultural competency. The pursuit of cultural competency represents a window of opportunity in America that expands traditional knowledge, skills, and abilities (KSAs) into more effective KSAs that promote a public sector workforce who possesses the knowledge, skills, abilities, awareness, and attitudes to eliminate the existing gap or divide that exists between cultural and social groups in the United States. If we fail to focus our efforts on the changing demography of America, we blindly widen the "cultural divide"—creating more profound disparities in education, employment, housing, justice, health (physical, mental, and emotional), citizen engagement, and overall quality of life.

Cultural competence as a standard of care is a very important strategy that embodies two main concepts: culture and competence. *Culture* is defined as "the integrated patterns of human behavior that include the language, thoughts, communications, actions, customs, beliefs, values and institutions of racial, ethnic, religious or social groups and *competence* implies having the capacity to function effectively as an individual and an organization within the context of the cultural beliefs, behaviors, and needs presented by consumers and their communities" (Cross et al. 1989a). As such, cultural competence should be pursued as a set of behaviors, attitudes, policies, and practices that collectively lead to improvements in the quality of services provided to consumer groups—recognizing that these competencies significantly impact the quality of services, influence consumer engagement, and improve overall outcomes for all consumers (Lewin Group 2002). Linguistic competence is the "capacity of an organization to communicate effectively, and convey information in a manner that is easily understood by diverse audiences which may (1) include persons of limited

English proficiency (LEP), (2) those who have low literacy skills or who are not literate, as well as (3) individuals with disabilities" (Cross et al. 1989b). Our public commitment to achieving cultural and linguistic competence plays a significant role in reducing disparities that continues to exist among cultural and social groups.

In assessing cultural competency in the field of public affairs and administration, we must focus our attention on three key approaches. First, public administrators must construct an operational definition that integrates their KSAs with their attitudes and awareness of cultural and social groups. Second, researchers and practitioners in the field of public administration and affairs must recognize that the process of achieving cultural competence evolves along a continuum and that the acquisition of cultural knowledge about cultural and social groups should be used to promote efficiency and effectiveness. Third, the pursuit of cultural competence must be connected to the standards of delivering culturally and linguistically appropriate services and the identification of cultural and social differences. These key suggestions go beyond establishing best practices for program development and service delivery. The process of promoting cultural competency dictates that public administrators must first obtain cultural information about themselves, their organizations, and their constituents before applying that cultural knowledge to the development and delivery of culturally and linguistically appropriate goods and services serving distinct social and cultural groups. While achieving cultural competency in the public sector requires the development of theoretical, technical, and practical knowledge, a cultural inventory of public administrators serves to strengthen an agency's ability to solve problems, adapt to change, and effectively and efficiently serve its constituents. These behaviors, attitudes, practices, and policies allow public sector agents to understand, appreciate, and work with individuals from cultures other than their own as long as those agents demonstrate awareness and acceptance of cultural differences, self-awareness, and knowledge of the consumer's culture and have the ability to adapt their professional skills to meet the needs of the consumers (McManus 1988). To bridge the cultural divide, it is then necessary for systems, agencies, and service providers to develop the capacity to respond to the unique needs of populations whose cultures are different from mainstream America and to interact effectively with individuals from a wide array of cultures (Isaacs and Benjamin 1991).

This chapter explores cultural and linguistic competency as a strategy to reduce health-care disparities among cultural and social groups. Using health care as a case study, it begins by offering practical suggestions for public sector professionals and encouraging organizational assessments to bridge the cultural divide. The author of this chapter promotes national standards for culturally and linguistically appropriate services (CLAS) in health care as we begin our journey toward cultural proficiency—emphasizing public sector professionals to increase their own awareness and understanding of cultural differences when implementing culturally and linguistically responsive programs. More importantly, this chapter offers a framework through which progress on cultural proficiency in public service can be evaluated. Along our journey toward culturally proficiency, we face two important evaluative questions: How do we measure for cultural competency in our journey toward cultural proficiency? And what does our public sector journey toward cultural proficiency look like?

PERSPECTIVES ON HEALTH AND HEALTH CARE

O'Sullivan, Rassel, and Berner note that case studies are often "the preferred research strategy if one wants to learn the details about how something happened and why it may have happened." In fact, these researchers assert that public administrators who want to investigate a social phenomenon should utilize a case study approach to examine a program or a policy that has had remarkable success; programs or policies that have unique ambiguous outcomes; and situations where actors' behavior is discretionary (O'Sullivan, Rassel, and Berner 2008, 40). Cultural competency policies and programs that address disparities in health and health care are unique in that a *national standard* has been developed for health and health care to promote cultural competency care, suggest organizational mandates, and recommend organizational infrastructure. As a case study, the use of cultural competence standards to improve health and health-care outcomes for Americans has had some success, especially in service areas where the status quo has been challenged. The use of cultural competence standards in the delivery of health and health care challenges public sector professionals to reexamine the unique characteristics of those cultural and social groups served, to develop programs that promote a new *standard of care* in an effort to improve the delivery of public goods and services, and to address the social implications of missed opportunities to care for America's underserved populations.

Using the health-care industry as a case study, research on cultural competency in health care highlights key perspectives on public policy, programs, and initiatives. For example, researchers at the Center for Health Equity Research and Promotion (CHERP) report that disparities in health and health care result from many factors. Accordingly they define *health disparities* as "differences in the prevalence, mortality, and burden of disease and other adverse health conditions that exist among specific population groups" and distinguish them from *health-care disparities*, which are "differences in access, process, and structure of healthcare among specific population groups" (CHERP 2010). According to CHERP, the following four factors have led to health and health-care disparities:

1. *Social and environmental factors*, whereby social factors include racial segregation, social cohesion, and income disparity and environmental factors involve living or working in contaminated or unsafe communities;
2. *System and policy factors*, whereby system factors refer to insurers, public health, Medicare, Medicaid, and the Veterans Administration and policy factors refer to organizational and clinical decision making, staff of health-care facilities, and the lack of health insurance for specific population groups;
3. *Individual factors*, referring to the genetic or biological differences among racial, ethnic, and gendered groups, including aspects of culture or religion that might prevent people from seeking treatment for a certain illness; and
4. *Provider factors*, referring to the knowledge, attitudes, practice patterns, communication, and cultural competence of doctors, nurses, and treatment staff.

Among cultural and social groups, differences in care contribute to health disparities that affect consumer morbidity, mortality, health status, and functional status and can also contribute to health-care disparities, which affect consumers' access to care, the structure of care, the process of care, and consumer satisfaction (CHERP 2010).

Researchers continue to identify how individual perceptions and institutional practices impact treatment outcomes for cultural and social population groups. In *Unequal Treatment: Confronting Racial and Ethnic Disparities in Health Care*, published by the National Academies Press, Smedley, Stith, and Nelson found that "racial and ethnic minorities tend to receive a lower quality of health care when compared to non-minorities, even when access-related factors, such as patient's insurance status and income, are the same or similar" (2003, 1). Provider prejudice and stereotyping continue to affect clinical decision making; research in this area suggests that some physicians believe that minority patients are less likely to comply with medical advice and are more likely to abuse alcohol and drugs (Van Ryn and Burke 2000). Clinical encounters that involve stereotyping, biases, and uncertainty on the part of health-care providers contribute to the health-care gap between racial and ethnic groups in the United States (Smedley, Stith, and Nelson 2003). The link between provider treatment and client outcomes, especially among minority clients, continues to be a significant one.

Over the past five years, trend data from the National Healthcare Disparities Report (NHDR) describe access to health care and quality of health care as a major challenge for cultural and social groups, particularly for racial and ethnic minorities, low-income groups, women, children, the elderly, residents of rural areas, and individuals with disabilities and special health-care needs. In the most recent report of 2007, the NHDR indicates that quality of health care and access to health care for cultural and social groups have gotten significantly worse or remained unchanged over a five-year period. To report progress in this area, researchers at the Agency for Healthcare Research and Quality (AHRQ) measure quality in four dimensions (effectiveness, patient safety, timeliness, and patient centeredness) over four stages of care (staying healthy, getting better, living with illness or disability, and coping with the end of life) and measure health-care access in two dimensions (facilitators and barriers to care and health-care utilization) (AHRQ 2007). Despite progress made on some grounds, AHRQ (2007) suggests that "disparities in quality and access for minority groups and poor populations remain unchanged since first measures were reported in 2000." In fact, trend data on quality of health care and access to health care appear to suggest that noticeable gaps are widening and persistent gaps still exist among minority groups regarding new AIDS cases, immunizations against pneumonia, lack of prenatal care, and communication with health-care providers. Further, better quality of health care is positively correlated with patients who have insurance. This news is consistent with similar trend analysis of NHDR data in 2005, 2004, and 2003. Researchers working on the NHDR found black and Hispanics reported that health-care professionals lacked the cultural and professional competence to reduce disparities and close health-care gaps (AHRQ 2005). When quality of care was examined in relation to issues of cultural competence, these data showed that higher proportions of black and Hispanic parents and guardians (of adolescent clients) reported that health-care providers "sometimes or never" listened carefully to them, "sometimes or never" explained things clearly to them, "sometimes or never" respected what the adult had to say, and "sometimes or never" spent enough time with them (AHRQ 2005). Inasmuch as health and health-care disparities are pervasive in our health-care system, differences in provider treatment and patient outcomes represent a national crisis for the United States (AHRQ 2003). Health-care disparities, in particular, carry a significant "personal and societal price"—including lost productivity, needless disability, and early death (AHRQ 2003, 2004b). Our journey toward cultural proficiency must remain focused on eliminating health and health-care disparities for cultural and social groups—embracing cultural competence as a standard of care is essential to eliminating the persistent gaps in access to health care and quality of health care. Focusing our national efforts and initiatives on improving the overall health of America's cultural and social groups translates into policy and programs that speak to the greater good.

The U.S. Office of Minority Health (OMH) has focused on reducing health disparities by facilitating conversations with health-care organizations to embrace holistic approaches like "cultural competence" as a standard of care. Following the work of OMH, several federal agencies within the U.S. Department of Health and Human Services (HHS) have adopted cultural competence as an initiative that is central to their mission to provide effective services to health-care consumers. The Substance Abuse and Mental Health Services Administration (SAMHSA), for example, has long recognized the correlation between cultural competence and eliminating health disparities. SAMHSA (2010) continues to assert that "American Indians and Alaska Natives, African Americans, Asian Americans, Native Hawaiian and Other Pacific Islanders and Latinos bear a disproportionately high burden of disability from mental and substance use disorders due to barriers to access and poor engagement in services compounded with endemic social risk factors" (16). According to SAMHSA, effective practices in the behavioral health system must "respect and understand the histories, traditions, beliefs, language, sociopolitical contexts and cultures of diverse racial and ethnic populations and use this information to improve access, quality of services and outcomes of care" (SAMHSA 2010, 16). SAMSHA's community-based service delivery model to help young children and their families uses a "systems of care" approach to ensure that the mental health and health-care needs of children and youth and their families are met. The "systems of care" approach focuses on youth services that are family-driven, youth-guided, and evidence-based and that emphasize clinical excellence as well as cultural and linguistic competence (U.S. DHHS 2010; Goode and Jackson 2003). SAMHSA's systems of care approach includes a network of family, school, and community members as key partners to address the physical, emotional, intellectual, cultural, and social needs of youth seeking treatment for mental health needs (U.S. DHHS 2010). Based on this new standard of care for America's youth, the systems of care approach is seen as a community partnership to provide comprehensive support for families of youth who are living with or at risk of experiencing serious emotional disturbances (U.S. DHHS 2010).

CULTURAL COMPETENCE AS A STANDARD OF CARE

The National Standards for Culturally and Linguistically Appropriate Services (CLAS) consist of fourteen recommended standards organized into three broad areas: (1) culturally competent care, (2) language access services, and (3) organizational supports for cultural competence (see Figure 11.1). Standards 1 through 3 are *guidelines* to ensure that health-care organizations provide consumers with culturally appropriate health care, promote staff diversity, and encourage staff education and training. Standards 4 through 7 were originally developed as *mandates* that minimized cultural, language, and communication barriers for health-care consumers with limited English proficiency. Standards 8 through 14 are *guidelines* for health-care organizations to develop culturally responsive environments that integrate self-assessments, organizational assessments, and needs assessments into the delivery of culturally and linguistically appropriate programs and activities.

CULTURALLY COMPETENT CARE

CLAS standards 1 through 3 focus on "culturally competent care" that health-care organizations can use to attract, retain, and promote personnel that possess the knowledge, skills, abilities, attitudes, and awareness to ensure that respectful, understandable, and effective care is provided to all consumers. Several researchers have focused on strategies that promote culturally competent care. For example, Goode (2000) and the National Center for Cultural Competence (2004) recommend that health-care organizations promote cultural diversity and cultural competence by paying particular attention to the physical environment of the service area, the materials and resources given to health-care consumers, the communication style used to address families seeking care, and the values and attitudes of health-care staff. As a best practice, Goode suggests that culturally competent organizations and/or programs use print and media resources that reflect the diversity of their health-care consumers, use written materials that reflect the level of education and English-proficiency levels of health-care consumers, and speak plainly to health-care consumers and their families when communicating important information about assessments, treatments, and interventions. Ultimately, culturally competent care will depend on staff's ability to remove stereotyping, cultural insensitivity, racial bias, and prejudice in health care, according to Goode (2000). In addition to the best practices noted above, organizations seeking to become more culturally competent must (1) value cultural diversity; (2) have the capacity to conduct a cultural self-assessment; (3) be able to manage the dynamics of difference; (4) be willing to institutionalize cultural knowledge; and (5) be willing to adapt service delivery to diversity within a cultural context (Cross et al. 1989b).

Developing cultural competence is a continuous process, whereby individuals and organizations move through stages of cultural destructiveness, cultural incapacity, cultural blindness, cultural pre-competence, cultural competence, and cultural proficiency (Goode 2004).

LANGUAGE ACCESS SERVICES

To significantly impact clinical care, the pursuit of cultural competency accompanies the "language access services" previously mandated by the federal government in CLAS standards 4 through 7. In their original form, these language mandates were supported by Title VI of the Civil Rights Act of 1964, which "required that all enti- ties receiving Federal financial assistance, including health care organizations, take steps to ensure the limited English proficiency persons have meaningful access to the health services that they provide" (U.S. DHHS 2001a, 8). Health-care consumers who were unable to read, speak, or understand English and consumers who needed American Sign Language were protected by this mandate. To comply with the law, organizations provided consumers with qualified language assistance services, either orally or in writing. Organizations also provided written notices to patients and con- sumers of their right to receive language assistance services, such as translation by a credible source. In addition, organizations were directed to use qualified bilingual language interpreters who had language certifications by accredited bodies and/ or who qualified as a bilingual/language interpreter through some formal process. CLAS standards 4 through 7 were the only mandated culturally competent "stan- dards" required for programs receiving federal funds. Some very practical ways in which organizations ensured that they complied with the language access services mandated by these standards included hiring bilingual and certified interpreters and advising consumers of their right to receive these services. In past years, the U.S. Department of Health and Human Services, Office of Minority Health (2001a, 9) suggested that organizations use one or all of the following methods to implement the language access standards: (1) using language identification or "I speak . . . " cards; (2) posting and maintaining signs in regularly encountered languages at all points of entry; (3) creating uniform procedures for timely and effective telephone communication between staff and LEP persons; and (4) including statements about the services available and the right to free language assistance services in appropriate non-English languages in brochures, booklets, outreach materials, and other materials that are routinely distributed to the public.

While the original method for language assistance services promised to quickly level the playing field for LEP persons, organizations reportedly found it difficult to comply with LEP mandates, citing hardships to comply with standards, unease when relying on family members as interpreters, and other concerns about coverage for LEP persons. After review of public comment, the Department of Justice helped to develop the revised HHS LEP Guidance. Rather than utilizing the methods identi- fied in the initial HHS Guidance (see Figure 11.1), the revised HHS Guidance joins other federal agencies when adopting and applying Title VI balancing factors for compliance with the language access services mandates. Four factors are now used to weigh whether health-care organizations must adhere to the Title VI provisions of the LEP mandate: (1) the number or proportion of LEP persons eligible to be served or likely to be encountered by the program or grantee; (2) the frequency with which LEP individuals come in contact with the program; (3) the nature and importance of the program, activity, or service provided by the program to people's lives; and (4) the resources available to the grantee/recipient and costs (U.S. Department of Health and Human Services 2002, 1). Some health-care organizations have become "universal model organizations" in adopting best practices to improve service access for cultural and social groups who have limited English proficiency or are literacy-challenged. For example, researchers have partnered with designers of hospital facilities to promote

Figure 11.1
National Standards for Culturally
and Linguistically Appropriate Services

Guidelines for Culturally Competent Care

1. Health-care organizations should ensure that patients/consumers receive from all staff members effective, understandable, and respectful care that is provided in a manner compatible with their cultural health beliefs and practices and preferred language.
2. Health-care organizations should implement strategies to recruit, retain, and promote at all levels of the organization a diverse staff and leadership that are representative of the demographic characteristics of the service area.
3. Health-care organizations should ensure that staff at all levels and across all disciplines receive ongoing education and training in culturally and linguistically appropriate service delivery.

Mandates for Language Access Services

4. Health-care organizations must offer and provide language assistance services, including bilingual staff and interpreter services, at no cost to each patient/customer with limited English proficiency at all points of contact, in a timely manner during all hours of operation.
5. Health-care organizations must provide to patients/consumers in their preferred language both verbal offers and written notices informing them of their right to receive language services.
6. Health-care organizations must assure the competence of language assistance provided to limited English proficient patients/consumers by interpreters and bilingual staff. Family and friends should not be used to provide interpretation services (except on request by the patient/consumer).
7. Health-care organizations must make available easily understood patient-related materials and post signage in the languages of the commonly encountered groups and/or groups represented in the service area.

Guidelines for Organizational Supports for Cultural Competence

8. Health-care organizations should develop, implement, and promote a written strategic plan that outlines clear goals, policies, operational plans, and management accountability/oversight mechanisms to provide culturally and linguistically appropriate services.
9. Health-care organizations should conduct initial and ongoing organizational self-assessments of CLAS-related activities and are encouraged to integrate cultural and linguistic competence-related measures into their internal audits, performance improvement programs, patient satisfaction assessments, and outcomes-based evaluations.
10. Health-care organizations should ensure that data on the individual patient's/consumer's race, ethnicity, and spoken and written language are collected in health records, integrated into the organization's management information systems, and periodically updated.
11. Health-care organizations should maintain a current demographic, cultural, and epidemiological profile of the community as well as a needs assessment to accurately plan for and implement services that respond to the cultural and linguistic characteristics of the service area.

12. Health care organizations should develop participatory, collaborative partnerships with communities and utilize a variety of formal and informal mechanisms to facilitate community and patient/consumer involvement in designing and implementing CLAS-related activities.

13. Health care organizations should ensure that conflict and grievance resolution processes are culturally and linguistically sensitive and capable of identifying, preventing and resolving cross-cultural conflicts or complaints by patients/consumers.

14. Health care organizations are encouraged to regularly make available to the public information about their progress and successful innovations in implementing the CLAS standards and to provide public notice in their communities about the availability of this information.

Source: U.S. Department of Health and Human Services, Office of Minority Health (2001b).

the use of universal symbols throughout hospitals. When used in addition to bilingual interpreters, multilingual signs, words, numbers, and other universal symbols (i.e., word pictures) remove barriers for LEP or literacy-challenged health-care consumers (Berger n.d.). In addition, OMH and HHS have sponsored an implementation guide to assist health-care organizations in improving access to services for LEP persons. Specifically, the Patient-Centered Guide to Implementing Language Access Services in Healthcare Organizations provides a step-by-step approach to implementing language access services (LAS) in health-care organizations seeking to close the language disparities gap. The steps and resource units to LEP implementation include the following: (1) assessing the language needs of patients; (2) assessing organizational capabilities; (3) planning and implementing language access services; and (4) evaluating the quality of language access services (U.S. Department of Health and Human Services 2005, 19–20). The LAS components support the initial HHS methods and universal symbols when broadening LEP services—they are interpretation services, written materials, signage and wayfinding, notice of LAS to LEP patients, community involvement, and written language assistance plans. The Patient-Centered Guide systematically promotes monitoring and evaluating quality of care and patient satisfaction at every stage of the process, advocating for an organizational needs assessment as well as collecting process and outcome measures to assess program compliance and service delivery. For example, at the initial stage (Step 1: Patient Language Needs Assessment), health-care organizations are encouraged to conduct a needs assessment that accounts for population trends, shift patterns, and population growth projections. At the second stage, leaders in the health-care organizations are encouraged to monitor progress toward cultural competency to ensure that staff demonstrate acceptance and respect for different people and different customs. At the third stage, organizations are encouraged to focus on interpretation services, written materials, signage and wayfinding, notice of language access services provided to LEP patients, community involvement, and written language assistance plans. At the final stage, health-care organizations are encouraged to monitor and evaluate program performance using patient satisfaction and community outreach data so that midcourse corrections in service delivery can be made (U.S. Department of Health and Human Services, 2005, 19–20).

ORGANIZATIONAL SUPPORTS

In addition to the standards that govern clinical care (culturally competent care) and nonclinical care (language assistance services) for consumers, *organizational supports* for cultural competence span across CLAS standards 8 through 14. These standards provide recommendations that public or private health-care organizations should follow to begin the process of becoming culturally proficient. Organizational support standards provide practical suggestions on how organizations can implement the CLAS standards, assess individual and organizational competence, and collect information that documents the process of becoming culturally proficient. As a starting point, health-care organizations should incorporate CLAS standards into their written strategic plan as well as conduct organizational self-assessments of CLAS-related activities. In addition, organizations should regularly conduct needs assessments to ensure that their programs and services reach the community served. To ensure that the organization's medical record system accurately captures important client information, the medical record system should be updated to include the race, ethnicity, and spoken and written language of the health-care consumer. Finally, the ability of the health-care organization to meet the cultural needs and expectations of the community should be documented through a cultural assessment process and regularly shared with members of the community.

The following suggestions were adapted from the National Center for Cultural Competence and other models to help organizations begin the journey toward cultural competency. According to the National Center for Cultural Competence, organizations should focus on the following six steps:

1. Convene a workgroup to develop a *cultural competence plan* for assessing competence in your organization, addressing disparities among your consumers and your employees, institutionalizing cultural competence at all levels of the organization, and identifying measurable objectives that will be reviewed annually, evaluated (and reevaluated), and disseminated widely in order to get feedback from all, stakeholders (employees, consumers, and community leaders) in the organization.
2. Revise organizational *mission statements* to include a defined set of culturally competent values and principles.
3. Create new *policies and procedures* to demonstrate behaviors, attitudes, processes and structures that enable and support effective cross-cultural practices as well as identify personnel and performance measures, including skill sets that recognize and support cultural and linguistic competency.
4. Improve *service delivery* to ensure that cultural and linguistic services can be provided to those you serve.
5. Incorporate the cultural competence plan into all aspects of policy development, administration, and service delivery and *dedicate resources* to implement it.

6. Systematically *involve consumers and personnel* in evaluating organizational competence through consumer review committees, community outreach efforts, and consumer and personnel satisfaction surveys.

Many cultural and social groups living in the United States seek specialized services from health-care organizations—often, treatment is multidimensional and complex, even when cultural and linguistic barriers do not exist. To ensure culturally effective health care, providers first must possess the knowledge, skills, and abilities that correlate with effective health-care delivery (Tirado 1998). Communication with cultural and social groups begins by developing a rapport and trust with family members; by demonstrating that providers have the ability to assess relevant cultural factors in the patient's health history (socioeconomic influences, educational attainment, family structure and dynamics, cultural beliefs and practices, ethnic origin and identification, and language preferences); by understanding patients' perspective on their health problems; and by recognizing any cultural misunderstandings (Fleming and Towey 2003). In its broadest sense, cultural competence involves the willingness of individuals and organizations to learn about people or groups of people who differ based on race, ethnicity, language, gender, religion, and class in order to provide essential services to address health, behavioral, and social needs. This knowledge, coupled with the right attitude and awareness of self and others, can then be transformed into specific standards, policies, practices, and attitudes that can be embraced by those who interact with health-care systems—those who work in health-care systems as well as those who are consumers of health-care systems. The most qualified professionals are aware of the distinctions between cultural and linguistic groups and possess at minimum the knowledge, skills, and abilities to translate this professional perspective into culturally appropriate approaches designed to treat health-care consumers from culturally and linguistically diverse communities.

The collective knowledge, skills, and abilities of health-care professionals help shape the way we develop and deliver programs. These essential elements are manifested in the type of care that is provided to cultural and social groups (Tirado 1998). Because of our cultural and linguistic differences, we have a remarkable opportunity to expand our knowledge base, to identify our similarities, and to recognize our differences as strengths. Families seeking treatment, education, and care can rely on a systems of care approach with the hope that intervention, prevention, and treatment will lead to improvements in emotional, mental, and physical health as well as quality of life. As a community of partners, we should see cultural competence as the paradigm through which we view social problems, create public policies, and implement programs and services. In this regard, we are able to build a legacy of exceptional service through our cultural KSAs—cultural knowledge, cultural skills, cultural abilities, cultural attitudes, and cultural awareness.

BIG QUESTIONS FOR THE FIELD: WHAT IS *IT* AND CAN WE MEASURE *IT*?

In the field of public affairs and administration, we are struggling to answer the big questions—what is cultural competency and can we measure cultural competency?

In our quest to rely on scientific inquiry to assess cultural competency, we seek valid measures that help us understand health-care disparities. In theory, our journey toward cultural proficiency broadens our knowledge base on group differences in such a way that we develop, implement, and evaluate the effectiveness of health-care programs. However, in practice we seek implementation measurements that help us compare "where we are" with "where we ought to be." Even without an agreed-upon measurement standard for cultural competency, what we know is that disparities among cultural and social groups continue to exist in health and health care. These racial, ethnic, gender, and language disparities have profoundly impacted the delivery of public goods and services and encouraged those interested in closing the cultural divide to ignore a one-size-fits-all strategy or one-best-way approach. While the big questions in our field are often cast in terms of "what is" and "what ought to be," the utility of cultural knowledge moves us along the continuum toward cultural proficiency. If social science is concerned with the discovery of truth, we must use what we know about cultural and social differences to assess these cultural matters to help us evaluate the effectiveness of our public policies. Our ability to describe, explore, explain, and predict cultural competency in the public sector is a developmental process that examines the role of the public sector professional within the context of an organization that supports (or fails to support) program implementation efforts to incorporate new knowledge into a wider range of practice (Goode 2004).

In *Evaluating Public Policy*, Fischer (1995, 1) points out that public policy analysis is a practical deliberation that integrates empirical and normative inquiry into the evaluation process. Fischer's policy deliberation model involves assigning a value or worth to a policy so that we explore how policy goals contribute to the values established for our society. Empirically, our cultural competency framework examines the collective knowledge, skills, abilities, awareness, and attitudes of public sector professionals as policies are crafted and programs are delivered to serve a culturally diverse citizenry. From a normative perspective, our cultural competency framework focuses on the standards that were developed to link our collective social action to our social values. According to Fischer, public policy defines the problem to be addressed, identifies the policy evaluation in terms of whether or not a program achieves its stated goals and objectives, and, more importantly, considers whether the program is what society *ought* to be doing. Fischer points out that factual knowledge often influences how society views whether policies achieve social good. From this perspective, he asserts that factual knowledge influences our judgments about social policies even as we exchange ideas around our civil right to culturally appropriate and linguistic services. Doing what is right will be a matter of social choice, especially as we struggle to assess and evaluate our journey toward cultural competency within all aspects of an organization.

In the public health sector, we must use an evaluative framework that is set against the CLAS standards of care adopted by the Department of Health and Human Services. Merit, worth, and significance help to separate policy goals from political promises. Responsible governance promotes the use of measures for cultural competency among four levels of discourse as identified in the policy deliberation model—we must verify through quasi-experimental research the impact of culturally and linguistically appropriate services; we must validate how social phenomena contribute to cultural disparities; we must further explain how the behaviors of public sector professionals and the practices of organizations contribute to disparities in health and health care; and finally, we must make the social choice to adopt laws and develop regulations that end disparities in health and health care for cultural and social groups. The significance of promoting cultural competency as a social good may seem farfetched and difficult to achieve given that public service organizations continue to struggle with assessing where their attitudes, practices, and policies fall on the cultural competence continuum.

In summary, our journey toward cultural proficiency is complicated by the fact that politicians, public administrators, and public sector advocates continue to grapple with these basic questions: what is cultural competency and can we measure cultural competency? To set the research agenda for cultural competence in health care, Fortier and Bishop (2003) suggest that we need to employ universal evaluation approaches that link performance activities to improved health-care delivery and better health outcomes for cultural and social groups. Health-care providers and policy makers seek answers to questions related to access and outcomes, quality and reduction in errors, cost, and comparative analyses for approaches and interventions (Fortier and Bishop 2003, 4). Applying a quantitative framework to assess how health-care organizations use cultural knowledge to improve the delivery of health care is important to measuring the journey toward cultural proficiency. However, one of the major challenges facing the field of public affairs and administration is the inability of researchers to conduct a comprehensive assessment of the impact of culturally competent approaches, programs, and practices. We lack an agreed-upon approach that links program resources, activities, outputs, audiences, and outcomes (short-term, intermediate, and long-term) related to the problem of cultural and social disparities. In health care, however, there is an agreed-upon standard or guideline that describes cultural competence as a journey where contemplation of cultural competency begins with discovery. To prevent individual perspectives and institutional practices from translating into barriers to effective service delivery, the journey toward cultural competency begins with self-awareness. Many instruments are widely available to measure our progress toward cultural competency—some of which yield data that provide insight into our ability to justify how scarce resources are used to close the cultural disparities gap. Yet some social scientists question whether these tools really measure what they intend to measure or measure the same cultural phenomenon over and over again since they lack reliability and validity. As a single-source repository, the *Cultural and Linguistic Competence Implementation Guide* is the most comprehensive guide found in the literature to date. The *Guide*, developed by Martinez and Van Buren (2008), operationalizes cultural competency in the public health sector and identifies the ways in which culturally competent processes can be fully implemented at the policy, administrative, practice, and consumer levels. To assess cultural competency from an organizational framework, the researchers link implementation strategies, community examples, best practices, resources and tools, and performance indicators and measures to six areas within organizations: governance and organizational infrastructure; services and supports; planning and continuous quality improvements; collaboration; communication; and workforce development (Martinez and Van Buren 2008, 5–6).

When we ask the question "Where do we go from here?" we must realize that our journey is measured by our ability to achieve our social goals—life is individual, life is social, and ultimately our progress is measured by our social choices. Where we go from here rests with our ability to conduct self-assessments, promote organizational assessments, and develop a cultural knowledge base to meet the needs of consumers of public goods and services. Our quest to provide meaningful solutions to the cultural divide should include an evaluative framework that measures, empirically and normatively, where we are along the cultural competency continuum.

References

Adams, Diane L., ed. 1995. *Health Issues for Women of Color: A Cultural Diversity Perspective.* Thousand Oaks, CA: Sage.

Agency for Healthcare Research and Quality (AHRQ). 2003. National healthcare disparities report. U.S. Department of Health and Human Services. Rockville, MD. www.ahrq.gov/qual/nhdr03/nhdr03.htm.

———. 2004a. Letter from Director Carolyn Clancy on the national healthcare disparities report. U.S. Department of Health and Human Services. Rockville, MD. www.ahrq.gov/qual/nhdr03/letter.htm.

———. 2004b. National healthcare disparities report, 2004. U.S. Department of Health and Human Services. Rockville, MD. www.ahrq.gov/qual/nhdr04/nhdr04.htm.

———. 2005. National healthcare disparities report, 2005. U.S. Department of Health and Human Services. Rockville, MD. www.ahrq.gov/qual/nhdr05/nhdr05.htm.

———. 2007. 2007 national healthcare quality report—at a glance. Rockville, MD. www.ahrq.gov/qual/nhqr07/Glance.htm.

Berger, Craig. n.d. *Universal Symbols in Healthcare Workbook: Best Practices for Sign Systems.* Executive summary. www.hablamosjuntos.org/signage/PDF/Best%20PracticesFINALDec05.pdf.

Center for Health Equity Research and Promotion (CHERP). 2010. Introduction to the health disparities primer. Office of Veterans Affairs. www.cherp.org/primer3.php.

Cross, Terry. 1998. *Towards a Culturally Competent System of Care: A Monograph on Effective Services for Minority Children Who Are Severely Emotionally Disturbed.* Washington, DC: Georgetown University Child Development Center, CASSP Technical Assistance Center.

Cross, Terry, Barbara Bazron, Karl Dennis, and Mareasa Isaacs. 1989a. Cultural competence in serving children and adolescents with mental health problems. Substance Abuse Mental Health Services Administration, Washington, DC. www.eric.ed.gov/PDFS/ED461221.pdf.

———. 1989b. *Towards a Culturally Competent System of Care*, vol. I. Washington, DC: Georgetown University Child Development Center, CASSP Technical Assistance Center.

Fischer, Frank. 1995. *Evaluating Public Policy.* Chicago: Nelson-Hall.

Fleming, Missy, and Kelly Towey. 2003. Delivering cultural effective health care to adolescents: A guide for primary health care providers. American Medical Association. www.ama-assn.org/ama1/pub/upload/mm/39/culturallyeffective.pdf.

Fortier, Julia P., and Dawn Bishop. 2003. Setting the agenda for research on cultural competence in health care: Final report. Rockville, MD: U.S. Department of Health and Human Services Office of Minority Health and Agency for Healthcare Research and Quality.

Goode, Tawara D. 2000. Promoting cultural competence and cultural diversity in early intervention and early childhood settings and promoting cultural competence and cultural diversity for personnel providing services and supports to children with special health care needs and their families.

Washington, DC: National Center for Cultural Competence, Georgetown University Center for Child and Human Development. www11.georgetown.edu/research/gucchd/nccc/documents/Checklist. CSHN.doc.pdf.

———. 2004. Cultural competence continuum. Washington, DC: National Center for Cultural Competence, Georgetown University Center for Child and Human Development. www.nccccurricula. info/documents/TheContinuumRevised.doc.

Goode, Tawara, and Vivian Jackson. 2003. Getting started and moving on: Planning, implementing and evaluating cultural and linguistic competency for comprehensive community mental health services for children and families: Implications for systems of care. Washington, DC: National Center for Cultural Competence, Georgetown University Center for Child and Human Development. http:// nccc.georgetown.edu/documents/Getting_Started_SAMHSA.pdf.

Goode, Tawara, Wendy Jones, and James Mason. 2002. A guide to planning and implementing cultural competence organizational self-assessment. Washington, DC: National Center for Cultural Competence, Georgetown University Center for Child and Human Development. http://gucchd.georgetown. edu/products/OrganizationalSelfAssessment.pdf.

HHSLEP Guidance. www.hhs.gov/ocr/civilrights/resources/laws/revisedlep.html.

Isaacs, Mareasa R., and J.P. Benjamin. 1991. *Towards a culturally competent system of care*, vol. 2. Washington, DC: Georgetown University Child Development Center, CASSP Technical Assistance Center.

Lewin Group. 2002. HRSA indicators of cultural competence in health care delivery organizations: An organizational cultural competence assessment profile. Report, April. www.hrsa.gov/Cultural-Competence/healthdlvr.pdf.

Martinez, Kenneth, and Erika Van Buren. 2008. *The Cultural and Linguistic Competence Implementation Guide*. Washington, DC: Technical Assistance Partnership for Child and Family Mental Health. www.tapartnership.org/COP/CLC/implementationGuide.php.

McManus, Marilyn C., ed. 1988. Services to minority populations: What does it mean to be a culturally competent professional? *Focal Point: A National Bulletin on Family Support and Children's Mental Health* 2(4): 1–16.

National Center for Cultural Competence. 2004. Planning for cultural and linguistic competence in state Title V programs serving children and youth with special health care needs and their families. Washington, DC. http://nccc.georgetown.edu/documents/NCCC%20Title%20V%20Checklist%20 %28CSHCN%29.pdf.

Ohio Department of Alcohol and Drug Addiction Services. 2006. Strategic plan update on cultural competence. Unpublished document, 33–34.

O'Sullivan, Elizabethann, Gary Rassel, and Maureen Berner. 2008. *Research Methods for Public Administrators*. 5th ed. New York: Pearson Education.

Roizner, Monica. 1996. *A Practical Guide for the Assessment of Cultural Competence in Children's Mental Health Organizations*. Boston: Judge Baker Children's Center.

Smedley, Brian, Adrienne Y. Stith, and Alan R. Nelson. 2003. *Unequal Treatment: Confronting Racial and Ethnic Disparities in Health Care*. Washington, DC: National Academies Press.

Substance Abuse and Mental Health Services Administration (SAMHSA). 2006. Results from the 2005 national survey on drug use and health: National findings. Office of Applied Studies, NSDUH Series H-30, DHHS Publication No. SMA 06–4194. Rockville, MD.

———. 2010. Leading change: A plan for SAMHSA's roles and actions, 2011–2014. Draft report, October 1. www.samhsa.gov/about/sidocs/SAMHSA_SI_paper.pdf.

Tirado, Miguel D. 1998. *Monitoring the Managed Care of Culturally and Linguistically Diverse Populations*. Vienna, VA: National Clearinghouse for Primary Care Information.

U.S. Census Bureau. 2000. Fact sheet—Census 2000 demographic profile highlights. http://factfinder. census.gov/servlet/SAFFFacts.

———. 2004. U.S. interim projections by age, sex, race, and Hispanic origin. www.census.gov/ population/www/projections/usinterimproj/natprojtab01a.pdf.

U.S. Department of Health and Human Services (U.S. DHHS). 2002. Fact sheet on guidance to federal financial assistance recipients regarding Title VI prohibition against national origin discrimination affecting limited English proficient (LEP) persons. www.hhs.gov/ocr/civilrights/resources/special-topics/lep/factsheetguidanceforlep.html.

U.S. Department of Health and Human Services, Center for Mental Health Services. 2010. Addressing the mental health needs of young children and their families: Systems of care. Substance Abuse and Mental Health Administration. http://store.samhsa.gov/shin/content//SMA10-4547/SMA10-4547.pdf.

U.S. Department of Health and Human Services, Office of Minority Health. 2000. Assuring cultural competence in health care: Recommendations for national standards and an outcomes-focused research agenda. www.omhrc.gov/clas/finalpo.htm.

———. 2001a. National standards for culturally and linguistically appropriate services in health care: Final report. Washington, DC.

———. 2001b. National standards for culturally and linguistically appropriate services in health care. Executive summary, March, 5–18. www.omhrc.gov/assets/pdf/checked/executive.pdf.

———. 2005. A patient-centered guide to implementing language access services in healthcare organizations. https://hclsig.thinkculturalhealth.hhs.gov/Documents/HCLS-IG.pdf.

Van Ryn, Michelle, and Jane Burke. 2000. The effect of patient race and socio-economic status on physicians' perceptions of patients. *Social Science Medicine* 50: 813–828.

Cultural Competency in Disasters

Frances L. Edwards

There is no point in "doing good badly." Examples of well-meant intervention in disaster that turns into disaster in itself are legion. Recently, Nancy Gibbs wrote in *Time* magazine about the frequently well-meant, but ill-received, responses to disasters, including woolen blankets sent to the 2004 Asian tsunami victims, and outdated or unneeded medicines that had to be discarded by the receiving government. The victims of the 2005 Pakistan earthquake used the inappropriate donated clothing, including ball gowns and Santa Claus suits, as fuel for their fires while they faced the freezing fall temperatures in their mountain community living in military tents (Gibbs 2010).

In many cases the urge to "do good badly" is based on a lack of cultural competency. American donors of wool blankets to Southeast Asia did not understand how hot and humid it is there all year round. The donors of inappropriate clothing did not understand the climate and lifestyle of the people of northern Pakistan. The well-meant urge to assist actually became an impediment to assistance, as logistics support was wasted transporting the useless donations, and the beleaguered local emergency response agencies had to cope with discarding unwanted donated goods along with the disaster debris already in the community.

While it may not be reasonable to expect the average American donor to appreciate the nuances of cultural differences, it is crucial that emergency management professionals recognize the differences among cultural, ethnic, and special need groups in a community, and their varying needs across all four phases of emergency management.

CULTURAL COMPETENCY CONSIDERED

Cultural competency is essential for anyone providing emergency mitigation, planning, and response or recovery services to people whose ethnicity, education level, and socioeconomic circumstances differ from the provider's. "Cultural competence may best be described by three characteristics: obtaining knowledge about specific people and groups of people; integrating and transforming this knowledge into specific standards, policies, practices, and attitudes; and using these tools to increase the quality of services and produce better outcomes" (Davis 1997).

The importance of cultural competency in delivering effective postdisaster mental health services was noted by Jones et al. (2008) in the report on their postdisaster services to a predominantly African American community after Hurricane Katrina in 2005. They noted that minority groups and marginalized populations will receive the most effective assistance from people they already know: "Thus, psychologists will benefit from partnering with established community organizations within a disaster area … [C]ollaborating with community agencies allows psychologists to obtain valuable information on the most effective ways to reach out to minority group members in a disaster area" (Jones et al. 2008, 105). Similarly, emergency managers should look to the leaders of diverse communities for guidance in developing and delivering services across all four phases of emergency management.

Jones et al. note that while help is readily accepted from anyone during the acute phase of a disaster response, after the crisis people are more selective about the sources of assistance that they are willing to access. This provides a second rationale for creating partnerships between government programs and existing community resources. "Relatives, friends, churches, and community agencies are more likely to be called on than outsiders" in the postdisaster phase (Jones et al. 2008, 105), so community emergency managers should work with these resources in the development phase of emergency management recovery programs.

Cultural competency has also been addressed in the international business literature, where a lack of cultural competency is blamed for many of the failures of international business ventures. Johnson, Lenartowicz, and Apud (2006, 526) note that "contextual influences can impede effective cross-cultural communication" in a business environment, and this is equally true in a postdisaster environment. This business-related literature should inform the development of emergency management programs, where understanding the community "customers" is crucial to getting their cooperation during a disaster.

There is substantial literature on cross-cultural communication in the American environment, triggered by the federal government's interest in the delivery of effective medical and education services to American minority populations. A notable example is the cultural competency training created by the Department of Health and Human Services' (DHHS) Office of Minority Health (OMH). The federal OMH has created online training programs in cultural competency to equip emergency responders and volunteers to provide effective services to diverse communities during disasters. Cultural Competency Curriculum for Disaster Preparedness and Crisis Response emphasizes "working with an interpreter, locating translated materials, negotiating cultural differences" as a means to improve the outcome for minority disaster victims, who have historically experienced greater disaster impacts (DHHS 2008a).

OMH created a standard called CLAS to enhance the delivery of disaster services: *c*ulturally competent care, *l*anguage access services, *a*nd organizational *s*ervices. The goal was to lessen the disparities in care and safety experienced by racial and ethnic minorities during disasters. Looking at all hazards and three phases of disaster—preparedness, response, and recovery—the cultural competency course "focus[es] on facilitating communication during all phases of a disaster" (DHHS 2008b). The course defines five aspects of cultural competency: (1) awareness and acceptance of difference; (2) awareness of one's own cultural values; (3) understanding and managing the "dynamics of difference"; (4) development of cultural knowledge; and (5) ability to adapt activities to fit into different cultural contexts (DHHS 2008c). Applying these principles to emergency planning for all three phases will enhance the services provided to culturally diverse communities.

Hurricane Katrina provided a highly visible example of the importance of cultural competence in the delivery of emergency management services. As a result of the failure of the New Orleans evacuation process in the poor and minority neighborhoods, notably among the elderly who reportedly expressed fear of the unknown, having never left the city (Kiefer 2010), the emergency management community has reconsidered the need for predisaster training of emergency management workers and volunteers in the issues of cultural competency.

Sociologists have long described the special needs of vulnerable community members in disasters. This work both highlights the importance of cultural competency for emergency managers and provides important insights into vulnerabilities in disaster that require the application of cultural competency principles. Susan Cutter has created a Social Vulnerability Index that defines the factors likely to enhance a disaster's impact for an individual or subset of the community (Cutter and Smith 2009).

> For emergency response planning and hazard mitigation, populations can be assessed from a perspective of their vulnerability to various hazards (fire, flood, etc.). Physical vulnerability refers to a population's exposure to specific potential hazards, such as living in a designated flood plain. Social vulnerability refers to potential exposure due to population and housing characteristics: age, low income, disability, home value, or other factors. For example, low-income seniors may not have access to a car to simply drive away from an ongoing hazard such as a flood. (Cutter 2010)

Elaine Enarson has written about the special needs of women and children in disasters. Her recent work on Hurricane Katrina points to the invisible challenges of family and community recovery that are managed almost entirely by women (Enarson 2006). She was the lead author for a college-level course for the FEMA Higher Education Project called *A Social Vulnerability Approach to Disasters* (Enarson et al. 2003). This course is available as a free download at the FEMA higher education website. Brenda Phillips has also written about social vulnerability to disasters (Phillips et al. 2009) and with Betty Morrow has written about the special needs of women in disasters (Phillips and Morrow 2008).

CULTURAL COMPETENCY IN EMERGENCY MANAGEMENT'S FOUR PHASES

In the United States, the emergency management community understands emergencies in the context of four phases: mitigation, preparedness, response, and recovery. Mitigation refers to steps taken to lessen the impact of disasters that cannot be prevented. For example, levees mitigate the potential for flooding along low-lying portions of rivers, building codes strengthen a building's resistance to wind or earthquake-related shaking, while flood insurance mitigates the economic losses from flooding of property. Preparedness refers to steps taken to get ready for disasters, such as creating a community emergency operations plan, public education on the hazards in a community, and creating a family disaster plan and an emergency kit of supplies. Response refers to the activities undertaken when a disaster occurs. This includes evacuating to higher ground for an individual or family, or opening the emergency operations center, sending out search and rescue teams, and providing emergency shelters at the community level. Recovery refers to repairing the damage and getting community economic activities restarted. This includes rebuilding housing and restoring the environment.

The American "salad bowl" of cultures demands that its public administrators understand the variety of cultural norms and community expectations of residents based on their previous life experiences and cultural values. This is especially true during disaster response and recovery, when the affected population is already stressed.

Emergency management professionals need to develop cultural skills that will enable them to work with communities in a predisaster setting to provide effective public education on community threats and the need for self-reliance and resilience during response.

Sensitivity to economic, social, and religious norms that impact community outreach and education is the key to experiencing receptivity from the target population and creating an effective action agenda that leads to actual disaster preparedness across all community segments. For example, the Army Corps of Engineers has worked with Cutter to create *Social Vulnerability and Place: Vulnerability Methods and Application for Corps Planning*. "SoVI was intersected with storm surge inundation areas and 100-year floodplains to illustrate where and what contributed the most (social or hazard exposure)" to the disaster's impact on various groups (Hazards and Vulnerability 2010).

Predisaster steps include the development of relationships within the diverse community, recruitment of public employees from various backgrounds with language skills and cultural competency in other cultures, and the recruitment and training of cadres of emergency management volunteers with bilingual and bicultural skills to be available to support disaster response activities and the sheltering and temporary housing of survivors. Predisaster training is crucial to effective response and outreach during the emergency.

Emergency response in life-threatening circumstances requires the ability to effectively and clearly communicate with the affected population in a language and format that will provide lifesaving information. Both the right words and the right context are essential for engendering community action, and they may have to be delivered by nongovernment leaders, depending on the community. Clergy, educators, and nongovernment organization (NGO) leaders will be key to successful evacuation, sheltering, mass care, and movement to temporary housing. Interpreting the American emergency response and its differences from previous experiences in residents' nation of origin can be essential to achieving appropriate participation of community members in their own safety.

Recovery requires interaction not only with the local, known government bureaucracy but also with state and federal governmental agencies, disclosure of information to bureaucrats to get assistance, use of technology to register for aid, and the management of expectations among the survivors for the aid coming from various potential sources. Understanding of cultural norms and community expectations can assist in a smoother transition and lessen stress for the survivors and their families.

Cultural competency is crucial to success in all four phases of emergency management.

UNDERSTANDING AMERICAN CULTURE IN THE TWENTY-FIRST CENTURY

Years ago the United States was called a melting pot. People came to the New World from many nations with the goal of becoming "Americans." In this quest they often forfeited the language and customs of the land of their birth in favor of fitting in with the new country. Today the United States is a salad bowl of cultural expressions. People from around the world immigrate to the United States to participate in the economic milieu, but often they strive to maintain the language and traditions of their home country within the family group. Antidiscrimination legislation has enabled people to succeed in the workplace while retaining the cultural identity of their lands of origin.

CULTURE AND ETHNICITY

In earlier generations, most immigrants to the United States were young men seeking their fortunes or their young brides who joined them after some years of planning and saving (U.S. Census Bureau 1999a). Adapting to the new land was possible because they were young and highly motivated to become part of the vibrant new country. Today, many of the new residents of the United States are fleeing oppression, war, famine, or disruption in their home countries, but have no desire to assimilate. Today's immigrant may be a child or senior citizen, as well as an adult in the working years. For some of the older people, adapting to a new language and new customs is too difficult. They make a community among themselves for support and may never develop a working knowledge of written English. Many possess only a limited spoken English vocabulary (Edwards and Wong 2010).

Until the middle of the nineteenth century, most immigrants to the United States came from Western Europe (U.S. Census Bureau 1999b). These cultures of origin had many similarities to the developing "American culture." Language groups generally shared Germanic or Romance roots. If literate, most of the immigrants used the Roman alphabet and were accustomed to a phonetic written language. Since English has many words from these European roots and shared the phonetic alphabet approach to writing, immigrants could learn spoken English based on common words from their birth language and could learn to read English using a bilingual dictionary. Today, people come from cultures with languages using entirely different alphabets, including symbolic representations. The result is that many immigrants have a greater challenge learning to read and speak English because the alphabet and word roots are radically different than their birth languages.

In the early days of the American republic, most immigrants came from countries with religious practices based on Judeo-Christian traditions. As a result, cultural norms related to personal behavior and community interaction tended to be similar among the immigrant groups. In contrast, the religious backgrounds of the immigrants of the later part of the twentieth century included almost every religion and cultural tradition in the world. The cultural norms of their birth cultures may preclude interaction of some members of the culture with strangers or members of the opposite gender, in some cases leading to isolation and slowed acclimation to American cultural norms. Behavior that is unremarkable to an American may be offensive or shocking to a new resident.

The increasing diversity in American culture means that all emergency planners must be prepared to provide essential services under a variety of constraints—language barriers, literacy barriers, and special needs within a cultural context. Cultural competency will enable them to create and implement plans to serve the needs of all community members.

CULTURE AND VULNERABILITY

In addition to ethnic minorities, there are also other minority groups, sometimes referred to as "vulnerable populations," for whom cultural competency may be needed. Older people have special needs. Physically limited people of all ages will have different considerations in lifestyle and access issues. Some Americans of any ethnicity are illiterate or have only limited reading ability because of either learning disabilities or lack of effective educational opportunities. A successful emergency management program must take into account the development of methods of reaching out to the whole community in order to effectively involve residents in the development of culturally competent emergency management programs, including the ability to convey essential emergency planning and response information. The state of Missouri has created a Special Needs Toolkit with checklists like "Planning and Response Strategies for Culturally Diverse Populations" to assist emergency planners with evaluating the many types of services and materials that should be planned for (Missouri 2006).

Seniors, children, those living with physical and learning disabilities, and those unable to read English must also be considered in developing emergency management resources. Seniors can be addressed through special publications that are distributed both at general public events and at special events that draw seniors, such as health fairs. Senior centers and clubs are also effective distribution points for emergency preparedness and response information aimed at the older residents. Sometimes there are senior clubs for specific populations, such as the Vietnamese Senior Center and Japanese Senior complex in San Jose, California. These organizations may assist with the preparation and translation of appropriate materials, as well as the distribution of written materials during programs that teach emergency preparedness principles.

Children can be educated about emergency management through comic books and puzzle books. Simple picture books without words can also be used that show people behaving appropriately during an emergency. Such wordless materials are also effective for illiterate adults and non-English readers to illustrate the appropriate response to a variety of life-safety issues. The Los Angeles Chapter of the American Red Cross created an earthquake education booklet using only illustrations. That booklet was augmented with video presentations in several different languages, including English, Spanish, and Vietnamese.

Sometimes a comic book approach with words and illustrations is a good way to communicate to people of all ages with limited literacy. For example, the Southern California city of Irvine commissioned a flier on gas meter safety that extensively uses cartoons. A flier on nonstructural hazard mitigation uses illustrations to show how to accomplish the necessary tasks. Adults with limited reading ability will appreciate the simple format of a comic book like the earthquake preparedness series created by Hanna-Barbera featuring Yogi Bear. Illustrated materials can convey a serious message about earthquake preparation and response through meaningful illustrations and few words, making them more broadly accessible.

Earthquake preparedness materials for people living with disabilities are available through the Federal Emergency Management Agency (FEMA) and often from state-level emergency management agencies. Videos are also oriented toward educating people with special needs on how to prepare for disasters. For example, *Silent Quake* is a video with captions that is an excellent resource for people with hearing disabilities (American Red Cross n.d.) while also appealing to hearing audiences. Volunteer groups like Irvine's Guardian Angels for People with Disabilities can receive emergency preparedness training and then assist their special needs "buddy" with preparing the home for emergencies. Activities would include reorganizing belongings to minimize the potential for personal injuries or becoming trapped after an earthquake, and storing water, medications, and other essential items where they can be easily reached.

Psychological trauma suffered at an earlier time will affect the ability of the individual to withstand a new trauma. Researchers have described an "echo effect" (Abueg et al. 1990) that causes people to react to the current crisis by reverting to the experiences of an earlier trauma. For example, someone who has experienced an earthquake will react more strongly to a subsequent earthquake, especially if the first experience carried with it severe consequences or personal loss. Someone who has lived through a war will react more strongly to any subsequent disasters.

Some groups of immigrants are in the United States today specifically because of some tragedy in their birth country. Many Americans who were born in Southeast Asia have personal memories of wars in Cambodia, Laos, and Vietnam. Should they experience an earthquake, for example, the previous traumatic event will influence their psychological response to the new stimulus. Americans born in Central America may have similar memories of wars in Nicaragua and El Salvador. People from Nicaragua and Guatemala may also have experienced the earthquakes there in 1972 and 1976, respectively. Residents from Mexico may have experienced the Mexico City earthquake in 1985 (Dufka 1988). These individuals may have a much stronger psychological response to new trauma than will their neighbors who have not suffered a previous traumatic event.

Finally, it is important to be sensitive to economic issues within a community. Public officials should analyze the socioeconomic balance in the community before launching any program that includes a significant amount of self-help or citizen financial participation. For example, in a community with a large population of low-income renters, it may not be effective to hand out fliers on nonstructural retrofitting of the home. In such a community it would be more helpful to contact landlords regarding the importance of strapping the refrigerator so it will not fall over in an earthquake. The $25 strapping kit might be beyond the financial means of a low-income family, while in a more affluent community the homeowner might find the strap a good investment. Similarly, before launching a program to collect classroom emergency supplies like water and food bars for schools, school emergency management officials should consider whether the families can afford to donate several dollars' worth of goods that may never be used. A family of limited means with several children in the school may find that the financial burden of providing food and water donations for each child's classroom prohibitive. It might be better to contact the major industries in the community to see if they would donate the basic necessities of water and first aid supplies to the schools. For example, in the early 1990s, the Coca-Cola Bottling Company in Southgate, California, donated the emergency supplies for that city's schools.

AMERICAN CULTURAL LANDSCAPE IN THE TWENTY-FIRST CENTURY

The city of San Jose has a population of just over 1 million people, with no ethnic majority, residents with a variety of special needs, and many immigrants with limited English proficiency. This cultural diversity is today found throughout Silicon Valley. This profile can be extended to most of the rest of the state of California, as well as many other states. For emergency managers whose professional work depends on meeting the needs of every member of the community, recognition of the impact of language and cultural factors, as well as special needs, can be critical to the success of emergency and disaster response and ultimate community recovery.

An effective emergency management program requires a comprehensive evaluation of the community that the program will serve. Are there groups of non–English-speaking residents in the community? Are there people with physical disabilities, learning disabilities, lack of literacy in English, or young children, all of whom will need special planning and developmental or cultural considerations? Each of these groups needs to be considered in developing public education materials during all four phases of emergency management: (1) types of mitigation that will lessen the impact of disaster, (2) public education that will prepare all residents for the disaster, (3) premade public information messages in multiple languages to guide their response, and (4) plans for multilingual support in shelters and disaster application centers.

MEETING THE CHALLENGE OF CULTURAL COMPETENCY

How many languages and formats should an emergency management program develop and maintain? When all materials had to be printed and stored in advance of need, the cost of printing and storage had to be considered in selecting the number of languages and formats. Today, the use of websites and electronic notification systems may make it possible to have many more messages stored in multiple languages for dissemination through electronic means to those households with the appropriate technology to receive them. However, in disasters that destroy the power grid and telecommunications capabilities, the paper versions maintained in careful storage may be the only way to communicate with the public.

BENCHMARKING FOR LANGUAGE SELECTION

San Jose, California, the nation's tenth largest city, uses a benchmark of 1 percent to determine in which languages it will prepare disaster education materials. Public educational materials for all departments are prepared in each language used by a mono-lingual, non–English-speaking population equal to 1 percent of the total population, or about 10,000 people. The Department of Environmental Services takes a periodic community survey to determine which language groups fall into the 1 percent size range. As an example, it uses this information to label the storm drains with warnings against dumping, stenciling the message "This drain goes to the Bay" on the curb in the appropriate language. Emergency managers use the information to develop and acquire appropriate written and videotaped public outreach and education materials.

As the most culturally diverse large city in America, San Jose has over 100 languages spoken in the homes of the children who attend school in the community. State-level Department of Education language census reports can provide information on the number of languages spoken in the homes of schoolchildren in a community. This census information may also be a good guide for selecting which languages, other than English, should be included in the public education program.

Many state-level emergency management agencies have prepared emergency management information in multiple languages. For example, the California Emergency Management Agency has provided basic earthquake preparedness information in the languages commonly spoken in California homes, including Spanish, Korean, Mandarin Chinese, Vietnamese, Lao, Cambodian, and Hmong. Local ethnic cultural and religious associations may be willing to provide the translation of sets of fliers into other languages of the community. For example, in Irvine, a Japanese cultural group translated a flier for senior citizens into Japanese—a language not available through the state office—for use in the community outreach program.

The United Nations Office of Disaster Assistance in New York and the Pan American Health Organization in Washington, DC, are sources of educational materials in languages other than English. Earthquake, tsunami, cyclone/hurricane, and pandemic flu are just a few of the subjects that are available. Ethnic associations within a community may have access to resources about emergency preparedness in their languages, or they may provide reliable culturally competent translators for community-generated emergency response materials. Cartoon artists, including students from community college graphics programs, are a good resource for interpreting life safety information into simple graphic formats or even cartoon materials.

CULTURAL COMPETENCE IN TRANSLATIONS

It is very important to ensure that all translations into languages other than English are done by culturally competent individuals who also speak the language idiomatically and ideally as their first language. At least two other native speakers of the language should read the translation to ensure that it is accurate and at an appropriate level of difficulty for the target audience before the new translation is printed and distributed. Resident monolingual non-English speakers may not understand the language when it is translated into a scholarly format, such as that taught at the university level. Using computer-based translations is also likely to create stilted verbiage that may not convey the desired message or may actually have incorrect words. When San Jose held a grand opening for a new building in 1990, a banner was created that said "Best wishes for a successful celebration" in English, Spanish, and Vietnamese, but in Tagalog it said "Have a happy circumcision"—not the message that the city wanted to send to the community.

CADRE OF TRANSLATORS

In addition to providing preparedness information in several languages, the Office of Emergency Services (OES) should ensure that the emergency plan includes a point of contact for recruiting translators during the event, preferably people who are native speakers of the non-English language. In many cities, employees with bilingual capabilities receive differential pay for being available to provide emergency translations of city-created materials of all types. Rather than trying to maintain a list of such employees independently, the OES should have a point of contact within the human resources department who can access the latest list of bilingual city employees.

In addition to providing written translations, these bilingual speakers will be a critical resource in a medical-aid center, public information branch of the Emergency Operations Center, and in mass-care shelters. Potential translators for emergency management programs should receive pre-event training in the Incident Command System (ICS) and National Incident Management System (NIMS) so that they can not only directly translate materials, but also enhance the translations by providing information to fill knowledge gaps that may exist in a specific community. For example, there is no Vietnamese word for *earthquake*, so an earthquake preparedness brochure might have to start with an explanation of the phrase in Vietnamese being used for the English word *earthquake*.

If a building must be posted as dangerous and occupants are unable to read English, it would be helpful to have a culturally competent speaker of the language accompany the building inspector to the site to discuss the problem with the occupants and to post the official notice on the building in the occupants' languages.

After 1989's Loma Prieta earthquake in the San Francisco Bay area, people entered unsafe buildings, even though they were marked with "red tag" signs, which were often accompanied by an explanation in English and Spanish only. Others refused to enter perfectly safe buildings because of their inability to understand the instructions posted on the building's green (for safe) placard. In addition to relying on color-coded signs, major languages spoken in the community might be included on the life safety signage. For example, Los Angeles has used signs with English, Spanish, and Chinese.

CULTURAL COMPETENCY IN DELIVERY OF MEDICAL CARE

Cultural competency is especially important in the delivery of disaster health care. First, it is crucial to have a clear conversation with the victim. It may be necessary to have a three-way conversation among the victim, the caregiver, and an interpreter, in either spoken language or sign language. Clear and well-understood communication is essential during medical care, where a complete medical history, list of medications, and statement of symptoms may be a life-and-death issue. First responder and medical care agencies are mandated by Title VI to have competent interpreters available, either in person or by phone, to ensure effective communication in the medical setting (DHHS 2008d).

In the past, it was common to use children as interpreters in medical settings. This is no longer recommended. First, the need to communicate deeply personal information may put both the adult and the child in an embarrassing situation. Also, cultural norms may prevent the child from communicating unwanted information to an elder, causing the child to change the message to make it more acceptable to the hearer. Finally, the seriousness of the message may frighten the child, adding to the disaster-related stress and possibly inducing psychological harm (DHHS 2008d).

Because of religious or cultural norms, female victims may not be permitted to be alone in a room with a man to whom they are unrelated or to be touched by a strange man. These cultural taboos may inhibit the delivery of lifesaving care by male medical professionals. Communities need to assess in advance whether such cultural taboos are likely to exist in a postdisaster environment in the community, and plan for gender-specific care areas for women who need to be secluded (Edwards 2009, 262).

CASE STUDIES IN THE FOUR PHASES OF EMERGENCY MANAGEMENT

The following case studies offer insight into the four phases of emergency management: (1) mitigation, (2) preparedness, (3) response, and (4) recovery.

MITIGATION: NEW ORLEANS

Mitigation Before Katrina: Evacuation of the Elderly

Hurricane Katrina was disproportionately fatal for the elderly. Seventy-one percent of the fatalities were over the age of sixty, with 47 percent of those over the age of seventy-five. Although most of the elderly dead had lived independently, most had disabilities and mobility limitations. Frequently living alone, they were often invisible to the community (Cahalan and Renne 2007, 7).

During the storm preparations, many of New Orleans's older residents without cars were rescued through a church-based program in the African American community called Brother's Keeper. Starting in July 2005, the community's leaders, including Mayor Ray Nagin, explained that the city lacked the transportation resources to move the estimated 135,000 people without cars out of harm's way in the event of a hurricane. The message: you are responsible for yourself, your family, and friends. Because the Red Cross had moved the shelters for New Orleans to the higher ground north of Interstate 10, the option of sheltering in the city was gone. As a result of this message, the African American churches mounted a campaign to organize congregations to evacuate each other, under the leadership of Total Community Action and the American Red Cross (Nolan 2005). The older people who were evacuated as part of Brother's Keeper were willing to leave their familiar surroundings because they were surrounded by friends.

Mitigation After Katrina: Elder Education

Following the return of population to New Orleans, disaster researchers and emergency managers interviewed residents to understand their behavior during the hurricane and its aftermath. Some older people reported that they did not follow the evacuation order because they had never left New Orleans or even their own neighborhoods. They had no idea where they would stay, what they would eat, or how the residents of the outlying areas would treat them (Kiefer 2010).

In an effort to create more disaster resilience among the elderly, the University of New Orleans led an effort to educate older people about how to evacuate (Kiefer 2010). Residents who participated in programs at the senior centers were offered a free day trip to a hurricane shelter north of Interstate 10. Each tour guest was given a camera and a scrapbook to document the trip. The willing travelers took an Amtrak train north and were transported by local bus to a Red Cross shelter, where they received a shelter lunch and a talk about disaster preparedness and mass care plans. They took photos along the way of everything that was interesting and different: the train station, the inside of a train, the town where the shelter was located. Most of the travelers expressed pleasure at the welcome and services that they had received.

A few weeks later, with their scrapbooks completed, the travelers gave a program on their trip to their colleagues at the senior center. The fear engendered by a trip out of the familiar neighborhood, the worry about the welcome they would receive, the concern about strange food were all dispelled by the reports of the outing.

Thus, the concerns of seniors were recognized as legitimate, and people who shared the socioeconomic culture did the "research" to ensure that disaster evacuation was a lifesaving activity that even seniors with disabilities could participate in. The younger care givers and trip organizers learned about the needs of evacuating seniors, including special food, adult diapers, and paratransit, so that these needs could be written into future evacuation plans. With this new cultural competence, New Orleans emergency planners can plan for "no one left behind."

PREPAREDNESS: CADRE TRAINS THE NGOS

In the weeks following 1989's Loma Prieta earthquake, Nina McCrory of the Santa Clara Valley Chapter of the American Red Cross recognized the need to gather the nonprofit community to coordinate the services that they were providing to the disaster victims. In response, Collaborating Agencies Disaster Relief Effort (CADRE) was formed. NGOs collaborated to ensure that resources were used for the greatest benefit to the disaster victims. Disaster response was divided into areas expressed as spokes of an umbrella: disaster feeding, mass care, clothing and household goods donations management, volunteer management, and similar subdivisions.

CADRE's NGO members included the traditional nonprofits like the American Red Cross, as well as the Center for Living with Dying, the Volunteer Center of Silicon Valley, and the Council of Churches. Clergy represented the Roman Catholic diocese, the Buddhist congregations, Latter-day Saints stakes, and Protestant denominations. The Boys and Girls Club, the Santa Clara Valley Humane Society, and church-based soup kitchens joined to receive training about emergency planning, including cross-disciplinary support like storage, translations, and transportation. CADRE engaged in Memoranda of Understanding (MOUs) with the local communities, providing support to them in local emergencies.

After about ten years of community service in apartment fires, community-wide floods, and wildland interface fires, CADRE's leadership recognized a need to have not only a common emergency umbrella plan, but also common training on emergency response for each agency internally. The post–9/11 mandate for the use of the National Incident Management System (NIMS) by all organizations receiving federal disaster preparedness funding was another incentive. The local Emergency Managers Association's Emergency Management Performance Grant funded a consultant who developed a common emergency plan template for all the NGOs in the county, now numbering over 100 member organizations, and organized the required training.

RESPONSE: SAN JOSE, IRVINE, NORTHRIDGE

Hurricane Katrina Survivors in San Jose

In 2005 the City of San Jose was contacted by FEMA to ask how many Katrina survivors it could house and care for. The city offered to take 100 FEMA-sponsored people and immediately activated CADRE to provide emergency services. The common planning and training enabled organizations as disparate as the Jewish Community Center, African American clergy, San José State University (SJSU), and the Volunteer Center of Silicon Valley to organize housing, casework services, and rides to church for the anticipated survivors.

While awaiting FEMA-sponsored people—who never arrived—CADRE began providing services to Katrina survivors who found their way to Silicon Valley on their own. About 60 percent of the Katrina survivors who went to the Silicon Valley were African Americans, while about 30 percent were Vietnamese who had come to stay with family members and friends (Edwards 2010). African Americans from Louisiana often had family ties to East Palo Alto. Some of the Katrina survivors went to the Silicon Valley because they had once been there for a convention or a job interview.

SJSU provided two-bedroom graduate student dormitories (Spartan Village, since demolished), complete with furnishings, linens, and kitchenware. The American Red Cross provided casework services at the community room at Spartan Village. Volunteers from the Jewish Community Center created "welcome" backpacks for each new resident: man, woman, or child's. The adult bags included prepaid phone cards and Valley Transportation Agency bus passes.

The Volunteer Center, whose leaders included a retired naval officer and a twenty-five-year navy wife, donated sweatshirts for the new residents imprinted with "New Orleans Neighborhood Association," which represented the height of cultural competency. The U.S. Navy provided a paradigm for being involuntarily relocated to strange surroundings, which creates a need for a sense of belonging to a larger group. Changes of climate from the Gulf Coast to the Bay area made these Navy veteran leaders aware of how cold the summer in Silicon Valley would feel with its 75-degree highs and 35 percent humidity.

CADRE provided common training on NIMS and, most important, cross-cultural awareness among volunteer leaders. When Katrina rendered thousands homeless, San Jose was ready for people to make a new home in Silicon Valley.

Whittier Narrows Earthquake in Irvine

After the Whittier Narrows earthquake in California in 1987, St. John Knits in Irvine, California, suffered a significant disruption of production because most of the workers refused to reenter the building. These workers did not speak much English, so there was limited communication between them and the supervisor regarding the safety of the building. When a bilingual employee was able to translate the workers' protests, it was discovered that many had experienced earthquakes in Nicaragua in 1972 or Guatemala in 1976. Because these nations lack strict building codes, the workers' experience was of wholesale building failure, and they were now afraid that the St. John building would collapse in the first aftershock.

Cultural competency in Central American disaster experience might have led the corporation to offer employee education about American building codes and workplace safety in an earthquake, perhaps delivered during new employee orientation. Employees could have been reassured about seismic building codes in California and the likelihood that most commercial buildings would withstand even relatively strong shaking without significant damage. Recognizing such a potential problem in advance can prevent some of the psychological trauma to the workers after an earthquake, and can benefit the company by restarting work faster after a seismic event.

Northridge Earthquake in Los Angeles

At 4:30 A.M. on Monday, January 17, 1994, the Northridge earthquake shook the greater Los Angeles area awake. With no moonlight and the electricity cut off, residents stumbled around in the dark collecting children and valuables before fleeing their homes. Aftershocks continued all day, with some aftershocks almost as strong as the initial 6.7 Richter scale shake (Southern California Earthquake Data Center n.d.).

Los Angeles is home to a multicultural community, with Hispanic neighborhoods generally receiving higher vulnerability scores for earthquakes (Rashed and Weeks 2003). Young Hispanic families took a few possessions and their cars and set up camps in area parks and school fields. Although Red Cross shelters were readily available with hot showers and hot meals, the Hispanic residents stayed in the parks.

By Friday, January 21, the park encampments had become a public health problem. Young children were living in unheated cars and even sleeping on the ground in the Los Angeles winter. Although the daytime temperatures were in the eighties, the nighttime temperatures dipped into the fifties; the weather was damp, and it was intermittently raining. In addition, the parks with community centers had restrooms available only during operating hours, usually 9 A.M. through 8 P.M., while many parks had no restroom available at all. Consequently, people took shovels and dug latrines, unaware of the poor drainage qualities of the clay soil and the proximity of groundwater. By Saturday, January 22, the Public Health Mobile Clinic in one Northridge park had a line of over 100 parents waiting for medical care for children with earaches, runny noses, and coughs. Researchers for the California Seismic Safety Commission traveled to the parks to determine what could be done to get the people into the Red Cross shelters or even back into their homes, most of which were undamaged.

One researcher interviewed a woman who appeared to be about forty years old and had five children less than ten years of age in her care. They were sitting on a blanket next to a car, with a plastic tarp strung between the car window and a small tree. The researcher greeted the woman in Spanish, presented a business card from the commission, and asked if they could have a conversation about the disaster. Readily agreeing, the woman introduced the ten-year-old boy as her youngest son and the four younger children as her grandchildren.

When the researcher asked why the families were living in the park, the woman told this story. She had been living in Guatemala in 1976 during its deadly earthquake. When the shaking stopped, she took her youngest brother out of the house and went with her father to check on her grandmother, who lived on the hillside. As they were walking up the hill there was a strong aftershock and a resounding crack, and suddenly a wall of water and mud from the broken dam swept through the valley village, killing the family members whom they had left at home. She then paused, looked at the researcher, and said, "So we come to the park so that when the dam breaks I can put my babies in the trees." When the researcher tried to explain that there was no dam, the woman just smiled.

A researcher went to speak with young people who had formed a long line next to the FEMA Disaster Application Center, set up at a community center. The entrance was guarded by a Los Angeles Police Department sergeant, an African American woman. A young man in the line told the researcher that they were lined up waiting for help from FEMA. The researcher asked if they had called the 800 number for appointments. One young woman said that she had been in several disasters in the Caribbean, where you line up and go into the building and get food and blankets, and sometimes money. When the researcher said that was not the case in the United States, the young woman gave a knowing smile and said, "Then why do all the Koreans go into the building?" When the researcher tried to explain about the paperwork application system and the Red Cross shelter, the young people just laughed at her naïveté.

In the afternoon, the researcher noted that the line was about half the length it had been, a Von's supermarket truck was distributing baby food, and an African American church was preparing barbequed food. Thinking that people had been given appointments, the researcher spoke to the police sergeant, who explained what had happened. About 11 A.M., a very angry young Hispanic man had confronted the sergeant, demanding immediate admission to the community center. He stated that he had been the first in line since 7 A.M. and was done with waiting. He said that if she did not start letting the people in line enter the building, they would take it by force. He said that he saw that she was afraid of the Koreans (noting the racially motivated shootings during the 1991 Rodney King verdict riots) and of her "own people" and that he was tired of being disrespected because he was Hispanic.

The sergeant was alone at the community center, so she radioed for backup and went into the building. In a few minutes uniformed officers with bulletproof vests arrived, many of whom spoke Spanish. One officer had a bullhorn. He explained in Spanish that the community center was a place for people to register with the federal government for disaster assistance. He listed the documents that applicants would have to show: proof of residence (such as a utility bill), some proof that the home or apartment was uninhabitable, and the driver's license for each adult and birth certificate for each child in the family. He told them that it would take several days to get a decision and that money would be deposited into a checking account, for which the applicant had to provide a deposit slip.

Shortly there was an undercurrent of conversation about "La Migra" (the Border Patrol), and most of the people left the line. Those remaining had been given cards with appointments for that afternoon. The situation had been defused, but it was unclear whether those waiting in line really understood that they would get nothing tangible from the community center.

That afternoon the National Guard arrived with tents, portable latrines, and portable showers, and a camp was set up by evening. Because the Red Cross manages only indoor mass-care centers, the Salvation Army was registering families for the tents. Some additional local NGOs were distributing cooked food, diapers, and blankets. Finally, five days after the earthquake, some organization was coming to the park and its refugee campers.

The Flood in Rock Springs

After several weeks of rain, on Super Bowl Sunday in 1997, a freeway in San Jose, California, unexpectedly flooded. Although the rain had stopped, the director of emergency services (DES) was notified that the fire department wanted the Emergency Operations Center (EOC) opened in case things got worse.

About two hours later, the San Jose Police Department (SJPD) reported to the EOC that water was now rising in the Rock Springs neighborhood next to Coyote Creek.

SJPD's chief sent several cars to Rock Springs to organize an evacuation of the population at risk. By the time a second patrol car arrived, it was clear that the water was rising too fast to use the cars to notify the community. The fire department set up Incident Command in preparation for a rescue and offered to use the fire apparatus with tall tires to drive through the neighborhood with a loudspeaker to tell people to evacuate on foot. SJPD established a roadblock to prevent additional people from entering the neighborhood—and here the controversy began.

At the time, SJPD had one Cambodian officer, and there were no Cambodian firefighters. Cultural norms in the Cambodian community did not promote going into public safety services as a career. The Rock Springs neighborhood was about half-Hispanic and half-Cambodian. The Cambodian population spoke and understood very little English, though within the mostly undocumented Hispanic population, many were fluent in English.

The police captain called for the Cambodian officer to come to the scene. The captain stationed the Cambodian speaker at the roadblock to explain the situation to Cambodian residents trying to go home. But the incident commander requested that the Cambodian officer be assigned to the fire apparatus that was driving through the community making evacuation announcements in English and Spanish. He wanted to add Cambodian announcements. As a compromise, the Cambodian officer rode on the fire engine for thirty minutes until evacuation became too dangerous, and then returned to the road block. At the after-action meeting, the incident commander said he felt like Solomon dividing the baby and that the fire department needed some help from the Neighborhood Development Center to create a firefighter recruitment program in the Cambodian community.

The Cambodian officer stated that the fire department did not need to work on recruiting the young people—the problem was "old-fashioned parents" who did not view firefighting as a profession. This insight into the barrier to Cambodian police and fire recruitments led to the creation of a campaign aimed at parents. Because Cambodian is a script-based language, the literacy rate among the community is very low. The recruitment campaign was placed on Cambodian radio and television, along with wordless posters of happy police and fire personnel providing services for happy customers.

RECOVERY: NORTHRIDGE, CALIFORNIA

Three weeks after the Northridge earthquake, the housing stock had been inspected, and most post-1960s homes and apartments—except for soft-story structures, those with inadequate support of the first floor of a multi-story building—were deemed habitable. Many of the earthquake's survivors had returned home and begun repairing and cleaning up the nonstructural earthquake damage to their properties or apartments.

The Hispanic encampments in the parks, however, were not much smaller than when the National Guard set them up. Los Angeles city officials were eager to restore the park programming and especially anxious to clean up the illegally dug latrines. Schools with encampments wanted the refugees to leave so they could clear the athletic fields of human waste and refuse and restart spring sports programs. City and school district leadership made appeals over radio and television in all community languages, asking everyone to go home or to get new temporary housing through the FEMA 800 number—these appeals had no effect. Next, building inspectors went to the parks to explain the building inspection process and urge people to check the inspection tags on their homes to see if they were safe to return to—but to no avail. Finally, the City of Los Angeles created "reassurance teams" composed of building inspectors, mental health counselors or clergy, and culturally competent Spanish language translators. They went through the parks to encourage people to return to their safety inspected homes (Bolin and Stanford 1998, 144)—and were finally successful.

CONCLUSION

When disaster strikes, those not affected are often motivated to acts of charity. Unfortunately, the donors often do good badly because of a lack of cultural competency. They offer inappropriate material goods, further burdening the disaster area, while misunderstanding the real needs of the disaster survivors.

Educational programs for emergency planners, including programs in universities, must include information on cultural differences, sensitivities, and special needs in order to ensure that emergency management programs are designed to meet the needs of all the members of a community. Community-based organizations, especially those serving English-as-a-second-language communities and people with special needs, must partner with the community emergency management organization to ensure that disaster-response issues unique to their clients are adequately addressed in emergency plans.

Emergency management planners must be given the information necessary to be sensitive to the challenges of providing community disaster education for people from many cultures and language groups, and of various ages, economic strata, and special needs. Culturally competent translations and presentations are essential to communicating the safety messages to every member of America's richly diverse communities and to creating response and recovery plans that meet their disaster-related needs. In this way communities may be assured of doing good well.

NOTE

Portions of this chapter originally appeared as Frances E. Winslow (now Frances L. Edwards), *Meeting the Needs of Diverse School Populations: Issues in Earthquake Education*, ed. Katharyn E.K. Ross, Technical Report NCEER-92–0003 (Buffalo, NY: NCEER, 1992). Used by permission.

REFERENCES

Abueg, Francis R., Terence M. Keane, Jessica Wolfe, Rock Pfotenhauer, and Robert Agella. 1990. Predicting the range of adjustment to earthquake trauma in Santa Cruz. Paper presented to the International Society for Traumatic Stress Studies, New Orleans, LA.

American Red Cross. n.d. *Silent Quake: Preparedness for the Hearing-Impaired.* Los Angeles Chapter, Audio Visual Department, 2700 Wilshire Boulevard, Los Angeles, CA, 90057.

Bolin, Robert, and Lois Stanford. 1998. *The Northridge Earthquake: Vulnerability and Disaster.* London: Routledge.

Cahalan, Clare, and John Renne. 2007. Emergency evacuation of the elderly and disabled: Safeguarding independent living. *Intransition* (Spring): 7.

Cutter, Susan. 2010. Social vulnerability index map set. Redlands, CA: ESRI. www.arcgis.com/home/item.html?id=0a85781f7890497185d6cde6760a20c5.

Cutter, Susan L., and Mark Smith. 2009. Fleeing from the hurricane's wrath: Evacuation and the two Americas. *Environment* 51(2): 26–36.

Davis, Kenneth. 1997. *Exploring the Intersection Between Cultural Competency and Managed Behavioral Health Care Policy: Implications for State and County Mental Health Agencies.* Alexandria, VA: National Technical Assistance Center for State Mental Health Planning.

Dufka, Corinne L. 1988. The Mexico City earthquake disaster. *Social Casework: The Journal of Contemporary Social Work* 69 (March): 162–170.

Edwards, Frances L. 2009. Effective disaster response in cross border events. *Journal of Contingencies and Crisis Management* 17(4): 255–265.

———. 2010. At home in Silicon Valley. In *How Ethnically Marginalized Americans Cope with Catastrophic Disasters: Studies in Suffering and Resiliency,* ed. Jason D. Rivera and DeMond S. Miller. Lewiston, NY: Edwin Mellen Press.

Edwards, Frances L., and Yvonne Wong. 2010. Silicon Valley's elderly Chinese immigrants and disaster vulnerability. In *How Ethnically Marginalized Americans Cope with Catastrophic Disasters: Studies in Suffering and Resiliency,* ed. Jason D. Rivera and DeMond S. Miller. Lewiston, NY: Edwin Mellen Press.

Enarson, Elaine. 2006. Women and girls last? Averting the second post-Katrina disaster. Social Science Research Council. http://understandingkatrina.ssrc.org/Enarson/.

Enarson, Elaine, Cheryl Childers, Betty H. Morrow, Deborah Thomas, and Ben Wisner. 2003. *A Social Vulnerability Approach to Disasters.* Emmitsburg, MD: FEMA Higher Education Project. http://training.fema.gov/EMIWeb/edu/sovul.asp.

Gibbs, Nancy. 2010. There's no point in doing good badly. *Time,* February 22.

Hazards and Vulnerability Research Institute. 2010. Social vulnerability and place: Vulnerability methods and application for corps planning. http://webra.cas.sc.edu/hvri/research/vulnerabilitymapping.aspx.

Johnson, James P., Tomasz Lenartowicz, and Salvador Apud. 2006. Cross-cultural competence in international business: Toward a definition and a model. *Journal of International Business Studies* 37(4): 525–543.

Jones, Russell T., Christopher S. Immel, Rachael M. Moore, and James Hadder. 2008. Hurricane Katrina: Experiences of psychologists and implications for future disaster response. *Professional Psychology: Research and Practice* 39(1): 100–106.

Kiefer, John. 2010. Personal interview, April 10.

Missouri Department of Health & Senior Services. 2006. Planning and response strategies for culturally diverse populations. www.dhss.mo.gov/SpecialNeedsToolkit/EmergencyPlanning/SpecPopStrategyGrid1-24-06LC4CDtoolkit.doc.

Nolan, Bruce. 2005. In storm, N.O. wants no one left behind. *New Orleans Times-Picayne,* July 24.

Phillips, Brenda D., and Betty H. Morrow. 2008. *Women and Disasters.* Bloomington, IN: Xlibris.

Phillips, Brenda, Deborah Thomas, Alice Fothergill, and Lynn Blinn-Pike. 2009. *Social Vulnerability to Disasters.* New York: Taylor and Francis.

Rashed, Tarek, and John Weeks. 2003. Assessing vulnerability to earthquake hazards through spatial multi-criteria analysis of urban areas. *International Journal of Geographical Information Science.* http://geography.sdsu.edu/Research/Projects/IPC/publication/Rashed_Weeks_IJGIS.pdf.

Southern California Earthquake Data Center. n.d. Northridge earthquake. www.data.scec.org/chrono_index/northreq.html.

U.S. Census Bureau. 1999a. Table 7: Age and sex of the foreign born population: 1870–1990. www.census.gov/population/www/documentation/twps0029/tab07.html.

———. 1999b. Table 2: Region of birth of the foreign-born population: 1850 to 1930 and 1960 to 1990. www.census.gov/population/www/documentation/twps0029/tab02.html.

U.S. Department of Health and Human Services (DHHS). Office of Minority Health. 2008a. Cultural competency curriculum for disaster preparedness and crisis response. https://cccdpcr.thinkculturalhealth.org/Content/Course1/Course1_Intro2asp.

————. 2008b. Cultural competency curriculum for disaster preparedness and crisis response: Introduction, 4 of 6. https://cccdpcr.thinkculturalhealth.org/Content/Course1/Course1_Intro4.asp.

————. 2008c. Cultural competency curriculum for disaster preparedness and crisis response: Module 1.1, 5 of 5. https://cccdpcr.thinkculturalhealth.org/Content/Course1/Module1/Module1_1_5.asp.

————. 2008d. Cultural competency curriculum for disaster preparedness and crisis response: Course One, Module 6. https://cccdpcr.thinkculturalhealth.org/Content/Course1/Module6/Module1_6_1.asp.

Part III

Educating for Cultural Competence

Cultural Competency as a Standard for Accreditation

Nadia Rubaii and Crystal Calarusse

The demographic changes that are contributing to increases in the racial, ethnic, religious, cultural, and linguistic diversity of the workforce and the citizenry of the United States are well documented (Riccucci 2002; U.S. Census Bureau 2010; U.S. DOL Bureau of Labor Statistics 2004). The corresponding imperative for cultural competence among public administrators as a means to ensure service quality, enhance organizational effectiveness, redress disparities, comply with mandates, and reduce liabilities has been articulated repeatedly throughout this book and in other venues (Bailey 2005; Benavides and Hernandez 2007; Johnson and Rivera 2007; Kellar 2005; Rice 2007; Rubaii-Barrett 2006). That case is therefore not restated in this chapter. Instead, the focus here is on educating for cultural competence and, more specifically, on the role that accreditation standards can and do play in facilitating change and monitoring the progress of schools and programs as they strive to meet this challenge.

As the accrediting body for professional education in public affairs, the National Association of Schools of Public Affairs and Administration (NASPAA) plays a leading role in defining key values for the profession and in guiding the discourse about corresponding knowledge, skills, and abilities required of public service professionals in response to the ever-changing work environment. Since NASPAA began conducting peer reviews and then formal accreditation of professional public affairs programs, the association has required programs to engage in efforts to promote diversity among their faculty and student bodies. In 2007, the accreditation standards were amended to include a requirement that diversity be addressed in courses, curriculum materials, and other program activities. While nondiscrimination and diversity were identified as concerns within the NASPAA accreditation standards from the beginning, the emphasis was generally on programmatic *efforts* rather than *results*.

In 2009, the membership of NASPAA overwhelmingly approved a comprehensive overhaul of the accreditation standards for professional master's degrees in public affairs, administration, and policy. Among other things, the standards now include a requirement that programs seeking accreditation operationally define and fully assess their students' competencies "to communicate and interact productively with a diverse and changing workforce and citizenry"—that is, to demonstrate cultural competence (NASPAA 2009, Standard 5.1). This represents a notable change in expectations in response to the changing demographic realities of the current and future environment of public administration. When considered in the context of prior unsuccessful efforts to expand the faculty and student diversity standards to require demonstrated outcomes, the shift to a competency and student learning focus generally, and the inclusion of cultural competency among the required student learning outcomes in particular, is significant.

The evolution of the accreditation standards and the process by which NASPAA reached this milestone of a cultural competency standard represents an interesting case study in the role of accreditation in the evolving discourse surrounding diversity and cultural competence within public affairs education. As such, a review of the historical developments leading to the current standards is warranted. Also notable in this process is what other ideas related to diversity and cultural competence were proposed but are not reflected in the final standards. Insights into the deliberations and controversies surrounding diversity and cultural competence are discussed as well. Finally, in addition to understanding the past, it is equally important to look forward and consider the implications and implementation challenges of this newly adopted standard. Only if these challenges are effectively addressed will the NASPAA accreditation process be able to contribute to ensuring that the next generation of public administrators is prepared for the challenges associated with increased diversity.

THE ROOTS OF ACCREDITATION: THE BIRTH OF NASPAA

NASPAA is a membership association of 267 graduate programs in public administration, public affairs, and public policy whose primary mission includes "ensuring excellence in education and training for public service and to promote the ideal of public service" (NASPAA 2011a). Founded in 1970, NASPAA currently provides a variety of services to its members, including an annual conference, a journal, a data center, and communications services, and has been at the center of discussions on the curriculum for public service education and the assessment of public service programs. The primary means by which NASPAA pursues its quality mission, however, is through accreditation.

A requirement of NASPAA's accreditation process is that all programs seeking accreditation must be at an institution that holds institutional accreditation through a recognized regional or national provider (or the equivalent in the non-U.S. context). As of 2010, 169 programs at 160 institutions (representing 59 percent of member institutions) were accredited by NASPAA (2010b). NASPAA is a professional programmatic accreditor, meaning that the scope of the accrediting process includes only professional graduate programs in public service, and the standards and process are deeply tied to the needs of the public service profession.

While the term *NASPAA accreditation* is generally used to refer to the process, the actual peer review is a semiautonomous process conducted by the Commission

Table 13.1

Key Institutional Actors in Public Affairs Accreditation

Organization	Structure	Purpose	Relationship to NASPAA accreditation
Council for Higher Education Accreditation (CHEA)	Nonprofit institutional membership association of over 3,000 degree-granting colleges and universities. Recognition conducted by the Committee on Recognition, composed of nine members, including public members. Governed by a twenty-person board of university presidents, academics, and public members. Led by a full-time executive director with a staff of seven full-time employees.	To promote academic quality through formal recognition of higher education accreditation bodies and to coordinate and work to advance self-regulation through accreditation.	Recognizes COPRA-NASPAA to accredit master's degree programs in public affairs, policy, and administration.
National Association of Schools of Public Affairs and Administration (NASPAA)	Nonprofit institutional membership association of over 260 graduate programs in public affairs, policy, and administration. Led by an executive council of eighteen academics from member schools and a full-time executive director with a staff of seven full-time employees.	To ensure excellence in education for public service and promote the ideal of public service.	Parent body of the accrediting arm. Does not participate in or intervene in accreditation review.
Commission on Peer Review and Accreditation (COPRA)	Quasi-independent standing committee of NASPAA composed of eleven academics and one practitioner. Members are appointed by the president of NASPAA on a volunteer basis for three-year terms. Two NASPAA staff members provide full-time support.	To ensure quality in graduate public service programs with respect to a set of defined accreditation standards.	Responsible for making accreditation decisions and policies. Performs a somewhat judicial role in interpreting and applying standards.
NASPAA Standards Committee	Standing committee of NASPAA. Twelve-member committee with both academics and practitioners. NASPAA staff members provide support as needed.	To develop and maintain appropriate standards for master's programs in public affairs, policy, and administration.	Responsible for drafting new standards as needed and providing broad analysis on future needs. Performs a somewhat legislative role within NASPAA.

Sources: CHEA (2006, 2011); NASPAA (2002, 2011b).

on Peer Review and Accreditation (COPRA). COPRA oversees the rigorous process that begins with the program's submission of a hard copy or online self-study report (SSR) and includes a peer review site visit and then a final decision on accreditation. COPRA must act within the confines of rules established by three other institutional actors both within and outside of NASPAA. The roles and responsibilities of the Council on Higher Education Accreditation (CHEA), NASPAA, NASPAA Standards Committee, and COPRA are described in Table 13.1. Collectively, these four groups provide the framework for accreditation of professional public affairs degree programs.

The Power and the Limitations of Accreditation to Motivate Change

In many respects professional accreditation is a powerful force to motivate change. This regulatory process can be a lever to move a professional field toward the aspirations of those designing the accreditation standards, in part due to the scale of the operation and widespread level of participation. Programs generally consider the standards legitimate guidelines developed by professional peers whom they respect. Even those programs that are not accredited look to the accreditation standards for guidance on appropriate indicators of program quality. Equally important, students and employers value the status of accreditation as an external assurance of quality. That said, however, there are limits to the power of accreditation.

First, accreditation for graduate public service programs is voluntary and programs are not compelled to seek or maintain accreditation as a condition of awarding degrees within the public administration profession. In some professions, such as law or nursing, attending an unaccredited program would jeopardize a graduate's employability, as a student from an unaccredited program would not be able to sit for an important entry exam or obtain a license to practice. NASPAA accreditation does not carry the same weight among prospective employers of Master of Public Administration (MPA) and Master of Public Policy (MPP) graduates since there are no required gateways to enter the profession. Roughly 60 percent of the graduate public service programs in the United States are accredited by NASPAA. Among the public service graduate programs that have elected to forgo accreditation, some do so because they are too small, others may have a curriculum that diverges from NASPAA standards, and some have sufficiently high visibility and institutional reputation even without accreditation.

Beyond the voluntary nature of accreditation, there is the logistical matter of the periodic review cycle that ranges from five to ten years, depending on the profession. NASPAA uses a seven-year review cycle for professional public service degree programs. When a comprehensive review of a program occurs only periodically, it takes considerable time for changes to disperse throughout all programs. While programs report annually on substantive changes and continued conformance, they do not respond to new standards until their next full review.

Another limiting factor is the dual role that the Commission on Peer Review and Accreditation takes during its evaluations of programs. On the one hand, as an accreditor, COPRA is responsible for evaluating programs under the standards and issuing decisions regarding whether a program is in "substantial conformity." At the same time, NASPAA accreditation has always been explicitly formative by design and COPRA has an additional goal of advancing the development and continuous improvement of programs through education, not simply punitive assessments. As new standards are adopted, COPRA generally applies a relatively lenient and educational approach when assessing programs under that standard during a phase-in period. Only over time does the commission increase its expectations for conformity.

Taken together, the voluntary nature of public affairs accreditation, the periodic review cycle, and the long-standing practice of phasing in enforcement of new standards creates a situation in which there is often a lag of three to seven years before all accredited programs can be expected to understand and conform to a new standard. The changes may take longer to be applied to nonaccredited programs, if they are applied at all. That said, accreditation can and does play a significant role in facilitating discipline-wide changes and forcing programs to improve continuously and respond to changing conditions.

THE EVOLUTION OF NASPAA STANDARDS

The cultural competency standard approved by NASPAA in 2009 cannot be examined in isolation; the broader context of evolving philosophical approaches to accreditation standards must be examined as well. In the case of NASPAA standards, this means understanding the conditions leading to the development of standards and the peer review process that served as a precursor to accreditation, as well as three clear and distinct generations of accreditation philosophy.

In the early to mid-1970s, NASPAA began to develop standards that could be used on a voluntary basis by institutions interested in evaluating the quality of their programs. In 1974, NASPAA adopted the *Guidelines and Standards for Professional Master's Degree Programs in Public Affairs/Public Administration* to "foster the development of the overall profession of public management" (Henry 1995). Interestingly, this early document included a lengthy list of recommended competencies, including some that had components of cultural competency; however, as the document progressed from a set of guidelines for voluntary review to formal standards for accreditation, the competency provisions were removed.

NASPAA began peer reviews of programs in 1978–79, and in 1980 it published the first list of programs "in substantial conformity." Three years later, at the 1983 annual meeting, the members voted to convert the process to a formal accreditation and to seek official recognition of NASPAA as an accrediting agency. In 1986 the Council on Postsecondary Accreditation (COPA), a nongovernmental organization, formally recognized NASPAA as the accrediting body for professional master's degree programs in public affairs, administration, and policy. Since 1996 oversight and recognition of NASPAA's accreditation authority has rested with the Council for Higher Education Accreditation, COPA's successor. Since its initial recognition, NASPAA accreditation has progressed through three distinct periods or generations that are described below, followed by a discussion of the extent to which and manner in which diversity and cultural competence have been addressed within the three accreditation frameworks.

FIRST-GENERATION NASPAA ACCREDITATION (1986–1992): INPUTS AND PROGRAM RESOURCES

The standards during the initial years of accreditation were those that had previously been used for the peer review process. Programs were required to demonstrate that they had resources sufficient to provide a high-quality education. In assessing conformity with the standards, COPRA largely examined input measures in the form of prescribed subject areas included in the curriculum; minimum number of faculty, credit hours, budgets, and library resources; and expectations that faculty and programs have sufficient autonomy and authority. The implicit expectation was that desired outputs and outcomes would result from programs that demonstrated adequate commitment to public affairs education in the form of the specified inputs.

Although the standards allowed for some flexibility, there was some concern they were too limiting and did not meet the needs of the diverse array of programs. Curriculum was the defining accreditation element of this period and it was rigidity in interpretation that led to the need for a change in philosophy. The Standards Committee sought a compromise that would maintain the measures of quality but allow programs to emphasize their distinct foci; the result was mission-driven accreditation.

SECOND-GENERATION NASPAA ACCREDITATION (1992–2009): MISSION-BASED

A philosophical and practical shift in the accreditation standards took place in 1992 when NASPAA placed the program's own mission and goals as the central and guiding point from which conformity to all other standards would be interpreted. Programs were granted greater flexibility to articulate their specific missions and to adapt other standards within the framework of their mission. Some bright lines of input requirements remained in place, and much of what was reported and assessed by COPRA still was in the form of inputs, but most thresholds of sufficiency were generated from a program's own mission and goals. The shift to mission-based accreditation was motivated by desire to accommodate diversity among public service programs, most notably to allow NASPAA to accommodate public policy programs in the fold. It was also intended to allow for and encourage innovation.

The implementation of mission-driven accreditation also ushered in the requirement of a systematic assessment process. Programs were asked to document how they utilized relevant constituencies in the development of a mission, how they assessed the extent to which the program achieved its stated mission, and how they modified the program in response to data gathered on program performance. Although this initial layer of evaluation was included, the focus was still on the program level, not necessarily competencies of students.

During this time, the standards also reflected a maturation of the idea of ongoing assessment and continuous improvement. COPRA responded by supplementing the periodic seven-year full accreditation review with more careful monitoring of changes documented in annual reports. This began as a way to simply monitor whether and how programs responded to concerns identified during the accreditation or reaccreditation review. It evolved to a formal process by which COPRA can monitor program changes and, if deemed necessary, require programs to undergo a full-scale review before the scheduled seven-year interval. The enhanced monitoring process allows COPRA a means of balancing its development and evaluative roles described earlier.

Second-generation standards and supporting documents began to use the language of competencies, but they were not the focus of the accreditation process or the basis for accreditation decisions. Specifically, the instructions for preparing a self-study report required programs to identify "general competencies that are consistent with the program mission" and to "summarize how the common and additional curriculum components shall develop in students general competencies that are consistent with the program mission" (NASPAA 2010a, Standard 4.23). COPRA's expectation for conformity was largely that programs articulate some general competencies related to their mission and that they describe the courses designed to provide students with those competencies. There was minimal emphasis on operationalizing or measuring attainment of competencies.

THIRD-GENERATION NASPAA ACCREDITATION (2009 AND BEYOND): PUBLIC SERVICE VALUES AND STUDENT COMPETENCIES

In April 2006, the NASPAA Executive Council launched the NASPAA Standards 2009 initiative to conduct a comprehensive reassessment and revision of the accreditation standards with a goal of voting on new standards at the fall 2009 annual conference. A set of guiding principles was developed before revising the standards, and the three-and-a-half-year process provided numerous opportunities for participation by academics and practitioners.

The impetus for this change was multifaceted and reflected a recognition that the standards in existence could not keep pace with changing external demands and conditions. As a professional accreditor, NASPAA has a strict obligation to continuously ensure that its standards match the need of the public service profession. Additionally, institutions of higher education, as well as individual degree programs, faced increasing pressures to demonstrate accountability, comparability, and transparency. In practical terms, these external pressures required programs to assess student learning outcomes, to provide information in terms that would allow student consumers to compare programs, and to be more open about the abilities and accomplishments of graduates.

Additionally, changing demographics, increased complexity of management, and global interdependencies represented an environment of rapid change to which the standards were not well equipped to respond. Second-generation standards also lacked the capacity to effectively review emerging delivery mechanisms (online programs, distance campuses, executive education, fast-track or combined undergraduate-graduate degree programs, etc.). Throughout the entire process, it was also important for NASPAA to be able to articulate the distinctive qualifications of graduates of NASPAA-accredited programs—that is, what makes professional public service degrees unique.

The result of this process was a set of third-generation accreditation standards, overwhelmingly approved at the fall 2009 annual conference, that articulate a more central role for public service values and student competencies within the previous mission-based framework. These standards do not represent a purely outcomes-based approach but rather a shift toward a performance measurement focus. Neither inputs nor mission-based accreditation is abandoned with the application of the new standards; rather, a new layer of emphasis is added. In this way, the standards represent a clear link to what public administration professionals must increasingly contend with in measuring performance, demonstrating accountability, and maintaining transparency.

While the evolution of NASPAA standards is described here as consisting of three generations, each successive philosophical approach to accreditation builds upon and adds to the previous stages and does not completely disregard the earlier generations. As such, even within the current competency framework, many inputs are still measured. Similarly, while a program's mission must now be framed in terms of public service values, the unique program mission is still expected to guide how competencies are defined and measured and how COPRA determines threshold levels of conformity with the standards.

DIVERSITY AND CULTURAL COMPETENCE WITHIN THE THREE GENERATIONS OF NASPAA ACCREDITATION

As NASPAA has progressed through first-, second-, and now third-generation accreditation philosophies and standards, the manner in which diversity and cultural competence have been addressed has evolved as well. Not surprisingly, the trends in accreditation standards parallel somewhat the policies in professional public administration practice.

As with early personnel policies, the initial emphasis was on ensuring that programs avoided discriminatory practices and engaged in efforts to provide equal employment opportunities for persons of color, women, and individuals with disabilities. Programs were required to report the diversity of their faculty and student bodies in terms of specific diversity characteristics (race, gender, and disability status) and to describe their policies and practices that would promote diversity in recruitment or admissions. As the profession expanded its notion of relevant diversity characteristics, NASPAA standards and guidelines also began to mention ethnicity, sexual orientation, and other indicators of diversity. Similarly, as the profession focused more on the organizational climate and how it affected the work experience of women and minorities, NASPAA standards also placed a greater emphasis on program efforts to provide a supportive environment for diverse faculty and students.

Standards regarding faculty and student diversity are not sufficient to advance cultural competency, but commitment to diversity and conformity with these standards can be considered necessary preconditions. Additionally, the discourse surrounding how to assess conformity with the faculty diversity and student diversity standards—specifically, whether to accept generic policies or require program-specific activities and whether to be satisfied with program efforts or to insist on results—provides valuable insights into the challenges of implementing a cultural competency standard.

The faculty and student diversity standards are similar in several notable ways. First, both have been present in the standards since the earliest generation. Second, the language of both standards has been modified over time, but the meaning and interpretation of the standards have remained relatively stable over time. Third, in both cases, the emphasis continues to be on inputs and efforts. Finally, despite recurring discussions about the importance of results, there has been resistance within the Standards Committee and within COPRA to insisting on results in either of these areas. Standards surrounding diversity and cultural competency in the curriculum have followed a much different path and have encountered a very different response within the association. For these reasons, the evolution of the faculty diversity and student diversity standards is discussed before directly examining NASPAA's more recent cultural competency standard and the deliberations surrounding public service values.

Throughout the subsequent sections of this chapter, the emphasis is on general characterizations of the generations as they relate to diversity and cultural competence. More detailed examples of the language utilized in both the accreditation standards and the self-study instructions are provided in Table 13.2.

DIVERSITY AND CULTURAL COMPETENCE WITHIN FIRST- AND SECOND-GENERATION ACCREDITATION

Beginning with the peer review process that preceded formal accreditation, faculty diversity has been among the variables considered to assess program quality. First-generation accreditation processes required programs to provide a list of minority, female, and handicapped faculty and to explain the program's plans for developing and/or maintaining diversity of the public affairs faculty with respect to those same three categories. These two requirements can be considered an accreditation equivalent of the human resource practice of equal employment opportunity (EEO).

It soon became clear that this initial approach, while important, did not fully express the diversity goals of the association. Nondiscrimination as a diversity policy simply did not go far enough as a strategy for developing or maintaining diversity at accredited programs. In the late 1980s, the NASPAA Standards Committee channeled this concern into the Diversity Guidelines, a best practice document that describes what "plans" for ensuring diversity might look like, including developing a diverse pool of applicants, providing a positive and supportive environment, and supplemental efforts outside of hiring. Essentially, the accreditation standards transitioned from an EEO approach to one more closely approximating an affirmative action (AA) perspective. The Diversity Guidelines were approved by the NASPAA Executive Council in 1992, and corresponding to the transition to mission-based accreditation, they were the guidepost of COPRA's interpretation of both the faculty and student diversity standard throughout the second generation of NASPAA accreditation. COPRA directly included language from the guidelines in its self-study instructions that articulated the types of evidence programs should submit to demonstrate conformance with standards. These instructions play a significant role in the accreditation process as they provide one of the clearest articulations of how COPRA actually interprets a given standard.

Every phrase of the instructions represents a deliberative policy discussion around the COPRA table; a careful discussion interpreting the faculty diversity standard occurs at nearly every accreditation decision meeting. Several aspects of interpreting standards related to diversity have proved particularly vexing, and none more so than the desire to look at results or outcomes rather than efforts. The standard itself is written in terms of effort and plans (i.e., inputs), yet the self-study instructions require programs

Table 13.2

Three Generations of NASPAA Standards

Generation	Years	General philosophy	Corresponding practitioners' priorities	Illustrative language from standards and self-study instructions regarding diversity and cultural competence
First generation	1986–1992	Inputs and program resources	Non-discrimination and equal employment opportunity	**Faculty diversity** "There should be evidence that specific plans have been developed to assure the diversity of the composition of the faculty with respect to the representation of minorities, women, and handicapped individuals" (Standard 4.5, 1977). Programs are asked to list full-time faculty with primary responsibility for the program and other full-time faculty teaching in the program, and to indicate affirmative action status ("Indicate whether minority, female, or handicapped") (Self-Study Instructions, 1984). **Student diversity** "Admission goals, policy and standards, including academic prerequisites, should be clearly and publicly stated, specifying the differences for pre-service, in-service or other categories of students, and reflecting specific concern for the representation of minorities, women and handicapped individuals" (Standard 6, 1986). Programs are asked to provide a chart of applications and admissions by part- and full-time, and "if data are available, please include minority, female, and handicapped subtotals" (Self-Study Instructions, 1984). Similarly, programs are asked to provide a student attrition chart that includes students that have graduated, are still actively pursuing the degree, or are no longer active, with a note that " if possible, include identification that allows comparison by minority, female, and handicapped status" (Self-Study Instructions, 1984). In required tables of student applications, admissions, enrollment, and graduations, programs are asked to list number of women and minorities (Self-Study Instructions, 1984). **Curriculum** "The common curriculum components shall provide each student with a basic understanding of the environment of public policy and the ability to deal with: political and legal institutions and processes; economic and social institutions and processes; organization and management concepts, including human resource administration; concepts and techniques of financial administration; techniques of analysis, including quantitative, economic, and statistical methods" (Standard 4.21, 1986).

Second generation	1992–2009	Mission-based accreditation	Supportive environment for diversity and affirmative action	

Faculty diversity

"There should be evidence that specific plans are being implemented to assure the diversity of the composition of the faculty with respect to the representation of minorities, women, and persons with disabilities. Programs and plans to insure faculty diversity shall generally reflect NASPAA Diversity Guidelines" (NASPAA 2008, Standard 5.5).

"Regardless of whether they exist as a written programmatic document, provide evidence that program-based 'specific plans' to assure faculty diversity with respect to the representation of minorities, women, and persons with disabilities are being implemented. Programs should also discuss their efforts to provide a positive and supportive atmosphere for women, minorities, and persons with disabilities on the faculty, to enhance their participation and to increase their retention. . . . Describe supplemental diversity efforts with respect to practitioners, speakers, adjunct faculty, part-time faculty and others" (NASPAA 2010, Standard 5.5(A) Self-Study Instructions).

"Note that this standard does not necessarily require historically black colleges and universities to hire non-black faculty members" (NASPAA 2010, Standard 5.5(A) Self-Study Instructions).

Student diversity

"Admission goals, policy and standards, including academic prerequisites, should be clearly and publicly stated, specifying any differences for pre-service, in-service or other categories of students, and reflecting specific concern for the representation of minorities, women, and person with disabilities. Programs and plans designed to insure student diversity shall generally reflect NASPAA's Diversity Guidelines" (NASPAA 2008, Standard 6.1).

Curriculum

Common curriculum components to "enhance students' values, knowledge, and skills to act ethically and effectively" in the "management of public service organizations," in the "application of quantitative and qualitative techniques of analysis," and "with an understanding of the public policy and organizational environment" (Standard 4.21).

"Program activities must prepare students to work in and contribute to diverse workplaces and communities. Consequently, courses, curriculum materials, and other program activities should expose students to differences relating to social identity categories such as race, ethnicity, gender, class, nationality, religion, sexual orientation, disability, age, and veterans status" (NASPAA 2008, Standard 4.21).[1]

(continued)

Diversity Across the Curriculum (adopted in 2007, near the end of the second generation):

Table 13.2 *(continued)*

Generation	Years	General philosophy	Corresponding practitioners' priorities	Illustrative language from standards and self-study instructions regarding diversity and cultural competence
Third generation	2009 and beyond	Public service values and competencies	Managing for diversity and cultural competence	**Faculty diversity** "The program will promote diversity and a climate of inclusiveness through its recruitment and retention of faculty members" (NASPAA 2009, Standard 3.2). **Student diversity** "The program will promote diversity and a climate of inclusiveness through its recruitment, admissions practices, and student support services" (NASPAA 2009, Standard 4.4). **Curriculum** Cultural competence in curriculum: Programs must define and measure student competencies • To lead and manage in public governance; • To participate in and contribute to the policy process; • To analyze, synthesize, think critically, solve problems and make decisions; • To articulate and apply a public service perspective; • *To communicate and interact productively with a diverse and changing workforce and citizenry.* (NASPAA 2009, Standard 5.1; emphasis added).

[1] Interestingly, the initial proposal for the Diversity Across the Curriculum standard was limited to race, ethnicity, gender, class, nationality, religion, and disability. Sexual orientation was added to the list midway through the committee's deliberation process. The proposal that was presented to the membership for a vote did not include age or veterans status; these were added to the standard as friendly amendments from the floor prior to voting to approve the standard.

to submit data on the demographic composition of their faculty (outputs). Among the questions that repeatedly challenge COPRA are these: Do programs that describe a diverse faculty still need to have a plan? Can a program achieve conformance if it has adopted an excellent plan on paper and provides evidence of implementation efforts yet has no success in achieving a diverse faculty?

As NASPAA progressed through the second-generation mission-based standards, the idea of tying the diversity plan to program mission increased in importance. At one time, a program may have achieved conformance with the faculty diversity standard if it adopted an umbrella university or college plan for achieving diversity. By the end of the second generation, COPRA was sending the clear message to programs that, while a program can adopt a university plan, it must also articulate plans specific to the program and must explicitly articulate how those plans relate to the program mission.

The faculty diversity standard continues to be one to which programs struggle to conform; as of 2010, 20 percent of accredited programs were being monitored by COPRA on the faculty diversity standard in their annual reports. Every year since 2005, more than one-third and generally more than one-half of all programs in the accreditation cycle have been cited by COPRA on the faculty diversity standard at the stage of the interim report, peaking at 65 percent in 2009–10. The percent of accredited programs cited on this standard in the final accreditation decision letter and subject to ongoing monitoring has ranged from 12 to 36 percent (Commission on Peer Review and Accreditation 2010).

The faculty diversity standard was effective in improving awareness and requiring that all programs actively plan for diversity. Yet programs did not achieve the levels of diversity once imagined, prompting a general sense that something more was required. In response to a series of reports from NASPAA's Diversity Committee and in order to assist COPRA with its interpretive challenges, in 2003 the NASPAA Standards Committee began drafting a comprehensive new diversity standard, one that included language for a stronger results-oriented faculty diversity standard, a stronger results-oriented student diversity standard, and a new curriculum standard regarding diversity.

One proposal stated that "the faculty shall be diverse" and would have required programs that did not meet that criterion to present evidence of plans to implement actions to increase diversity. It also included for the first time a standard on faculty environment, stating, "Programs must demonstrate openness to faculty from differing intellectual perspectives and diverse cultures and identities." Similarly, the proposed student diversity standard asserted that the "composition of students shall be diverse" and also included a statement on student environment and openness to differing perspectives and cultures.

The slate of proposed diversity standards was submitted for feedback from the public at large as well as from accredited programs and practitioners. While the feedback generally indicated positive support for the broad notion of a stronger diversity standard, support for particular methods of potential implementation was not as easily gained. Program directors criticized the slate as a one-size-fits-all strategy, in that standards would not allow programs to pursue diversity goals with respect to their specific mission. Others expressed fears that the proposed standards would require programs to pursue diversity goals in ways that were legally prohibited in their states. Still others cited the pipeline problem or other concerns that would prevent them from showing results in achieving diversity in the short term. Many questioned how programs could effectively demonstrate to an accrediting body their openness to diverse perspectives, cultures, and identities.

The Standards Committee met several times over a four-year period to revise the language and discuss feedback. As the time to propose final language for the vote neared, many aspects of the proposed standards continued to vex the committee. Members of the committee pointed out that the standard, while moving away from "efforts," did not move the assessment any closer to outcomes, as counting faculty members or students was still a component of an inputs-based process, and it left no room for mission-based or situational contingencies. The only element of the standard that embraced the trend of moving toward outcomes was the proposal on "Diversity Across the Curriculum," since it explicitly referred to preparing students "to work in and contribute to diverse workplaces and communities." Thus, while the faculty and student diversity components of the proposals would have held programs to stronger thresholds, they represented two steps backward in accreditation philosophy.

These concerns weighed on the Standards Committee's deliberations but none was more troubling than the legal analysis undertaken by experts in accreditation law to see whether these changes were possible for programs in all states. It appeared that a results-based standard would be very challenging to implement consistently, given the constraints that many programs operated under. The standard was criticized as being too quantitatively focused on a very narrow definition of diversity. A results-based standard did not appear to be held up as a best practice in accreditation, and accreditation law experts advised that a superior option would be an efforts-based standard that requires programs to address diversity in the context of their mission and program objectives.

By this time, the comprehensive standards revision to move NASPAA toward the third generation was already well under way. Given the number of concerns expressed by programs, the legal analysis, and the questions that arose in the committee itself, it became clear that some of the proposed language was problematic and should not move forward as written. The committee decided to recast the faculty and student diversity standards within the constructs of the larger standards revision. However, the Diversity Across the Curriculum standard was retained as a proposal because it was deemed a very important step forward in NASPAA's understanding of diversity in graduate public service programs, and one that should not wait until the next generation of accreditation standards.

The curriculum components required of a NASPAA-accredited program remained relatively consistent during the first and second generations of accreditation and they did not include any explicit reference to diversity or cultural competence. Since the earliest generation, programs have been required to document how the common curriculum components of their degrees "enhance student's values, knowledge, and skills to act ethically and effectively" in the "management of public service organizations," in the "application of quantitative and qualitative techniques of analysis," and "with an understanding of the public policy and organizational environment" (NASPAA

2008, Standard 4.21). Diversity and cultural competence can be inferred in several of these areas—for example, as a part of human resources management that is expected in public service organizations, or as part of the social, legal, and organizational context in which policies are developed and implemented, but it is notable that they were not explicitly required during the entire first generation of accreditation or most of the second generation.

In 1998, a small grant from NASPAA's Diversity Committee helped support a research project to determine the extent to which diversity was addressed in the curricula of programs within NASPAA and the Association for Public Policy Analysis and Management (APPAM). The results of the survey, conducted by Walter Stafford, documented that fewer than 10 percent of programs had a required course on some aspect of diversity or multiculturalism and that roughly half of all programs address diversity in the context of a broader course (e.g., on human resource management) (Stafford 2000). The findings of that report and another on faculty diversity prepared by Jorge Chapa served as the basis for a series of breakout sessions and a plenary session at the 1999 Annual Conference. The research findings, summaries of the conference discussions, and a series of action items were included in a May 2000 report from the Diversity Committee to the Executive Council of NASPAA. Among the recommendations contained in the Diversity Committee report was that "NASPAA should encourage programs to incorporate diversity in the required core curriculum components" (NASPAA Diversity Committee 2000). This came to fruition in 2007 when the Diversity Across the Curriculum provision was added to the standards. The Diversity Across the Curriculum standard was the sole surviving proposal from the Standards Committee's deliberations of 2003–7 related to strengthening diversity standards.

Due to COPRA's practice of phasing in enforcement of new standards, Diversity Across the Curriculum barely had time to move from education to enforcement with any rigor before the transition to the third-generation accreditation standards. Since the standard was approved only in 2007, programs in the 2008–9 accreditation cycle were not expected to demonstrate much by way of conformity with the new standard. COPRA identified this as a concern in 58 percent of the interim reports issued during that cycle, but fewer than 5 percent of the programs were ultimately monitored on this standard as part of their accreditation decisions. Either programs were tremendously successful in meeting the standard in response to feedback received in the interim reports or, more likely, COPRA opted to apply its lenient educational perspective. In 2009–10, COPRA again cited more than half (51.4 percent) of programs on this standard at the stage of the interim report (Commission on Peer Review and Accreditation 2010). The commission also articulated its intent to take seriously the requirement that programs address diversity in courses, curriculum, *and* program activities (emphasis added) (Commission on Peer Review and Accreditation 2010).

Diversity and Cultural Competence Within Third-Generation Accreditation Standards

Under the third generation of NASPAA standards, faculty and student diversity are addressed using slightly different language from earlier versions of the standards, but the self-study instructions suggest they continue to apply largely the same foci. For both faculty and student diversity, programs are required to promote diversity and a climate of inclusiveness.

In preparing a self-study report to document conformity with this standard, programs will be asked to document specific strategies used in recruitment of faculty, strategies for retention of faculty, and other strategies to expose students to diverse views and perspectives. Programs will also have to document the diversity characteristics of their faculty to the extent permissible by law. For U.S.-based programs, a set of reporting categories related to race, ethnicity, disability, gender, and international status are provided. Programs based outside the United States are allowed to define the relevant demographic categories of diversity with respect to their own cultural context. Under the standards, programs must also provide narrative descriptions of their current faculty diversity efforts linked to the program mission, and any changes in faculty diversity experienced over the previous five years (NASPAA 2010a, Standard 3.2).

With respect to students, programs must provide narratives describing ongoing diversity activities and how the program's recruitment efforts include outreach to historically underrepresented populations and serve the program's mission. Like the faculty diversity requirements, programs must document the demographic characteristics (race, ethnicity, international status, disability, and gender) of the student body in the self-study year and previous year, while programs based outside the United States may define their own categories of diversity (NASPAA 2010a, Standard 4.4).

In contrast to the continuity in the areas of faculty and student diversity, the language and reporting expectations are notably different with respect to curriculum. The focus is no longer on subject area context and material to which students are exposed; instead, the emphasis is on student learning and competencies. This represents a clear shift from diversity to cultural competence, again demonstrating that the accreditation standards are paralleling the changes and challenges that practitioners are confronting in the workplace.

Under the standards adopted in 2009, a set of "universal required competencies" has been articulated that encompasses five broad domains, one of which directly addresses cultural competence in that it requires that programs assess for their students' abilities to communicate and interact productively with a diverse and changing workforce and citizenry. In each of these domains, programs must adopt a set of required competencies related to the program mission and public service values. For each of the universal competencies—as well as others that the program may identify specific to its mission or its advertised specializations—the program must engage in ongoing assessment of student learning. Specifically, programs must identify how they have defined learning outcomes for a competency, gathered evidence of learning, analyzed evidence of learning, and used evidence to make programmatic decisions. Programs must also document which required courses cover each competency. In this way, the third generation of NASPAA accreditation standards will serve as a driving force for ensuring that public affairs education develops the cultural competencies of the next generation of public service professionals.

A summary of the three generations of NASPAA accreditation standards and the evolution of standards surrounding issues of diversity and cultural competence is provided in Table 13.2. This table also illustrates how the changing terminology of accreditation standards and self-study instructions reflects a response to changes in the profession.

Cultural Competency in Other Professional Accreditation Standards

NASPAA is not alone in its shift toward the inclusion of cultural competency in its standards. Several other peer accreditors have a head start on assessing competencies, having adopted competency-based standards prior to NASPAA's shift. Some cultural competency standards appear particularly well-developed, especially in fields where an emphasis on cultural competency might be expected as a core aspect of developing effective professionals, such as counseling (CACREP), planning (Planning Accreditation Board [PAB]), social work (Council on Social Work Education [CSWE]), and library sciences (American Library Association–Committee on Accreditation [ALA-COA]). For example, the accreditation standards for social work state: "Social workers recognize the extent to which a culture's structures and values may oppress, marginalize, alienate, or create or enhance privilege and power; gain sufficient self-awareness to eliminate the influence of personal biases and values in working with diverse groups; [and] recognize and communicate their understanding of the importance of difference in shaping life experiences" (CSWE 2010). And the planners require that their graduates

> understand the different values and ethical standards affecting the practice of planning, demonstrating knowledge for: comprehending and discriminating among the goals that an individual, group, community and organization holds when considering the future including the values of justice, equity, fairness, efficiency, order and beauty; assessing and choosing among different forms of democratic decision making that support and improve the quality of plans and planning related activity including the values of fair representation, equal opportunity and non discrimination by race, ethnicity, gender, age, religion, nationality, sexual orientation or disability; and comparing and respecting the complex social, historical and ecological legacies that accompanies urban settlement across the globe including the values of social equity, cultural and historical preservation and environmental conservation and sustainability. (Planning Accreditation Board 2006)

Other fields and accreditors, such as business (Association to Advance Collegiate Schools of Business [AACSB]), take a more explicitly global perspective when looking at cultural competency. An eligibility standard for business school accreditation states: "Consistent with its mission and its cultural context, the institution must demonstrate diversity in its business programs" (AACSB 2011). The interpretive clarification for this requirement further explains that the "school must first define and support the concept of diversity appropriate to its culture, historical traditions, and legal and regulatory environment . . . Every graduate should be prepared to pursue a business or management career in a global context. That is, students should be exposed to cultural practices different than their own. The school must document how it achieves diverse viewpoints among its participants and as a part of students' learning experiences" (AACSB 2011).

Clearly, accrediting bodies are choosing an array of strategies to define cultural competency, each according to the ways they believe will contribute to graduates' success in their field and that match the accrediting goals of the agency. However, effective practice and taking into consideration the context of the program appear to be a common thread. NASPAA, COPRA, accredited programs, and the entire public administration profession will be able to learn from the experiences of other accrediting bodies, while also developing unique strategies appropriate to public service and individual program missions.

THE PUBLIC SERVICE VALUES DEBATE REGARDING DIVERSITY AND CULTURAL COMPETENCE

The third generation of accreditation is characterized not only by greater emphasis on student learning and demonstrated competencies, but also by placing competencies and the entire mission-based accreditation within a framework of public service values. In so doing, NASPAA intends to better brand the professional public affairs, administration, and policy degrees it accredits and to help distinguish them from other professions.

In sharp contrast to the manner in which the Diversity Across the Curriculum and the cultural competency standards proceeded from idea to official standard with widespread support and minimal opposition, the discussion of what should be explicitly included in the definition of public service values was considerably more controversial. Ultimately, the precondition statements to the standards that were approved by the NASPAA membership included the following statement about public service values: "They include pursuing the public interest with accountability and transparency; serving professionally with competence, efficiency, and objectivity; acting ethically so as to uphold the public trust; and demonstrating respect, equity, and fairness in dealings with citizens and fellow public servants" (NASPAA 2009, Preconditions for Accreditation Review). Notably absent from the description is any explicit reference to appreciating diversity or demonstrating cultural competence. As with earlier curriculum standards, diversity and cultural competence can be inferred in the more generic statements about competence, respect, fairness, and equity, but it is important to note that explicit reference is omitted not by accident or oversight, but rather in response to the degree of controversy that the inclusion of more specific values elicited.

The discussion surrounding public service values was at the heart of defining quality in public service education for the new standards. In fact, the theme of the 2009 NASPAA conference where the final vote took place was "Public Service Values." On the one hand, there was much debate and considerable resistance to the notion of the accrediting body defining for a program the public service values to which it should aspire. At the other end of the spectrum, some expressed concern that a failure to define any values in the standards would force COPRA to accept any public service values that the program proposed. The challenge was whether members could agree on some central universal values; however, what seemed to many like values clearly shared by all quickly became problematic. For example, a commitment to democratic governance seemed like an important goal, yet it conflicted with the early principle that the NASPAA standards not be designed in a way to arbitrarily preclude international accreditation.

Should a high-quality public administration program in a monarchy automatically be excluded from the process? Equity was another problematic value; some advocated for social equity to be included in the list of values, while others argued that it conflicted with the value of efficiency. The argument was that a program should have the option to decide for itself how to balance and pursue these goods and that COPRA should not be in the business of deciding which is the most acceptable good for the program.

The other problem with adding specificity to acceptable values was a bit more pragmatic, in that the list of potential values was growing. With the list becoming longer, it became clear that at some point the list of values itself would cease to have value in the accrediting process. The Standards Committee concluded that the sheer number of potential values would render the list useless when it came time for CO-PRA to assess conformance, subscribing to the maxim that if you value everything, you ultimately value nothing.

What resulted was a compromise solution. The revised standards themselves require the program to define its mission in terms of public service values, but no specific values are listed. The preconditions language includes a very broad set of values but stops short of explicitly listing diversity. With this compromise came the understanding that this was a snapshot in time of a conversation that has been ongoing and will continue as programs and COPRA attempt to wrestle with this standard. There was a strong sense that this was not a discussion that could be resolved in the few years over which the standards were penned.

Ironically, while diversity, social equity, and cultural competence did not fare well in the definitions of public service values, it was the overall commitment to a public service values focus that ultimately led to the inclusion of cultural competency in the standards. As of January 2008, the original draft of the competency domain that would ultimately become the cultural competency standard read, "to communicate and interact in multi-person environments"; in February 2008 this phrase was revised to emphasize that graduates should be able "to communicate and interact in groups." During this time period, the Standards Committee formed a small task force to analyze the standards in terms of the public service focus and to see if the concept of public service values was sufficiently captured throughout the standards. Concluding that the public service values focus was not infused strongly enough throughout, the committee's internal report offered a number of suggestions, one of these being a proposal to add diversity as a curricular or competency element. The next draft of the standards, presented to the public in March 2008, included the cultural competency language that passed into the final standards, which moved beyond reference to the ability to communicate and interact in "multiperson environments" and "groups" to include the stronger and more explicit reference to "a diverse and changing workforce and citizenry."

LESSONS LEARNED: IMPLICATIONS FOR PROGRAMS INTERESTED IN CULTURAL COMPETENCE

The evolution of NASPAA accreditation standards surrounding the issues of diversity and cultural competence can inform curriculum development and programmatic improvements for a wide array of professional degree programs, not simply those in public affairs or those that are accredited. Just as the NASPAA standards have struggled to move from an emphasis on inputs to mission to competencies, so too must programs progress in their thinking and action. It is no longer sufficient to define programs in terms of the courses that students must complete, even if those courses are substantively linked to a program's mission. Programs must invest time and energy in defining what students will be able to do upon completion of a course or program (i.e., what competencies they will have) and how the program will assess student achievement of those competencies (i.e., how to measure and assess competencies).

With respect to the transition from diversity to cultural competence, it will no longer be sufficient for programs to tout the diversity of their faculty rosters or student bodies or to identify how course modules or even entire courses expose students to the issues of diversity. To adequately prepare students for the current and future challenges of professional public service, programs will need to reexamine their curricular and extracurricular activities for their ability to instill in students the competencies to effectively work with individuals from a variety of cultures. Grading criteria for course assignments and evaluation criteria for degree completion must be revised to include measures of how well students demonstrate their ability to communicate effectively across cultural differences.

LOOKING AHEAD: SPECIAL CHALLENGES OF THE CULTURAL COMPETENCY STANDARD

Accreditation standards have the potential to provide a motivation for change across the discipline, and the goal of NASPAA's cultural competency standard is to ensure that future graduates of public affairs programs are capable of working effectively in an environment of increasing diversity. NASPAA-accredited programs should be preparing individuals who are fully equipped to manage people and projects; to develop, implement, and evaluate policies; and to provide essential services to populations characterized by cultural, racial, ethnic, linguistic, religious, generational, and other forms of diversity.

It is too soon to know if the standard will have that intended effect; past experience would suggest that the new standard will be in place several years before it is fully enforced, allowing time for programs and COPRA to develop the expertise and capacity to meet the expectations of the standard. While it is too soon after adoption of the cultural competency standard to assess its effectiveness, it is not too early to identify the most likely challenges that will be encountered along the way. Two challenges stand out as deserving particular attention: (1) the capacity of programs, COPRA, and site visitors to effectively operationalize and assess cultural competencies, and (2) the meaning of cultural competencies in nontraditional settings such as minority-serving institutions (MSIs) or programs based outside the United States.

CAPACITY TO DEFINE AND ASSESS CULTURAL COMPETENCIES

In recognition that the increased emphasis on student competencies may represent a burden to programs, a task force responsible for crafting self-study instructions under the standards also developed an extensive list of potential operational definitions in each domain. While programs are tasked with developing operational definitions that are specific to their own mission, examples are provided to assist programs in thinking about possible definitions. So, for example, cultural competency may be demonstrated in the form of "sensitivity and responsiveness to beliefs and behaviors associated with differences among people because of their ethnicity, nationality, race, gender, physical characteristics, religion, age, etc." or the ability to utilize a process that "discerns the interests and values of others; surfaces assumptions; secures agreement on ground rules and tolerable outcomes; gains cooperation of others to accomplish goals" (NASPAA 2010a, Appendix B). This list is not meant to constrain how programs define cultural competency, but simply to suggest some options.

Defining what constitutes cultural competency is a challenge, but it is eclipsed by the difficulty of measuring that competency. This challenge faces not only programs, but also COPRA and site visitors. Before COPRA can insist on conformity with the standard, members of the commission as well as the site visitors who gather information on behalf of COPRA will need to have the capacity to evaluate cultural competency measures reported by programs. The qualifications of site visitors are particularly important as NASPAA moves forward because programs are only required to summarize their assessment of one of the universal required competencies in their own self-study reports; reporting the program's assessment of the other competencies will be the responsibility of the site visitors. For each of these actors—program directors, COPRA members, and site visitors—measuring competencies for any domain is difficult enough; measuring cultural competencies is among the most complex tasks.

The question remains whether COPRA is equipped to review program conformity with respect to cultural competency. COPRA members are, after all, peers of the programs under review. Prior experience suggests that COPRA, like programs, must travel a learning curve. Standards are aspirations and in that respect they catalyze and provide guidance on what is needed. Future scholarship in the profession as well as ongoing activities of the Diversity Committee will inform and assist programs and COPRA in developing the abilities to assess cultural competencies. It is also likely that many programs will be cited on cultural competencies in the early years, particularly at the stage of the interim report as COPRA works with programs to enhance understanding and conformity.

CULTURAL COMPETENCY IN MINORITY-SERVING INSTITUTIONS AND INTERNATIONAL SETTINGS

Implementation of the cultural competency standard is further complicated when one considers how it applies in nontraditional settings. Programs housed in minority-serving institutions (MSIs), particularly those in historically black colleges and universities (HBCUs), as well as those outside the United States present some interesting interpretation and implementation challenges for NASPAA and COPRA.

Challenges of Implementation in Minority-Serving Institutions

Institutions of higher education that serve large proportions of minority students are classified as minority-serving institutions (MSIs). Three categories of MSIs—

historically black colleges and universities (HBCUs), Hispanic-serving institutions (HSIs), and tribal colleges and universities—play a role in providing access to higher education for African Americans, Hispanics, and American Indians, respectively. The most visible debates surrounding the implementation of NASPAA standards in MSIs have focused on HBCUs.

As NASPAA has observed with respect to the faculty diversity and student diversity standards, there is some disagreement within the membership regarding how such standards should be applied to programs based in HBCUs. In the realm of the faculty and student diversity standards, the issue has been whether a program based in an HBCU—with a faculty and student body that are largely or entirely composed of the groups that are often woefully underrepresented at other institutions—has met the diversity standards. On the one hand, the programs are clearly employing and serving members of groups who have historically faced discrimination. On the other hand, there may be limited diversity within the faculty or student body. A review of the available self-study reports from 2005–10 shows that all but one of the graduate programs at HBCUs applying for NASPAA accreditation reported that the population of African American students exceeded 88 percent of the enrolled student body in the self-study year.

As stated earlier, COPRA added a statement to the self-study instructions during the second generation to clarify that HBCUs are not necessarily required to hire nonblack faculty members because their mission may emphasize the employment of and service to African Americans. Similarly, programs that have large minority representation in their student body are not generally expected to demonstrate efforts to recruit and admit more white students. As interpreted and applied to HBCUs, the faculty and student diversity standards have tended to prioritize serving historically underrepresented groups (at a societal level) rather than ensuring diversity within a given program.

A similar challenge may arise when interpreting the cultural competency standard for programs within HBCUs. In programs that provide students with regular opportunities to interact with African American faculty and practitioners, and in which students can point to their own personal experience bridging a minority culture with the majority culture, is there a need to prepare students to work with other cultures? Can a program at an HBCU claim that African American students have a lifetime of demonstrating cultural competencies by functioning as a minority within the majority white society? If the discourse surrounding the evolution of NASPAA standards to date is any indicator, this will continue to be a matter of discussion and debate for many years.

Challenges of Implementation in International Institutions

Similar challenges will apply to how the diversity and cultural competency standards apply to programs in an international context. In 2011 COPRA will begin a pilot program of accepting its first self-study reports from programs based outside of the United States. The cultural and historical assumptions regarding diversity in the United States either do not apply or manifest themselves differently in these contexts that are new to COPRA. How, then, can COPRA ensure consistency in its decision making between domestic applicants and those based outside the United States?

From a purely definitional standpoint, the demographic characteristics used for reporting on conformity with the faculty and student diversity standards that are relevant in the United States may not be meaningful in other countries. COPRA's early self-study instructions to programs ask international applicants to define their own diversity categories, in accordance with the norms of their country. Similarly, the knowledge, skills, and abilities related to diversity—that is the cultural competencies—required of graduates of public affairs programs in non-U.S. settings may be quite different.

Once the hurdle of communicating information on diversity and cultural competency has been crossed, COPRA then faces the exceptional challenge of evaluating a program's conformance to these standards with respect to its mission and unique cultural context. To do this, the commission will have to familiarize itself with the nuances of each country and program. To reasonably assess international programs, the commission itself will need to be more diverse in its membership. COPRA members and site visitors will need to have the ability to consider multiple cultural viewpoints and to interpret program characteristics within the context of both the accreditation standards and the cultural and legal environment in which an individual program operates.

Many questions surround the implementation of cultural competencies standards in an international context. Among the most pressing questions are these: What will constitute conformance to diversity and cultural competency standards in the international context? Is the intent of this standard primarily to address the need for greater representation of traditionally underrepresented groups, or should it address broader goals of diversity? And how far is COPRA willing to tread into nondiscrimination issues outside of the United States? For example, will it be acceptable for a program in a Muslim country to exclude women from either its faculty or student body? The debates surrounding how best to advance the interests of historically underrepresented groups are heated even within the United States, and it is unclear how COPRA will weigh in on such questions in an international setting with very different laws and societal values.

A further and very important component of the diversity standard in the international context goes beyond the physical location of the applicant program. During the 2003–7 deliberations regarding diversity standards, as well as during the 2006–9 comprehensive standards revision process, the Standards Committee discussed at length the relationship between international or globalized education and the diversity standard. More programs are beginning to conceive of themselves as explicitly internationalized, with international faculty and student bodies, an internationally focused curriculum, and alumni that work on international issues in countries worldwide. Should the diversity and cultural competency standards be applied uniquely for these types of programs, defining diversity explicitly from an international viewpoint? Will these programs be expected to conduct the same proactive efforts as primarily nationally focused programs in terms of recruiting underserved groups and preparing students for the unique cultural context surrounding the geographic location of the program?

Is this a progressive evolution to capture innovative programs, or will something be lost from the original intent of the standard in the U.S. context?

Although NASPAA accreditation will be open to international programs under the third-generation standards, the accreditation model is still explicitly U.S. style, essentially meaning any inherent values and/or baggage that motivated the current accreditation standards in the traditionally U.S.-focused organization will be applied worldwide. What that means in exceptionally difficult cases is hard to predict. Will the commission accept that a program that discriminates by gender, class, or ethnicity may indeed serve an important purpose and mission in the country in which it operates, even if the commission does not necessarily agree with the politics? The commission will need to find a balance between its commitments to consistency in interpretation and its recognition of quality in alternative models worldwide.

SUMMARY

As NASPAA transitions to the third-generation standards, cultural competency has joined faculty diversity, student diversity, and diversity across the curriculum as a requirement for accreditation. In the area of diversity and cultural competence, it is not always clear whether the accreditation standards are leading or following the profession, but standards and the accreditation process certainly facilitate discussion and provide an incentive for change and responsiveness. As the profession and the association confront the challenges of implementing the cultural competency standard, the experiences of other professional accreditors who started this journey earlier and have progressed further can provide some guidance. Additionally, NASPAA's Diversity Committee and the scholarship of individuals dedicated to promoting cultural competence will continue to play an important role in pushing the Standards Committee, COPRA, and the broader membership to elevate the priority of diversity and cultural competence through publications, conference sessions, and accreditation decisions.

Having cultural competence in the standards will not guarantee that all graduates of accredited MPA/MPP programs will be culturally competent, but it will force programs to think deliberatively about how cultural competency relates to their specific program mission, what they need to include within the curricular and noncurricular elements of the program to improve the cultural competencies of students, and how they can assess the level of cultural competence among their students. Just as previous chapters in this volume provided the rationale for the increased emphasis on cultural competencies in public affairs, the following chapters serve as excellent resources for programs and individual faculty involved in the education of public administration professionals.

REFERENCES

The Association to Advance Collegiate Schools of Business (AACSB). 2011. AACSB standards 2011 update report. www.aacsb.edu/accreditation/standards.asp.

Bailey, Margo. 2005. Cultural competency and the practice of public administration. In *Diversity and Public Administration: Theory, Issues, and Perspectives*, ed. Mitchell F. Rice, 177–196. Armonk, NY: M.E. Sharpe.

Benavides, Abraham David, and Julie C.T. Hernandez. 2007. Serving diverse communities: Cultural competency. *Public Management Magazine* 89(6): 14–18.

Commission on Peer Review and Accreditation. 2010. Internal documents and summary reports.

Council for Higher Education Accreditation (CHEA). 2006. CHEA at a glance. www.chea.org/pdf/chea_glance_2006.pdf.

———. 2011. 2010–2011 directory of CHEA-recognized organizations. May. www.chea.org/pdf/2010_2011_Directory_of_CHEA_Recognized_Organizations.pdf.

Council on Social Work Education (CSWE). 2010. Educational policy and accreditation standards. www.cswe.org/File.aspx?id=13780.

Henry, Laurin L. 1995. History. National Association of Schools of Public Affairs and Administration. www.naspaa.org/about_naspaa/about/history.asp.

Johnson, Richard G., and Mario A. Rivera. 2007. Refocusing graduate public affairs education: A need for diversity competencies in human resource management. *Journal of Public Affairs Education* 13(1): 15–27.

Kellar, Elizabeth. 2005 Wanted: Language and cultural competence. *PM: Public Management* 87(1). http://icma.org/en/icma/knowledge_network/documents/kn/Document/4918/Wanted_Language_and_Cultural_Competence.

National Association of Schools of Public Affairs and Administration (NASPAA). 2002. Bylaws. www.naspaa.org/about_naspaa/about/bylaws.asp.

———. 2008. General information and standards for professional master's degree programs. January edition. www.naspaa.org/accreditation/document/OFFICIAL_DOCUMENTS_2008_standards_only.pdf.

———. 2009. Accreditation standards for master's degree programs. October 16. www.naspaa.org/accreditation/NS/naspaastandards.asp.

———. 2010a. General instructions for the self-study report. 2010 edition. www.naspaa.org/accreditation/NS/OFFICIAL_DOCUMENTS_2010_Self_Study.pdf.

———. 2010b. Official roster of NASPAA accredited programs 2010–11. www.naspaa.org/accreditation/NS/roster.asp.

———. 2011a. NASPAA. www.naspaa.org/about_naspaa/naspaa.asp.

———. 2011b. NASPAA overview. www.naspaa.org/about_naspaa/about/overview.asp.

NASPAA Diversity Committee. 2000. Examining what we teach and how we teach it: Diversity in the NASPAA curriculum. In *NASPAA Diversity Report*, 8–9.

Planning Accreditation Board. 2006. The accreditation document: Criteria and procedures of the planning accreditation program. November. www.planningaccreditationboard.org/index.php?id=46.

Riccucci, Norma M. 2002. *Managing Diversity in Public Sector Workforces*. Boulder, CO: Westview Press.

Rice, Mitchell F. 2007. Promoting cultural competency in public administration and public service delivery: Utilizing self-assessment tools and performance measures. *Journal of Public Affairs Education* 13(1): 41–57.

Rubaii-Barrett, Nadia. 2006. Teaching courses on managing diversity. *Journal of Public Affairs Education* 12(3): 361–383.

Stafford, Walter. 2000. Principle findings of the diversity survey 1997–1998. In *NASPAA Diversity Report*, 29–35.

U.S. Census Bureau. 2010. *The 2010 Statistical Abstract of the United States*. Washington, DC: Government Printing Office.

U.S. Department of Labor (DOL), Bureau of Labor Statistics. 2004. Workforce diversity: Opportunities in the melting pot. *Occupational Outlook Quarterly* (January): 28–37.

14

Cultural Competency in Public Administration Programs

PAMELA H. LEWIS, ALLEN N. LEWIS
AND FELECIA D. WILLIAMS

Recent changes in U.S. demographics have underscored the demand for cultural competency in all settings (Genao et al. 2003). Since 1976 the percentage of minority students in U.S. colleges and universities has more than doubled from 15 percent to 32 percent in 2007 (U.S. Department of Education 2009). In addition, the racial and ethnic makeup of faculty at U.S. colleges and universities is gradually becoming more diverse. Eighty percent of full-time faculty in 2010 is white compared to a faculty that was 89 percent white in 1987 (American Association of State Colleges and Universities 2006). Although the percentage of faculty that is nonwhite is increasing, it is anticipated from these trends that in coming years many students will experience a cultural mismatch with their faculty.

The anticipated demographic changes in the United States will challenge the capabilities of America's universities and public serving agencies, and new approaches are needed to address cultural differences among consumers (Lewis and Lewis 2010). Public administration programs and public serving agencies face many challenges in the twenty-first century. Therefore, public administration programs are redefining their roles and aligning their structures with other components of the changing demographics in the United States, where they must proactively and strategically position themselves for the coming years.

ORGANIZATIONAL FRAMEWORK OF CULTURAL COMPETENCY IN PUBLIC ADMINISTRATION PROGRAMS

Addressing critical issues such as "How can cultural competency effectively be implemented in a public administration program?" and "How does the faculty know that students are able to demonstrate cultural competency upon completion?" presents challenges for faculty and administrators (Drummond, Nixon, and Wiltshire 1998; Shavelson and Huang 2003). This chapter provides a strategy for distilling the issues and integrating the concepts of cultural competency into public administration programs and public serving agencies by providing a framework for public servants and faculty to utilize in their journey toward cultural competency.

Adapted from the Department of Nutrition at the University of Tennessee, Knoxville (Eckley et al. 2004), a strategy for integrating cultural competency into public administration programs is demonstrated in Figure 14.1. Figure 14.1 offers users a simple, yet explanatory model incorporating the principles of cultural competency and providing a foundation upon which to base a public administration program's plan for cultural competency. The main objectives are to (1) identify strengths and weaknesses of the program; and (2) use the strengths and weaknesses identified to enhance cultural competency.

Figure 14.1 illustrates eleven domains that focus on the mission and program policies; governance and organization; student, faculty, and practitioner preparation and development; campus and community; environment and communication; curriculum development; integration of cultural competency; translating research; and technical assistance and consultation.

The mission, policies, practices, recruitment, and retention illustrate the importance of integrating populations from diverse communities and including activities so that faculty and students can develop cultural competency skills. Notably, access to services cannot be achieved if the physical environment is not accessible to everyone. Also, the curriculum should be evaluated for evidence of cultural competency and research should address and recognize culturally diverse populations. As a final point, consultants with cultural competency skills can assist the program in incorporating the above elements in all aspects of policy making, administration, practice, and service delivery. Integrating congruent values, policies, behaviors, and practices will enable public administration programs to become culturally competent and perform effective cross-cultural work (Eckley et al. 2004). However, before this can be accomplished, faculty and staff must develop certain foundational skills for further learning.

MISSION AND PROGRAM POLICIES

Mission and program policies refer to all of the "documentation that governs the academic unit including mission statements, strategic plans, handbooks, policies, and procedures" (Eckley et al. 2004, 8). Some employees view mission statements as documents that are simply displayed and strategic plans as documents that collect dust on managers' shelves because some staff are not aware of the contents (Williams 2007). Therefore, it is important that a process for integrating cultural competency into a program's mission statement, policies, and procedures be developed in such a way that actively promotes student, faculty, and practitioner involvement. For example, language in the mission statement, policies, and procedures should reflect the diversity of the students, faculty, and community served. Importantly, policies and procedures should be in a usable mode of communication, such as Braille for persons with blindness.

Figure 14.1   Cultural Competence Framework in a Public Administration Program

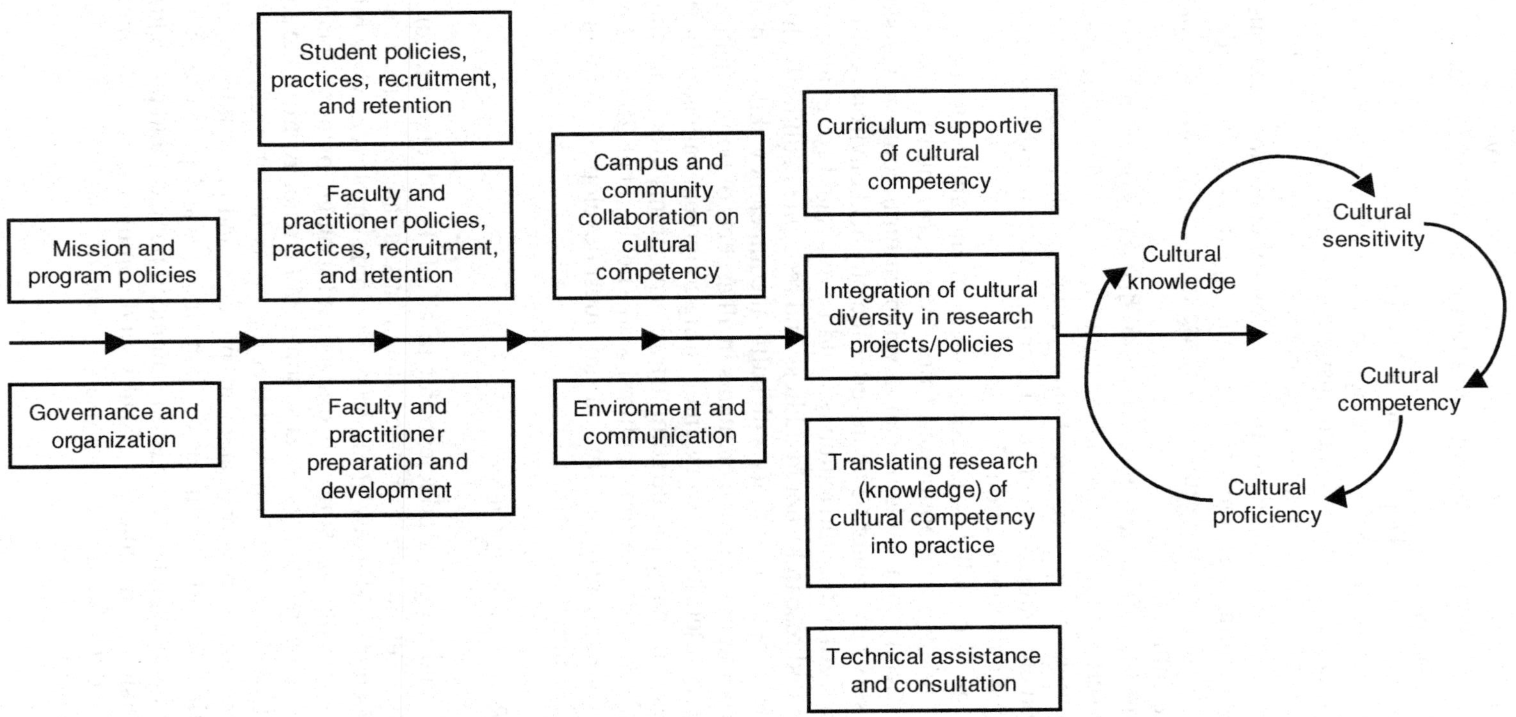

Source: Adapted from Eckley et al. (2004).

Figure 14.2
Methods of Providing Culturally Competent Services

1. Gather demographic information about students in order to provide advising, and translation and interpretation services if needed.
2. Seek input from students of diverse backgrounds in developing policies.
3. Recruit students from diverse backgrounds.
4. Actively implement student policies on harassment, racism, and discrimination.

GOVERNANCE AND ORGANIZATION

"Governance involves cooperation and collaboration among multiple governmental and nongovernmental actors with diverse economic and non-economic interests" (Halachmi 2005, 308). Governance refers to the way the public administration program is organized. The system of governance in the university setting is unique because it includes components from corporate, nonprofit, and government systems. Subsequently, each field of study may define university governance differently (Halachmi 2005). While universities typically have a hierarchal structure, each level must be in agreement regarding cultural competency in the respective departments, programs, and units. A political framework is often applied to university governance (Maitlis 2004; Sasso 2003). Recognizing the innately political nature of governance (Reed 2002), an academic program needs to be diligent in order to incorporate the principles of cultural competency.

One of the most important features of effective university governance is a committee, task force, or program area that addresses issues of cultural competency. It is equally important to involve a diverse group of stakeholders as appropriate in the planning of the academic unit. Commitment, by all, to positively moving along the continuum is critical to the success of efforts toward cultural competency. Senior administrators, including presidents, vice presidents, deans, and directors, set the agenda and signal the importance of cultural competency as a goal when they actively participate in or appoint members to the task force.

STUDENT POLICIES, PRACTICES, RECRUITMENT, AND RETENTION

Student policies, practices, recruitment, and retention refer to advising and mentoring students in a culturally competent manner. Students are affected by the policies and practices of the university and the program. For this reason, commitment to cultural competency should be evident in all student policies, practices, recruitment, and retention practices (Eckley et al. 2004). It is important that the public administration program respects students' cultural differences and provides mentoring, advising, and support for their academic needs. This can best be achieved by obtaining the demographic information of the student population (see Figure 14.2). For example, translation and interpretation services should be available to students from diverse backgrounds. Also, student organizations should reflect the diversity of the student population.

Faculty and Staff Policies, Practices, Recruitment, and Retention

Faculty and staff policies, practices, recruitment, and retention refer to a diverse workforce and the elimination of barriers to job recruitment (Eckley et al. 2004). The public administration program should have an employment equity policy that eliminates discriminatory barriers when hiring faculty and staff. Typically, the human resources department is the unit charged with developing position descriptions, implementing personnel practices, and investigating complaints of unfair and discriminatory barriers to accessibility to jobs. Human resources policies, procedures, and practices should be supportive of cultural competency and include specific provisions to address multiculturalism, racism, harassment, and discrimination. Also, performance evaluations should be sensitive to cultural differences and reflect skills related to cultural competency.

Faculty and Practitioner Preparation and Development

Faculty and practitioner preparation and development refer to increasing awareness, knowledge, and skills through cultural competency training (Eckley et al. 2004). Faculty and practitioner development falls under the broad category of human resources development (HRD). HRD is the widely accepted idea of bolstering organizational infrastructure and capacity through comprehensive workforce development. HRD includes various strategies. First, preservice programs should give staff and faculty the necessary tools to function in a culturally competent manner. Second, once individuals become a part of the faculty and workforce, there must be ongoing efforts to retool them and ensure continuous quality improvement in their ability to remain culturally competent. To meet this obligation requires public administration programs and agencies to invest in sufficient on-the-job training opportunities as well as workshops and training sessions outside of work on a routine basis. Precursors for further learning for faculty and practitioners alike require developing perceptual flexibility, valuing diversity, cultivating awareness, and gauging readiness. They provide a critically needed beginning point that is foundational for further understanding.

Developing Perceptual Flexibility

As human beings, we are all prone to generalizing, stereotyping, and drawing wrong conclusions. This is because our minds are designed to make sense of diversity in a manner that is predictable and that routinely helps us to efficiently promote a sense of order in how we view difference in the world. The two main processes that we utilize to promote a sense of order among the individual differences we encounter in the world are cognitive schemas and the formation of our own subjective reality.

Cognitive schemas are unconscious structures that we develop that represent the world around us mentally. This concept was first introduced by Piaget (1972). Cognitive schemas are mental categories that speak to the physical dimensions of the things we experience in life. These categories are very useful because they allow us to not have to examine and identify the same physical stimulus each and every time that we encounter it. For example, imagine a world in which every time we saw a person we had to figure out what that physical entity was, or each time we approached a traffic signal, we had to experience it for the first time and figure out what our actions needed to be. Cognitive schemas are based on the physical attributes of some phenomenon, and they work with subjective reality, which provides the meaning or interpretive part of what the object is once we have determined it to be something familiar based on cognitive schemas.

Subjective reality is sometimes called phenomenology, which is also known as metaphysics (after the physical)—a branch of philosophy associated with Aristotle that is concerned with the fundamental nature of reality and being. Phenomenology or subjective reality is a means of seeking understanding through philosophy, focusing on the nature and essence of a phenomenon without ontology (exploring the nature of existence or being). So, essentially, phenomenology and subjective reality are the same thing. The bottom line on subjective reality is that (1) reality is based on perception; (2) all things and experiences have two levels of reality: level one is the physical description and level two is the subjective interpretation of the meaningfulness of that which is perceived in level one, and finally; (3) subjective perception is the intervening variable in determining what constitutes reality.

So schemas help faculty and practitioners identify that something is based on preformed categories in our brains based on experience, and subjective reality helps to place meaning on that something. Subjective reality or phenomenology helps to explain why as members of particular groups (drawn along racial, ethnic, cultural, gender, sexual orientation lines), we have common group experiences and thus common subjective realities. Conversely, subjective reality also helps explain why as faculty and practitioners we have distinct experiences and thus individualized subjective realities, which account for both within-group and across-group differences.

VALUING DIVERSITY

Valuing cultural diversity is a big part of functioning successfully in a culturally competent manner. The reality is that the demographics in the United States are rapidly changing, rendering the nation more culturally diverse. Census projections indicate that by the year 2050, more than half of the U.S. population will be nonwhite (U.S. Census Bureau 2004). Thus, to truly value cultural diversity, faculty and practitioners must come to realize that cultural diversity is much more than a superficial acknowledgement of ethnic differences. Faculty must understand that cultural diversity speaks to substantive differences in worldview.

According to noted psychologist Edwin Nichols (1989), there are stark differences in worldview across cultural lines. In his unpublished paper, "The Philosophical Aspects of Cultural Difference," he makes the case for differences in the key philosophical dimensions of axiology (the study of the nature of values versus value judgments or that which has value), epistemology (the study of the grounds for knowledge), logic (the science or study of formal principles of reasoning), process (a series of actions or operations that lead to an end), pedagogy (the art or science of teaching), and methodology (a body of methods and rules used for analysis and inquiry in a particular field). These differences, he asserts, are based on ethnic group or how one affiliates with a particular worldview.

Cultivating Awareness

To function in a culturally competent manner, the first step is for faculty and practitioners to understand their stage of readiness. This entails identifying their personal biases, which requires a systematic and intentional process of becoming self-aware through self-evaluation. The goal of the self-evaluation process is to explore those biases that may negatively influence their ability to work effectively across cultural lines. To effectively identify such biases requires an active and candid introspective process in which faculty members or practitioners take an inventory of those issues that may negatively impact their effectiveness in working with specific culturally diverse groups. While the process is not intended to be overly prescriptive, there is some benefit to embarking on this exploration using a somewhat systematic approach. Apply the four steps as shown in Figure 14.3 to each personal bias or issue identified.

Part of what will happen in the processes below is that faculty members and practitioners will achieve a greater understanding of self as they endeavor to clarify as needed their own values (a principle or standard that one considers important and that typically premises how one lives), judgments, attitudes (an emotionally charged idea that leads to particular action in certain situations; therefore, it has cognitive, affective, and behavioral aspects), and stereotypes (a general judgment about a group based on experience, but a very small sample of experience).

The above process must be engaged in on an ongoing basis in an effort to overcome biases that may contraindicate working with culturally diverse individuals effectively. The reality is that we change all the time, so we have to be willing to devote time and energy toward routinely invoking this self-awareness process.

Culturally Responsive Andragogy

Andragogy is the branch of education that addresses educating adults. It is both an art and a science (Knowles [1970] 1980). While pedagogy specializes in how to teach children, andragogy is based on the following four characteristics of adults (1) being self-directed, (2) having life experience that helps learning, (3) having a high readiness to learn that is based on social roles and developmental tasks, and (4) having readiness to apply knowledge immediately. With these attributes in mind and as the delivery of information changes quickly, there is a need for the adult learner to have a dynamic engagement with it in order to keep pace. This means that the adult learner must be multifaceted and effective at handling multiple demands and tasks. The learning process has to be purposefully parsimonious, so as to give the adult learner the "right" amount of exposure to critical new content, not too much or too little.

Because many adult learners possess a broad and knowledgeable base of information about many things, it is no longer necessary for faculty to maintain the role as the sole expert on the application of the subject matter being learned. Many adult learners have sufficient experience to be experts themselves in the application of

---

Figure 14.3
Self-Evaluation Process

Apply four steps to each personal bias or issue identified separately.

Step 1. Understand the true nature of the bias or issue
A. Identify and describe the bias or issue
B. Acknowledge how long you have been aware of the bias or issue
C. Provide a personal hypothesis on why this is a bias or issue
D. Determine the extent to which this bias or issue is permanent or amenable to change, and if amenable to change, what will modify it

Step 2. Understand the potential impact of the bias or issue
A. Evaluate how this bias or issue impacts you as a professional
B. Evaluate how this bias or issue could impact those who interface with you

Step 3. Identify strategies for successfully managing the bias or issue
A. Determine how you will mitigate the potential negative impact of the bias or issue
B. Decide to proactively monitor and mitigate the potential negative impact of the bias or issue in an ongoing manner

Step 4. Realize the personal learning that the bias or issue provides
A. Identify the lesson learned about who you are as a result of having the bias or issue
B. Describe the implications of the lesson you have learned for overall career development

---

learned content. In fact, many adult learners have experiences and information that can augment the learning process for them, other adult learners, and faculty, especially where practical experience is concerned.

Life experiences for adult learners provide a ripe context within which learning can be optimized. This optimization is often called the "teachable moment." The concept of the teachable moment was mainstreamed by Robert Havighurst in his book *Human Development and Education* (1952). For adult learners, the teachable moment represents the intersection between new content and life experience. Therefore, the teachable moment represents the nexus of discovery, but the precise moment is individually driven; therefore, it varies from one adult learner to the next.

Given that the culture provides much of the variation in the learning process, it is not difficult to see how culture is inextricably intertwined with the concept of the teachable moment, its optimization is key. Maximizing the number of teachable moments that adult learners experience is the best way for faculty to address the permanence of learning. A three-step process is ideal for this purpose. To make learning permanent for adult learners, it is necessary to (1) provide the key content, (2) ask the adult learners to pinpoint the intersection where the course content and their career or life expectations meet, and (3) ask the adult learner to apply their learning to the real-world going forward.

Motivation for Change

The changing demographics of students in U.S. colleges and universities alone may not necessarily provide the impetus for faculty to become more culturally competent. Assessing the applicability of McGregor's Theory X and Theory Y may be an initial step to address the needed change. Theory X and Theory Y are two different assumptions identified by McGregor (1960) that superiors in the workplace hold about their subordinates. Superiors with a Theory X orientation assume that subordinates must be forced to work, seek direction from other organizational members, and avoid taking responsibility for work performed. Superiors with a Theory Y orientation assume that subordinates have a natural desire to work, are self-directed, can satisfy higher-order needs (Maslow 1954) through their work, and take responsibility for work performed. These theories have proven to be effective in helping management create programs and solutions that introduce change and increase productivity in the workplace, particularly within the business sector. Other positive outcomes associated with the application of these theories include an improvement of people skills, a feeling of empowerment, and improved ethical behavior (Heil, Bennis, and Stephens 2000).

Given that management has not considered in depth what is entailed in managing a public administration program composed primarily of people whose prime contribution is a creative intellectual effort (Heil, Bennis, and Stephens 2000), McGregor's X and Y theories have implications for the modern organization and include challenges and opportunities. As we learn from these theories and work to apply them in academia, faculty must be aware of the modern issues of working with people from different cultures. Learning is enhanced in settings where individuals are a part of a diverse group of people who are not like themselves (Chisolm 2004). Diversity in training environments improves the cross-cultural training and cultural competencies of all participants (Chisolm 2004; Cohen 2003). Interaction among people from different backgrounds challenges preconceived notions and broadens perspectives with regard to race, ethnicity, and cultural differences (Smedley, Butler, and Bristow 2004), thereby facilitating professionalism (Chisolm 2004). Within a higher education setting, the governance should have provisions to ensure that the faculty is committed to moving along the continuum (Cross et al. 1989).

Gauging Readiness

Determining readiness requires that faculty members and practitioners take a candid look at where they are on a continuum from being ethnocentric, to culturally open, to culturally relevant, to culturally efficacious. Faculty members or practitioners who are functioning in an ethnocentric manner basically do not acknowledge cultural difference and function in the world as if everyone shared their culture, values, worldview, and way of experiencing the world. These people rarely if ever consider the existence of cultural differences. Alternatively, faculty members or practitioners who are culturally open have an intellectual understanding and observance of cultural pluralism, but this is only a cognitive matter. That is, it is acknowledged cognitively. It does not influence the faculty member or practitioner to act or behave any differently. Further along are the faculty members or practitioners who are culturally relevant because they actually begin to take some basic steps to look at themselves to see how cultural difference may influence the things that they do. These faculty members and practitioners are beginning to take action on that basic awareness; that is, they functioning in a somewhat more sensitive manner. Faculty members or practitioners who are at the stage of being culturally efficacious are more advanced and will essentially take routine steps to learn about other cultures while simultaneously keeping their own cultural perspective from becoming overly influential in interactions with others. Therefore, faculty members or practitioners need to be honest and make an earnest effort to assess current readiness in an accurate manner. The goal is to move as close to being culturally efficacious as possible.

UNDERSTANDING RESISTANCE

To be effective, faculty must possess the necessary skills to provide a classroom environment that adequately addresses student needs, validates diverse cultures, and advocates for equitable access to educational opportunity for all (Banks 1995; Irvine 1992). Educators emphatically state that faculty must be able to teach and interact with students from different cultures and that faculty should teach and encourage concepts that foster cultural competency. However, faculty resistance is a major concern (Brown 2004).

Resistance manifests itself in inadequate preparation, reluctance to participate in mentoring activities, and an overall lack of commitment to cross-cultural interactions and research (Banks 1995; Irvine 1992). Many prejudices and preconceived notions are developed in early childhood through various socialization agents. At some point, faculty may assume a dual role as they work their way across the continuum. While participating in professional development activities geared toward cultural competency, faculty will become the students.

TEACHING STRATEGIES

What is the best method to integrate practices that will help students achieve cultural competency skills? Table 14.1 as cited in *Cultural Competence in the College Biology Classroom* (Tanner and Allen 2007, 252) Jennifer Klump and Steve Nelson (2005) describe common teaching approaches and the characteristics of each that are used by culturally competent and responsive educators.

Jennifer Klump and Steve Nelson (Tanner and Allen 2007, 251) describe the most effective classroom practices as hands-on, cooperative, and culturally aligned. Cooperative, problem-based, and experiential learning strategies incorporate hands-on learning and the approaches identified above. Cooperative learning includes developing a climate of cooperation and community in the classroom. Building a learning community where students from different backgrounds are broken into smaller groups is a major component of cooperative learning. Students are able to gain a different perspective and learn from one another. Cooperative learning gives students opportunities to solve problems together and share their successes and experiences. This

Table 14.1

Common Characteristics of Culturally Responsive and Competent Educators

Employing active learning and hands-on teaching	"The most effective classroom practices are hands-on, cooperative, and culturally aligned. There is less emphasis on lecture. As Ladson-Billings says, educators should 'dig knowledge out of students' rather than 'fill them up with it.'"
Developing a learning community among students	"A climate of inclusion, respect, connection, and caring is fostered in the school and classroom. Interpersonal relationships are built and fostered, and a learning community culture is developed."
Building knowledge of students and differentiating instruction	"Teachers find out as much as possible about their students' culture, language, and learning styles so they can modify curriculum and instruction accordingly."
Maintaining high expectations for all students	"High expectations and high standards are set for all students. Remedial work for students is not acceptable. Activities are designed to foster higher order thinking."
Viewing culture as an asset to academic learning	"Bridges are built between academic learning and students' prior understanding, knowledge, native language, and values. Culture and native language (and cultural dialect) are valued and used as assets in learning, rather than deficits. 'Empower students intellectually, socially, emotionally, and politically using cultural references to impart knowledge, skills and attitudes'" (Ladson-Billings, 1995).
Being explicit about cultural competence	"Teachers realize that students are at different stages of acculturation: Lesson plans need to blend information on how students can become more comfortable with American culture with ways that other students can become culturally responsive to members of diverse cultures."

Source: Adapted and quoted from Klump and Nelson (2005), as cited in Tanner and Allen (2007, 252).

is important for public administration students in that some of the issues they will address in their careers are interdisciplinary in nature; also, the public sector provides services for people from many cultures and cultural backgrounds.

Problem-based learning (PBL) is based on the constructivist approach to learning that stresses active learner participation and self-directed learning (Van Berkel and Dolmans 2006) and is characterized by the high expectations and high standards that are set for all students (Tanner and Allen 2007). Collaboration among learners in a meaningful context is also part of the PBL foundation. Implementing PBL, public administration students will gain practical knowledge and problem-solving skills. They will be able to conceptualize and think at the macro- and microlevels when needed. Simulations of real situations may be used to facilitate PBL.

The experiential learning approach posits that experience is transferred into concepts and that knowledge is gained in settings other than the academic classroom. Experiences gained in the workplace and, in part, outside of the workplace supplement the theory and practice gained in the classroom. Progressing through the four-stage learning cycle—concrete experience, reflective observation, abstract conceptualization, and active experimentation—the learner is gaining experience that will aid in the future (Kolb 1984). Internships, paid or unpaid, will give students the opportunity to gain experience and interact with people from different cultures. Government agencies, at all levels, are sites where students of public administration can receive training and experience.

CURRICULUM SUPPORTIVE OF CULTURAL COMPETENCY

THE HIDDEN CURRICULUM

The hidden curriculum is the set of assumptions that are responsible for inequities within the classroom and beyond. It is also the knowledge of how to behave and use language in a way that is esteemed by students of the dominant culture but unknown to other students from nondominant cultures (Cheng 1995). Negative effects of the hidden curriculum take place when students from the nondominant group are held to lower expectations while students from the dominant group are held to a higher level of expectation. Often, these assumptions are below the level of conscious awareness (Trumbull et al. 2001). Culturally competent faculty members fully embrace and have a commitment toward high expectations for all groups. Faculty thus will not accept the premise that some students will do better than others because of their culture, ethnicity, gender, or group differences; instead, culturally competent faculty want and expect all students to achieve at their maximum level.

CULTURALLY RESPONSIVE CURRICULUM

Culturally responsive curriculum communicates that education has relevancy in students' lives (Villegas 1991). A culturally responsive curriculum is designed to integrate the learners' values, knowledge, and method of learning while taking into account the needs of students to succeed in school and become productive citizens. Integration assumes that learning in higher education is a complex social and cognitive process of discovering and mastering knowledge, making rules and practices, values and roles, that integrate the various disciplines (Warren et al. 2001). Any review of curricula requires not only an examination of textual materials, but also the idea of content integration and knowledge construction through curricula review and redesign (Villegas 1991). Integrating various disciplines facilitates acquisition of new knowledge (Hollins 1996).

Culturally responsive curriculum cannot be an add-on; it must be integrated. Making use of Cross et al.'s (1989) definition of cultural competence, curriculum integration should achieve the following objectives (Pilcher, Charles, and Lancaster 2008):

1. Identify individual cultural biases and stereotypes.
2. Define cultural competence.
3. Demonstrate value for the importance of diversity in public administration and practice.
4. Demonstrate knowledge of the diverse cultures encountered by accessing community-appropriate resources.
5. Identify students or consumers' requirements for interpreter services and have the ability to effectively communicate using interpreters.
6. Demonstrate respect for student's cultural beliefs.

Once these questions have been answered, the next step is to identify the gaps and infuse the curriculum with opportunities to explore questions of fairness and equity (Figure 14.4). Involving students in the curriculum design process and identifying current faculty who are willing to integrate and develop content within existing curriculum is a strategy to demonstrate cultural competency. Acquiring resources and training materials that engage faculty development and workshops that will assist faculty in reshaping their curricula will be important. In addition, having a diverse faculty is necessary because diversity fosters learning, knowledge, and skills that are vital to curriculum development. Further, the development of a curriculum design committee for developing appropriate measuring tools for assessing multicultural content is a strategy to reshape and measure the effectiveness of the curriculum; however, this suggestion may be met with resistance. Institutional and community resources should be committed to the curriculum, and community leaders should be sought out and involved in designing the curriculum and providing feedback (Association of American Medical Colleges 2005).

INTEGRATION OF CULTURAL COMPETENCY INTO PROGRAM DEVELOPMENT

Integration of cultural competency into program development refers to the integration of cultural competency into each program process. This section describes a four-step process for integrating cultural competency into each key program process. The first step in integrating cultural competency into the public administration program is to define what is central to the program's operation; that is, it is a process or program that would be identified as integral to the operational definition of the organization's mission. Within the context of organizations, processes or programs are those curricula, interventions, or activities targeted toward some improvement or benefit that have clear beginning and end points, have steps in between, and happen over and over again within the organization (Lewis et al. 2009). The integration approach will involve answering four questions relative to each organizational program or process (Lewis, Bethea, and Hurley 2009). Each question represents a discrete step and will involve answering a key question based on Stufflebeam's decision-oriented model of educational evaluation (Stufflebeam 2000). Stufflebeam's framework, originally developed in 1971 and updated more recently, forms the basis of a four-step process for infusing cultural competency into program curricula (Lewis et al. 2009; Table 14.2).

The first question that administrators, faculty, staff, and students should ask themselves is this: What is cultural competency in the context of the program or process? Those involved should attempt to define cultural competency relative to the program or process. The answer to this question essentially sets a range on the extent of relevance of cultural competency within the context of the program or process.

Once key intersections between cultural competency and the specific process or program are identified, then the second question must be addressed: What strategy could be utilized to appropriately address cultural competency in the context of the

Figure 14.4
Strategy for Reshaping the Curriculum

To reshape curriculum to be culturally responsive, faculty must first ask four questions:

1. What do you already do? Examine what you already do. The texts and instructional activities should represent diversity in terms of everyday, real-life activities of various groups.
2. Does your curriculum have an additive approach? The texts and instructional activities should be essential to the curriculum and not structured as an add-on.
3. Does your curriculum have a transformational approach? The texts and instructional activities should promote or provoke critical questions about the societal status quo. (Do they present an alternative point of view worth considering?)
4. Does your curriculum provoke social action? The texts and instructional activities should lead to students' exploring ways that they can effect social change.

program or process? The goal here is to develop or identify a strategy to align cultural competency with the process or program and, in particular, the key point of intersection between cultural competency and the process or program.

The third question is as follows: To what extent could the strategy identified in question two be subjected to implementation monitoring? The goal here is to have the strategy serve as a means for indicating how well the implementation goes. This will ensure that actual deployment occurs and has fidelity to what was originally intended. This is an evaluation concern with an emphasis on implementation and monitoring. The idea is to build in some accountability mechanism to ensure routine monitoring of the delivery of the identified strategy, with an eye toward making any needed midcourse adjustments and modifications.

The final question is then asked: How much impact could the strategy identified in question two have in positively addressing cultural competency for the program or process in the organization in an ongoing manner? The goal in this step is to see whether the strategy will produce any positive impact, and if so, whether it is likely to be sustainable. Again, this is an evaluation concern, but here the focus is on how effective the strategy will be in going forward with the option of making modifications as needed. These last two questions, with their strong evaluative focus, are intended to ensure a proactive, monitoring role. After completing these four infusion steps, the program or process would then be requested to implement any lessons learned going forward (Lewis et al. 2009; Table 14.2).

OUTCOME-FOCUSED

Since the 1980s, the focus on producing outcomes among public organizations seems to have been unwavering (Lewis et al. 2006). In many instances during the 1980s and the 1990s, there was a challenging situation of lean resources and heightened

Table 14.2

Stufflebeam's Decision Oriented Model of Educational Evaluation

Public administration program or process	Corresponding structure of question(s)
Context/need decisions	Plan or context questions to address the extent of need
Input/programming decisions	Structuring/programming or input questions to determine what should be done anew
Process/implementation and monitoring decisions	Implementation or process monitoring questions to assess how well programming/service delivery is going
Product/recycling decisions	Product also known as recycling/impact or outcome/effectiveness questions to know whether the service/program should continue

accountability concerns, and these were managed concomitantly amid changing and expanding service needs (Lewis 2009a). During the dawning years of the twenty-first century, neither the austere economic times of the 1980s and 1990s nor the concerns for programmatic accountability of the 1990s have relented for public agencies.

Today, publicly funded programs face unprecedented demands related to accountability (Lewis et al. 2006). These demands take on four primary forms: (1) limited and uncertain funding, (2) increasing demands for services, (3) an insistence on the part of customers that public services meet their needs, and (4) a requirement imposed by citizens and by legislative and governmental bodies that public funds be expended responsibly and in ways that maximize the reach of such resources (Lewis 2009a). Although there appears to be a craze to pursue and measure outcomes in the public arena, it is clear that not all organizations are at a point developmentally to withstand the intense scrutiny that comes with outcome evaluation (Lewis et al. 2006).

STANDARDS-BASED

Practitioners today live in an era when the quality of services is almost guaranteed by the imposition of professional standards, and public administration organizations are no exception. These standards often come in the form of standards of professional practice or accreditation standards and serve the purpose of ensuring that services are of high quality. The professional landscape these days is replete with accrediting bodies and other kinds of organizations that are in business to provide a "good housekeeping" seal of approval of sorts for almost any kind of service organization in the open marketplace in this new century. This movement toward standardization is not expected to ease in the near future; therefore, it is critical to structure public administration professional development activity according to established standards in order to ensure quality.

JOB-EMBEDDED

All professional development activity must also be firmly anchored within the milieu of one's job. The context of one's job provides the domain within which efforts toward success must play out. The extent to which professional development activity shares a close kinship with the job environment is the extent to which improved proficiency and competence as a result of development activity will be relevant to the aspects of job performance that are most salient to success.

Campus and Community Collaboration

In order to better integrate cultural competency into program development and prepare students for working with increasingly diverse populations, curriculum development, activities, or programs, should be used as a tool for collaboration and developing partnerships with other campuses, local, regional, or national resources. Also, public administration programs should promote cultural competency by actively engaging other organizations and academic programs in the research process. Such engagement promotes the delivery of culturally competent curricula, activities, and programs. Importantly, campus and community engagement results in the exchange of knowledge and skills among students, faculty, and staff.

Environment and Communication

An excellent strategy for institutionalizing cultural competency is to create promotional materials that reflect the diversity of the public administration program. This includes the Internet and associated applications, course descriptions in the course catalogue, and other materials marketing the program to prospective students and current university students who are contemplating public administration as their program of study. At a minimum, the campus admissions office, advising offices, career development offices, and community engagement programs should be aware of the public administration program's commitment to achieve cultural competency, and this message should be presented consistently in all forums.

Translating Research (Knowledge) of Cultural Competency into Practice

The process of translating research findings into a form that is usable by frontline workers is called knowledge translation. Research that has the capacity to be translated into usable results is called translational research. Both terms are synonymous with the process of moving research findings from the laboratory to the point of being used by end users. Perhaps the definitive authority on the process of knowledge translation is the Canadian Institutes of Health Research, which is analogous to the Centers for Disease Control in the United States. The Canadian Institutes propagate this view of knowledge translation (paraphrased): "the appropriate integration and implementation of knowledge in a context where researchers and end-users of research engage in a constant interplay in order to minimize the time from new innovation to everyday evidence-based practice" (2004). In short, it is not enough to merely disseminate the results of new research. In addition, there must be a systematic and intentional process to ensure full integration and timely use of new research findings among end users, as well as evidence through formal evaluation that the use of findings improves practice. Of equal importance for the purposes of this discussion is that when new research findings reach end users quickly and afford positive benefits to practice, such findings must also be culturally competent—that is, efficacious in the face of cultural nuances.

To promote knowledge translation on a consistent basis in public administration organizations, it is important to address the five levels of the social ecological model (SEM) by McLeroy et al. (1988). With each of those five levels there is a key output that manifests if the knowledge translation process has occurred successfully, as follows: (1) at the individual level, the output is behavior; (2) at the interpersonal level, the output is relationship; (3) at the institutional or organizational level, the output is procedure; (4) at the community level, the output is collaboration; and (5) at the public policy level, the output is policy. The final step in ensuring the link between knowledge translation and cultural competency will be to answer these two questions for each output at the corresponding SEM level: What does cultural competency mean at each level? What is the cultural competency alignment strategy at each level?

Moreover, faculty should keep in mind that the strategy for translating knowledge into practice varies according to the target audience and the type of knowledge being translated. In summary, the awareness and sensitivity approach (attitude), the multicultural approach (knowledge), and the cross-cultural approach (skills) all have different goals and focuses, yet each interacts harmoniously with the social ecological model to increase a faculty member's level of cultural competency (Betancourt 2003).

Technical Assistance and Consultation

Technical assistance and consultation refers to seeking consultation from experts with culturally competent skills and working with diverse groups in a culturally competent manner (Eckley et al. 2004). One important aspect is that technical assistance needs can be provided directly by faculty, staff, practitioners, or outside consultants with culturally competent skills. Public administration programs providing advice, supporting project preparation and implementation, or enhancing the capacity in communities should utilize members who have the knowledge and experience reflecting the diverse cultural makeup of the community. Every effort should be made to train key personnel by developing culturally competent training materials designed to be useful to the community.

Conclusion

The success of every program depends upon strong administrative support. Effective leaders have the skills to motivate others by communicating a clear vision. In addition, active leadership is demonstrated in setting priorities, allocating time and resources, and creating policy change to integrate and infuse cultural competency throughout the program. Cultural competency is a skill that develops over time, and public administration programs that effectively pursue cultural competency as a goal must value and be committed to diversity; be aware and sensitive to differences, learning and understanding the students' culture; engage in a cultural competency self-assessment; integrate cultural competency into existing educational programs and services; and institutionalize cultural knowledge (Isaacs and Benjamin 1991; Mays, Siantz, and Viehweb 2002; U.S. Department of Health & Human Services 2010).

Cultural differences must not be overlooked, ignored, or merely tolerated. The differences should be celebrated as diversity is embraced. Effective programs "place diversity front and center" (Nieto 2000, 180). Professional development in cultural competency must include a self-evaluation component so faculty members and practitioners can review their own history as it relates to their current beliefs, cross-cultural interactions, and the experiences of others (Banks 1995; Martin 1991). It is not sufficient or equitable for educators to ignore the students' culture. A commitment to reciprocity regarding the students' culture must be present (Buber 1970). The leadership role of key administrators at the program level or specifically, the chair of the public administration program and senior personnel (Schoorman 2000)—such as the university president, provost, vice president for academic affairs, and deans—will be critical to attaining cultural competency.

Public administration programs must accept and respect differences among and within their students, continually assess program policies and practices regarding culture, expand cultural knowledge and resources, and adapt service models to better meet the needs of different racial or ethnic groups. Public administration programs must hire faculty and staff who are unbiased and those who represent the racial and ethnic groups of students being served and seek the advice and counsel from their students within the program. The public administration program must be committed to policies that enhance services to a diverse student body. Public administration programs must conduct original research, develop new approaches based on culture, and publish and disseminate their results to add to the knowledge base of culturally competent practices. Culturally competent public administration programs hire faculty and staff who are specialists in culturally competent practice.

Understanding this continuum may help administrators and staff, as well as faculty, to assess and improve the public administration program. Learning to evaluate the level of cultural competency of the faculty and the public administration program must be part of an ongoing effort to provide better services to our students.

REFERENCES

American Association of State Colleges and Universities. 2006. Faculty trends and issues. *Policy Matters* 3(4). www.aascu.org/policy_matters/v3_4/.

Association of American Medical Colleges. 2005. Cultural competence education for medical students. www.paeaonline.org/index.php?ht=a/GetDocumentAction/i/73944.

Banks, James A. 1995. Multicultural education: Historical development, dimensions, and practice. In *Handbook of Research and Multicultural Education*, ed. James A. Banks and Cherry A. McGee Banks, 3–24. New York: Simon & Schuster.

Betancourt, Joseph R. 2003. Cross-cultural medical education: Conceptual approaches and frameworks for evaluation. *Academic Medicine* 78(6): 560–569.

Brown, Elinor L. 2004. What precipitates change in cultural diversity awareness during a multicultural course: The message or the method? *Journal of Teacher Education* 55(4): 325–340. http://jte.sagepub.com/cgi/content/abstract/55/4/325.

Buber, Martin. 1970. *I and Thou*. New York: Scribner's.

Canadian Institutes of Health Research. 2004. Knowledge translation strategy 2004–2009: Innovation in action. www.cihr-irsc.gc.ca/e/26574.html.

Cheng, Lilly, ed. 1995. *Integrating Language and Learning for Inclusion: An Asian-Pacific Focus*. San Diego, CA: Singular.

Chisolm, Mary A. 2004. Diversity: A missing link to professionalism. *American Journal of Pharmaceutical Education* 68(5).

Cohen, Jordan. 2003. The consequences of premature abandonment of affirmative action in medical school admissions. *Journal of the American Medical Association* 289(9): 1143–1149.

Cross, Terry, Barbara Bazron, Karl Dennis, and Mareasa Isaacs. 1989. *Towards a Culturally Competent System of Care*, vol. 1. Washington, DC: National Center for Technical Assistance Center for Children's Mental Health, Georgetown University Child Development Center.

Drummond, Ian, Iain Nixon, and John Wiltshire. 1998. Personal transferable skills in higher education: The problems of implementing good practice. *Quality Assurance in Education* 6(1): 19–27.

Eckley, Emily, Andrea Graves, Eriko Grover, Shelese McMillan, Amber Mosely, Marsha Spence, and Betsy Haughton. 2004. Manual for self-assessment of cultural competence of an academic department or unit. Department of Nutrition. University of Tennessee, Knoxville. http://nutrition.utk.edu/culture.

Genao, Inginia, Jada Bussey-Jones, Donald Brady, William Branch, and Giselle Smith. 2003. Building the case for cultural competence. *American Journal of the Medical Sciences* 326(3): 136–140.

Goode, Tawara, and W. Jones. 2009. Linguistic competence. National Center for Cultural Competence, Georgetown University. http://nccc.georgetown.edu/documents/DefinitionofLinguisticCompetence.pdf.

Halachmi, Arie. 2005. Governance and risk management: Challenges and public productivity. *International Journal of Public Sector Management* 18(4): 300–317.

Havighurst, Robert J. 1952. *Human Development and Education*. New York: Longman.

Heil, Gary, Warren Bennis, and Deborah C. Stephens. 2000. *Douglas McGregor Revisited: Managing the Human Side of the Enterprise*. New York: Wiley.

Hollins, Etta R. 1996. *Culture in School Learning: Revealing the Deep Meaning*. Mahwah, NJ: Erlbaum.

Irvine, Jacqueline J. 1992. Making teacher education culturally responsive. In *Diversity in Teacher Education*, ed. M.E. Dilworth, 79–92. San Francisco: Jossey-Bass.

Isaacs, Mareasa, and Marra Benjamin. 1991. *Towards a Culturally Competent System of Care*, vol. 2. *Programs Which Utilize Culturally Competent Principles*. Washington, DC: Georgetown University Child Development Center, CASSP Technical Assistance Center.

Jackson, M. 2005. Breaking the barriers to overseas study for students of color and minorities. *Institute of International Education Networker* (Fall): 16–17.

Klump, Jennifer, and Steve Nelson. 2005. Cultural competency of schools and teachers in relation to student success. In *Cultural Competence in the College Biology Classroom*, Kimberly Tanner and Deborah Allen, 252. Northwest Regional Educational Laboratory (NWREL). www.ode.state.or.us/opportunities/grants/saelp/cuturlcmptencebibnwrel.pdf.

Knowles, Malcolm S. [1970] 1980. *The Modern Practice of Adult Education*, revised and updated. Chicago: Follett.

Kolb, David A. 1984. *Experiential Learning: Experience as the Source of Learning and Development*. Englewood Cliffs, NJ: Prentice-Hall.

Lewis, Allen N. 2009a. Disability disparities: A beginning model. *Disability and Rehabilitation* 31(14): 1136–1143.

———. 2009b. The logic model: A vocational rehabilitation program manager's best friend. *Journal of Rehabilitation Administration* 33(1): 19–31.

Lewis, Allen N., Amy J. Armstrong, Angela H. Taylor, and Susan Spain. 2006. Determining a vocational rehabilitation program's readiness for outcome-focused program evaluation. *Journal of Rehabilitation Administration* 30(1): 245–257.

Lewis, Allen N., James Bethea, and Jessica Hurley. 2009. Integrating cultural competency in rehabilitation curricula in the new millennium: Keeping it simple. *Disability & Rehabilitation* 31(14): 1161–1169.

Lewis, Allen N., Sarah J. Brubaker, Ariana S. Karp, and Brian Ambrose. 2009. Community assets assessment: Evaluating a community's readiness to engage in youth risk avoidance programming. *Journal of Adolescent and Family Health* 4(3): 138–143.

Lewis, Pamela H., and Allen N. Lewis. 2010. A profile of cultural awareness and sensitivity among behavioral healthcare professionals in a state behavioral healthcare organization. *Journal of Minority Disability Research and Practice* 1(2): 3–33.

Maitlis, Sally. 2004. Taking it from the top: How CEOs influence (and fail to influence) their boards. *Organization Studies* 25(8): 1275–1311.

Martin, Renee J. 1991. The power to empower: Multicultural education for student teachers. In *Empowerment Through Multicultural Education*, ed. Christine E. Sleeter, 287–297. Albany: State University of New York Press.

Maslow, Abraham. 1954. *Motivation and Personality*. New York: Harper

Mays Rose, Mary Siantz, and Stephan Viewheg. 2002. Assessing cultural competence of policy organizations. *Journal of Transcultural Nursing* 13(2): 139–144.

McGregor, Douglas. 1960. *Human Side of Enterprise*. New York: McGraw-Hill.

McLeroy, Kenneth R., Daniel Bibeau, Allan Steckler, and Karen Glanz. 1988. An ecological perspective on health promotion programs. *Health Education and Behavior* 15(4): 351–377.

National Prevention Information Network. 2011. Cultural competence. Centers for Disease Control and Prevention. www.cdcnpin.org/scripts/population/culture.asp.

Nichols, Edwin J. 1989. The philosophical aspects of cultural difference. Unpublished paper delivered at Evergreen State College, Tacoma, Washington.

Nieto, Sonia. 2000. *Affirming Diversity*. New York: Longman.

Piaget, Jean. 1972. *The Psychology of the Child*. New York: Basic Books.

Pilcher, Elizabeth, Laurine Charles, and Carol Lancaster. 2008. Development and assessment of cultural competency curriculum. *Journal of Dental Education* 72(9): 1020–1028.

Reed, Michael I. 2002. New managerialism and new forms of organisational control in UK higher education. *Management Research News* 25: 158–162.

Sasso, Peggy. 2003. Searching for trust in the not-for-profit boardroom: Looking beyond the duty of obedience to ensure accountability. *UCLA Law Review* 50: 1485–1546.

Schoorman, Dilys. 2000. Internationalization: The challenge of implementing the organizational rhetoric. Educational Resources Information Center Higher Education Clearinghouse.

Shavelson, Richard, and Leta Huang. 2003. Responding responsibly to the frenzy to assess learning in higher education. *Change* 35(1): 10–19. www.stanford.edu/dept/SUSE/SEAL/Reports_Papers/Paper.htm.

Smedley, Brian D., Adrian S. Butler, and Lonnie R. Bristow, eds. 2004. *In the Nation's Compelling Interest: Ensuring Diversity in the Health Care Workforce*. Washington, DC: National Academies Press.

Stufflebeam, Daniel L. 2000. The CIPP model for evaluation. In *Evaluation Models: Viewpoints on Educational and Human Services Evaluation*, 2nd ed., ed. Daniel L. Stufflebeam, George F. Madaus, and Thomas Kellaghan, 279–317. Boston: Kluwer.

Tanner, Kimberly, and Deborah Allen. 2007. Approaches to teaching biology in the college biology classroom. *Cell Biology Education* 6: 251–258.

Trumbull, Elise, Carrie Rothstein-Fisch, Patricia Greenfield, and Blanca Quiroz. 2001. *Bridging Cultures Between Home and School: A Guide for Teachers*. Mahwah, NJ: Erlbaum.

U.S. Census Bureau. 2004. United States interim projections by age, sex, race, and Hispanic origin. www.census.gov/ipc/www/usinterimproj.

U.S. Department of Education, National Center for Education Statistics. 2009. *Digest of Education Statistics, 2008* (NCES 2009020), Chapter 3. http://nces.ed.gov/pubs2009/2009020_3a.pdf.

U.S. Department of Health & Human Services. 2005. The role of cultural competence in family-centered care. Maternal and Child Health Bureau, Division of Services for Children with Special Health Needs. www.neserve.org/maconsortium/pdf/Medical Home/Family_Centered_Care.pdf.5.

Van Berkel, Henk, and Diana Dolmans. 2006. The influence of tutoring competencies on problems, group functioning and student achievement in problem-based learning. *Medical Education* 40: 730–736.

Villegas, Ana. 1991. Culturally responsive pedagogy for the 1990s and beyond. Washington, DC: ERIC Clearinghouse on Teacher Education.

Warren, Beth, Cynthia Ballenger, Mark Ogonowski, Ann Rosebery, and Josiane Hudicourt-Barnes. 2001. Rethinking diversity in learning science: The logic of everyday languages. *Journal of Research in Science Teaching* 38: 529–552.

Williams, Felecia. 2007. Study abroad and Carnegie doctoral/research extensive universities: Preparing students from underrepresented racial groups to live in a global environment. PhD diss. Center for Public Policy, Virginia Commonwealth University.

Cultural Competency in "Everyday" Public Policy Research

SUSAN T. GOODEN

A quick quiz: Cultural competency is an important consideration in each of the following research studies except:

A. Examining satisfaction with public health services among tribal communities
B. Evaluating the K–12 educational experiences of Latinos
C. Evaluating a community policing program in an African American community
D. Assessing job counseling services provided by the state labor department to recently unemployed workers

If you are inclined to select D, you are not alone. When an area of research involves a specific minority group, a red warning flag goes up: "Cultural competency is important to this research project. We need to make sure our research design, questionnaire construction, and data analysis are culturally sensitive, appropriate, and accurate." Previous scholarship that examines cultural competency in research focuses heavily on the need for culturally appropriate research techniques when a cultural minority group is the focus of the research (see, e.g., Caldwell et al. 2006; Skaff et al. 2002; Tillman 2002). Definitely, cultural competency is vital to such research designs. But what consideration is given to cultural competency in general "everyday" public policy research? When conducting a study in an area such as D listed above, researchers may be less likely to focus on cultural competency as a primary concern.

Cultural competency is an important consideration in general public administration and public policy research designs, not just those that are focused on minority or underrepresented populations. By highlighting some of the primary ways cultural competency considerations are overlooked in common public policy research and offering suggestions to incorporate such considerations, we can collectively strengthen "everyday" research approaches in public administration.

FAILING TO LOOK AT OURSELVES IN THE MIRROR

Despite our fiercest objections and thorough academic training, each of us is deeply shaped by our own lived experiences. Put simply, we remain subjective researchers. Often unacknowledged directly as such, these experiences become a silent influence in our research design and approach. Fejos (1959, 35) describes culture as "the sum total of socially inherited characteristics of a human group that comprises everything which one generation can tell, convey or hand down to the next; in other words, the nonphysical inherited traits we possess." Culture is an integrated pattern of human behavior that includes language, thoughts, communications, actions, customs, beliefs, values, and institutions of racial, ethnic, religious, or social groups. At its essence, culture involves our values, beliefs, and norms, including personal perceptions of what is good or useful.

Cultural competency includes the learning of skills that can be applied in research domains to make our program evaluation and research work more effective and accurate. It includes our ability as researchers to understand the beliefs, language, interpersonal styles, and behaviors of those individuals or organizations that are the target of our research. Adapting a definition from Purnell and Paulanka (1998), we could say that cultural competency in a research context involves both developing an awareness of our own existence, sensations, thoughts, and environment without allowing them to have an undue influence on people from other backgrounds and demonstrating knowledge and understanding of the cultures represented in our research sample. The lived experiences of researchers, as determined by their class background, racial and ethnic identity, and educational background, help to shape the assumptions and frames of reference that they bring to the research process (Cuthbert 1985; Guzman 2002; Hood 2001; Merryfield 1985). Cultural competency is essential to the delivery of high-quality research. This is particularly true of research related to public institutions, management, and policies, as such research can significantly influence the future delivery of public services.

The Cross model (1988) of cultural competence is based on a continuum of six stages: cultural destructiveness, cultural incapacity, cultural blindness, cultural precompetence, basic cultural competence, and advanced cultural competence. This model offers an excellent framework against which researchers can assess their cultural competency. Cultural destructiveness is the most negative end of the continuum. Individuals in this phase view culture as a problem. This group assumes that one culture is superior to other cultures and that people from minority cultures should be more like the "mainstream." Cultural incapacity includes individuals who lack cultural awareness and skills. Perhaps shaped largely by a homogeneous society, individuals in this stage may have low expectations of people from other cultures. In the third stage, cultural blindness, individuals and organizations see others in terms of their own culture. They generally believe that culture makes no difference—"we are all the same." In the cultural precompetence stage, individuals and organizations recognize that there are cultural differences and start to educate themselves and others concerning these differences. Individuals who accept, appreciate, and accommodate cultural differences have reached the basic cultural competency stage. They accept the influence of their own culture in relation to other cultures. For example, Anglo researchers in this stage may seek advice from communities of color in order to assess the appropriateness of their research design to individuals from these communities. In the final stage, advanced cultural competency, individuals move beyond accepting, appreciating, and accommodating cultural differences and begin to actively educate others. Researchers in this stage actively seek out knowledge about diverse cultures, specifically develop research skills to apply to diverse research environments, and feel comfortable conducting research in multicultural settings. Often, they seek out multiple researchers with specific cultural specializations in order to better inform their overall research designs.

As researchers, our first step in achieving cultural competency is to determine where on the continuum we lie. What is the relationship between our individual cultural values and the cultural values we consider, appreciate, and seek out in our research projects? Specifically, what values do we privilege in standard public policy research? As Babbie (2005, 7) notes: "Each of us inherits a culture made up, in part, of firmly accepted knowledge about the workings of the world." He continues: "Like tradition, authority can both assist and hinder human inquiry. We do well to trust in the judgment of the person who has special training, expertise, and credentials in a given matter, especially in the face of controversy. At the same time, inquiry can be greatly hindered by the legitimate authority who errs within his or her own special province" (7).

Faced with the research project outlined in selection D above, do we adopt a "one size fits all" approach to job counseling services? Does our research design consider multicultural aspects of job counseling services, the labor market, and employment options that various groups of the public may face? Does our research design ignore, discount, or consider, for example, differences in employment options that vary for perspective employees due to employer discrimination, language abilities, or criminal record? Unlike the scope of the research design identified in options A, B, and C above, the cultural aspects of option D are not glaringly obvious. Rather, they require greater cultural awareness and sophistication from the researcher. Placed in the hands of a researcher without cultural competency, the cultural dimensions of the research design may not be identified by either the agency or the researcher, therefore resulting in incffective and inaccurate public policy research. As public sector researchers, we must routinely assess each of our research designs along cultural competency dimensions. It is particularly important to provide this assessment of "everyday" research designs where the cultural dimensions of the design are not obvious.

USE OF "NON" CATEGORIES IN RESEARCH DESIGNS

Many years ago, when I was giving a presentation at a large state university, I observed that faculty members in the department referred to each other as "lawyers" and "nonlawyers." I found the term *nonlawyer* very interesting because it captured only the background that these faculty members lacked, conveying nothing about the expertise that they possessed. The "nonlawyer" category could include all sorts of individuals, including those who held terminal degrees in fields such as public administration, economics, political science, engineering, or even medicine, but the description failed to capture specific areas of faculty training and expertise.

Similarly, researchers often use the term *non-* to describe a particular subgroup in a sample. One of the most commonly used is the term *nonwhite* to describe survey respondents who are racial or ethnic minorities. What does *nonwhite* tell us? Not much. Does the "nonwhite" group consist primarily of African Americans, American Indians, Asians, or Latinos? Does the sample contain a relatively even distribution of each of these groups or is the "nonwhite" group in this sample nearly all African American? By collapsing all minorities into the nondescript category of "nonwhite" or "minority," we not only fail to accurately describe our sample, but leave the reader to speculate and draw dangerously inaccurate conclusions about our findings.

Let us assume that an economic development practitioner reads in one of our studies that "nonwhite" or "minority-owned" businesses have significantly lower levels of success than majority owned businesses. The practitioner shares these findings with her agency and concludes that investing in minority-owned businesses in their community may be risky. Perhaps the data upon which the original study was based did not include any businesses owned by Latinos. However, the businesses in the practitioner's community are largely Latino-owned, so, absent additional information, she translates the study using the "minority" context of her community, which is primarily Latino. She decides not to prioritize investing in Latino owned businesses because the results suggest they have a high failure rate. Although we can rightly criticize the practitioner for making incorrect assumptions and applications of our sample, we as researchers are also to blame for using terms that are too vague and subject to incorrect interpretation and application in the decision-making process.

Beyond the methodological dangers of using ambiguous terms like *nonwhite* or *minority*, it also delivers a troubling message: There are not meaningful distinctions between various cultural and ethnic groups; there are only white and "everything else." Researchers adopting this approach align with Cross's cultural destructiveness stage. White culture is represented in the data analysis as the superior or dominant culture, and other cultures are not worthy of distinct consideration. The primary concern is to align "nonwhite" cultures with the "white" mainstream.

FAILING TO FULLY EXAMINE POPULATION SUBGROUPS

A related concern involving data analysis in "everyday" public policy research is failing to adequately examine population subgroups. An improvement over the "nonwhite" categorization above, groups may be identified by racial or ethnic strata. However, important cultural differences within these strata may be masked. Suppose we are comparing findings from two large-scale research studies that note very different experiences for Latinos. The first study comprises primarily Mexican Americans living in Texas. The second study comprises primarily Cuban Americans living in Florida. Although most U.S.-based research adopts the term "Latino" or "Hispanic" to describe both groups, the cultural distinctiveness of each of these groups, which could offer powerful explanations of the findings, is not uncovered.

These important cultural differentiations and complexities may be largely ignored by the researcher, thus leaving this task of "connecting the dots" to the savvy consumer of research.

Pan-ethnic labels (Latino or Asian) represent crude categorizations that can mask the complex and multidimensional nature of socioeconomic and cultural factors, including discrimination (Stewart and Nápoles-Springer 2000). As these authors detail, "Factors such as gender roles, cultural norms, and language differences could systematically inflate or deflate response levels. If these factors operate differentially across demographic strata, then group differences or similarities assessment by instrument scores could be partially the result of response bias" (Stewart and Nápoles-Springer 2003, 1212).

Acculturation is multidimensional and includes such items as lifestyle behaviors, gender roles, fundamental beliefs, language, cultural norms, and attitudes. Yet most acculturation measures are unidimensional, primarily language-based (Stewart and Nápoles-Springer 2003). Interpreting results of policy research without assurances of equivalence of concepts and measurement properties is risky, especially given the potential applications of such findings.

A primary challenge for public policy researchers is to first understand the population being studied. If the study population is very large and diverse, using a standard method such as the Office of Management and Budget (OMB) Federal Standards for Racial and Ethnic Data facilitates comparative ethnic research consistent with federal data, rather than the use of pan-ethnic labels. If the study population is more localized to a specific community, researchers should work in partnership with individuals from these specific communities to develop quality research designs that are inclusive of local demographics.

> Determining how to define a community or minority population group is more than an academic exercise . . . the definition of key variables affects interpretation of findings. For example, the magnitude of a difference between African Americans and white Americans might be reduced if the study population were defined to include Latinos who report their race as white. Measures of race/ethnicity should be treated with the same methodological rigor applied to other variables. (Lillie-Blanton and Hoffman 1995, 231–232)

Additionally, longitudinal studies reported by state and local governmental agencies have to be carefully examined. For example, vital records are an invaluable source of data; however, states vary in their definitions of race and ethnicity. As late as 1988, only thirty states included a Hispanic identifier on death certificates (Lillie-Blanton and Hoffman 1995, 230). Reporting of data in a comparative state longitudinal context necessitates careful examination and explanation of these measures.

Understanding specific cultural differences, rather than relying on pan-ethnic comparisons, could lead to more effective delivery of public sector programs. Buki et al. (2004) were concerned about the late detection of breast cancer in Latinas. Their study examined how screening behaviors differed among women of Mexican, Puerto Rican, Cuban, Salvadoran, and South American ancestries. For example, secrecy was a major factor among women from Puerto Rico and Mexico as open discussions of breast-related topics were considered taboo. Other factors, such as general distrust of health-care providers, affected a larger group of Latina women, including participants from Cuba, El Salvador, Mexico, and Puerto Rico.

Often we must rely upon administrative or secondary data that includes only pan-ethnic or collapsed racial and ethnic data. In these cases, it is important for us to understand what groups are included in these categories and in what proportions. It is particularly important to discuss these population proportions when reporting our findings and comparing our findings to those of previous researchers. We need to avoid making broad, sweeping conclusions that may neglect important cultural norms or nuances.

USING THE DOMINANT CULTURAL GROUP TO SET THE OUTCOME STANDARD

When examining public policy outcomes, researchers often compare outcomes across groups. In the area of education, for example, we may compare graduation rates of low-income students to those of middle- and high-income students. Or we may examine course completion rates of first-generation college students to those of students whose parents earned a college degree. We may compare the grades of female students in science courses to those of their male counterparts. In cases like these, researchers have traditionally examined the performance of one "inferior" group compared to another "superior" group. Data analysis proceeds along an important cultural dimension: the superior group sets the desired level of achievement for all other inferior groups.

> Given that most research has been conducted on European-American samples, by predominantly European-American researchers, this has become the 'gold standard.' In a sense, this form of ethnocentricity, whether methodological or conceptual, may set up inappropriate assumptions that affect all aspects of research, including recruitment, constructs, and the instruments to measure them, language, and interpretation of data. (Skaff et al. 2002, 305–306)

The stage is set whereby the reputational status of the "superior" group begins as a default assumption of the research design. Whites, males, heterosexuals, and abled individuals enter the research design with a position of cultural privilege. They set the bar for all other groups, virtually ensuring a first-place outcomes finish of the dominant group within the research design.

If white, middle-class community college students have a degree completion rate of 50 percent, upon what logical basis does this become the desired community college completion rate for all students? Is a 50 percent completion rate acceptable or do we need to establish higher levels of completion rates that educational policy makers and the public find desirable? Allowing the dominant group to set the outcomes standard not only provides a cultural privilege to that group, but it can also lead to an across-the-board lowering of agency outcome expectations for all. The challenge here is for public administrators to think very carefully about the establishment of performance measures and goals in examining outcomes.

NOT INCLUDING SMALL SAMPLES

We all learned in research methods courses to be wary of small samples—and for good reason. Small sample sizes limit the types of statistical analysis and have limited statistical power. But what happens over time when the data from a cultural group get discarded in routine public policy research because the sample is not sufficiently large? Consider this example: Public agencies routinely collect data from all their clients, but the number of American Indians is always very low because they are a relatively small percentage of the overall population. An agency routinely assesses outcomes among client groups but routinely discards data from American Indians due to the overall small sample size. Although the agency has served American Indian clients for many, many years, what have researchers learned about the experiences of these clients? Unfortunately, very little. The cumulative effect of eliminating American Indians from the research design (or combining them with other groups) leaves the agency and public policy makers uninformed about the experiences of these groups. Over time, this limits researchers' and the agency's ability to assess how well or poorly these clients are being served.

A related concern is that researchers avoid examining populations that are either hard to reach or have small overall populations to study. Crosby et al. (2010, 3) identify this as an important concern in health policy research:

> Thus, it is important to consider whether there is a tendency within our discipline to overvalue findings derived from large samples and undervalue findings stemming from small samples. Such bias could inadvertently steer research interest and focus away from studies involving under-served and hard-to-reach populations. Although smaller samples may be limited in their statistical power to effectively test hypotheses and the precision of effect estimates may be less stable, a key consideration is the value of these findings in addressing gaps in the empirical literature as these gaps may be valuable for informing public health policy and practice.

A worrisome pattern emerges: Researchers give far less attention to small subgroups or hard-to-reach populations due to the statistical limitations associated with small sample sizes. Our knowledge base of how these populations experience our public programs or policies is underdeveloped. These populations become less well understood. We are unable to gauge the effectiveness of public sector programs or services for these groups. Crosby et al. (2010, 1) suggest a need to balance methodological rigor against inherent practical limitations: "This stark difference demands that the scholars involved in designing and conducting research, as well as researchers and practitioners involved in utilizing the published research findings, be aware of the need to judge research based on a balance between methodological rigor and the inherent limitations imposed by working with any given hard-to-reach population."

As Lillie-Blanton and Hoffman (1995, 230) suggest, data derived from large-scale surveys may need to be buttressed with community- or population-specific data in order to design and deliver public services more effectively:

Some states and localities have field survey data that can be used to assess the health needs of a community or populations group. However, with the exception of recent national surveys, population-based surveys seldom have sufficient numbers of a racial/ethnic minority group for subgroup analysis. If data are needed to estimate service needs for planning purposes, national surveys that have focused exclusively on or oversampled specific racial/ethnic minority groups may serve as better information sources than state surveys.

Do No Harm

Our medical colleagues are governed by the Hippocratic oath to "do no harm." Similarly, ethical treatment of human subjects in research is governed by three basic principles contained in the Belmont Report, established by the National Commission for the Protection of Human Subjects of Biomedical and Behavioral Research (1979). The second of these principles—beneficence—requires doing no harm, maximizing possible benefits, and minimizing possible harm.

Some practices to assist us to "do no harm" include having a culturally diverse research team, conducting a cultural orientation, developing culturally appropriate research designs, and considering the cultural implications of certain research norms, such as the use of pan-ethnic labels and the cumulative effects of routinely not analyzing data from small or difficult-to-reach populations. As O'Sullivan, Rassel, and Berner explain: "Researchers are expected to be especially vigilant if potential subjects represent a distinctly different population from themselves. For example, researchers may underestimate the potential harm in studying recent immigrants. In such cases the researcher is more likely to misjudge what constitutes a risk or a benefit for a participant" (2008, 255). These are important considerations in "everyday" public policy and administration research, not just studies that are focused on particular underrepresented groups or studies strictly governed by institutional review boards.

Table 15.1 offers guidelines for valuing cultural competency in public administration and public policy research. Incorporating the perspective of the study population is vitally important and may best be achieved by deliberately seeking cultural diversity in the research team. Abramowitz and Murray (1983) conclude that ethnic minority and white researchers who examine the same data usually come up with completely opposite conclusions that are basically drawn along ethnic lines. "We each have our own way of interpreting data based on the cultural lenses through which we view the world, and we must guard against this bias when we as researchers, regardless of our ethnicity, study cross-cultural issues" (Atkinson 1993, 220).

It is important to have knowledge of the individuals in our research as "cultural beings." Cultural orientation information prior to evaluation allows us to know whether the assessment technology and style of service delivery developed in the dominant culture is applicable to particular subgroups (Dana 1996). As Dana details:

> Hispanic Americans respond to the cultural script of *simpatía*. . . . This style contains *respeto* (i.e., respect shown by women to men, younger to older persons, and to persons in authority), *personalismo* (i.e., preference for informality in relationships), and *platicando* (i.e., chatting) to convey a sense of *ambiente* or warmth and acceptance. A more leisurely pace facilitates acceptance of the person providing assessment services prior to engagement with the tests. (476)

Table 15.1

Cultural Competency Guide for "Everyday" Public Administration and Policy Research

Item	Description/examples	Assessment questions	Ways to improve
Researcher orientation	Level of baseline cultural competency of researcher; cultural subjectivity	• Which of the six stages in the Cross model most accurately describes me? • Do I routinely prioritize cultural competency in my professional development activities?	• Acknowledge the importance of cultural competency in every research design • Commit to rigorous cultural competency standards in research design • Assess cultural competency of self and all research team members • Frequently invest in cultural competency professional and social development
Research design	Research questions; survey questionnaires; semi-structured interviews; focus groups; spatial mapping	• Do I routinely consider cultural competency in "everyday" research designs that do not have a primary cultural focus? • Are my questions congruent with the cultures of my respondents? • Are my questions reviewed by a variety of subgroups for language, meaning, context, and appropriateness? • What category labels do I include as options for respondents to identify racial or ethnic minorities and why? • Do I use self-reported demographic data, especially in focus groups or semistructured interviews?	• Make cultural competency assessment a standard component of all research designs • Solicit input from individuals who are more culturally knowledgeable about the subgroups included in the research design • Use racial and ethnic labels that are most appropriate for the populations included in the research design • Avoid collapsing multiple groups into a single "non" or "minority" category • If only broad pan-ethnic categorical labels are available from the public agency, be sure to understand and report which groups are specifically included within each category • Allow individuals to self-report demographic data (e.g., racial and ethnic data, disability status)
Data analysis	Statistical analysis; content analysis; mapping	• Does my data analysis consider the dominant group's performance as the gold standard? If so, based upon what justification? • How do I handle small sample sizes of population subgroups? • If data are longitudinal or comparative, does my analysis consider operational differences in categories?	• Consider and justify appropriate comparative performance standards • Recognize the value of small samples in public policy research, especially for underrepresented or hard-to-reach populations • Balance methodological rigor with practical population considerations
Report of findings	Discussion of findings; recommendations; conclusions	• Does my report of findings reflect cultural knowledge and understanding? • Are my recommendations relevant and appropriate for the population subgroups in my analysis?	• Solicit input on recommendations from individuals who are more culturally knowledgeable about subgroups in the study • Use a cross-cultural lens when contextualizing findings and developing recommendations

Researchers conducting studies of Hispanics only might seek out and implement these cultural norms, but these considerations may be overlooked in large-scale agency questionnaires designed to utilize a "one size fits all" data collection approach that does not consider cultural norms among subcultures. This may result in inappropriate or ineffective service delivery. As Stewart and Nápoles-Springer note, it is important to find a balance between "obtaining a single set of items that are comparable across all cultures and creating culture specific measures" (2000, II–117).

All researchers should routinely invest in improving their cultural competency. This includes professional development, such as attending conference sessions and workshops that include cultural competency training, as well as social development acquired by intentionally spending time with cultural groups that do not align with the researchers' dominant cultural reference. Additionally, senior researchers should assess and invest in the development of cultural competency within their research team. Just as senior researchers expect analysts to be knowledgeable about data analysis tools such as SPSS, NVIVO, or GIS, they should also expect analysts to value and exhibit knowledge across cultural groups. Within the specific research design, cultural considerations should be routinely assessed during the development of survey questionnaires, focus group protocols, or semistructured interviews. Researchers should prioritize self-reported demographics and routinely solicit input on developing questionnaires from individuals who are most knowledgeable about the cultural groups included in the study. When performing the data analysis, researchers should carefully consider how to analyze small sample sizes from underrepresented or difficult-to-reach populations. Methodological rigor should be evaluated in a context of providing *public* policy research that is practically useful. Similarly, researchers should consider and justify the standard that is used to compare groups.

Many of the norms that govern our research designs need to be reexamined through a cultural competency lens. Providing a critical assessment of our cultural biases as researchers is an essential first step. As we formulate, analyze, and interpret our research questions and findings, we should be aware of our general cultural orientation. We must also question the cumulative cultural effect of some common practices such as the use of the term *nonwhite* to describe minority populations, allowing the dominant cultural group to serve as the standard for performance outcomes, and failing to analyze data from small samples of underrepresented cultural groups. Cultural competency is not limited to research studies that are squarely focused on ethnic or racial minorities or disadvantaged populations. Cultural competency in "everyday" public policy research is far too often hidden in plain view, challenging us to strengthen our research rigor by incorporating more cultural complexity into our typical research designs.

REFERENCES

Abramowitz, S.I., and J. Murray. 1983. Race effects in psychotherapy. In *Bias in Psychotherapy*, ed. J. Murray and Paul R. Abramson, 215–255. New York: Praeger.

Atkinson, D.R. 1993. Who speaks for cross-cultural counseling research? *Counseling Psychologist* 21(2): 218–224.

Babbie, Earl. 2005. *The Basics of Social Research*. 3rd ed. Belmont, CA: Thomas Wadsworth.

Buki, Lydia P., Evelinn A. Borrayo, Benjamine Feigal, and Iris Y. Carrillo. 2004. Are all Latinas the same? Perceived breast cancer screening barriers and facilitative conditions. *Psychology of Women Quarterly* 28: 400–411.

Caldwell, Joyce Y., Jamie D. Davis, Barbara DuBois, Holly Echo-Hawk, Jill Shepard Erickson, R. Turner Goins, Calvin Hill, Walter Hillabrant, Sharon R. Johnson, Elizabeth Kendall, Kelly Keemer, Spero M. Manson, Catherine Marshall, Paulette Running Wolf, Rolando Santiago, Robert Schacht, and Joseph B. Stone. 2006. Culturally competent research with American Indians and Alaska Natives: Findings and recommendations of the first symposium of the work group on American Indian research and program evaluation methodology. *Culturally Competent Research* 12(1): 1–21.

Crosby, Richard A., Laura F. Salazar, Ralph J. DiClemente, and Delia L. Long. 2010. Balancing rigor against the inherent limitations of investigating hard-to-reach populations. *Health Education Research* 25(1): 1–5.

Cross, Terry L. 1988. Services to minority populations: Cultural competence continuum. *Focal Point: A Publication of the Research and Training Center on Family Support and Children's Mental Health* 3(1): 1–2.

Cuthbert, Marlene. 1985. Evaluation encounters in third world settings: A Caribbean perspective. *New Directions for Program Evaluation* 1985(25) (special issue): 29–35.

Dana, Richard H. 1996. Culturally competent assessment practice in the United States. *Journal of Personality Assessment* 66(3): 472–487.

Fejos, Paul. 1959. Man, magic, and medicine. In *Medicine and Anthropology*, ed. I. Galdston. Freeport, NY: Books for Libraries Press.

Guzman, B.L. 2003. Examining the role of cultural competency in program evaluation: Visions for new millennium evaluators. In *Evaluating Social Programs and Problems: Visions for the New Millennium*, ed. Stewart I. Donaldson and Michael Scriven, 167–181. Mahwah, NJ: Lawrence Erlbaum.

Hood, S. 2001. Nobody knows my name. In praise of African American evaluators who were responsive. *New Directions for Evaluation* 92: 31–43.

Lillie-Blanton, Marsha, and Sandra C. Hoffman. 1995. Conducting an assessment of health needs and resources in a racial/ethnic minority community. *Health Services Research* 30(1): 225–236.

Merryfield, Merry M. 1985. The challenge of cross-cultural evaluation: Some views from the field. *New Directions for Program Evaluation* 1985(25) (special issue): 3–17.

The National Commission for the Protection of Human Subjects of Biomedical and Behavioral Research. 1979. The Belmont report: Ethical principles and guidelines for the protection of human subjects of research. April 18. Washington, DC: Department of Health, Education, and Welfare [now the U.S. Department of Health and Human Services], 4–6.

O'Sullivan, Elizabethann, Gary R. Rassel, and Maureen Berner. 2008. *Research Methods for Public Administrators*. 5th ed. New York: Pearson Longman.

Purnell, Larry D., and Betty J. Paulanka, eds. 1998. *Transcultural Health Care: A Culturally Competent Approach*. Philadelphia: F.A. Davis.

Skaff, Marilyn McKean, Catherine A. Chesla, Victoria de los Santos Mycue, and Lawrence Fisher. 2002. Lessons in cultural competence: Adapting research methodology for Latino participants. *Journal of Community Psychology* 30(3): 305–323.

Stewart, Anita L., and Anna M. Nápoles-Springer. 2000. Health-related quality of life assessments in diverse population groups in the United States. *Medical Care* 38(9): II-102–II-124.

———. 2003. Advancing health disparities research: Can we afford to ignore measurement issues? *Medical Care* 41(11): 1207–1220.

Tillman, Linda C. 2002. Culturally sensitive research approaches: An African-American perspective. *Educational Researcher* 31(9): 3–12.

A Dialogic Model for Cultural Competency in the Graduate Classroom

Mario Rivera
Richard Greggory Johnson III
and Glenda Kodaseet

In this study we ask—from a critical standpoint—whether cultural competency can be taught. This question presupposes another, pertaining to our definition of the term *cultural competency*. We address each of these questions based on our combined reflections and classroom experience, providing what are admittedly provisional, partial, and tentative answers. We then go on to propose a pedagogical framework that incorporates both cultural and diversity competencies, one that is organized around the interplay of multiple perspectives in the classroom—a dialogic model for cultural competency.

Cultural competency is broadly defined for purposes of our study to incorporate diversity competencies—with the caveat that we are here principally concerned with diversity issues connected with race and ethnicity, and only secondarily (though no less importantly) with culture as such. We take cultural competency to be an open—accepting—and welcoming attitude toward other group cultures, defined broadly as the normative, behavioral, and communicative values of racial, ethnic, nationality, gender, and other groups different from one's own. Acceptance is ideally coupled with understanding of the nuances of specific group cultural norms and practices. However, we believe that it is more reasonable to expect students to come to greater *acceptance* of other groups, rather than a substantially greater *understanding* of other groups, in the course of a typical classroom experience. Insistent as we are on the prospect of attitudinal change rather than knowledge acquisition, we hope to avoid hackneyed treatment of any group and especially to avoid stereotyping others. From this standpoint, cultural competency cannot be taught, as a matter of discrete course *content*. Instead, what is desirable and feasible, in our view, is to bring students to the beginning of a process of cognitive development and personal growth, in their regard for others whom they consider different from themselves.

CULTURAL, MULTICULTURAL, AND DIVERSITY COMPETENCIES

We regard cultural competency as a cognitive capacity that some people attain more fully than others, as a matter of life experience and by dint of socialization, learning, and maturation. For Antonio and his collaborators, cultural competency is an indicator of *integrative complexity*, "the degree to which cognitive style involves the differentiation and integration of multiple perspectives," a way of perceiving, thinking, and acting that allows one to take up alternative viewpoints on issues, while regarding one's own as but one such viewpoint (Antonio et al. 2004, 508; see also Tuckman 1966). Integrative complexity is therefore a kind of *perspectivism*, the ability to evaluate issues at once from one's own perspective (which one regards as partial and limited) and those of others. Integrative complexity cannot be taught; it can only be "grown into" by those willing and able to do so.

Consequently, we argue that cultural competency is a cognitive as well as emotive capacity that can be strengthened through diversity and cultural education, but not transmitted in formulaic ways or in a narrow sense taught as course content. Our working definition of cultural competency is broader than most, since it deliberately includes racial and ethnic diversity, and it concerns itself with personal, attitudinal change. For us, there is but one integrated competency, one that involves much greater acceptance of other racial, ethnic, nationality, and other groups. While this subject is often relegated to discussions of diversity narrowly defined, sometimes under the rubric of "diversity competencies," we take an expansive view of cultural competency, one that is somewhat more concerned with personal maturation than with learning as such.

The Tilford Group (2001) of Kansas State University similarly identifies cultural competencies with cosmopolitan perspectives that appreciate and genuinely value racial and ethnic diversity (Figure 16.1). The Tilford Group defines cultural competency as the knowledge, attributes, and skills required in order to live and work in a diverse and globalized world. To arrive at this perspective, the Tilford Group evaluated training programs, interviewed specialist diversity and multicultural trainers and managers, reviewed literature from a variety of disciplines (from social work to education and management), and conducted focus group research with faculty and students at Kansas State. Its effort resulted in the identification of the following essential cultural, multicultural, and diversity competencies. It should be noted that even the knowledge and skills categories that follow involve changes in awareness, behaviors, and communicative and collaborative abilities, and not mastery of any particular subject matter.

Consistent with the Tilford framework, as well as a typology developed by Rice (2006), for our purposes cultural competencies incorporate diversity competencies, as previously suggested. We find that the two kinds of competency are inextricably tied together, essentially equivalent as a set of cognitive, attitudinal, and behavioral capacities. Neither is a set of discrete skills. So conceived, the development by individuals of cultural competencies can be fostered but not, strictly speaking, imparted in the way that particular skills may be transmitted in training courses for technical competencies. It is our conviction, born of experience but also a matter of principle, that cultural competencies cannot be taught in any classroom, unless

---

Figure 16.1
Tilford Group Cultural Competencies

I. KNOWLEDGE: Awareness and understanding needed to live and work in a diverse world
1. Cultural self-awareness: The ability to understand one's ethnic self-identification
2. Diverse ethnic groups: An understanding of different cultures and ethnic groups
3. Social/political/economic/historical framework: Understanding how sociopolitical, economic, and historical factors and events impact racial groups around the world
4. Changing demographics: Understanding how changing demographics impact race
5. Understanding population dynamics of race and ethnicity

II. PERSONAL ATTRIBUTES: Traits needed by to live and work in a diverse world
1. Flexibility: Being able to adapt to a changing world
2. Respect: An appreciation for differences in others
3. Empathy: The ability to respect another person's culture and perspective

III. SKILLS: Behaviors and performance tasks needed to live and work in a diverse world
1. Cross-cultural communication: Verbal and nonverbal communications with different groups
2. Teamwork: The ability to work with diverse groups toward a common goal
3. Conflict resolution: The ability to resolve cultural conflicts
4. Critical thinking: Being able to use inductive and deductive reasoning
5. Language development: Being able to speak and write more than one language
6. Leadership development: The ability to provide diversity leadership

Source: Tilford Group (2001).

---

such competencies are somehow redefined as processes of cognitive development and personal maturation.

In this regard, we take the view of Anderson and Collins (2004, 1) that diversity and cultural awareness is about increased sensitivity to "the intersections of race, social class and gender," about seeing "linkages to other categories of analysis, including sexuality, age, religion, physical disability, national identity and ethnicity," and about appreciating the disparities of power "that produce social inequalities." There is a sense in which shared experiences of discrimination or oppression allow us to find empathy with others. We do not want to suggest, however, that experiences of racism, sexism, discrimination on the basis of nationality, and so on are somehow equivalent. Nor are they in any way reducible to one another. Every instance of discrimination is singular in its individual and social impacts, and objectionable. Nevertheless, almost everyone can tap into a commonality of human experience so as to better appreciate others.

The celebrated (and controversial) study *The Future of Multi-Ethnic Britain,* commonly known as the *Parekh Report* (Parekh, 2000), named after Bhikhu Parekh, chair of the Commission on the Future of Multi-Ethnic Britain, provides a series of contrasting attitudes toward those of other faiths, races, ethnicities, and cultures. The commission was established in January 1998 by the Runnymede Trust, a think tank devoted to the promotion of racial justice in Great Britain. Parekh and his commission set out to analyze the state of race and ethnic relations in that nation and to propose ways of countering racial discrimination and advancing multicultural diversity. They did so in the *Report*, published in 2000. Their analytical and advocacy framework, like ours, lays stress on attitudinal modalities rather than skill sets, in addressing cultural competencies. These modalities turn on polar dichotomies between rejection of and identification with others. The resulting construct, which we find has much to recommend it, is shown in Table 16.1 (with some paraphrasing, for brevity).

IDENTITY AND IDENTIFICATION

The notion of identification with others is key to our discussion, since the promotion of cultural and diversity competency should be to go beyond simple tolerance, or even empathy, to a sense of identification (identity) with others. There is an arc that carries one from awareness to emotive engagement with others. Self-awareness needs to carry one into other-awareness and identification with others, a conversion process that brings a real depth of acceptance with it.

Identity as the assertion of individual autonomy on the basis of respect for one's own culture is the political side of a coin whose obverse is ethical, the valuing of others' cultural norms and values through identification with them; this presupposes a dialectic movement from cultural rootedness to cultural transcendence. Culture is constitutive of identity, just as are race, ethnicity, gender, age, and disability: Taken together, these help constitute the self. Identity is also political in that it is tied to power, the relative power of individuals and groups. But these very factors, while constituting identity, do not exhaust it. Identity is more than its constituent parts, and it is this transcendent quality of identity that allows us to go beyond who we are in moments of identification with others.

IDENTITY, DIVERSITY, AND PLURALITY

Identity is bound up with what Kwame Anthony Appiah (2004) calls the "irreducibly plural nature of human values." As Jürgen Habermas proposes (1992, 130–131), "identity formation depends upon relations of reciprocal recognition." Identity is plural, perspectival, transactional, and dialogical. One should reject reductive essentialism with regard to race, ethnicity, gender, or the other qualities here discussed (Stasiulis 1999), since no one is exhaustively defined by such traits. Stasiulis would counter race or gender essentialism with relational awareness, or awareness of the "intersectionality" of the *plural* vectors of race, gender, class, and identity. Not only is it undesirable to define people reductively by race or gender or other traits, but also many of us have come to identify ourselves with plural dimensions of personal identity.

When it comes to sexual orientation and gender identity, to take one instance, there is great diversity reflecting different life experiences and experiences of discrimination

Table 16.1

The Parekh Report Framework: Closed and Open Views of the Other

Distinctions	Closed views of the Other	Open views of the Other
Monolithic/diverse	The Other is seen as a monolithic bloc, static and unresponsive to new realities.	The other is seen as diverse and progressive, with internal differences, debates, and developments.
Separate/interacting	The Other is seen as separate: (a) not having any aims or values in common with the self; (b) not affected by it; (c) not influencing it.	The Other is seen as interdependent with the self: (a) having certain shared values and aims; (b) affected by it; (c) enriching it.
Inferior/different	The Other is seen as inferior to the self.	The Other is seen as different but of equal worth.
Enemy/partner	The Other is seen as threatening, to be defeated and perhaps dominated.	The Other is seen as an actual or potential partner in solving shared problems.
Manipulative/sincere	The Other is seen as manipulative and deceitful, bent only on gaining advantage.	The Other is seen as sincere in its beliefs, not hypocritical.
Criticisms of the self rejected/considered	Criticisms made by the Other of the self are rejected out of hand.	Criticisms of the self are considered and debated.
Discrimination defended/criticized	Hostility toward the Other is used to justify discriminatory practices and social exclusion of the Other.	Debates and disagreements with the Other do not diminish efforts to combat discrimination and exclusion.
Hostility toward the Other seen as natural/problematic	Fear and hostility toward the Other is accepted as natural and normal.	Critical views of the Other are themselves subjected to critique, lest they be inaccurate and unfair.

among lesbians, gays, bisexuals, and transgender and transsexual (LGBT) people. There are also considerable divergences in the political loading of public agendas that relate precisely to questions of sexual orientation versus gender identity, down to questions of issue definition, strategy, tactics, and priorities (Aspinall and Mitton 2008). It would be simplistic, therefore, to regard as homogeneous all who would accept the LGBT acronym, as though they amounted to a single identity group or community of interest. Their extraordinary diversity and widely differing contexts and circumstances make for great differences in political positioning as well, whether the issue at hand is marriage equality, employment equity, party politics, or anything else.

In fact, what are treated as groups for the sake of convenience are usually far from monolithic. That is true of Latinos, for example, who encompass hundreds of communities, nations, races and ethnicities, cultural groups, and languages, and of African Americans, and of virtually every superficially homogeneous group. Questions of group identity are exceedingly complex, and setting out to master them in a single academic or training class is futile and naive.

To take still another example of complexity tied to identity, Rockquemore and Brunsma (2002) examine the multidimensionality of biracial identity in the United States; the authors consider how biracial individuals construct their identity, which shifts between single identity (e.g., black), exclusively biracial, "protean" or multiple identity, and "transcendental identity" beyond race. It is very common as well to be bicultural, or biracial and bicultural, and many other permutations of race, ethnicity, nationality, and culture. There is also complexity in the "intersectional" discrimination undergone by individuals who combine more than one relevant identity trait, such as a member of an ethnic minority group who also has a disability, or a person of color who is also gay or lesbian (McCall 2005; Turner 2002).

There is a difference, therefore, to be found in our pedagogical approach, beyond incorporating diversity in the concept of cultural competency. We insist that cultural and diversity education should not aim to bring classroom participants to a substantial understanding of other groups or cultures, although obviously the greater the depth of knowledge, the better. No one academic or training class can bring students close to an adequate understanding of other cultural groups. But a single class *can* be a point of departure in an open-ended journey toward much greater acceptance of others in their difference and toward valuing difference as such.

Particular instances and cases explored in dialogue in the classroom should be seen as emblematic of the entire phenomenon of difference, beyond the particular subjects of inquiry in that particular classroom. The overriding aim, contrary to the emphasis in much of the literature, is not so much to comprehend others as to gain in *self*-comprehension. The lens held to other groups and their cultures also holds a reflection of the perceiving subjects and their culture. When there is resistance to exploration of these issues in the classroom, it does not occur because students are in any way forced to look at others more acceptingly, but because students are made uncomfortable by beholding themselves in that lens *qua* mirror. It is painful to have to recognize prejudices in oneself that have to be overcome, but that is nonetheless a critical moment of self-discovery that needs to be traversed by students and instructors alike.

In these distinct emphases, on cognitive and personal growth in particular, we sidestep what we consider to be overreaching in the theories and methods that have become standard fare in the diversity and cultural competency field. There is everything from "expectation" and "communication-accommodation" theories to dozens of theory-based training methods. There are numerous testing methods in use, such as Developmental Model of Intercultural Sensitivity, and assessment devices such as the Multicultural Awareness-Knowledge-Skills Survey and the Organizational Climate and Diversity Assessment and Climate QUAL™ survey protocols developed by the University of Maryland (Kyrillidou et al. 2009). The Interdisciplinary Cross-Cultural Communication Project of Tulane University's Southern Institute for Education and Research has comprehensively examined a compendium of these theories, methods, and instruments (see Hill 2004). To be sure, these have been widely used and validated, and they may work well in conjunction with educational curricula where the development of specific skill sets is somehow the rationale and goal.

In our own teaching endeavors, however, we espouse aims that are at once more modest and more far-reaching. As suggested earlier, what we try to accomplish is to bring students to greater insight about others, to openness toward other groups. We try to bring students to a kind of humility, in the etymological sense of the word, which is to say to a fuller self-awareness in their relationship with others. We are unaware of any standard test protocols for these capacities; rather, we sense the growth in awareness and sensitivity among our students, when we succeed.

Dynamics of Difference in the Classroom: Specifications of Our Experience

The dynamics of difference unfold in sometimes congenial and sometimes contentious classroom exchanges. The contexts differ for authors Mario Rivera and Richard Johnson in particular, as active faculty members in their respective universities. For Johnson, the context is classroom courses at the University of Vermont variously devoted to issues of race and diversity or topics that include diversity concerns among a number of other subjects. In treating the subjects of diversity and equity, Johnson asks students to consider and critically discuss racial, ethnic, gender, and socioeconomic class stereotypes, an exercise that typically generates vital discussion, if also occasional resistance, in a largely Anglo-American, Caucasian student cohort. Johnson also has been teaching a course on race and racism at the undergraduate level since 2002, a course that would be required of much of the student body (irrespective of major) beginning in 2007. (For the most part, students cannot opt out of this class with substitution of other experiences, though many do creatively attempt to do so, with such activities as going to Jamaica for a week.) While contentiousness has lessened in these classes in recent years, students are still typically disengaged from the subject matter and unconvinced that it should be addressed academically at all. Yet student engagement is absolutely essential for these classes to function as intended.

For Rivera, the setting is the School of Public Administration at the University of New Mexico (UNM), in graduate professional courses whose subject matter includes but is not devoted principally to questions of diversity. Courses include Comparative Public Administration, Organizational Behavior, and Intergovernmental Administration. UNM is a minority-serving ("Hispanic-serving") institution, and the master of public administration (MPA) program is a so-called "majority-minority" program: more than half of the students in the School of Public Administration are Hispanic (or Latino), Native American, African American, and Asian or Asian American, including international students. Two-thirds of the MPA students are women, and the program's faculty is itself majority-minority. There is greater ease here to classroom treatments of diversity-related topics such as immigration or tribal nation sovereignty, and less need to offer stand-alone diversity courses (although a new course called Diversity Management has been instituted as an occasional elective in a newly restructured MPA curriculum).

Classroom makeup makes a difference, in these and other contexts, as research confirms, and it makes a difference as well for the role of the instructor in guiding dialogue in the directions already suggested, toward fruitful exploration of diversity and cultural difference. As may be expected, classroom interaction around issues of race and ethnicity differs significantly in classrooms where students of color are in the majority versus those where they are in a small minority. When they are at least a substantial minority, and certainly when they constitute the majority in the classroom, there obtains what some scholars call a "critical mass" of students of color (or, in other contexts, women). These students may then be expected to speak their minds more assertively, whereas in classrooms where they are a small minority, students of color (or women) may be more diffident. Regardless of numbers, when there is a classroom climate that values diversity and difference, the prospect for productive dialogue improves dramatically.

In the following sections, the germane experiences of the three authors of this chapter are recounted, followed by further explication of the dialogic pedagogical model (Rivera, Johnson, and Ward 2010).

Johnson's Experience

At the University of Vermont, Johnson has taught a graduate course called Human Resources Management (HRM) since 2003, as well as the undergraduate course Race and Racism in the United States required for all students by the university. For three successive years, graduate students taking the HRM course were surveyed at the beginning of the semester so as to identify social attitudes toward people of color, as well as toward social class. There was, in the vernacular, some "pushback," or resistance, from some white students, who were overwhelmingly in the majority demographically. A large majority of these students reported not fully understanding the connection between HRM and the survey. Three percent of the total reported feeling uncomfortable about discussing such issues in a graduate seminar and therefore opted out of the survey. However, the remaining 97 percent did complete the survey.

There were two principal questions, which read as follows: (1) Please identify commonly found social stereotypes for African American men, Hispanic men, Asian men, Native American men, white men, and working-class men; and (2) Please identify commonly found social stereotypes for African American women, Hispanic women, Asian women, Native American women, white women, and working-class women.

Table 16.2

Stereotypical Perceptions of Men

African American men	Asian men	Native American men	Hispanic men	White men	Working-class or poor men
1. Thrives	1. Intelligent	1. Drunks	1. Macho	1. CEOs	1. Large family
2. Sexy	2. Quiet	2. Spiritual	2. Uneducated	2. Nonathletic	2. Not ambitious
3. Athletic	3. Small	3. Uneducated	3. High sex drive	3. Cheaters	3. City resident
4. Rappers	4. Autocratic		4. Greasy	4. Privileged	

Table 16.3

Stereotypical Perceptions of Women

African American women	Asian women	Native American women	Hispanic women	White women	Working-class or poor women
1. Loud	1. Intelligent	1. Nurturing	1. Loud	1. "Barbie doll"	1. Born that way
2. Many children	2. Quiet	2. Spiritual	2. Curves	2. Smart	2. Absent father
3. Good cooks	3. Small	3. "Absent from America's landscape"	3. Good dancers	3. Catty	3. Lives in a trailer park
4. Strong	4. Subservient		4. Many children	4. Ambitious	
5. Sexy					

It was made clear in the survey instructions that these were stereotypes of which students were aware, not ones that would be imputed to them personally.

The resulting survey findings suggest that 98 percent of the students responding were aware of a number of race, gender, and class stereotypes in American society, as Tables 16.2 and 16.3 indicate.

It is interesting to note that, notwithstanding the dissociation of responses from personal attitudes, people of color were more often than not described with reference to negative stereotypes, while their white counterparts were more often characterized as ambitious and high achievers. Poor and working-class people—across racial lines—were also cast negatively. While gender was included in the survey, sexual orientation, age, disability, and other categories were not addressed. Respondents at times noted that they themselves did not share the perceptions reported, but that they were aware of them as persistent social stereotypes. Nonetheless, the class was left to contend with jaundiced images of people of color and women in the workplace.

A peculiarity of some prominent treatments of diversity and cultural competency topics is the extent to which they unwittingly propound racial and ethnic stereotypes. Potter (2009) makes reference to a Likert-scale typology from a management text from the 1990s that ascribes a number of stereotypical cultural outlooks to unspecified minority groups. Broadly paraphrasing, these include a belief in predestination, an assertion that punctuality is relatively unimportant, and a declaration that individual needs are *always* subordinate to those of family and friends. These are but three of nine such invidious characterizations (which the author does not present as her own); the "punctuality" reference is presumably made to Latinos, who are often caricatured as chronically late. The polar options, clearly corresponding to majoritarian values, are as follows (again, paraphrasing): Actively preparing for the future is important and reflects maturity; punctuality and efficiency are characteristics of intelligent and concerned people; and individual independence *must* come before family needs. The pervasiveness of stereotyping is evident in this intercultural education material, however well-meaning it may have been in its original formulation in a 1990s-era text.

While Johnson's HRM course survey on stereotyping was first conducted in 2007, he has consistently found mixed attitudes expressed by participants in this majority white graduate course. Students seem unconvinced that questions of diversity and cultural difference, related issues of social equity, and queries about stereotypes have a compelling connection to the study of HRM. However, as classroom pedagogy and textbooks increasingly include discussions of race, gender, and other forms of discrimination and connect them to the topics of social equity and professional and managerial concerns, this way of thinking is likely to change.

In contrast to this graduate course, the undergraduate course Race and Racism in the United States has had a higher proportion of students of color, who (perhaps because of the nature of the course) have displayed a high degree of self-confidence in their assertion of counterviews. White students have not generally tried in this class to confront students of color with their own biases, to the extent that these are present at all.

Instructors dealing with controversial questions such as these, entailing as they do the historic disenfranchisement of oppressed groups, must set ground rules. Johnson has done this with the following articulation of policy in his course syllabus for the Race and Racism class: "Safe Space Policy: Students will speak and be full participants in this class without fear of verbal or physical abuse from any other student. Any student violating this policy will be sent before judicial affairs department of the University of Vermont." The policy is not only prominently printed in the syllabus, but also it is pointedly addressed on the first day of class. It allows students the freedom to express their ideas without fear of retaliation from classmates. Some may not like the policy, but they do understand the importance of having it.

RIVERA'S EXPERIENCE

In Rivera's Comparative Public Administration and Administrative Behavior graduate courses at the University of New Mexico (UNM), cultural competency issues are principally addressed through student presentations of case studies, for instance the following two from the Electronic Hallway website at the University of Washington (http://hallway.evans.washington.edu):

1. "Preventing Drilling in the Arctic Wildlife Refuge: The Gwich'in Tribes and Their Role in the National Policy Debate": the impact on the Gwich'in Native people of Alaska of federal policies dating to the 1970s affecting their economy, culture, and corporate status and sovereignty

2. "Managing a Health Project: HIV/AIDS in Thailand," sometimes coupled with "Science, Discrimination, and the Blood Supply: San Jose State University's Blood Drive Ban": close parallels in the effects of cultural prejudice on the ability of people with HIV/AIDS to participate in health services

Case presentations generate discussion among students of all backgrounds (though, as suggested previously, it ought to be considered that in UNM classrooms upward of two-thirds of the students are women, 90 percent are in-service/working students, and a substantial majority is comprised of Hispanic, Native American, and international students). Student-led discussions drive the joint exploration of cultural competency, diversity, and social equity questions. These questions are both negative in nature—the persistence of stereotypes, loss of identity, the dissipation of power over resources—and positive—the prospects for improvement in intergroup relations, capacity-building in cultural awareness, and the enduring strength of community.

As does Johnson, Rivera insists on open discussion and on respect for the persons and views of others in the classroom. With rare exceptions, these conditions obtain. In one memorable instance when they did not, the student responsible for disruptive behavior was sanctioned. Upon being given an opportunity to apologize in writing for a totally unwarranted accusation of racism leveled at another student during a class, the offending party did so, and then the sanction was removed. Rivera's equivalent in his syllabi to Johnson's "Safe Space" policy reads as follows: "It should be noted that civility toward everyone in the classroom is a definite expectation for this course. All should feel free to express their views thoughtfully, and to summon evidence for their arguments. Moreover, they should do so without fear of interruption or any kind of denigration from others, especially when there are difficult questions of cultural, racial, or other difference at issue."

In leading a student presentation of the Gwich'in case, author Glenda Kodaseet, a candidate for a master's in public administration, made an important distinction between Native spirituality and historic impositions of religion. Kodaseet developed the issue persuasively in establishing the background facts of the case. If her characterization of missionary Christianity discomfited anyone, there was no sign of it as she made her way through the case presentation. Kodaseet's own account of her case presentation experience follows.

KODASEET'S EXPERIENCE

When presented with case summaries in order to select a case study for a presentation in Mario Rivera's graduate Comparative Public Administration course, Kodaseet chose Dodge and Walters (2004), "Preventing Drilling in the Arctic Wildlife Refuge: The Gwich'in Tribes and Their Role in the National Policy Debate: Rebirth of a Nation." She did so because of her affinity and familiarity with Native American (NA) cultures, her awareness of the many challenges facing NA tribes, and her comfort level in engaging peers in discussions of these linked topics.

It was already her experience in the School of Public Administration that the manifold diversity enjoyed by students and faculty allowed for sustained and motivated student-initiated inquiry on issues of race and culture. Indeed, when presenting the Gwich'in case, she discovered that the dialogue between her and her classmates reinforced her confidence as an NA student in leading this particular class discussion.

Gwich'in culture was the motive force behind the tribe's success in staving off oil drilling within its historic homelands. Kodaseet's case presentation emphasized the vibrancy and strength of culture in this and many other NA communities. It further emphasized that cultural values, beliefs, outlooks, and practices are linked to the underlying bond between individuals, community, land, and natural environment. It was in this vein that Kodaseet provided her peers with a comprehensive foundation from which case discussion could develop (Ah Nee-Benham and Mann 2003). As indicated, her presentation of cultural descriptors distinguished cultural life-ways from mainstream religion, native spirituality from imposed institutional forms of religion, thereby clarifying a critical factor in cultural difference.

To the Gwich'in, identity, life-ways, and survival are directly connected to the Porcupine River caribou and its migration pattern. Serving as their source of food, clothing, and tools, the caribou is at the center of Gwich'in life. These cultural elements were pivotal discussion points in the author's presentation because they reinforced an irreducible link between individual and community, and land and natural environment. This thematic strain deepened understanding on the part of non-Native students in that classroom of the unique qualities of Native spirituality and community that helped the Gwich'in galvanize broad-based national and international support for their ultimately successful political efforts to stave off drilling. Such mobilization was a critical component of the Gwich'in case study, since oil interests were threatening Gwich'in life and gaining federal policy support at the time of the case narrative. Connecting corporate lobbying to federal policy threatening a Native way of life bared the disparities of power that for NA populations continue to result in social inequities. Taking the opportunity to explore these concerns with her peers in the classroom, the author drew strength and voice from her own NA identity.

In the Gwich'in case, historic assimilation policies had devastating consequences (Deyhle and Swisher 1997; Havighurst 1957), but when the tribe came together to resist the threat of oil drilling, a kind of cultural rebirth occurred which all at once strengthened community, pride of heritage, and tribal identity. Class discussion of the impact of adverse policies on Gwich'in culture shed light on present-day challenges facing Native communities in general, as well.

It may be helpful in this same context to note the importance to Native students of the tribal college and university (TCU) movement. This movement arose in the 1960s, in large part to counter the high dropout rates of tribal members attending mainstream colleges and universities. TCUs introduced cultural relevancy into the Native American educational agenda through a curriculum that blended tribal knowledge and wisdom with mainstream academic study (Ah Nee-Benham and Mann 2003). The aim of this advocacy was educational parity as defined by Native traditions and values. At TCUs, the learning environment was to be made to support every student's cultural identity. While the author's case presentation did not specifically address TCUs, it drew nonetheless from the movement's premise of the importance of the Native student's own cultural identity and sense of self-efficacy (Lomawaima and McCarty 2002).

While mainstream colleges and universities do not often incorporate indigenous knowledge and experience into curricula, the University of New Mexico prides itself on welcoming dialogue that engages Native cultural perspectives. The author's case presentation in this Comparative Public Administration course was consistent with the effort of the instructor, Mario Rivera, to extend the traditional scope of this academic subfield so as to include NA cultural and public policy concerns, consistent with the university's mission with regard to multicultural diversity and students and communities of color.

From the author's point of view, diversity among her classmates allowed for a dynamic discussion without fear of either undue criticism or indifference. Animated class discussion made for real dialogue on cultural concerns, furthering student awareness and appreciation in a relatively easy classroom atmosphere. Through inquiry, students discovered similarities between their own experiences of adversity and the threats faced by the Gwich'in.

In another Electronic Hallway (2009) case study, an examination of the microlender *Compartamos* and microcredit programs in Mexico and the United States, the impediment represented by American individualism to group-based lending was explored. Insight came from the interaction of students of all backgrounds, a couple of whom had had experience with local microcredit programs, as had the instructor himself in his consulting practice. In both this and the Gwich'in case, what was essential was the uncovering of points of contact between the students' experience and that of the case protagonists. In the process, students discovered the ways that taken-for-granted values might either advance or impede policy initiatives, often with paradoxical outcomes. Understanding—of what was desirable as a matter of public policy—came from exposition and exploration of the case material and from the classroom dialogue that ensued.

A COMMON MODEL FROM DIFFERENT SETTINGS

As a consequence of these experiences, we have elaborated a preliminary teaching model for cultural competency in the graduate classroom, one that is adequate to academic and training classrooms of any demographic composition. Following the literature, Rivera and Johnson characterize it as a *dialogic pedagogy*. Other terms of art for this approach to cultural competency include *interdiscursive pedagogy*, *perspectival pedagogy*, and *transactional pedagogy*, all of which denote the fact that it is critical to have dynamic interaction among a multiplicity of personal and cultural perspectives in classroom dialogue.

The dialogic model appears to work roughly as well in cohorts with large and small minority-student numbers, contrasting UNM and the University of Vermont (UVM). The dialogic approach appears to work in these different settings—notwithstanding somewhat different classroom experiences—because it turns on the interaction of discussants of varied backgrounds and not on any set classroom profile. There must be face-to-face discussion of the issues among students of diverse backgrounds for the model to work, because other group and national and social cultures are instantiated in the persons of participants in the classroom. This does not mean that every culture

Table 16.4

University of Vermont Faculty by Race, 2008

Full-time tenure/tenure track faculty	Number	Percentage of total
African American	17	2.8
Asian	41	6.7
Hispanic/Latino	11	1.8
Native American	4	0.6
Subtotal: Faculty of color	73	11.9
International	24	3.9
White	517	84.2
Total	614	100.0

Source: University of Vermont Office of Institutional Research (2010).

under consideration must be represented there, however. What is essential, as Antonio argues (Antonio et al. 2004), if the salutary effects of these kinds of interactions are to become evident, is at least a minimum of diversity in the classroom itself.

It *is* the case that in the University of New Mexico graduate classroom there appears to be a greater ease of interaction among students of color and white students, less resistance, and greater ease in the development of issues of race; the University of Vermont appears less amenable to dialogue about race. Interestingly, the politics of sexual orientation (questions, for example, relating to marriage equality in law) appears to be somewhat less readily approachable at UNM than at UVM. Nonetheless, UNM has a significant and growing number of advocacy and associational programs for LGBT students and faculty and a clear institutional commitment to them and their concerns.

At University of Vermont there is still not a critical mass of students of color or faculty of color, which makes it difficult for such dialogue to occur. Taking, for example, the fall of 2008, Table 16.4 shows the disparity in the numbers of faculty members by race.

ALANA (Asian Latino African American Native American) students represented 862 out of a total of 9,513 undergraduate full-time students attending UVM. By way of contrast, in that same semester, University of New Mexico tenured and tenure-track faculty of color (self-identified, for Main Campus, excluding the medical school) totaled 269 of 1,200 faculty members, or 24 percent (eighteen faculty members had given no response to optional race/ethnicity) categories when submitting applications for employment. And at UNM there were 9,249 students of color out of a total of 18,394 undergraduate students, or 50.3 percent, and 1,177 ALANA students of a total of 4,231 graduate students, or 27.8 percent (University of New Mexico 2009). The demographic contrast between the two institutions is therefore rather stark, and those disparities are reflected in the quality of discourse on race and racism in particular.

CRITICAL MASS

As previously suggested, the critical variable in obtaining more assertive dialogue in the classroom, rather than either diffidence or indifference, is the presence of students of color among white students. The experimental research conducted by Antonio and colleagues (Antonio et al. 2004, 507) confirmed earlier (largely anecdotal) findings by other scholars that group interaction incorporating at least some students of color makes for increases in integrative complexity among majority-opinion members in particular, which is also to say among majority group members. Other researchers (e.g., Anderson, Daugherty, and Corrigan 2005) have found that a "critical mass" of students of color in the classroom, beyond a minimal presence, makes a critical difference in the quality of those students' participation in class discussion. Critical mass allows for much greater "integrative engagement" (Keiner and Burns 2010), and it has been found to help women and racial and ethnic minorities in the science classroom to be more confident in participation (Beichner 2006; see also Anderson, Daugherty, and Corrigan 2005).

As suggested by Johnson's explicit "Safe Space" ground rules—which are echoed in Rivera's syllabi by his requirement for civility of dialogue—contentiousness must be limited even while vital discourse is encouraged. Unsupported generalizations, invidious characterizations, assertions of stereotypes, and undue antagonism must not be permitted. This is not at all a matter of political correctness, which underestimates students' ability to have intelligent conversation. On the contrary, instructors need to encourage candid exploration of issues, but on the premise that dialogue requires respect for other interlocutors. Avery and Steingard (2008) similarly argue for authentic dialogue, in a "zone of understanding," beyond strictures of political correctness.

In either kind of setting, the role of the instructor, and in particular the instructor of color, is critical. In our experience there are differences in the role responsibilities of instructors, based on their race or ethnicity. One difference is that the instructor, when a person of color, may carry more of a burden than white instructors in defining topics for discussion, down to the selection of materials to be discussed, and in setting the right tone for productive dialogue, modeling it in his or her own discourse whenever possible (Ortiz and Jani 2010). It is our experience that in the "majority-minority" classroom the instructor may be well served to take a lower-profile role, allowing discussion to proceed as it may, with the expectation that all students will join in, without undue concern for disagreement as such. What is of concern is the *quality* of disagreement, as well as consensus, in the discussion of germane issues.

Conclusion: The Role of the Instructor in Establishing Ethical Dialogue

In classrooms where those of color are distinctly in the minority, the instructor, particularly the instructor of color, may be in effect the equalizer, pressing issues volubly and intervening to steer discussion toward dialogue. As Brookfield and Preskill (2005) argue, it is important to keep student and instructor voices in reasonable balance when exploring potentially contentious questions. There are alternative roles the instructor can take, as advocate or arbiter or moderator, that suit the demands of the classroom situation (Blum 1998; Larson and Schermerhorn 1989).

We agree with Jackson (2008) that one must avoid being overly prescriptive in the classroom. Instructors and trainers can frame issues and, to an extent act as advocates without preempting discussion or rendering it undemocratic. Milovavic (1995) insists that, ultimately, knowledge is "coproduced" by teachers and students as they develop "a language of possibility" together. Leistyna and Mollen (2008) similarly call for "a dialogic pedagogy." Learning is transactional and accountable. Instructors and students have to answer to each other for the way in which they approach these sensitive subjects and for the manner of conclusions they reach together.

Finally, we agree with Robert Nash (2010) when he argues that one should construct dialogue in such a way as to find "the commonalities in our different views on social justice." However, as Nash further suggests, when it is not possible to find common ground we must agree to suspend rather than end the conversation, with the hope of returning to it at a more propitious time. It is in both the nature of conversation and the ends of dialogue that the study of diversity and cultural difference can become an ethical undertaking for all involved.

To pick up an earlier proposition, it is feasible for instruction relating to cultural and diversity competencies to bring students to an attitudinal threshold—one that is more about valuing than understanding difference, more about respect for others than about comprehension of others. This aim is more realistic than setting out to impart extensive knowledge of other cultural and group norms, values, and interests. It is virtually impossible to literally *teach* cultural competency. The stress, as Nash suggests, should be on dialogue as an end in itself, rather than as a means to the learning of content. Dialogue is a way to negotiate and thereby appreciate difference; it does not bring about any exhaustive comprehension of difference (Gardiner 1996; Pettit 1989).

In the end, therefore, cultural competency is what Carol Falender and Edward Shafranske (2007, citing Weinert 2001, 235) call a "metacompetence." A metacompetence is the capacity to "introspect about one's personal cognitive processes [that depends] on self-awareness, self-reflection, and self-assessment"; one needs it in order to determine "which skills or knowledge are missing, [and] how to acquire these" for oneself. For these authors, and for us, cultural competency is nothing less than an ethical principle, one that refers to "requisite knowledge, skills, and values for effective performance" in a diverse and global society (232). While it cannot be taught as such, it does entail an open-ended process of learning.

REFERENCES

Ah Nee-Benham, Maenette K.P., and Henrietta Mann. 2003. Culture and language matters: Defining, implementing, and evaluating. In *Renaissance of American Indian Higher Education*, ed. Maenette K.P., Ah Nee-Benham, and Wayne J. Stein, 167–191. Mahwah, NJ: Lawrence Erlbaum.

Anderson, Gregory, Eleanor J.B. Daugherty, and Darlene M. Corrigan. 2005. The search for a critical mass of minority students: Affirmative action and diversity at highly selective universities and colleges. *Good Society* 14(3): 51–57.

Anderson, Margaret L., and Patricia Hill Collins. 2004. *Race, Class, and Gender*. 5th ed. Boston: Thomson/Wadsworth.

Antonio, Anthony Lising, Mitchell J. Chang, Kenji Hakuta, David A. Kenny, Shana Levin, and Jeffrey F. Milems. 2004. Effects of racial diversity on complex thinking in college students. *Psychological Science* 15(8): 507–510.

Appiah, Kwame Anthony. 2004. *The Ethics of Identity*. Princeton, NJ: Princeton University Press.

Aspinall, Peter J., and Lavinia Mitton. 2008. Kinds of people and equality monitoring in the UK. *Policy and Politics* 36(1): 55–74.

Avery, Derek R., and David S. Steingard. 2008. Achieving political trans-correctness: Integrating sensitivity and authenticity in diversity management education. *Journal of Management Education* 32(3): 269–293.

Barden, Jack. 2003. Tribal colleges and universities building community: Education, social, cultural, and economic development. In *Renaissance of American Indian Higher Education*, ed. Maenette K.P., Ah Nee-Benham, and Wayne J. Stein, 99–119. Mahwah, NJ: Lawrence Erlbaum.

Beichner, Robert J. 2006. Instructional technology research and development in a U.S. physics education group. *European Journal of Engineering Education* 31(4): 383–393.

Blum, Lawrence. 1998. Can we talk? Interracial dialogue in the classroom. *Change* 30(6): 26–37.

Brookfield, Stephen D., and Stephen Preskill. 2005. *Discussion as a Way of Teaching: Tools and Techniques for Democratic Classrooms*. 2nd ed. San Francisco: Jossey-Bass.

Deyhle, Donna, and Karen Swisher. 1997. Research in American Indian and Alaska Native education: From assimilation to self-determination. *Review of Research in Education* 22: 113–194.

Dodge and Walters. 2004. "Preventing Drilling in the Arctic Wildlife Refuge: The Gwich'in Tribes and Their Role in the National Policy Debate: Rebirth of a Nation." Electronic Hallway. Daniel J. Evans School of Public Affairs, University of Washington. http://hallway.evans.washington.edu.

Falender, Carol A., and Edward P. Shafranske. 2007. Competence in competency-based supervision practice: Construct and application. *Professional Psychology: Research and Practice* 38(3): 232–240.

Gardiner, Michael. 1996. Alterity and ethics: A dialogical perspective. *Theory, Culture and Society* 13(2): 121–144.

Habermas, Jürgen. 1992. *Justification and Application: Remarks on Discourse Ethics*, trans. Ciaran Cronin. Cambridge, MA: MIT Press.

Havighurst, Robert J. 1957. Education among American Indians: Individual and cultural aspects. *Annals of the American Academy* 311: 105–115.

Hill, Lance. 2004. Working paper: Interdisciplinary cross-cultural communication project. May 24. Southern Institute for Education and Research, Tulane University, New Orleans, LA. www.southerninstitute.info/discuss/wp-content/uploads/2007/07/working-paper-web-version-7-25-2007.doc.

Jackson, Liz. 2008. Dialogic pedagogy for social justice: A critical examination. *Studies in Philosophy and Education* 27(2–3): 137–148.

Keiner, Louis E., and Teresa E. Burns. 2010. Interactive engagement: How much is enough? *Physics Teacher* 48(2): 108–111.

Kyrillidou, Martha, Charles Lowry, Paul Hanges, Juliet Aiken, and Kristina Justh. 2009. *ClimateQUAL™: Organizational Climate and Diversity Assessment*. www.libqual.org/documents/admin/ACRL_Paper_FINAL_20091.doc.

Larson, Lars L., and John R. Schermerhorn Jr. 1989. Alternative instructor roles in cross-cultural business and management training. *Journal of Teaching in International Business* 1(1): 7–21.

Leistyna, Pepi, and Debra Mollen. 2008. Teaching social class through alternative media and by dialoging across disciplines and boundaries. *Radical Teacher* 81(1): 20–27.

Lomawaima, K. Tsianina, and Teresa L. McCarty. 2002. When tribal sovereignty challenges democracy: American Indian education and the democratic ideal. *American Educational Research Journal* 39(2): 279–305.

McCall, Leslie. 2005. The complexity of intersectionality. *Signs* 30(3): 1771–1800.

Milovanic, Dragan. 1995. Dueling paradigms: Modernist v. postmodernist thought. *Humanity and Society* 19(1): 1–22.

Nash, Robert J. 2010. What is the best way to be a social justice advocate: Communication strategies for effective social justice advocacy. *About Campus* 15(2): 11–19.

Ortiz, Larry, and Jayshree Jani. 2010. Critical race theory: A transformational model for teaching diversity. *Journal of Social Work Education* 46(2): 175–193.

Parekh, Bhikhu. 2000. *The Future of Multi-Ethnic Britain.* London: Profile Books. www.runnymede-trust.org/projects/meb/report.html.

Pettit, Philip. 1989. Consequentialism and respect for persons. *Ethics* 100(1): 116–126.

Potter, Patricia A. 2009. *Fundamentals of Nursing.* 7th ed. St. Louis, MO: Mosby.

Rice, Mitchell F. 2006. Promoting cultural competency in public administration and public service delivery: Utilizing self-assessment tools and performance measures. Annual Conference of the National Association of Schools of Public Affairs and Administration, Minneapolis, MN.

Rivera, Mario, Richard Greggory Johnson III, and James D. Ward. 2010. The ethics of pedagogical innovation in diversity and cultural competency education. *Innovation Journal* 15(2).

Rockquemore, Kerry Ann, and David L. Brunsma. 2002. Socially embedded identities: Theories, typologies, and processes of racial identity among black/white biracials. *Sociological Quarterly* 43(3): 335–356.

Stasiulis, Daiva. 1999. Theorizing connections: Gender, race, ethnicity, and class. In *Race and Ethnic Relations in Canada*, ed. Peter S. Li, 269–305. Toronto: Oxford University Press.

Tilford Group. 2001. *Multicultural Competency Development: Preparing Students to Live and Work in a Diverse World.* Manhattan: Kansas State University. www.tilford.ksu.edu/p.aspx?tabid=32.

Tuckman, Bruce W. 1966. Interpersonal probing and revealing and systems of integrative complexity. *Journal of Personality and Social Psychology* 3(6): 655–664.

Turner, Caroline Sotello Viernes. 2002. Women of color in academe: Living with multiple marginality. *Journal of Higher Education* 73(1): 74–93.

University of New Mexico. 2009. *UNM Fact Book 2008–2009.* Albuquerque: University of New Mexico, Office of Institutional Research. www.unm.edu/~oir/factbook/2008fb.pdf.

University of Vermont, Office of Institutional Research. 2010. Full-time faculty and staff headcount by race/ethnicity: 2008. Faculty Headcount and FTE Reports.

Weinert, Franz Emanuel. 2001. Concept of competence: A conceptual clarification. In *Defining and Selecting Key Competencies*, ed. Dominique Simone Rychen and Laura Hersh Salganik, 45–65. Seattle, WA: Hogrefe & Huber.

Educating for and Assessing Cultural Competence

JAMES FRANCISCO BONILLA
LEAH ANN LINDEMAN
AND NAOMI RAE TAYLOR

This chapter describes the development, implementation, and assessment of a model graduate course called Cultural Competence & Managerial Leadership offered through Hamline University's School of Business in the spring of 2010.[1] The literature on cultural competence makes clear that cultural competency training is necessary for the success of any type of organization. In the private sector, training in cultural competence (usually called "diversity training") focuses on how to work effectively with diverse coworkers and is seen as a necessity to improve the bottom line because a skilled and collaborative work team contributes to a better product. Cultural competency has long been seen as imperative for professionals in social service and health-care since having a better understanding of the clients who are being served can improve the services that are offered.

In designing the course, we began from the premise that skills in cultural competence would enhance leadership capacities of those working in the public administration and nonprofit fields. We began our course design process by asking these questions: Is cultural competency measurable? If so, which approaches to cultural competence do we choose and how do we assess the results?

A review of the literature demonstrated that there is not enough research to answer these questions definitively, nor enough research to guide teachers, trainers, and organizations on what is most effective. As one author states, "cultural competency poses difficult measurement challenges in part because its meaning is so broad" (Geron 2002, 41). Because there is no one common definition or universal standard to describe cultural competency, we found numerous assessment tools, each pegged to a particular definition of cultural competency. A variety of programs, curricula, and training models are available.

Scholars do agree that "prejudice reduction" is key (Paluck 2006, 579). Geron (2002, 39) suggests that prejudice reduction (or "an opportunity to correct the incomplete and often inaccurate presentation of people of color and other historically underserved and undervalued populations") is important when improving cultural competency of employees or simply offering diversity training. However, most training programs are based on the goal of overcoming ignorance, expressing one's hidden assumptions, or feeling empathy for an oppressed group or individual (Paluck 2006). Few are based on actual theories about best practices or demonstrable outcomes (Nagda, Tropp, and Paluck 2006, 441).

To address the dual dilemmas of varying definitions and assessment instruments, we chose to incorporate into our course five distinct approaches to defining cultural competence based on our review of the literature. We then selected five assessment instruments that corresponded to the five different approaches. The five approaches to cultural competency that framed the course were (1) the umbrella model of oppression (Adams, Bell, and Griffin 2007; Haro 1997, 81), (2) the cultural studies approach (LeBaron 2003; Ting-Toomey 2000), (3) the social identity development approach (Jackson and Hardiman 2007; Wijeyesinghe and Jackson 2001), (4) the managing diversity approach (Thomas 2008; Williams 2001), and (5) the multicultural organizational development approach (Chesler 1996; Holvino, Ferdman, and Merrill-Sands 2004; Jackson and Holvino 1998). The five corresponding instruments used to assess student learning were (1) the social group membership profile, (2) the intercultural development inventory, (3) the social identity development stage diagnostic, (4) the Williams ten lenses survey, and (5) the multicultural organizational development stage diagnostic. What follows is an explanation of course goals and related learning outcomes, brief descriptions of the five frames, showing how each approach defines cultural competence in a somewhat different and distinct manner, and a brief description of the five associated assessment instruments. We conclude with implications for educating students in, and assessing, cultural competence.

COURSE GOALS

The course was designed to provide learners with an opportunity to examine issues of cultural competence and conflict in managing and leading organizations in changing times. The course engaged students in a series of reflective dialogues exploring cultural competence on the interpersonal, cultural, and institutional levels and their impact on management, work, and the organization. Emphasis was on workplace issues of race, ethnicity, and gender and included discussions of issues of sexual orientation, disability, and social class.

In designing the course, our goals were that students would be able to

1. Compare and critique multiple theoretical understandings and perspectives on social identity, cultural competence, and managerial leadership
2. Assess how issues of cultural competence manifest in their own lives as well as professionally in their the professor is a co-learner and "our" creates an environment of all of us as learning, not just students—critical to building a safe classroom climate roles as managers and leaders in organizations
3. Apply a range of strategies and resources to help them develop their cultural competencies more fully so as to contribute to professional and organizational change

Ten associated learning outcomes (Pope, Reynolds, and Mueller 2004) that were spelled out in our syllabus were that students would be able to

1. Define the dynamics of oppression
2. Explain how race, culture, and other social identities may affect a wide range of behaviors, attitudes, feelings, and interventions
3. Demonstrate content knowledge about various cultural groups
4. Articulate their own values, attitudes, and assumptions
5. Explain the dynamics of and relationship of self to others
6. Articulate their own biases
7. Analyze how their own culture and heritage influence their worldview
8. Demonstrate improved proficiencies in cross-cultural communication
9. Reflect on and demonstrate an ability to recover from cultural errors
10. Demonstrate increased tolerance for ambiguity in managing and addressing cultural conflict

As we will discuss toward the end of this chapter, our analysis unearthed an eleventh important outcome regarding organizational cultural competence.

THE FIVE MODELS

Why opt for five models? Our purpose in utilizing these five approaches and their related assessment instruments was grounded in our observation that cultural conflicts are often, if not always, multidimensional. They often involve a range of social identities and can manifest either individually, interpersonally, culturally, or at the organizational or institutional level. The decision to utilize five approaches rested in our belief that graduate students would be better able to see and appreciate the complexity of cultural conflicts through multiple lenses. To paraphrase an old organizational theory adage, "The only thing better than a good theory is a lot of good theories." By exploring multiple perspectives on cultural competence, students can be empowered to choose from a host of approaches to seeing, understanding, and eventually tackling cultural conflicts. This multi-lens approach to management studies is not new; it can be seen in the work of Gareth Morgan in his groundbreaking textbook, *Images of Organizations* (2006). Building from our literature review, we adapted Morgan's approach to reflect different perspectives for understanding cultural competency in the workplace. These approaches are summarized in Table 17.1.

Approach Number One: Umbrella Model of Oppression

The umbrella model of oppression (Adams, Bell, and Griffin 2007; Haro 1997) takes a sociological look at multiple social identities (race, class, gender, religion, age, ability, and sexual orientation) and explores their similarities, differences, and intersections. The umbrella model offers an analysis of power and privilege as well as a framework for understanding how various cultural differences can become socialized into categories of agent (dominant) and target of oppression. This approach focuses less on cultural differences and more on how differences become framed as

Table 17.1

Five Approaches to Cultural Competence

	Approach or model	Description or definition	Sample corresponding assessment instrument
1	The umbrella model (Adams, Bell, and Griffin 2007; Haro 1997)	Takes a sociological and social justice look at multiple social identities (race, class, gender religion, age, ability, and sexual orientation) and explores their similarities and differences. Focus is on examining how differences become framed as deficits and result in systemic forms of oppression. Goal is to interrupt oppression.	Social group membership profile (Adams, Bell, and Griffin 2007 and Haro, 1997)
2	The cultural studies approach (LeBaron 2003; Ting-Toomey 2000)	Looks at cultural competence primarily within the international, immigrant, and/or ethnic arena. Focus is on cultural differences and behavior with less explicit focus on oppression and social justice. Goal is increased cultural understanding and conflict mitigation.	Intercultural development inventory (Hammer 2008)
3	The social identity development approach (Jackson and Hardiman 2007 Wijeyesinghe and Jackson 2001)	Examines cultural competence as an individual, psychological development phenomenon. Posits a multistage process that results in the development of a specific social identity (race, gender, and other categories) either as target or as agent of oppression. Goal is interruption of oppression through individual development.	Social identity development diagnostic (Jackson and Hardiman 2007)
4	The managing diversity approach (Thomas 2008; Miller and Katz 2002; Williams 2001)	Takes a business perspective on cultural competence. Sees cultural competence as a process of increasing understanding of ourselves and others with the goal of helping employees to work more effectively in cross-cultural teams or workplace settings.	Williams ten lenses survey (Williams 2001)
5	The multicultural organizational development approach (Chesler 1996; Holvino 2004; Holvino, Ferdman, and Merrill-Sands 2004; Jackson and Holvino 1998)	Examines cultural competence as an organizational phenomenon rather than individual or group behavior with the goal of fostering structures, policies, and procedures that are socially just and equitable. Focus is on helping organizations move through a process of developmental stages from monocultural to multicultural.	The MCOD stage diagnostic (Jackson and Hardiman 2007)

deficits. The model explains how differences are systemically incorporated into a web (or umbrella) of oppression that privileges agents and disempowers targets on the interpersonal, cultural, and institutional levels.

Cultural competency within the umbrella model is defined as an ability to identify multiple social identities, recognize how they are intertwined and their unique forms of socialization, and acknowledge the interconnected nature of oppression. The model frames cultural competency as a continuum running between the endpoints of contributing to liberation or colluding with the many interconnected forms of oppression.

The related assessment instrument consists of a social group membership profile (Adams, Bell, and Griffin 2007) that allows individuals to analyze their multiple social identities and how they are socialized into either the agent and/or target role. It asks individuals to identify what groups they are associated with in a number of social identity categories (gender, race, ethnicity, etc.). Once all social identities are specified, there is a list of statements the individual connects to particular identities that provide further exploration into how various identities contribute to one's socialization and how they fit into categories of agent (dominant) and target of oppression.

Approach Number Two: Cultural Studies Model

The cultural studies approach (LeBaron 2003; Ting-Toomey 2000) looks at cultural competency primarily in an international or immigrant ethnic context. It focuses on cultural differences and behaviors. It also provides opportunities for individuals to develop greater cultural competence in relating to cultural identities outside their own. This model does not include an explicit interrogation of systems of power and privilege and defines cultural competence primarily as ethnically based while sometimes ignoring or playing down issues of power and privilege.

Cultural competency within the cultural studies approach is defined as the capability to shift cultural perspective and adapt behavior to cultural commonality and difference. This capability is demonstrated particularly through how people communicate, show respect, and work through conflict (Hammer 2008, 246; LeBaron 2003).

The intercultural development inventory (IDI) is one related assessment instrument. It measures an individual's (or group's) fundamental worldview orientation to cultural difference and thus the individual's or group's capacity for intercultural competence. The developers of the IDI believe it is a statistically reliable, cross-culturally valid measure of intercultural competence adapted from the developmental model of intercultural sensitivity. It consists of a fifty-question Likert scale along with contextualizing questions that capture personal examples in organizational or educational settings.

The IDI places individuals and groups in one of five orientations. These orientations are placed on a spectrum from denial to defense/reversal, minimization, acceptance, and adaptation. Defense/reversal are ethnocentric worldviews. The orientations that identify intercultural competency are acceptance and adaptation.

The developers of the IDI believe its strengths are that it is statistically reliable, cross-culturally validated, and provides quick generation of the results (Hammer 2008). In our course the IDI provided baseline data and a starting point for dialogue about differences in race and culture. The limitations of the IDI are that it focuses primarily on race and ethnic cultural differences and lacks an explicit interrogation of power and privilege. Categorical differences such as gender, sexual orientation, religion, and age are not as explicit. In order to administer the IDI, an individual must become trained and qualified. Through an optional one-on-one coaching session, an experienced, qualified administrator helped our students interpret their IDI scores and offered them individual strategies for improvement.

Approach Number Three: Social Identity Development Approach

The social identity development model (Jackson and Hardiman 2007; Wijeyesinghe and Jackson 2001) at first glance appears similar to the umbrella model, but is less a sociological approach than a psychological examination of individual cultural and social identity development. It provides a continuum of seven stages of social identity development applicable to individual cultural identities (race, gender, class, etc.). It also requires individuals to self-diagnose as either targets or agents of oppression and then identifies their own stage of identity development along an oppression-liberation continuum.

The social identity development model (SIDM) defines cultural competency as an individual's movement through the continuum of seven developmental stages that are behaviors that contribute to a specific social identity as either a target (the oppressed) or as an agent (the oppressor). It is particularly concerned with moving both targets and agents along a developmental continuum from more oppressive to more liberated. The final stages of development focus on an individual creating an identity independent of an oppressive and hierarchical system and incorporating that identity into everyday life.

The SIDM diagnostic assesses an individual's perspectives, beliefs, awareness of privilege, and consciousness of a specific identity (race, gender, sexual orientation, etc.). However, people do not necessarily move developmentally along from one stage to the next and may have different identities that are simultaneously at different stages.

One way we utilized this diagnostic tool in class was as a self-assessment. Participants picked a specific social identity, defined the identity in terms of either an agent or target of oppression, and then worked through each of the seven stages. They outlined any characteristics they once had or currently associated with each stage until they could specify their own stage of identity development. This tool was also used in conjunction with in-class case studies as well as a personal case study in which students analyzed case study characters and diagnosed what development stage they were in and how that affected the case. The general purpose of the diagnostic is to develop an understanding of different individual perspectives in order to work more effectively with coworkers at different stages.

Approach Number Four: The Managing Diversity Approach

The Managing Diversity Approach (Miller and Katz 2002; Thomas 2001; Williams 2001) is commonly found in business and management literature and is exemplified by Williams's ten lenses model (2001). Williams's model provides a framework of ten lenses or American views on race, ethnicity, and cultural differences. The Williams framework defines cultural competency as a process of increasing our understanding of ourselves and others with the belief that this understanding will help us work more effectively in cross-cultural environments and manage multicultural organizations.

This model is distinctive because of the nonjudgmental and nondevelopmental approach it takes to asking individuals to self-diagnose and review how best to manage different cultural perspectives in an organizational context. This model measures only what individuals think about themselves. Furthermore, it does not provide a development roadmap for individual growth as it identifies no continuum of cultural competence. While there is no explicit analysis of power or privilege, the model does provide opportunities for individuals to assess the strengths and shadows of their particular lens in the workplace.

The Williams ten lenses survey is the associated assessment instrument. It is a series of statements associated with ten different lenses. Individuals are asked to pick the statements that most identify with their beliefs and then add up the number of statements associated with each lens. The more beliefs that managers associate with a particular lens, the more inclined they are to work from that perspective. Williams provides an analysis of each lens's strengths and weakness, how individuals coming from each perspective can be useful or harmful to an organization, and strategies for working with each lens. Williams identifies each of the ten lenses as part of the diversity within organizations.

Approach Number Five: Multicultural Organizational Development Approach

The multicultural organizational development (MCOD) approach (Chesler 1996; Holvino, Ferdman, and Merrill-Sands 2004; Jackson and Holvino 1998) presents an organizational perspective on cultural competency. The MCOD model defines cultural competence as organizational rather than individual behaviors with the intent of fostering culturally competent systems, policies, and procedures. Rather than focus on individual managerial stages, it examines the broader context of how organizations set the stage (or organizational culture) within which issues of cultural competence play out. It provides users with a diagnostic roadmap that encourages a systematic analysis of power and privilege in organizations. It identifies a continuum of organizational behaviors from monocultural to multicultural, including three broad levels and six distinct stages.

The MCOD diagnostic is an organizational tool, separating it from the individual diagnostics used in the course. This diagnostic is intended to assess an organization's policies, practices, workforce demographics, norms, and culture to diagnose a stage of multicultural awareness or cultural competence.

CLASSROOM PEDAGOGY AND DATA GATHERING

The course pedagogy included analysis of readings, large- and small-group discussion, the use of case studies, course lecture, and written papers and reflections. Because the course was designed, in part, to provide substantive data about how (or whether it is possible) to assess improvements in students' cultural competency, a variety of formative and summative data was gathered during a three-stage assessment process (preclass, midpoint, and at the end of the semester).

Based on our years of teaching experience, we knew that cocreating a positive classroom climate needed to be ongoing and that including students in the process would contribute significantly to student learning (Adams, Bell, and Griffin 2007). A process technique employed for this course learned from twenty years of teaching and training on diversity issues was a preclass needs assessment that queried participants about their goals, expectations, concerns, and needs prior to the first class meeting. This information can be extremely helpful in anticipating special circumstances that might otherwise blindside a teacher or trainer. For instance, one student disclosed that she was in the midst of a legal battle involving diversity and felt especially vulnerable. Another confided that she was unsure if she would share her sexual orientation with the class (eventually she did). Two students disclosed hidden disabilities. This type of information can prove useful in anticipating and/or facilitating difficult moments in all types of classrooms as well as tailoring the teaching approach to address these and other emerging needs and concerns. An anonymous summary of the pre- and mid-course assessment data can be shared with the class to help establish a climate of transparency as well as build trust in the classroom community.

At the outset we endeavored to create a safe atmosphere in which students could explore their dilemmas with cultural competence without feeling they would be judged or gossiped about outside of class. Following the recommendations of Adams, Bell, and Griffin (2007) and Cannon (1990), on the first night the class collectively developed discussion guidelines, including items such as maintaining confidentiality, sharing air time, listening respectfully, and refraining from put-downs).

The course design incorporated both formative and summative assessment of student learning and, most importantly, used both quantitative and qualitative measures to answer our original questions about the feasibility of educating for cultural competence and which approaches and assessment measures are most effective. For instance, qualitative data were gathered through a student-participant observer who took weekly field notes and met with the instructor after each week's class to debrief the session. This participant observer input was particularly important since she, as a white, female, Generation X graduate student, provided a comparison perspective to that of the male, Puerto Rican, boomer-generation instructor.

Quantitative data were gathered in the form of the IDI, which was administered by an external assessment specialist. Twice the instructor used formative assessment questionnaires to ascertain how the course was unfolding and whether it was meeting the goals as expressed in the initial needs assessment (Brookfield 1995). In the final summative assessment, the data collected at the end of the semester (anonymous course evaluations and student learning outcomes papers) were incorporated into our data analysis to ascertain which approaches, cultural competency assessment instruments, and classroom activities significantly contributed to student learning outcomes.

Triangulation was another means utilized to factor in validity and generalizability so as to further ensure reliability in our observations and conclusions. By utilizing observer field notes, student final learning outcomes papers, and a variety of qualitative and quantitative assessment instruments, and comparing those to the literature in the field of teaching for cultural competence, we made a serious effort to achieve triangulation. The point here is that it was not possible to be "objective" researchers. Our goal was to remember that

> we see others as we know ourselves. . . . If the understanding of the self is limited and unyielding to change, the understanding of the other is as well. . . . The great danger to doing injustice to the quality of the "other" does not come about through the use of the self, but rather through lack of the use of a full enough sense of self, which . . . produces a stifled, artificial, limited and unreal knowledge of others. (Krieger 1985, 320)

The limited understanding of the self has profound implications not simply for the methodology of this study or a single course, but more broadly for the process of teaching for and assessing cultural competence. It is a point that we will return to shortly.

FINDINGS AND IMPLICATIONS

As we reviewed the results of our study with our participant observer, our external IDI administrator, student self-assessments and case studies, and anonymous course evaluations, several themes emerged as offering potentially significant implications to those interested in how to educate for and assess cultural competence. The five most consistently encountered themes from the findings were the following.

THEME NUMBER ONE: UTILIZE A MULTIPERSPECTIVE APPROACH

A multiperspective approach to educating for and assessing cultural competence has strong educational advantages that benefited student-learning outcomes. The class was organized so as to privilege no one approach to cultural competence. Rather, students were presented with five different lenses or approaches that each defined cultural competence somewhat differently. Our hypothesis was that a broader approach to the topic would lead to deeper and more complex understanding of conflicts involving cultural difference and therefore greater cultural competence. The data support that hypothesis. In the anonymous end-of-course evaluations, in response to the statement "The Five Model Approach contributed to my grasp of cultural competency," 73 percent strongly agreed and 27 percent agreed with the statement. In short, all the students involved in the course found that a multiperspective approach to the material increased their cultural competence. Further, having applied a minimum of three of those five lenses to their own real-world cultural conflict case studies, 100 percent of participants stated that the case study as a teaching strategy helped them apply the course concepts to the real world.

We did observe that although not all the models were equally embraced by all students, every participant expressed a level of comfort with at least two of the models. This finding has broad implications in that it suggests that one strategy for lowering student resistance to the study of cultural difference may be to provide them with some options about how they can choose to see, understand, and respond to cultural conflict. Some participants were willing to embrace the models that tackle issues of oppression, privilege, and injustice directly (the umbrella, SIDM, and MCOD models). Other students who were not as comfortable with these models were able to remain engaged by having early access to models that were less confrontational (the cultural studies and managing diversity approaches, but still allowed them to engage with the topic and work toward achieving some of the stated learning outcomes.

THEME NUMBER TWO: START WITH THE SELF

Effective education for and assessment of cultural competence begins with the self. As suggested earlier in our discussion of research methodology, there can be no effective understanding of the "other" without a full understanding of the self (Krieger 1985). Our data stressed that our students felt they needed to first understand themselves, their cultural identities, and their organizational cultures. Only then did they feel they could be in a stronger position to be aware of and understand others' differences. Only then could they be leaders and organizational change agents in their roles as managers. This finding has profound implications for teaching and assessing cultural competence. It poses a fundamental question and perhaps challenges the primacy of content knowledge as the essential component of effective education for cultural competence. While 100 percent of the participants reported that their content knowledge about different cultural groups had improved, far more key among the reported outcomes were those that focused on understanding their own biases and the dynamics of oppression. Our findings support the premise that critical to the acquisition of cultural competence is the understanding of the self and one's own cultural biases *before* one can effectively understand the other.

THEME NUMBER THREE: CREATE THE RIGHT CLIMATE

Some approaches to teaching and training in the area of cultural competence primarily focus on content, with little attention to the process of learning. Our data (as gleaned from the end-of-semester learning outcomes papers, course evaluations, and participant observations) suggest that attention to the learning process (the "how" of the class) is as important as attention to the learning of specific content about particular groups (the "what" of cultural competence).

Creating an affirming classroom climate is critical to the process of learning cultural competency. This finding is supported by other research that demonstrates the necessity of creating a safe space for students to work through what can be difficult and risky learning (Adams, Bell, and Griffin 2007; Cannon 1990; Goodman 2010). Goodman offers: "In order to create spaces that are respectful, supportive, and allow students to take emotional risks, faculty can establish guidelines, conduct warm-up activities, and encourage gradual amounts of personal sharing" (2010, 11). Key elements that were used to establish a safe space included the establishment of guidelines at the beginning of the semester, tactics that allowed students to gradually share and open up during the course of the semester, and regular debriefs and check-ins during class. Of the fifteen students who completed the course evaluation, 100 percent either "strongly agreed" or "agreed" that "the classroom climate contributed to my learning about the topic."

The participant observation journal noted that the review of the classroom guidelines occurred in the first two weeks of class. It was also observed that starting in the third week, students began opening up and it became rare that somebody did not participate. In addition, students with hidden, target identities (sexual orientation and disabilities) grew comfortable enough to open up to the class and share their experiences, particularly after guest speakers who shared the same identity came to the class.

The guidelines were also important in helping participants accept their privileged identities. As Goodman notes: "While self exploration can be difficult, exploring a privileged identity can be particularly hard for many people. Educators [and trainers] are likely to encounter resistance when asking students to undertake this kind of examination" (2010, 10). At the beginning of the semester there were white students in our course who openly admitted they did not know how to identify their own culture. "This may be because people who are part of privileged groups seldom have to think about their privileged identities," observes Goodman (2010, 10).

Beyond the classroom guidelines, we also focused on the systemic nature of oppression to help students feel more comfortable exploring their attitudes, prejudices, and stereotypes while avoiding the suggestion of individual blame. One example of a group activity we used to demonstrate the power of dominant ideology was having the class break up into racial and gender caucuses (with a large number of females, we broke down the female caucus into a white female caucus and women of color caucus). In the gender exercise, each group made a list of the "ten commandments" for appropriate behavior they heard growing up and linked those to organizational behavior (Adams, Bell, and Griffin 2007). Students found their experiences to be very similar within their gender group. We found this type of activity in line with Goodman's findings: "The approach reduces defensiveness and resistance. Although each person plays a role in systems of inequality, all systems are larger than any one individual" (2010, 12).

Regular debriefings (Brookfield 1995) and completion of a preclass needs assessment by students (Adams, Bell, and Griffin 2007) also contributed to building and maintaining a positive classroom climate. The preassessment in particular can provide valuable information on students' expectations and in some cases personal experiences that can allow instructors to appropriately guide the discussion and minimize any potentially unproductive challenges.

THEME NUMBER FOUR: IMPROVEMENT IN CULTURAL COMPETENCY IS POSSIBLE

A multiperspective approach, development of an understanding of self, and a positive classroom climate led to an improvement in students' overall cultural competence. At the end of the semester, 93 percent of the students reported an improvement in cultural competency as a result of this course. Furthermore, the IDI, completed at the beginning and the end of the course, demonstrated a quantifiable increase in the group's overall development. Given the few quantitative assessment measures currently in use, this 8 percent increase in developmental points makes this overall design all the more promising for those seeking demonstrably successful approaches to improving learning outcomes in cultural competence.

The IDI profile presented information about how this group made sense of and responded to cultural differences and commonalities. The IDI provided a point scale that measured the group's perceived and actual orientations. The perceived orientation score measured how far the group thought it was along the intercultural continuum whereas the actual orientation score measured where the group actually was on the continuum.

When we compared the scores between the pre-IDI and post-IDI assessment, we saw considerable change. In ten weeks this group gained 10.75, developmental points, on a scale of 145 total, toward intercultural competency. On the spectrum, the group started in the orientation of "minimization" and ended at the "cusp of adaptation" toward intercultural competency. Their "orientation gap" shrank 5.21 points, which means that this group recognized that they have made progress toward intercultural competency, but still had some work to do in order to become fully interculturally competent.

At the beginning of the semester, during an overview about the IDI and the group profile, culture was highlighted. Many individuals, especially those of white European ancestry, struggled with identifying their culture. Culture was often viewed as something "other people" had, with "other people" meaning persons of color. After this group profile presentation, every student had an individual coaching session with the external administrator. The individual coaching sessions provided a powerful opportunity for participants to unpack and make sense of their developmental orientation. The most common recommendation provided to individuals was for them to learn more about their own culture. Even something as basic as creating a family tree to learn more about one's family heritage is a step toward becoming interculturally competent.

The culture we work with every day is typically the tip of the cultural iceberg, the part of the iceberg or culture we can see. True interaction across differences gets at the other 90 percent that is under the surface, the part of the iceberg that sank the *Titanic*—communication styles, assumptions, attitudes toward difference, and conflict styles. The IDI served as a tool that allowed students to learn more about themselves and was a significant factor that contributed to the group's development of intercultural competency.

THEME NUMBER FIVE: THERE IS NO ONE "RIGHT" MEASURE

We began this study by asking the question "Is cultural competence measurable?" Our data indicates that the answer is a qualified yes—qualified because we found in our review of the literature as well as in our study results that there is no one way to measure cultural competence. Student learning outcome papers, course evaluations, case studies, and results of five different assessment instruments reinforced the finding that there exist several effective approaches to cultural competence. Each of these lenses or approaches to cultural competence offers its own assessment instruments and each measures cultural competence somewhat differently. Some emphasize ethnicity and race, others explore multiple social identities, and yet others examine cultural competence from an organizational perspective.

In our findings (specifically, the precourse needs assessment), we found that not all students began their journey toward cultural competence from the same starting point (Adams, Bell, and Griffin 2007; LeBaron 2003; Wijeyesinghe and Jackson 2001; Williams 2001). Therefore, to apply only one approach and assessment instrument risks not meeting students where they are on their own developmental journey. Indeed, one approach (the Williams model) avoids an explicitly developmental approach to cultural competence. While we were initially dubious (both the instructor and the student participant-observer were more oriented toward the developmental and social justice approaches), we have come to appreciate approaches that allow some students to venture into the topic from a starting place of nonjudgment and greater safety. While we did ask students to identify which models helped them see their case study conflicts in the newest light, we recommend avoiding an atmosphere that forces students to take sides and defend their favorite approach or lens. Instead, we encourage students to see that the various approaches all have value in and of themselves. It is important that students explicitly explore the strengths and weaknesses of each of the five models, and how each can assist them to "see and not see" cultural conflicts from varying perspectives. Articulating the various strengths and limitations of each lens is also an important exercise in building critical thinking skills.

Not only is the measurement of cultural competence dependent on which approach the educator or trainer employs, it is also highly dependent on the individual student's social identities and social and organizational context. Students with less exposure to certain types of cultural difference (personally and/or professionally) may feel disadvantaged by a design that emphasizes only those perspectives that advantage students with greater experience or exposure. By incorporating a wide range of approaches that underscore different aspects of cultural competence (race, gender, sexual orientation, disability, age, social class), all students can be empowered to uncover or explore at least one new aspect of their own multiple cultural identities. Using several approaches not only increases the participants' buy-in, but also simultaneously broadens their definition of cultural competence beyond the traditional "black-white" or simple ethnicity paradigms. It serves to underscore the reality that we all have multiple cultures and that we all should seek to uncover what those cultures are and how they may or may not privilege some and disadvantage others (Goodman 2010) in and outside the organizational context.

One final lesson from our analysis of this class experience came as somewhat of a surprise. As a result of incorporating the MCOD approach, an unanticipated eleventh outcome emerged from the student learning outcomes data, namely "the ability to analyze an organization's level of cultural competence." We strongly recommend that this be added to any list of student learning outcomes.

CONCLUSIONS

Our study corroborates the work of Adams, Bell, and Griffin (2007), Jackson and Hardiman (2007), Jackson and Holvino (1998), LeBaron (2003), Wijeyesinghe and

Jackson (2001), and Williams (2001), which suggests that cultural competency is a journey, not a destination. It is a process that is highly dependent on the individual, the cultural identities being explored, and the social and organizational context within which the exploration takes place.

We began our study by asking whether cultural competence is measurable. Our study suggests that the answer is a qualified yes. We found that there is no one way to measure cultural competence. Our review of the literature revealed at least five distinct approaches, definitions, and related ways of assessing cultural competence. Our experience indicates that an effective design for educating for and assessing cultural competence needs to incorporate a range of perspectives, models, and assessment instruments that can meet students where they are on that journey. Employing only one approach risks participant withdrawal, defensiveness, nonengagement, and other forms of resistance.

Our data lead us to conclude that the learning process (the "how" of cultural competence) can be as important as the learning of content about specific groups (the "what" of cultural competence). We must develop a complex understanding of our multiple social identities and our own cultural biases before we can effectively understand the "other."

Our study argues against the single workshop or "Diversity Day" approach to cultural competence. Even after a twelve-week course with numerous indicators of increased competence, our participants left with an understanding that for them, acquiring deeper levels of cultural competence had just begun. The broader implications of our study are that developing cultural competency must be designed as an ongoing process, both for individual employees and managers and, perhaps more importantly, for the parent organizations whose commitment it will require. This requires that top leadership is committed to conducting regular summative and formative assessments at the individual, team, and organizational levels.

Besides using a variety of approaches, we also recommend qualitative and quantitative assessment instruments to help students to constructively engage the contradiction between what they think they know and what they actually know about cultural competence. Since many of us think we know more than we actually do, this contradiction puts us all on somewhat equal footing and it can give students a safe as well as shared space for learning. By "safe" we recommend the confidential administration of the individual IDI instrument by an external assessor. This offers students an opportunity to collectively explore their scores and the related contradictions without worrying whether the results might affect their grades (or in the case of the workplace, the employees' status, raises, and/or promotions).

There is no question that students of public administration and management must develop skills in cultural competence if they are to be effective leaders for the future. We strongly believe that utilizing a variety of educational approaches and assessment techniques can lead to a robust classroom and/or training experience. More importantly, all participants involved reported that a multiperspective approach to the material increased their cultural competencies. When students learn to analyze and deepen their own cultural competencies, they are then in a better position to assess the levels of cultural competence in their own governmental, nonprofit, or private sector organizations. As managerial leaders they are then empowered to take the appropriate steps to move their institutions forward into our brave new multicultural world.

NOTE

1. The course was designed for graduate students in the departments of public administration and nonprofit management and was seeded by a small grant, which paid for a research assistant, from Hamline University's Committee on Learning Outcomes Assessment.

REFERENCES

Adams, Maurianne, Lee Ann Bell, and Pat Griffin, eds. 2007. *Teaching for Diversity and Social Justice: A Sourcebook*. 2nd ed. New York: Routledge.

Brookfield, Stephen. 1995. *Becoming a Critically Reflective Teacher*. San Francisco: Jossey-Bass.

Cannon, Lynn Weber. 1990. Fostering positive race, class, and gender dynamics in the classroom. *Women's Studies Quarterly* 18(1 & 2): 124–143.

Chesler, Mark. 1996. Strategies for multicultural organizational development. In *The Diversity Factor: Capturing the Competitive Advantage in a Changing Workforce*, ed. Elsie Cross and Michael Blackburn, 34–46. New York: McGraw-Hill.

Geron, Scott Miyake. 2002. Cultural competency: How is it measured? Does it make a difference? *Generations* 26(3): 39–45.

Goodman, Diane J. 2010. Helping students explore their privileged identities. *Diversity and Democracy: Association of American Colleges & Universities* 13(2): 10–12.

Hammer, Mitchell R. 2008. The intercultural development inventory (IDI): An approach for assessing and building intercultural competence. In *Contemporary Leadership and Intercultural Competence: Understanding and Utilizing Cultural Diversity to Build Successful Organizations*, ed. Michael A. Moodian, 219–232. Thousand Oaks, CA: Sage.

Haro, Roberta. 1997. The umbrella model of oppression. In *Teaching for Diversity and Social Justice: A Sourcebook*, ed. Maurianne Adams, Lee Ann Bell, and Pat Griffin, 81. New York: Routledge.

Holvino, Evangelina, Bernardo M. Ferdman, and Deborah Merrill-Sands. 2004. Creating and sustaining diversity and inclusion in organizations: Strategies and approaches. In *The Psychology and Management of Workplace Diversity*, ed. Margaret S. Stockdale and Faye J. Crosby, 245–276. Malden, MA: Blackwell.

Jackson, Bailey, and Rita Hardiman. 2007. Conceptual foundations for social justice courses. In *Teaching for Diversity and Social Justice: A Sourcebook*, 2nd ed., ed. Maurianne Adams, Lee Ann Bell, and Pat Griffin, 35–66. New York: Routledge.

Jackson, Bailey, and Evangelina Holvino. 1998. Developing multicultural organizations. *Journal of Religion and Applied Behavioral Science* 9(2): 21–26.

Krieger, Susan. 1985. Beyond subjectivity: The use of the self in social science. *Qualitative Sociology* 8(4): 309–323.

LeBaron, Michelle. 2003. *Bridging Cultural Conflicts: New Approaches for a Changing World*. San Francisco: Jossey-Bass.

Merriam, Sharon. 1998. *Case Study Research in Education: A Qualitative Approach*. San Francisco: Jossey-Bass.

Miller, Frederick, and Judith Katz. 2002. *The Inclusion Breakthrough: Unleashing the Power of Real Diversity*. San Francisco: Berrett-Koehler.

Morgan, Gareth. 2006. *Images of Organization*. 2nd ed. Thousand Oaks, CA: Sage.

Nagda, Biren (Ratnesh) A., Linda R. Tropp, and Elizabeth Levy Paluck. 2006. Looking back as we look ahead: Integrating research, theory, and practice on intergroup relations. *Journal of Social Issues* 62(3): 439–451.

Paluck, Elizabeth Levy. 2006. Diversity training and intergroup contact: A call to action research. *Journal of Social Issues* 62(3): 577–595.

Pope, Raechele L., Amy L. Reynolds, and John A. Mueller. 2004. *Multicultural Competence in Student Affairs*. San Francisco: Jossey-Bass.

Thomas, David, ed. 2001. *Harvard Business Review on Managing Diversity*. Boston: Harvard Business Review Press.

———. 2008. *Cross-Cultural Management: Essential Concepts*. 2nd ed. Thousand Oaks, CA: Sage.

Ting-Toomey, Sheila. 2000. Intercultural conflict competence. In *Competence in Interpersonal Conflict*, ed. William R. Cupak, and Daniel J. Canary, 121–146. New York: McGraw-Hill.

Wijeyesinghe, Charmaine, and Bailey Jackson. 2001. *New Perspectives on Racial Identity Development: A Theoretical and Practical Anthology*. New York: New York University Press.

Williams, Mark. 2001. *The Ten Lenses: Your Guide to Living and Working in a Multicultural World*. Sterling, VA: Capital Books.

Cultural Competency Across the Master's in Public Administration Curriculum

KRISTEN A. NORMAN-MAJOR

As has been noted by several authors in this volume, gaining cultural competency skills is an ongoing process, not something achieved in a single course or professional development seminar. A key part of increasing cultural competency in public administration and public service is building increased awareness on the part of public servants of the need to consider cultural differences among the public that is served.

While courses specifically focused on cultural competency are important, they are not sufficient to ensure that students of public administration leave programs ready to incorporate cultural competency into their daily practices. Issues involving cultural competency must be incorporated across the public administration curriculum so students see how it relates to all aspects of public administration practice.

This need to incorporate the study of cultural competency into the public administration curriculum has been increasingly recognized by several scholars. For example, Mitchell Rice notes: "When culture is ignored or not considered in the study of public administration or by a public agency, there is a very strong possibility that individuals, families and groups will not get the services or support they need, or, worse yet, they will likely receive services and assistance that is more harmful than helpful" (2007b, 50).

In her work on cultural competency in the practice of public administration, Margo Bailey writes: "In the long term, public administration should consider how its current training methods meet the future demands for culturally competent organizations, managers and professionals. . . . Undergraduate and graduate programs that prepare students for careers in the public sector should consider how they would change their curricula to provide graduates with the skills needed to develop and work within culturally competent agencies" (2010, 185). Finally, Susan White in her examination of a multicultural MPA curriculum states, "because of the role that public administrators have in protecting the public interest, students of public administration should be prepared to advocate for diverse populations" (2004, 114).

Despite this increased awareness of the need to incorporate cultural competency into the public administration curriculum, research shows mixed progress on the part of public administration programs in making cultural competency a central component of student learning (see, e.g., Hewins-Maroney and Williams 2007; Svara and Brunet 2004; White 2004). It is argued here that there are three critical phases to building cultural competency into the public administration curriculum at the master's level. First, program faculty must define goals and learning outcomes related to cultural competency. Second, a general framework for the types of information and learning related to cultural competency needs to be established. Finally, faculty must develop specific learning opportunities for their courses that expose students to key information, theory, and practice around cultural competency.

INCORPORATING CULTURAL COMPETENCY ACROSS THE MPA CURRICULUM: LEARNING OUTCOMES

As a first step in creating a public administration curriculum that makes cultural competency a core component, faculty must agree that helping students gain the knowledge and skills necessary to become culturally competent is a central and overarching goal of the curriculum as a whole and that all faculty are responsible for student learning on this front. As White writes: "In effect, diversity or cultural competency would have to be adopted by the department as a core value to ensure that all faculty members are aware that this is a step that must be made; this will help guarantee that the department's values are permeated throughout the classroom experience" (2004, 121).

This argument is particularly critical for schools under National Association of Schools of Public Affairs and Administration (NASPAA) accreditation since the NASPAA (2009) accreditation standards call for students in master's-level public administration programs to be able "to communicate and interact productively with a diverse and changing workforce and citizenry." Schools going through accreditation must be able to show how they meet this standard. However, given the increasing recognition of the importance of cultural competency in the delivery of public services, all schools, even those not going through accreditation, are well served by setting the cultural competency of students as a core goal and determining how they can best meet that goal.

One way of gaining faculty agreement on the goal of building cultural competency in the public administration curriculum is through the creation of learning outcomes that are then assessed in courses across the program. Learning outcomes are statements regarding the skills, knowledge, and values or attitudes that students should possess after completing a program. That is, learning outcomes identify what the students know, can do, and value as a result of their learning experiences. Once the outcomes are established, faculty members choose means of assessing student progress on the chosen outcomes. Establishing outcomes allows programs to provide faculty with agreed-upon goals for student learning that can be incorporated across the curriculum and assessed at different points in the students' learning.

To help schools with the process of establishing and measuring learning outcomes, the Association of American Colleges and Universities (AAC&U n.d.) has developed several sample outcomes as well as rubrics for assessing them. The outcome for Intercultural Knowledge and Competence" developed by AAC&U uses the definition of intercultural knowledge as "a set of cognitive, affective and behavioral skills and characteristics that support effective and appropriate interaction in a variety of cultural contexts." While this is a broad definition, it can serve as a starting point for developing learning outcomes specifically tied to public administration programs. The rubric developed to measure progress on this outcome is presented in Table 18.1 (see page 314). Faculty must select assignments that can be used to evaluate student development in the areas of (1) cultural knowledge and self-awareness, (2) knowledge of cultural worldview frameworks, (3) empathy skills, (4) verbal and nonverbal communication skills, (5) attitude of curiosity about other cultures, and (6) an attitude of openness to other cultures (AAC&U n.d.).

ONE PROGRAM'S EXPERIENCE

It its 2007–12 Strategic Plan, Hamline University included the goal of creating a university-wide learning outcomes assessment system. As a first step, the university established university-wide learning outcomes. The outcomes cover several aspects of student learning, including cultural competency. The university-wide outcome related to this issue states: "A Hamline graduate will be able to work and create understanding across cultural differences locally, nationally and internationally" (Hamline University n.d.).

Once the university-wide outcomes were adopted, programs were asked to develop program-specific outcomes that tied to the university-wide outcomes. In creating learning outcomes for the Master's and Doctorate in Public Administration programs at Hamline University, faculty developed the following outcomes for cultural competency:

Master's level   Students demonstrate cultural competency by identifying and analyzing the multicultural dimensions to relationships within governmental entities, between government and other sectors and between government and its constituencies.

Doctoral level   Students will have improved ability to engage diverse communities and to articulate public administration concepts in a sensitive manner; *and*
Students will have an awareness of and ability to implement and administer culturally appropriate public policies.

After the learning outcomes were developed, faculty determined in which of the core courses these standards would be introduced, emphasized, or reinforced. For example, it was determined that the ideas related to the cultural competency standard for the Master's in Public Administration would be introduced in the foundations course, emphasized in human resources, ethics, organizational theory, policy analysis, and research methods courses, and reinforced across all courses in the core. Introduction to the standard means that the course lays the groundwork for understanding related knowledge, skill, and values by exposing students to the concept, its definition, and its relationship to the theory and practice of public administration. Emphasis means that the course includes considerable time spent delving more deeply into the standard with more detailed readings, classroom activities, and assignments that are an integral part of learning in the course. Finally, reinforcement indicates that the concept is incorporated into the class, building on the groundwork laid in the courses where the concept is introduced or emphasized.

Once the extent of how the standard would be incorporated into each course was determined, faculty then identified course activities that exposed students to the related skills and information as well as specific assignments in courses across the master's and doctoral curriculum that could be used in assessing student progress on the learning outcome. Examples of activities include readings, lectures, use of movies and videos, case study analysis, and role-playing, as well as bringing in community members and public servants as guest speakers. To assess student progress, faculty use such items as research papers, policy analysis memos, literature reviews, online discussions, role-playing, comprehensive exams, dissertations and proposals, and written case study analyses. Similar to the AAC&U rubric, student work is assessed as to whether it (1) reflects no or minimal cultural competency skills, (2) is approaching the standard, (3) meets the standard, or (4) is exemplary. Assessing student learning at different points across the curriculum allows faculty to determine if students are progressing in meeting the learning outcomes as they advance in their program, as well as where adjustments need to be made to correct for weaknesses in the curriculum. While individual student assignments are assessed, it is the aggregate reflection of student learning that is used to evaluate program curriculum. This is a long-term process that requires regular review and reflection on the appropriateness of the learning outcomes, the assignments that are used to assess them, and adjustments that need to be made to the curriculum if the assessments show that students are not meeting the outcomes.

FRAMEWORKS FOR CULTURAL COMPETENCY IN THE PUBLIC ADMINISTRATION CURRICULUM

Once learning outcomes around cultural competency are established, faculty must develop ways to incorporate learning activities related to these outcomes into their courses. However, an intermediate step between learning outcomes and specific course practices is the development of a general framework around cultural competency education and what it should include in the larger perspective. Developing such a framework gives faculty a base through which to connect the goals of the learning outcomes to specific course practices across the curriculum.

One place to start the work of building a framework for cultural competency education in public administration is the components proposed by Tony Carrizales in his article "Exploring Cultural Competency Within the Public Affairs Curriculum" (2010). In this article Carrizales suggests that there are four key components to cultural competency in public administration.

The first of these components is a knowledge base that helps build a normative

Table 18.1

Intercultural Knowledge and Competence Value Rubric

Definition: Intercultural Knowledge and Competence is "a set of cognitive, affective, and behavioral skills and characteristics that support effective and appropriate interaction in a variety of cultural contexts" (Bennett 2009).

Evaluators are encouraged to assign a zero to any work sample or collection of work that does not meet benchmark (cell one) level performance.

	Capstone	Milestones		Benchmark
	4	3	2	1
Knowledge (*Cultural self-awareness*)	Articulates insights into own cultural rules and biases (e.g., seeking complexity; aware of how her/his experiences have shaped these rules, and how to recognize and respond to cultural biases, resulting in a shift in self-description).	Recognizes new perspectives about own cultural rules and biases (e.g., not looking for sameness; comfortable with the complexities that new perspectives offer).	Identifies own cultural rules and biases (e.g., with a strong preference for those rules shared with own cultural group and seeks the same in others).	Shows minimal awareness of own cultural rules and biases (even those shared with own cultural group[s]) (e.g., uncomfortable with identifying possible cultural differences with others).
Knowledge (*Knowledge of cultural worldview frameworks*)	Demonstrates sophisticated understanding of the complexity of elements important to members of another culture in relation to its history, values, politics, communication styles, economy, or beliefs and practices.	Demonstrates adequate understanding of the complexity of elements important to members of another culture in relation to its history, values, politics, communication styles, economy, or beliefs and practices.	Demonstrates partial understanding of the complexity of elements important to members of another culture in relation to its history, values, politics, communication styles, economy, or beliefs and practices.	Demonstrates surface understanding of the complexity of elements important to members of another culture in relation to its history, values, politics, communication styles, economy, or beliefs and practices.

Skills (*Empathy*)	Interprets intercultural experience from the perspectives of own and more than one worldview and demonstrates ability to act in a supportive manner that recognizes the feelings of another cultural group.	Recognizes intellectual and emotional dimensions of more than one worldview and sometimes uses more than one worldview in interactions.	Identifies components of other cultural perspectives but responds in all situations with own worldview.	Views the experience of others but does so through own cultural worldview.
Skills (*Verbal and nonverbal communication*)	Articulates a complex understanding of cultural differences in verbal and nonverbal communication (e.g., demonstrates understanding of the degree to which people use physical contact while communicating in different cultures or use direct/indirect and explicit/implicit meanings) and is able to skillfully negotiate a shared understanding based on those differences.	Recognizes and participates in cultural differences in verbal and nonverbal communication and begins to negotiate a shared understanding based on those differences.	Identifies some cultural differences in verbal and nonverbal communication and is aware that misunderstandings can occur based on those differences but is still unable to negotiate a shared understanding.	Has a minimal level of understanding of cultural differences in verbal and nonverbal communication; is unable to negotiate a shared understanding.
Attitudes (*Curiosity*)	Asks complex questions about other cultures, seeks out and articulates answers to these questions that reflect multiple cultural perspectives.	Asks deeper questions about other cultures and seeks out answers to these questions.	Asks simple or surface questions about other cultures.	States minimal interest in learning more about other cultures.
Attitudes (*Openness*)	Initiates and develops interactions with culturally different others. Suspends judgment in valuing her/his interactions with culturally different others.	Begins to initiate and develop interactions with culturally different others. Begins to suspend judgment in valuing her/his interactions with culturally different others.	Expresses openness to most, if not all, interactions with culturally different others. Has difficulty suspending any judgment in her/his interactions with culturally different others, and is aware of own judgment and expresses a willingness to change.	Receptive to interacting with culturally different others. Has difficulty suspending any judgment in her/his interactions with culturally different others, but is unaware of own judgment.

Note: Table 18.1 is excerpted with permission from *Assessing Outcomes and Improving Achievement: Tips and Tools for Using Rubrics,* ed. Terrel L. Rhodes (Washington, DC: AAC&U, 2010). Copyright © 2010 by the Association of American Colleges and Universities. For more information, please contact value@aacu.org.

understanding of the role cultural competency plays in the public sector, from basic definitions of cultural competence to demographics describing communities, discussions of disparities, and examinations of legal and policy implications of cultural competency. The knowledge base of cultural competency in the curriculum, according to Carrizales, builds understanding and context around these issues. In building this knowledge base, it is important that students and practitioners look at the varying definitions of cultural competency, the various stages of getting to cultural competence, and the broad array of cultural needs within communities. This is a point where discussions of diversity and cultural competency intersect. By examining multiple levels of diversity, students can then assess the cultural competency needs of constituencies that relate to the differences across many factors. This broad context to diversity is important because discussions of cultural competency often focus solely on the issues of race and gender. However, as the introduction to this volume shows, diversity goes well beyond these two components. It is also important to look at demographics and cultural competency skills related to ethnicity, class, sexual orientation, religion, education, age, access to technology, ability, and regional differences, to name a few. Gaining this context in terms of diversity will help students understand the broader implications of cultural competency in their communities.

Carrizales's second category consists of attitude-based components, which include the ability to self-reflect as well as examine societal biases. This component ties directly to the arguments in Chapters 16 and 17 of this book. The authors of those chapters note that in the lifelong process of becoming culturally competent, the most important aspect is the ability to self-reflect and understand one's own culture and biases as well as those of the broader society. Carrizales also recommends "reflecting upon the perceptions communities have of their public administrators" (2010, 600). So doing brings to the forefront issues of trust in one's government and the accepted roles of the public sector as well as how the delivery of culturally competent services might impact these perceptions. An understanding of self and society as well as the relationship between the government and the community it serves are important factors in grounding the development of cultural competencies at both the individual and agency level.

The third component of Carrizales's model is skills-based competencies such as the hard skills of communication, program development and assessment, and the role of technology when delivering public services. Besides the tools for self-reflection, teaching tools for organizational and policy assessment and evaluation that take cultural competency into consideration are important. Rice in particular emphasizes throughout his work a need to conduct cultural audits to help organizations diagnose the present culture, look at needed modifications, and build collaborations within organizations to effect change (2004, 2007, 2010). Hard tools such as these, along with communication skills and assessments of how technology can both help and hinder in the delivery of culturally competent policies, are critical to the practice of public administration in the twenty-first century and thus should be a key aspect of cultural competency education.

The final category in Carrizales's model includes community-based components. These emphasize direct interaction and cooperation between public servants and those they serve, include finding ways to involve constituents in the development and evaluation of policies and services. Including those served in the process of developing and implementing policies can go a long way to building trust and avoiding the kinds of unintended consequences and costly mistakes that can occur when policies are developed without taking cognizance of the cultural needs of the population served. As part of an overall framework for faculty in public administration, this component ensures the connection between theory and practice by providing opportunities to connect with and learn from the communities served.

Focusing on the knowledge, attitudes, skills, and community awareness students need to bring cultural competency to the practice of public administration provides a solid base on which faculty can build a specific course curriculum around cultural competency. Also helpful to the process of developing a framework for cultural competency in the public administration curriculum is the work of Christine Clark (2002) on bringing multiculturalism to courses across disciplines. In her work Clark sets forth a model of key parameters to develop multicultural curricula. The model is designed to apply to all disciplines and can be easily adapted to public administration.

For example, Clark calls on faculty to include and emphasize the experiences of traditionally underrepresented or oppressed groups in their teaching and to make sure that the everyday lives and cultural traditions of these groups are understood. Bringing the perspective of these groups to discussions of public administration and public policy highlights the differences in cultural needs across such groups. Issues of representative bureaucracy, civic engagement, the historical development of administrative and policy systems, and civil rights are natural areas to tie in to these discussions and the roles they play in culturally competent public service delivery. While public administration faculty may feel it is not their place to provide historical, cultural, sociological, or anthropological analysis of the population in their courses, it is important for students to gain an understanding of and knowledge about the cultures of the members of the communities in which they work. This is a key first step in building cultural awareness on the path to gaining cultural competence.

Along with a call to look at the work of diverse populations, Clark also suggests relating global issues and values to local issues and responses. Doing so allows students to break out of a limited paradigm and consider broader perspectives around cultural needs and responses. Given increasing globalization and interdependence of nations, this parameter is particularly important in teaching public administration. Global policies have local implications and vice versa. Students must be able to understand these relationships and bring varying perspectives on issues to the development of policy at the local level as well as be able to function in a culturally competent manner when dealing with a broad range of governments and constituents on the local, national, and international level.

The final two parameters in Clark's model relate to students' ability to self-reflect as well as empathize with others in considering the broad impacts of policies on individuals. As noted earlier, self-reflection, or autobiographical grounding, as Clark calls it, is an important step in building cultural competency. It is not possible to understand the "other" or different cultures and our feelings toward them unless we first understand ourselves and our own cultures. Building opportunities for self-reflection and personal cultural awareness into the public administration curriculum is important. After building a better understanding of self, Clark then calls for practices that get students to think critically and creatively about issues. This is vital in helping students make the connection between the theory and practice of public administration generally and particularly in incorporating cultural competency into practice. While students might understand theory or the importance of creating and implementing culturally competent public policy, they must then be able to convert that theory into practice.

A Sample Framework

By being exposed to the various aspects of cultural competency across the public administration curriculum, students hopefully come to value considerations of cultural competency and how public systems affect those served in relation to their cultural needs. Combining elements from both Carrizales and Clark's work, a sample framework for building cultural competency into the public administration curriculum would include activities and assignments that expose students to the following:

1. Definitions of cultural competency and how it has developed within the field of public administration.
2. The historical development of public administration systems and consideration of who was or is traditionally served by such systems, including histories of oppression and discrimination on the part of the public sector.
3. Demographic information that builds context around the diversity of cultural needs and an understanding of real or potential disparities in how these needs are met.
4. Information about and interaction with a wide range of cultures.
5. Diverse and comparative perspectives and critiques of public administration, especially those from traditionally underrepresented groups.
6. Reflection on culture from both personal or autobiographical and societal perspectives.
7. Skills related to communication, cultural audits, and technical assessments that aid in the delivery of culturally competent public services.
8. Opportunities to make the connection between theory and practice in working with diverse communities in the delivery of public service.

Cultural Competency in Public Administration: Examples Across the Curriculum

Once faculty members in public administration programs establish learning outcomes for and a framework around teaching cultural competency, they must then work to develop specific learning activities and assignments. Figure 18.1 and the following discussion are intended to provide some ways that cultural competency can be incorporated across courses traditionally found in the core curriculum of master's-level programs in public administration.

Figure 18.1
Incorporating Cultural Competency Across the Public Administration Curriculum

Foundations

1. Introduction to the values of public administration.

Discussion: How does cultural competency relate to providing economical, efficient, effective, and equitable public services?

2. Introduce various definitions of cultural competency.
3. Look at demographics of constituencies.

Discussion: What does cultural competency look like in the provision of public services in your community?

4. Introduction to representative bureaucracy.
5. Have students read selected chapters and articles on cultural competency in public administration.

Reading reflection paper: How do we develop cultural competency skills in public administrators?

Organizational Theory

1. Watch the videos "True Color" and "The Fairer Sex" (*ABC Primetime*).

Discussion: Do skin color, ethnicity, and gender still make a difference in how we relate to one another and organizational behavior?

2. Do organizational leadership and decision-making structures reflect cultural competency? How could you achieve this goal? What would a culturally competent leadership or decision-making structure look like?
3. What is a welcoming workplace? What qualities does it have? How does it reflect cultural competency?
4. Cultural audits and cultural self-awareness on the part of organizations.
5. How do organizations value diversity?

Reflection paper: According to Mitchell Rice, "the culture of a public organization determines its public service orientation" (2004, 145). This being the case, what is the public service orientation of your organization? Does it reflect cultural competency? How so or how not?

Ethics

1. Making decisions in an ethically diverse world.
2. How do people from different cultures and backgrounds view the world from different ethical points of view?
3. Are there universal principles of ethics that transcend time and cultures?
4. *Research paper:* Identify a significant ethical issue in the public sector and discuss it from both the dominant U.S. perspective and that of another culture, ethic group, or country.

Research Methods

1. Read Dvora Yanow, *Constructing "Race" and "Ethnicity" in America: Category-Making in Public Policy and Administration* (Armonk, NY: M.E. Sharpe 2002).

Discussion: What are the consequences of using race to classify a diverse population and what are the policy implications of categorization?

(continued)

Figure 18.1 *(continued)*

2. How does cultural competency relate to the selection of representative samples, survey questions, and focus groups?
3. *Final project:* Create a research design. Your design must cover how cultural competency and diversity issues will be addressed in your research.

Policy Analysis
1. Use case studies related to cultural competency to evaluate public policy and the policy-making process. Sample cases include the following:
   - "Robert Little and the Kinship Foster Care Program in New York City" (Harvard Case Studies)
   - "Zoning Restrictions on Social Services for the Poor" (Harvard Case Studies)
   - "Providing Obstetrical Services for Indigent Women" (Harvard Case Studies)
   - "Making Work Pay" (Electronic Hallway)
   - "Babcock Place" (Electronic Hallway)
2. Watch *Race: The Power of an Illusion* (California Newsreel/Public Broadcasting Station).
   Online discussion: What do you see as the role of public policy in either building differences or in resolving social conflicts around differences such as race, gender, religion, ability, ethnicity, and sexual orientation?
3. Review demographics of state and community.
   Discussion: What do the demographics that reflect the income, age, gender, race, religion, sexual orientation, immigration, education level, etc., of a population, mean for creating culturally competent public policies?

Administrative Law
1. What roles does multiculturalism play in implementation and enforcement of laws and rules?
2. How are diverse populations affected by laws and rules involved in the rule-making process?

Human Resources
1. How do organizations develop the elements needed to become culturally competent?
   - valuing diversity
   - self-assessment
   - impact of cultural interaction
   - institutionalized cultural knowledge
   - adapting services and activities for a diverse workforce (Bailey 2010)
2. Representative bureaucracy and welcoming workplace.
3. Equal Employment Opportunity Commission (EEOC) and antidiscrimination law.
4. How do demographic trends and generational issues affect the workplace and workforce planning?
5. How does motivation theory apply to diverse populations?

The article "Integrating Social Equity into the Core Human Resource Management Course" by Gooden and Wooldridge (2007) provides several ideas that can be related to cultural competency as well as social equity considerations in human resources management.

Capstone
1. Read Mitchell F. Rice, ed., *Diversity and Public Administration*, 2nd ed. (Armonk, NY: M.E. Sharpe 2010).
   Paper: How do issues of diversity and cultural competency affect your work as a public administrator? What challenges are most prevalent? How does your organization deal with issues of diversity and cultural competency both internally and in service to constituents?

Miscellaneous activities and resources that fit several courses
1. Bring in guest speakers from underrepresented groups or agencies that serve diverse constituencies.
2. Use case studies and role-playing featuring underrepresented groups or examine issues of cultural competence (White 2004). The Electronic Hallway (hallway.evans.washington. edu) is a particularly good source for such cases.
3. Have students participate in internship experiences in diverse organizations or "under the supervision of agency mentors that are typically marginalized" (White 2004, 121).
4. Have students interview public administration executives and ask their views on how diversity and cultural competency affect the work environment and public service delivery (Rice 2010).

Source: Examples are derived from various readings (noted), a survey of faculty, and review of course syllabi.

FOUNDATIONS

Given it is the first course and the one where issues of cultural competency are introduced, it is particularly important to set the grounding around the issue in the foundations course. This is an opportune time to expose students to definitions of cultural competency and the role it plays in public administration. In introducing public administration values such as efficiency, effectiveness, economy, and equity, discussions can include how cultural competency is related to these values and potential trade-offs among them. Introducing students to demographic information in the foundations course also helps set the context of why cultural competency is an important consideration in the practice of public administration. In introducing the historical study and practice of public administration, diverse perspectives and critiques, particularly those from traditionally underrepresented groups, can be used to help students analyze and reflect on the incorporation of cultural competence into the field. The foundations course is also a prime place to introduce students to self-reflection on their own culture and how it shapes ideas about the delivery of public service.

Here are three specific assignments that can introduce students to issues of cultural competency in public administration:

1. Review the demographics for your community or region. Pick one group, such as people over sixty-five, immigrants from a particular region or country, those with disabilities, or the GLBT community. Working with classmates,

create a list of factors that the public sector must consider in creating cultur-ally competent policies and services for the chosen group. Consider whether current policies and services adequately meet the needs of this community.

2. Conduct a literature review of two or three scholarly articles or book chapters on cultural competency issues in public administration. Compare the argu-ments of the authors. What do they raise as the key issues around cultural competency and public sector services? What are the strengths and weaknesses of the arguments? What are the needs for further research?

3. Conduct a site visit to an agency or organization that serves diverse popula-tions, such as a public health clinic, community center, youth support pro-gram, assisted living community, or nursing home. What public policies are involved in the provision of such services? What is the public sector's role or responsibilities in ensuring that culturally competent services are provided? This assignment can also be done through guest speakers who work with diverse communities.

ORGANIZATIONAL THEORY

Classes in organizational theory, change, and leadership provide opportunities to dig more deeply into issues of cultural competency. These courses can easily be designed to emphasize issues of cultural competency in the practice of public administration. In looking at the development of organizational theory and change, management stu-dents can reflect on various cultural perspectives as they relate to organizational and leadership structures and participation models. Learning in the class might include activities that assess how organizational missions and values reflect cultural com-petency for both employees and constituents. Giving students tools and developing hard skills for conducting cultural audits within organizations, assessment of cultural competency in how the agency delivers services, and development of strategic plans to improve cultural competency both internally and externally can help students make the connection between theory and practice. Other specific assignments might include the following:

1. Consider the formal and informal rules of an organization in which you work or with which you are familiar. Are these rules inclusive of all employees? Consider factors such as age, race, ethnicity, religion, gender, education level, and sexual orientation. Would all groups be included based on the formal and informal rules or is a predominant culture reflected?

2. Review the leadership and decision-making structure of your agency or or-ganization. Is it inclusive of all employees? What does the leadership of the organization look like? Can employees at all levels and from various cultural groups see themselves reflected in the leadership of the organization? If not, what are the barriers that limit movement to leadership positions? How might they be changed?

3. Considering the increasing need to replace public sector employees, particu-larly in senior positions, as the baby boomers retire, what types of hiring,

promotion, and motivational programs will the public sector need to attract new employees? What cultural factors need to be considered to make work in the public sector attractive to a broad array of potential employees?

ETHICS

The values that drive ethics vary across cultures. Such differences have implications for how decisions and actions by public servants and policy makers are interpreted. This is important to understand in the development of policies and their implementation and enforcement strategies. Ethics courses provide the opportunity to look at the varying perspectives on what constitutes ethical behavior in the provision of public services. This can be very important in contacts with diverse populations in local communities as well as in international interactions. Students can consider if there are universal values and principles of ethics that transcend culture and how different cultures interpret values and ethics. Course activities can help students consider how race, ethnicity, age, education level, gender, religion, sexual orientation, ability, or region might affect the morals, values, and ethics of individuals and communities. Cases that reflect different cultural perspectives on ethical dilemmas are helpful in getting students to analyze ethical issues from a broader perspective than their own. Specifics assignments might include the following:

1. Review the code of ethics from your professional organization or agency. Does it reflect cultural competency in setting ethical standards of behavior for employees and professionals? Does it consider cultural competency in the ethical standards underlying service to clients or constituents?
2. Pick an ethical dilemma related to public service raised in the news at a local or national level—for example, lawmakers arrested for drunk driving or another crime, fraud by employees or clients of public agencies, exposure of conflicts of interest or leaders' personal ties to groups they regulate. Examine the case from a wide range of ethical perspectives. How might people of different genders, ages, religions, ethnicities, income levels, and so on view the ethical issues raised by the case? Has the reaction been universal?

RESEARCH METHODS

In Chapter 15 in this book, Susan T. Gooden examines in depth issues related to cultural competency in public policy research. In general, however, research methods courses provide the opportunity for students to examine how diverse cultures are incorporated in research and program evaluation, including looking at categories of data that are collected, if they reflect the diversity of communities served, and how the categories of data collected might impact interpretation of results. For example, census data have not traditionally included information on sexual orientation, making it difficult to get accurate statistics on GLBT populations, and ethnic categories often lump together into one classification populations that might be very different on many levels, such as Asians or Hispanics. These are important factors to consider in the development of research and program evaluation as well as the interpretation of results as they relate to different cultures. Cultural competency in survey design, conduct of focus groups, and sample selection are also important issues for students to consider. Other specific assignments might include the following:

1. Read a research report or program evaluation from a cultural competency perspective. Does the research reflect a dominant cultural perspective or take a variety of cultural factors into consideration? Do the data used reflect cultural diversity? If not, what might the researchers have done differently to make the work more culturally competent?
2. Design an evaluation for a program that serves a traditionally underrepresented group. What cultural factors do you need to consider? How would you gather data? What questions need to be asked to reflect whether the culture needs of the group are being served?
3. Try to locate data on various groups in your community. What is available? What is missing? What are the implications of what is or is not available for developing public policies or evaluating programs in terms of cultural competency?

POLICY PROCESS OR ANALYSIS

Policy process or analysis courses are well suited to provide an emphasis on cultural competency in public administration. From problem definition to formulation of alternatives, implementation, and evaluation, considerations of cultural competency are vital. In discussions of the public good, agenda building and what is deemed appropriate for public sector versus private sector action, who should be served and what that means for cultural competency, are vital considerations to include in deliberations. What is the role of the public sector in providing culturally competent services and what are the limits to the public sector's ability to meet the cultural needs of the communities it serves? For example, many school districts serve children who speak various languages at home. In some districts, more than a hundred different languages are represented. Can a school district provide materials in all the languages? How does it decide which ones to include and how to serve families speaking other languages? Like foundations courses, policy courses provide an excellent opportunity to discuss how cultural competency relates to values such as efficiency, economy, effectiveness, and equity. How do they complement one another and what are some potential trade-offs?

Another area where cultural competency arises is in discussions of who is involved in the policy-making process, who influences it, and which groups' opinions are considered. Do the problems identified and alternatives considered involve a broad range of players representing diverse cultures and perspectives, particularly traditionally underrepresented groups or the groups directly affected by the policies when implemented? Finally, discussions of policy evaluation might include how to evaluate the cultural competence of programs and policies. That is, how well do they meet the cultural needs of the clients they serve? Here are some specific assignments:

1. Conduct a policy analysis from a cultural competency perspective. Who is the policy designed to serve? Who was involved in shaping the policy and implementation strategies? Was the affected community able to participate in the policy-making process? Do the implementation procedures for the policy reflect the cultural needs of the groups served?
2. Review the demographics of your community, state, or region. What do the data indicate about the likely demands the public sector faces? What factors will need to be considered in order to meet those demands in a culturally competent manner?
3. Attend a local government meeting or legislative hearing and evaluate it from a cultural competency perspective. Was the meeting accessible and welcoming to the whole community? Were diverse perspectives represented and welcomed? How was information about the meeting communicated? Were the people who would be affected by the policy debated represented or involved in the discussion? Were the differing cultural needs and perspective of the individuals who would be affected by the policy considered in the debate?

ADMINISTRATIVE LAW

Administrative law courses provide a vital link to help students examine the legal and policy implications of cultural competency. That is, how are diverse populations affected by laws and rules? How are communities involved in the rule-making process and development of administrative procedures? Cultural competence in policies and programs is enhanced when the communities affected are directly involved in program development and rule making. Courses in administrative law can build discussions, examples, and analysis of rule-making and administrative procedures as they relate to including underrepresented populations affected by the rules and procedures established and thus help students make the connection between theory and practice. Some ways to bring cultural competency into such courses might include the following:

1. Examine the administrative laws and procedures guiding a program that serves traditionally underrepresented groups. Do the regulations and procedures reflect the culture of the community served?
2. Review the administrative rule-making procedures for an agency. Do the rules provide clear and easy ways for diverse populations to participate in the process? Is the process driven by the cultural norms of the predominant population? Are there ways the process could be adjusted to include broader participation of diverse groups? You might consider issues of language, access to technology, communication, location of hearings, and so on.

HUMAN RESOURCES

Courses in human resources management are another place where cultural competency can be emphasized. From discussions of welcoming workplaces, representative bureaucracy, equal employment laws, and antidiscrimination policy to motivational and generational differences, the curriculum in human resources is inherently tied to questions of cultural competency. Issues of how religion, cultural dress, flexible work hours, technology, adaptations for disabilities, implementation of the Americans with Disabilities Act, and leadership and decision-making structures affect workplace rules are just some of the questions at the core of human resources training. Changing demographic trends will be reflected in the shape of the workforce, and human resources policies will need to take these changes into consideration to ensure strong, effective, and productive workplaces in the public sector. Increasingly diverse workplaces bring with them the need to understand cultural differences and to create human resources policies that demonstrate an awareness of these differences. This is a prime opportunity to help students make the connection between theory and practice. Potential class activities might include the following:

1. Define a "welcoming workplace." What qualities and characteristics would it have? Consider factors such as age, race, ethnicity, gender, religion, disability, education level, and sexual orientation. Do you think the organization in which you work is welcoming? If so, what makes it that way? If not, what are the barriers that need to be removed?

2. According to Margo Bailey (2010), a culturally competent organization is one that values diversity, conducts self-assessments, considers the impact of cultural interaction, institutionalizes cultural knowledge, and adapts services and activities for a diverse workforce. Given these qualities, evaluate your agency or organization as to how it meets these criteria.

3. Given the demographics of your state or region, what would a representative bureaucracy look like? Does the public sector or specific agencies in it reflect the community served? What might need to be done to attract a diverse workforce given the different cultural issues that are reflected in the demographics that make up the community?

CAPSTONE

As the last course in the public administration curriculum, the capstone provides students with the opportunity to synthesize their learning across the curriculum. In particular, activities should provide the chance for students to reflect on the role cultural competency plays in the practice of public administration generally, but, more importantly, the capstone course should provide opportunities to show how the practice of cultural competency is or will be reflected in the students' work as public servants. If the faculty has been successful in incorporating cultural competency across the curriculum, considerations of the role culture plays in the practice of public administration should be second nature to students by this point. Course assignments and activities should provide faculty with a means to assess whether students can make the connection between theory and practice around cultural competency and are ready to bring considerations of cultural competency to their daily activities in the public sector. For example, students can be asked to reflect how issues of cultural competency directly affect their work as public servants, including both their current practices as well as what they see as pending demands and challenges. The reflections can look both internally at the practices within their organization as well as externally at how the agency interacts with the community it serves. Students can also be required to address cultural competency in their final capstone projects. Depending on the issue addressed, their analysis could consider how issues of cultural competence are addressed and what needs to be improved.

Assessing the assignments in the capstone as part of the learning outcomes process will help programs assess the level of success in achieving a standard of cultural competency in the program as well as determine where adjustments to the curriculum need to be made.

CONCLUSION

One of the key factors distinguishing the public from the private sector is that public agencies have a responsibility to serve the public, regardless of race, ethnicity, age, gender, ability, region, education level, sexual orientation, or religion. In order to do this in an efficient, effective, and equitable manner, public services must reflect the cultural needs of a diverse community. While continuing changes in the population mean that gaining cultural competency skills is a lifelong process, the learning cannot continue without a solid foundation upon which to grow. Building this foundation in cultural competency should be a central goal for public administration programs. In order to do this, exposure of students to the concepts and skills that allow them to bring cultural competency into practice cannot be left to the chance that they will take the right electives. Instead, public administration programs must strive to build in cultural competency across the curriculum by creating learning outcomes, a curriculum framework, and specific course activities that recognize and emphasize the importance of learning around cultural competency. Doing so helps ensure that students of public administration will bring skills and knowledge to the practice of public administration that will allow them to best serve an increasingly diverse population in a culturally competent manner.

REFERENCES

Association of American Colleges and Universities. n.d. Intercultural knowledge and competence value rubric. www.intercultural.org/documents/InterculturalKnowledge.pdf.

Atwater, Mary M. 2010. Interview: Dr. Geneva Gay: Multicultural education for all disciplines. *Science Activities* 47:160–162.

Bailey, Margo L. 2010. Cultural competency and the practice of public administration. In *Diversity and Public Administration: Theory, Issues, and Perspectives*, 2nd ed., ed. Mitchell F. Rice, 171–188. Armonk, NY: M.E. Sharpe.

Bennett, J.M. 2009. Transformative training: Designing programs for culture learning. In *Contemporary Leadership and Intercultural Competence*, ed. M.A. Moodian, 95–110. Thousand Oaks, CA: Sage.

Carrizales, Tony. 2010. Exploring cultural competency within the public affairs curriculum. *Journal of Public Affairs Education* 16(4): 593–606.

Clark, Christine. 2002. Effective multicultural curriculum transformation across disciplines. *Multicultural Perspectives* 4(3): 37–46.

Gooden, Susan T., and Blue Wooldridge. 2007. Integrating social equity into the core human resource management course. *Journal of Public Affairs Education* 13(1): 59–77.

Hamline University. n.d. University-wide outcomes. www.hamline.edu/learning-outcomes/university-outcomes.html.

Hewins-Maroney, Barbara, and Ethel Williams. 2007. Teaching diversity in public administration: A missing component? *Journal of Public Affairs Education* 13(1): 29–40.

Mule, Nick J. 2006. Equity vs. invisibility: Sexual orientation issues in social work ethics and curricula standards. *Social Work Education* 25(6): 608–622.

NASPAA. 2009. Accreditation standards for master's degree programs. www.naspaa.org/accreditation/doc/NS2009FinalVote10.16.2009.pdf.

Rice, Mitchell F. 2004. Organizational culture, social equity and diversity: Teaching public administration education in a post-modern era. *Journal of Public Affairs Education* 10(2): 143–154.

———. 2007a. A post-modern cultural competency framework for public administration and public service delivery. *International Journal of Public Sector Management* 20(7): 622–637. www.emeraldinsight.com/journals.htm?articleid=1634404.

———. 2007b. Promoting cultural competency in public administration and public service delivery: Utilizing self-assessment tools and performance measures. *Journal of Public Affairs Education* 13(1): 41–57.

———. 2010. Teaching public administration education in a postmodern era. In *Diversity and Public Administration: Theory, Issues, and Perspectives*, 2nd ed., ed. Mitchell F. Rice, 120–139. Armonk, NY: M.E. Sharpe.

Svara, James H., and James R. Brunet. 2004. Filling the skeletal pillar: Addressing social equity in introductory courses in public administration. *Journal of Public Affairs Education* 10(2): 99–109.

White, Susan. 2004. Multicultural MPA curriculum: Are we preparing culturally competent public administrators? *Journal of Public Affairs Education* 10(2): 111–123.

Part IV

Conclusions

Challenges to Cultural Competency in Public Administration

Samuel L. Brown

In spite of the recognition of cultural claims of discrimination in international and regional human rights organization, the United States limits its claims to race, national origin, and religion and insists on treating its citizens the same. From a public administration perspective, this can be seen by examining the administrative responsibility literature and its normative assumption that makes a sharp distinction between politics and administration.

This chapter evaluates the topic of cultural rights by using a relevant court case. It posits that in an attempt to move beyond the assimilationist bias of current administrative practice, the approach of Cross and her colleagues generates a new set of dangers. Cross's regime of cultural competency calls upon administrators to engage in essentialism by identity. This means that in order to determine which cultural traits are deserving of administrative consideration, a significant amount of administrative discretion is warranted. Even if a public administrator could resolve the conflicting claims over which traits are essential to a group's identity, such recognition might support the notion that groups have essences.

The chapter proceeds as follows. The first part outlines Cross's framework for cultural competency and develops a critique of the lack of progress in addressing past discrimination. The second part develops and explores the complexity of defining culture and the competing values in cultural competence. By treating certain traits as constitutive of certain identities, Cross adopts an essentialist paradigm of identity and introduces the risk of reifying particular interpretations of racial, gender, and sexual identities of others. The third part of the chapter describes the shortfall of cultural competency to address past discrimination.

Cross and colleagues (1989) provided the influential philosophical framework that has given life to the idea of cultural competency in public administration. The authors recognized that racial and ethnic bias and prejudice are still pervasive in American institutions. They also recognized that groups of color (African Americans, Asian Americans, Hispanic Americans, and Native Americans) share similar social and historical experiences that often involve forms of discrimination. In doing so, the authors argued for the development of a system of mental health care that, in particular, is culturally competent.

THE CULTURAL COMPETENCY FRAMEWORK: A BRIEF ACCOUNT

Cross and his colleagues developed a monograph titled *Towards a Culturally Competent System of Care* (volume 1) in order to provide a philosophical framework for a culturally competent child mental health delivery system. Cultural competence is postulated to involve systems, agencies, and practitioners with the capacity to respond to the unique needs of populations whose cultures are different from the mainstream American form. The formal definition provided by Cross and colleagues is as follows:

> The word culture is used because it implies the integrated pattern of human behavior that includes thoughts, communications, actions, customs, belief, values, and institutions of racial, ethnic, religious or social groups. The word competence is used because it implies having the capacity to function in a particular way: the capacity to function within the context of culturally integrated patterns of human behavior as defined by the group. (1989, 3)

Cross and his colleagues posit that culturally competent systems must contain the following five essential elements manifested at every level of an organization (policy making, administration, and practice): (1) value for diversity, (2) the capacity for cultural self-assessment, (3) awareness of the dynamics inherent in cultural interactions, (4) institutional cultural knowledge, and (5) developed adaptations to service delivery reflecting an understanding of cultural diversity.

The values and principles assumed by this model to develop culturally competent systems for children and families of color include the following:

- Acknowledgment of culture as a predominant force in shaping behaviors, values, and institutions;
- Acknowledgment and acceptance that cultural differences exist and have an impact on service delivery;
- Recognition that the thought patterns of non–Western European peoples, though different, are equally valid and influence how clients view problems and solutions. (Cross et al. 1989)

The first challenge to the cultural competency framework is the lack of a clear and operationalized definition of the term *culture*. From a philosophical perspective, the great philosopher Wittgenstein informs us that words are best understood by the work that they are asked to perform. Hence, in a Wittgensteinian sense, the use of the term *culture* in the cultural competency framework results in a "language holiday" because its contextual meaning remains unclear. Some of the literature cited in Cross alludes to an impression that at least some of the difficulties encountered by the racial groups identified are due to factors deemed to be intrinsic, such as racial inferiority, incompatible values, and cultural pathologies. Political philosopher Appiah argues that the trouble with appeals to culture under such circumstances is that they conceal rather than elucidate the issues at hand. Concerning African Americans in particular, Appiah argues:

It is not black culture that the racist disdains, but blacks. There is no conflict of visions between black and white cultures that is the source of racial discord. No amount of knowledge of the architectural achievements of Nubia Kush guarantees respect for African Americans. No African American is entitled to greater concern because he is descended from a people who created jazz or produced Toni Morrison. Culture is not the problem and it is not the solution. (1997, 36)

In short, the cultural competency framework conflates cultural identities with racial ones. The broader discourse on multiculturalism refers to this practice as the "culturalization" of group identities (Barry 2001). The implicit assumption with this line of reasoning is that a group's distinctive cultural attributes are always the source of its problems. The challenge with this assumption is that it systematically neglects any alternative cause of the group's disadvantage. In the case of African Americans, race rather than culture has been, and will continue to be for quite some time, more central to their identity and the main source of African American disadvantage. Race as a social construct provides both a vocabulary and a theoretical framework for identifying the unique experiences of racial groups in a way that a cultural construct cannot because it simply obscures the social and historical significance of race.

A second challenge to the cultural competency framework of Cross and his colleagues is the absence of a connection to contemporary political philosophy to support the values articulated as critical to effective service delivery. While this framework advocates the recognition of group differences based on group cultures, it fails to provide a philosophical rationale for such recognition. There appears to be some movement toward a rationale in the authors' discussion of the failure of certain racial groups to fully assimilate into "traditional" American culture (or melting pot) coupled with the assertion that mental health treatment theories and practices lack the cultural pluralism demanded by changing demographics (Cross et al. 1989). Beyond providing a literature review that documents support for the value assumptions of the cultural competency framework, there is no contribution to the theoretical debates among philosophers and political theorists on group-based versus individual-based claims to economic, political, and social justice.

The need for recognition has been canonized since the 1994 publication of the Canadian philosopher Charles Taylor's essay, "The Politics of Recognition." It is this essay that provides the literature with a philosophical shape and substance for the idea of recognition. Essentially, Taylor argues that the fundamental idea of equal dignity for all human beings is rooted in the liberal tradition and that this tradition gives rise to two opposing thought strands: (1) commonality and universalism and (2) difference. It is the recognition of this difference that provides a liberal basis for the cultural competency that Cross and his colleagues espouse—that is, for an acknowledgment of a group's cultural claims to distinct treatment in health care and other institutional settings.

The claims advanced by Cross and his colleagues can be categorized as communitarian since they argue for the use of culture as the central focus for building the identity of racial groups. The opposing argument to group recognition and change in terms of service delivery (mental health and other services) is the liberal tradition of neutrality and individualism. According to liberal theory, the state should not pursue the kind of cultural competency that Cross and his colleagues advocate since it should provide a neutral framework for competing interests for the common good. In other words, the state should focus its efforts on ensuring the rights of individuals to be treated equally. In this sense, equality is taken to mean sameness in terms of treatment. The result is an equality/difference dichotomy that remains unaddressed for public debate on the normative value of cultural competency.

A third challenge for the cultural competency framework is its disconnection from the philosophical and sociological roots of cultural claims. The use of culture to define groups has deep roots in German nationalism. The philosopher Johann Gottfried Herder (1744–1803) is often cited as the forefather of nineteenth-century romantic nationalism because of his views on culture (Fredrickson 2002; Taylor 1993). According to Fredrickson, Herder was "a cultural pluralist who professed respect for all people, including Africans, explicitly disavowed scientific theories of human variation, and was personally opposed to slavery and colonization" (2002, 70). Herder's argument was that each ethnic group or nation possesses a unique and natural folk soul (*volkgeist*). As such, each group presumably contains incommensurable cultural essences manifested in language, poetry, arts, and folklore. Herder further asserted that in order to preserve and nourish its *volkgeist*, cultural groups should remain in their ancestral land to capitalize on the inspiration contained therein. Ironically, it is this philosophical line of reasoning that provided the foundation for the culture-coded form of racism, partly because of the view that cosmopolitan influences were deemed to be the source of contamination of a specific culture (Fredrickson 2002).

In the early to mid-nineteenth century, the United States developed a unique form of romantic nationalism from the biological theories of racial groups. Americans tend to racialize "others" based on what are assumed to be indelible marks of inferiority or unworthy ancestry in order to justify excluding any group perceived as less than human from the rights of citizenship promised to "all men" by the Declaration of Independence. The ethos of modernism has worked quite effectively to prevent racial groups of color from assimilating into the mainstream of the social and economic fabric of America. The mythology of the "premodern" attributes of backwardness and primitiveness has been ascribed to African Americans and other groups of color to rationalize their exclusion from meaningful participation in American government and industry. The political philosopher Charles Mills argued that the United States has become a racialized society in which "Western consciousness has been imprinted with the image of blacks as the paradigm subperson—ugly, uncivilized, of inferior intelligence, prone to violence, and generally incapable of serious contribution to global culture" (1998, 67).

It was against the background of scientific racism that the famed sociologist Robert Park developed the Chicago School of Race Relations, which sought to redefine the subordinated racial groups in cultural terms as opposed to genetic traits (Steinberg 2007). In his critical review of the Chicago School of Race Relations, Steinberg provides us with an insightful perspective on the theoretical turn of this school of thought. The race relations school of thought held that education was the linchpin for racial progress for African Americans, in response to which Steinberg argues the following:

At a time when racial segregation was encoded in law and blacks were denied elementary rights of citizenship, the practitioners of intergroup relations [the Chicago School of Race Relations] preoccupied themselves with reducing group tensions. This amounts to little more than a pacification program to promote interracial understanding and cooperation, but left the racist system intact . . . the race relations industry, consisting as it did of big-hearted and well intentioned men and women striving to mitigate the scourge of bigotry, utterly failed to address the core problem: entrenched racism that pervaded all major institutions of society. (2007, 82)

Steinberg offers a brief conceptual map of the use of the concept of culture to provide moral legitimacy to black subordination. He reminds us that the cultural portrayal of Africans as heathen and uncivilized was used to justify their enslavement long before the science of racism was invented. He also connects the 1950s "cultural deprivation" school to the "culture of poverty" theorists of the 1960s and 1970s and to the underclass discourse of the 1980s. According to Steinberg, the more recent sociological cultural theory termed "oppositional culture" (102) is more left of center in that it recognizes oppression as the source of racial resistance. In short, researchers across the political spectrum have used this newer theoretical lens to shift the blame for social disparities from race discrimination to culture deprivation. By the 1990s, the concept of "rational discrimination" (102) emerged to justify the evisceration of racism as a determinant of discriminatory treatment and as a target for government intervention.

Fredrickson argues that twenty-first century racism provides a new "way of thinking about difference that reifies and essentializes culture rather than genetic endowment or in other words makes culture do the work of race" (2002, 141). The newer forms of discrimination against African Americans are justified as a "rational" response to the "culture of poverty" that plagues certain segments of the African American community. In this sense, culture serves as the equivalent of biological racism.

The fourth challenge to the cultural competency framework is its separation from the broader concept of multiculturalism. The current discourse on cultural competency fails to acknowledge its multicultural roots and as a result appears decontextualized. In the United States, the more recent history of multiculturalism can be traced to the post–World War II era. Scholars such as Walzer (1997) have argued that America's liberalism, with its assimilationist policies, has always been more tolerant of cultural diversity than many other nations. America's civic institutions were designed to acculturate immigrant populations into the dominant U.S. culture through the stages of contact, conflict, accommodation, and assimilation (Omi and Winant 1986). Unfortunately, for much of its history, the assimilation model failed to incorporate people of color as full U.S. citizens. According to Omi and Winant (1986), in an attempt to establish the moral legitimacy of U.S. global leadership, a racial liberalism emerged after World War II with the aim of integrating African Americans into U.S. society. A political philosophy of racial liberalism would serve as the overriding value system to address the persistent challenge of racial inequality in the United States.

By the mid-twentieth century, assimilationist policies had all but lost credibility among racial minorities due to the persistence of racial inequality and racial disharmony (McCarthy 1991). As a result, the civil rights and other movements evolved to challenge major civic institutions. The primary targets for change were educational institutions. Among the racial groups existed the perception that schools and colleges were organized in a way that did not reflect the nation's cultural diversity and that the philosophical underpinnings of American college and K–12 curricula rested on European foundations at the expense of other cultural and/or national contributions. Subsequently, racial minority groups demanded more control of some institutions and increased representation among teachers and faculty, staff, and administrators in others. In addition, the cultural contributions of different racial groups were advocated for inclusion into the K–12 and college and university curricula throughout the United States.

The genesis of the more recent forms of multiculturalism is rooted in the movements of the 1960s and 1970s. With support from social researchers such as Glazer and Moynihan (1963) and educators such as Baker (1973) and Banks (1973), the assimilationist structure of the American school curriculum was changed to incorporate the value of cultural diversity. The resulting policy discourses on multicultural education all included culture as the most influential variable in addressing racial inequality and racial incivility. While this was not a new variable, it was now being used in a different context. Earlier liberal scholars had focused on notions of cultural deprivation. In multiculturalism, the resiliency and other positive characteristics of unique cultures were recognized and valued. In this early form of multiculturalism, the notion of cultural competency was the element that focused on the provision of a bilingual and bicultural education. This was to include the development of competencies in the language and culture of diverse groups among students, teachers, faculty, staff, and other administrators.

The context for the philosophical framework for cultural competency can be viewed from the standpoint of the broader literature on multiculturalism. This literature provides us with an insightful critique of the "equal culture" value of the cultural competency framework. In response to Taylor's "presumption" of equal value of all cultures in his 1994 essay "The Politics of Recognition," Blum (1998) reminds us that there are dangers inherent in the logic of requiring equal value judgments of all recognized cultures. Barry details the illogical nature of such demands more precisely, his main concern with valuing cultures equally being its logical contradiction with the idea that cultures are incommensurable. According to Barry, Taylor's reasoning to support his presumption of equal respect for culture is rooted in the doctrine of romantic nationalism: "typically, romantic nationalists . . . [conclude] . . . that cultures are incommensurable, because there is no transcultural standpoint from which they could be compared" (2001, 264). Barry refers to this line of reasoning as self-refuting because "the claim of incommensurability constitutes an explicit denial of the possibility of making the sort of comparative judgment that the claim of cultural equality embodies" (264). In other words, the presumption that every culture can be regarded as a self-contained moral universe to which a measure of value can be assigned and then compared with respect to the values it realizes is counterintuitive since there is no basis for assigning an overall value for individual cultures. Blum (1998) also rejects the assumption of equal value on the basis that we lack a justification for making value comparisons between and among different cultures. It is in light of such criticisms of the equal value of all cultures' assumption of multiculturalism that we need to reexamine the same assumption of the underlying philosophy of the cultural competency framework.

As fate would have it, in a recent U.S. case, a cultural claim was made by a parent who wished to withhold traditional medical treatment from a child recently diagnosed with cancer (*State of Minnesota v. Hauser* 2009). This case provides a useful example to evaluate the utility of the cultural competency framework. The overriding issue for public administration is whether the state should value equally the cultural and religious beliefs of the parents and the peer-reviewed standards for medical practice.

In January 2009, in Minnesota, a thirteen-year-old named Daniel was diagnosed with nodular sclerosis Hodgkin's disease. A referral to an oncology specialist at a children's hospital determined that the cancer was treatable by therapies including chemotherapy and radiation. Daniel began chemotherapy on February 5, 2009, as a direct result of his mother's consent to the treatment. It was established that she was adequately informed of her rights as a parent and consented in light of the gravity and imminence of Daniel's situation.

While Daniel's cancer responded well to the first round of treatment, there were severe side effects. As a result, Daniel's parents became concerned and sought a second opinion at the Mayo Clinic. The doctors from the Mayo Clinic concurred with existing medical advice. Still concerned, Daniel's parents sought a third opinion from the University of Minnesota Medical Center, and the medical advice was once again consistent: A second round of chemotherapy was recommended.

The medical solidarity of truth in this case was that Daniel had a very good chance of a complete recovery with chemotherapy and radiation treatments. The best estimate of remission with the course of recommended treatment was an 80–95 percent chance of five years without recurrence of the cancer. The established medical opinion was that Daniel would probably not survive five years without the recommended course of treatment.

Exploring alternative options to the traditional practice of medicine, Daniel's family consulted with an osteopathic physician, who also agreed with the recommended chemotherapy. In all, Daniel had the benefit of five different medical practitioners who all agreed upon the necessary medical treatment for him. Of the five physicians, three specialized in pediatric oncology. The medical consensus seemed to be that Hodgkin's lymphoma is best treated by chemotherapy and radiation. In April, in spite of being fully informed of the traditional practice of medicine in cases of Hodgkin's lymphoma, Daniel's family declined any further chemotherapy treatment on the basis of professing a strong religious belief in the holistic medicine of a Native American healing practice known as Nemenhah. Daniel's mother, after initially consenting to a first round of chemotherapy, subsequently contended that the traditional medical treatment methods would be "stripping the soul right out of [Daniel's] body."

After two months of no follow-up treatment for Daniel's cancer, the initial treating physician wrote a letter to Brown County Family Services (BCFS) about Daniel's case. In his letter, the oncologist informed BCFS that Daniel had a 90 percent chance of survival with standard chemotherapy and radiation and that time was critical, since the survival rate would decline if the tumor were allowed to regrow and possibly develop resistance to chemotherapy. Upon receipt of this report from the primary provider in Daniel's case, BCFS intervened.

The question here is essentially what the framework of cultural competency would suggest BCFS do to resolve this case—pursue the "conventional" course of treatment recommended by the physicians or permit the parents to use an alternative treatment for Daniel consisting of high-pH water, supplements, and an organic diet of greens, some protein, and no sugars? The cultural appeal in this case is essentially that Daniel's mother professed the family to be "traditional Catholics" who also subscribe to a belief in the alternative Native American medicine of Nemenhah. She argued passionately that her son would lose his soul if forced back into chemotherapy.

RECOGNIZING CULTURE

In the case of the Hauser family, it is difficult to accept the notion that culture is a predominant force in shaping its behavior because the mother acknowledged in court that she accepted the Nemenhah practice in March 2008. While she professed to believe in alternative medicine prior to getting married and accepted the Nemenhah core belief of "do no harm" before her son was diagnosed with cancer, no further articulations of the essences of this culture were made. Her belief that both chemotherapy and radiation are forms of poison was traced to sources on the Internet.

The fact that the Hausers professed to be Catholics who also chose to adopt a cultural practice with Native American roots poses an ethical dilemma for a service provider who attempts to use the cultural competency framework of Cross and colleagues (1989). If we interpret the cultural competency requirement to acknowledge culture as a predominate force, we are left unclear about whether the concept of culture rests on an essentialist or nonessentialist foundation. Under the former, the concept of culture is "valorized" in the sense that Herder claimed that each *Volk* has a *Geist* that is uniquely suited to it. As such, the Hausers would be expected to have "ancestral ties and geographic origins" in a Native American tribe to access the inborn cultural traits to be acknowledged. In the absence of such a biological tie to this culture, the extension of certain rights or treatment based on an appeal to culture is less clear. Under the nonessentialist foundation, we are left to identify a coherent social connection between Daniel and his newly adopted Native American culture. The challenge here is that Daniel and his family admit that they are not Native Americans and hence there is no reason to believe that there is a shared history that connects him to the Nemenhah practice. In fact, given how little Daniel or his mother knew about the Nemenhahl practice, it becomes less reasonable to expect that BCFS can acknowledge and accept the cultural needs and preferences of Daniel with respect to his cancer treatment. In this particular circumstance, it seems apparent that there is an appeal to culture in defense of the practice of alternative medicine.

TOLERATING AND RESPECTING CULTURAL DIFFERENCES

The larger issue here is how public service organizations can acknowledge the "cultural identity" of clients in cases where this identity is incoherent. In Daniel's case, the appeal to culture takes on an aboriginal tone. James Tully's book *Strange Multiplicity* (1995) is quite insightful on this issue. Tully makes the case for waiving general rules for aboriginal people whenever the application of such rules is incongruent with the form and substance of their culture. Acknowledging and accepting cultural differences in this case might involve assessing the value of a practice in relation to its centrality to the culture. If the general rule in mainstream society is to treat a cancer patient with chemotherapy and radiation, then we must identify a basis upon which this rule would interfere with Daniel's ability to enjoy his culture in an unchanged form. The one dimension of his adopted Native American culture that Daniel and his mother were able to articulate is "do no harm." As it turns out, Western medicine of the American variety has its roots in the Hippocratic oath to also "do no harm." Hence there does not appear to be an ethical conflict in this case on the face of it. More generally, in cases where individuals self-identify with a Native American culture while also professing to be American Catholics, the distinguishing properties that are in need of recognition become blurred. The cultural competency framework of Cross and colleagues (1989) provides very little guidance toward resolving such dilemmas.

THE EQUAL VALUE OF CULTURES

If we apply the cultural competency framework to the case of Daniel Hauser, with his cultural claim to an aboriginal practice of alternative medicine, in an attempt to value the culture of Nemenhah equally with the "standard of care" for the practice of pediatric oncology in the State of Minnesota, we reach a major point of disagreement on the course of treatment for his medical condition. On the one hand, Daniel's mother would like to treat his cancer by "starving" it with high-pH water to make the body more alkaline, with the understanding that cancer does not survive in an alkaline environment. This alternative treatment would also involve providing Daniel with supplements and a diet of organic greens and no sugars. On the other hand, we have the medical advice of five different medical and osteopathic providers who have all diagnosed Daniel with Hodgkin's lymphoma and recommended a course of chemotherapy and possible future radiation as the standard of care. The State of Minnesota, through BCFS, quite simply cannot value these practices equally because traditional policy analysis in health is dominated by the proposition that we can resolve health-care controversies in the health-care sphere through traditional economic reasoning, given the lack of a means to compare competing cultural values.

Under classic welfare economics it is argued that the systematic rationalization of medical and health policy decision making is possible when medical services are valued and weighed against the enhancement of biological functioning so as to maximize society's collective welfare (Epstein 1999). This view has been intensively criticized and its efficacy has been challenged on the grounds of effectiveness and policy direction.

INEFFECTUAL APPLICATION OF THE RATIONAL MODEL

The traditional policy analysis approach with its emphasis on the welfare economics model and its positivist foundations is inadequate to improve policy decisions addressing the ethical dilemmas posed by cultural claims. This framework lacks the tools to analyze this problem because of its complexity. The classic welfare economics framework is designed to identify efficient solutions at the expense of fairness and human dignity. Brown (1980) has argued that such models are incapable of incorporating the full complexity of people's thoughts about health policy issues. For example, as a society we lack a consensus on how to value the benefits and harms of therapeutic intervention. There are vast differences over which benefits and harms should be factored into a cost and benefits calculation. It remains unclear how such costs and benefits should be measured and how society's competing demands for social welfare should be mediated; in other words, how do we balance the maximization of social welfare and provide the level of health care that individuals desire without regard to cost? As a result, the model envisioned by classic welfare economics is beyond our cognitive and moral reach.

MISGUIDED ANALYSIS

The traditional policy analysis approach is argued to be antiquated because it does not accurately reflect the contemporary practice of medicine. We know too little about the efficacy of medical practice and the complexity and variability of patients' illnesses to make large advances in this knowledge likely for the foreseeable future. In light of this medical uncertainty, the cognitive constraints of individual physicians, the emotional needs of individual patients, and the persistent moral disagreements about the value of medical interventions, this model is not robust enough to capture the complexities involved in the practice of medicine. Hajer and Wagenaar (2003) argue that the traditional policy analysis approach reflects a positivist worldview with a focus on empiricism. Morcol (2002) suggests that such a view has been discredited by research in the fields of quantum mechanics, chaos theory, and cognitive science. Making a similar argument, Fischer (1995) has suggested that policy analysis in general needs to take into account the new realities of science.

Notwithstanding these criticisms, traditional administrative behavior, with its positivist orientation, has long served as the lodestar for health administration in the United States. The problem with the State of Minnesota using this rational approach to administrative behavior is that it is incongruent with the cultural practice of alternative medicine that Daniel Hauser and his parents demand. The evidence in support of the claim that a scientific model is at work in the practice of medicine is quite strong in this case, given that the medical decisions are empirically based. While there may be an astonishing amount of variation in clinical practice regarding multiple diagnostic and therapeutic procedures, there is a consensus among the five medical providers in Daniel's case about the appropriateness of his diagnosis of Hodgkin's lymphoma and the therapeutic measures of chemotherapy and possibly radiation primarily because of, quite simply, the strength of the scientific evidence.

In addition to the weight of this scientific evidence in support of the recommended clinical intervention in this case, BCFS is bound to comply with established Minnesota statutory law (Minn. Stat. Section 146A.025). In this instance, the statutory requirement seems quite clear that parents must provide "necessary medical care" for a child; according to multiple Minnesota statutes, the provision of "complementary and alternative health care" is not sufficient. The Minnesota legislature also requires any case in which a child is not receiving "necessary medical care" to be reported to child welfare authorities. At the same time, the Hauser family members are entitled to their freedom of belief and due process considerations in raising their child, as provided in the U.S. Constitution. These freedoms can be curtailed only when there is a compelling state interest at stake.

In this case BCFS did not attempt to value the cultural practices equally. It sought a court order for the protection of Daniel Hauser in light of his urgent need for medical treatment. While the parents asserted their constitutional rights to freedom of religion and due process, the State of Minnesota had determined through its legislature that ensuring that children receive necessary medical care was an important state interest. When the Minnesota statute was applied to this case, it was noted that medical opinion on Daniel's diagnosis and recommended therapeutic measures was unanimous and that the matter was one of life and death. Hence, the Fifth District Court of the State of Minnesota agreed with BCFS that the state had a compelling state interest of the magnitude required to impinge upon the parents' free exercise of religion and due process rights and could order the traditional medical treatment for Daniel's cancer.

There is very little federal or state legislation in the United States that mandates the kind of culturally competent care espoused by Cross and his colleagues (1989). While the national standards for culturally and linguistically appropriate services in health care emphasize the importance of cultural competence, these standards fall short in that organizations are only mandated to provide "language access services," as opposed to the tolerance, respect, and equal value of culture espoused by cultural competency proponents. The latter forms of cultural competence are available for voluntary adoption by interested organizations.

ONE SIZE DOES NOT FIT ALL

The framework of cultural competency as developed by Cross and his colleagues (1989) is not the common solution to the challenges facing all cultural groups in the United States because its philosophical foundations are simply not strong enough to overcome the tradition of American liberalism, with its focus on abstract individualism. As such, the political and social institutions associated with American liberalism are not accustomed to differentiating citizens based on cultural demands. Under law, policy, or regulation, all persons (without regard to their social identity) are to be treated equally. Past injustices are to be addressed with the removal of barriers to full inclusion into American society; however, state policy and law are to remain blind to differences in order to avoid the dilemma of stigma among the targeted beneficiaries and backlash among the resentful. Individual rights serve as the bedrock of American law, policy, and regulation. This is essentially the reason why American laws are written to redress issues that affect individuals as opposed to groups, notwithstanding the fact that individuals are often discriminated against because of a group characteristic. The U.S. Constitution, the Civil Rights Acts of 1866, 1875, and 1964, as well as the Voting Rights Act of 1965, all use the language of *citizens* or *persons* to reinforce the tradition of liberal individualism. While other nations have developed both legal and constitutional language to protect individuals who are harmed because of group affiliation, such efforts have been vigorously opposed in the United States. Group remedies were carefully avoided with the clear intention of the U.S. Congress and with the support of the majority of the American people.

Cultural competency in public administration is essentially a group-based approach to dealing with cultural diversity. It stands in stark contrast to the American approach in both legislation and Supreme Court decisions, which both use the language of individual rights. In fact, every major civil rights case in the twentieth century was litigated based on the damage to an individual resulting from individual discrimination (e.g., *Brown v. Board of Education*, where the litigant, Oliver L. Brown challenged Kansas's school laws in the U.S. Supreme Court as an individual). It could, however, be argued that when the courts act against an individual complaint of discrimination, they enhance the rights of an entire group. The action of a public agency is almost always focused on an individual as opposed to a group.

The central question for those who advocate culturally competent public services is whether it can bring about social equity for all groups that experienced some form of unjust treatment from public organizations in the past. America faces more challenges in its treatment of racial groups in public or private institutions than it does in its treatment of cultural groups. The tradition of liberal individualism has permitted many groups—for example, Chinese Americans and Japanese Americans—to assimilate into the mainstream of American society in ways that result in what might be called "overachievement." Americans of Italian and Polish origin have complained of past discrimination but were permitted assimilation in ways that groups of color were not. The cultural issues in the United States have more to do with language and bilingual education than with larger issues of political and economic justice. There have, historically, been legislative acts passed in favor of recognizing English as an official language. Some states such as Nebraska even went so far as to ban the teaching of all foreign language; however, this extreme version of "English only" was declared unconstitutional by the U.S. Supreme Court. In these cases, the individual approach to overcoming forms of discrimination permitted certain groups to overcome the obstacles of past discrimination. In the absence of federal rights legislation to protect such groups, is it unreasonable to expect groups of color to advance economically, educationally, politically, and socially with the outlawing of discrimination?

Contrary to the U.S. experience with cultural pluralism, many groups throughout the world experience culture- or religion-based discrimination, as opposed to race-based discrimination. It is truly a group's beliefs and behaviors, and not principally their physical characteristics or ancestry, serves as the marker for the differential treatment. In fact, in most cases religion is the most significant factor in determining the hierarchical ordering of some societies.

A central question for the United States as it relates to the challenges of an increasingly multicultural society (the challenges raised by the proponents of cultural competency in public administration) is not whether it should choose a path of individual or group rights but, rather, whether it should recognize different groups as permanent and distinct members of a people entitled to self-determination or whether it expects such groups to integrate fully into the fabric of a common society. Under the assimilationist ideal, group membership is simply a private matter and hence it makes no difference in social status, the advantages or disadvantages extended, or the manner of treatment by government, civil society, or other people (Wasserstrom 1980). Under this model, cultural pluralism would have no visible expression in the institutional structure of society, and hence public institutions, political or otherwise, would treat every person the same—equal treatment.

On the contrary, if America chooses a path of recognizing distinct cultural or other groups as permanent identity-based groups, then the challenge of defining precisely what each identity entails would have to be resolved, as well as determining what corresponding rights should be extended to each group. The Canadian example of Taylor (1994) comes to mind. As a federation founded by the English and the French, Canada's anglophones and francophones are roughly parallel in political and economic power and demand such different forms of recognition that the notion of assimilation into a common citizenship is unimaginable. The Canadian Charter, therefore, defines both individual and collective rights. Hence "English Canada" can pursue certain collective goals while the Quebec government actively seeks to preserve French culture.

Cultural competency as a concept does not provide the framework needed for the United States to pursue the kind of collective goals that Canada espouses because a consistent definition of culture is lacking. The narrower definition would encompass only groups of color (African Americans, Asian Americans, Hispanic Americans, and Native Americans); the broader definition incorporates a wider range of socially salient characteristics, such as gender, sexual orientation, and religion. When the term *culture* is used in recent public administration discourse, it is usually unclear which version of the term is being employed.

A significant difficulty with the use of the cultural competency framework in the public administration discourse is the lack of attention to the racial hierarchy established during the Enlightenment period to rationalize and justify the development of modernism with its current distribution of power and wealth. The current state of economic and political affairs remains unchallenged by the efforts of cultural competency in public administration. Postmodern racialism is not simply a slogan designed to market the new method of cultural competency designed to replace previous methods of addressing race relations; it is a complex system that works effectively to maintain a long-standing racial hierarchy with two fundamental forms of injustice: political and economic.

Taylor's essay "The Politics of Recognition" (1994) serves as a broad philosophical justification of cultural competency initiatives in the public sector in that it targets injustices "rooted in social patterns of representation, interpretation and communication (e.g., cultural domination, nonrecognition, and disrespect)" (Young 1998, 52), otherwise understood as cultural. The Taylorian remedy for cultural injustice is the valorization of cultural diversity embodied in cultural or symbolic change. On the other hand, Fraser argues that "as culture-based claims increase in salience, the focus on redistribution seems to subside" (1998, 21). She makes an analytical distinction between economic and cultural injustices, while recognizing that in practice the two are inseparable, to highlight the need for a remedy to address economic injustice. To get beyond the remedy of recognition, Fraser advocates for a form of politicoeconomic restructuring to address the economic dimension of modern-day injustices: "this might involve redistributing income, reorganizing the division of labor, subjecting investment to democratic decision making, or transforming other basic economic structures" (3). Recognition and tolerance of cultural differences certainly seem more acceptable to the current system than a fundamental transformation that a redistribution of power and wealth demands. The unfortunate reality is that demands for cultural change to address what is perceived as cultural injustice will often displace demands for economic and political change.

If public administration scholars are to advocate a replacement of the prescription of state neutrality that currently guides most public organizational behavior, should the focus be on the expansion of the American equal rights tradition to include cultural rights when the quest for the civil rights of its disadvantaged groups remains elusive? Would the quest for cultural competency adequately address the persistent low status of African Americans in what the sociologist Howard Winant refers to as the "new world racial system" (2001, 306)? Winant argues that the world racial system transformed "from domination to hegemony" and that this new system serves to "maintain much of the stratification and inequality, much of the differential access to political power and voice, much of the pre-existing cultural logic of collective representation and racial hierarchy, without recourse to comprehensive coercion" (307). Winant refers to the twenty-first century as "the age of racial hegemony" (308), when racism has been detached from its perpetrators.

Cultural competency initiatives in the public sector are not the solution to the problem of unequal treatment in public service for African Americans because their shared historical experience and social status have created social, political, and economic disparities that are so grim and substantial as to serve as a case for special preferences to protect this subordinated group, and to foster the development of the type of interracial harmony needed to more fully integrate them into the mainstream of American society. The cultural competency framework does not illuminate the unique circumstances of individual cultural groups and, as a result, treats all cultural groups of color as equally disadvantaged and in need of special consideration in order to receive full and effective treatment from government, resulting in cultural justice. This framework is insufficient to strengthen Americans' commitment to democracy and social justice in a manner that would permit the nation to achieve full justice and equality for African Americans and many other groups.

REFERENCES

Appiah, Kwame Anthony. 1997. The multiculturalist misunderstanding. *New York Review of Books* (October): 44.

Bailey, Margo. 2005. Cultural competency and the practice of public administration. In *Diversity and Public Administration: Theory, Issues, and Perspectives*, ed. Mitchell F. Rice, 177–196. Armonk, NY: M.E. Sharpe.

Baker, Gwendolyn. 1973. Multicultural training for student teachers. *Journal of Teacher Education* 24: 304–306.

Banks, James, ed. 1973. *Teaching Ethnic Studies: Concepts and Strategies*. Washington, DC: National Council for the Social Studies.

Barry, Brian. 2001. *Culture and Equality*. Cambridge, UK: Polity Press.

Benavides, Abraham D., and Julie T. Hernandez. 2007. Serving diverse communities: Cultural competency. *Public Management* 89(6): 14–18.

Betancourt, Joseph R., Alexander R. Green, J. Emilio Carrillo, and Owusu Ananeh-Firempong II. 2003. Defining cultural competence: A practical framework for addressing racial/ethnic disparities in health and health care. *Public Health Reports* 118(4): 293–302.

———. 2005. Cultural competence and health care disparities: Key perspectives and trends. *Health Affairs* 24(2): 499–505.

Blum, Lawrence. 1998. Recognition, value, and equality: A critique of Charles Taylor's and Nancy Fraser's accounts of multiculturalism. In *Theorizing Multiculturalism: A Guide to the Current Debate*, ed. Cynthia Willett, 73–99. Malden, MA: Blackwell.

Boyle, David P., and Alyson Springer. 2001. Toward a cultural competence measure for social work with specific populations. *Journal of Ethnic and Cultural Diversity in Social Work* 9(3/4): 53–77.

Brach, Cindy, and Irene Fraser. 2000. Can cultural competency reduce racial and ethnic disparities? A review and conceptual model. *Medicare Care Research and Review* 57 (Supplement 1): 181–217.

Brintnall, Michael. 2008. Preparing the public service for working in the multiethnic democracies: An assessment and ideas for action. *Journal of Public Affairs Education* 14(1): 39–50.

Brown, Stephen R. 1980. *Political Subjectivity: Applications of Q-Methodology in Political Science*. New Haven, CT: Yale University Press.

Center for Effective Collaboration and Practice. 2003. How does cultural competency differ from cultural sensitivity/awareness? http://cecp.air.org/cultural/.

Cross, Terry L., Barbara J. Bazron, Karl W. Dennis, and Mareasa R. Isaacs. 1989. *Towards a Culturally Competent System of Care*, vol. 1. Washington, DC: Georgetown University Child Development Center.

De Zwart, Frank. 2005. The dilemma of recognition: Administrative categories and cultural diversity in the Netherlands: Accommodation, denial and replacement. *Acta Sociologica* 50(4): 387–399.

Epstein, Richard A. 1999. Managed care under siege. *Journal of Medicine and Philosophy* 24(5): 434–460.

Fischer, Frank. 1995. *Evaluating Public Policy*. Chicago: Nelson-Hall.

Fraser, Nancy. 1998. From redistribution to recognition? Dilemmas of justice in a "post-socialist" age. In *Theorizing Multiculturalism: A Guide to the Current Debate*, ed. Cynthia Willett, 19–49. Malden, MA: Blackwell.

Fredrickson, George M. 2002. *Racism: A Short History*. Princeton, NJ: Princeton University Press.

Frederickson, H. George. 2007. Toward a new public administration. In *Classics of Public Administration*, 6th ed., ed. Jay M. Shafritz and Albert C. Hyde. Boston: Thomson Wadsworth.

Glazer, Nathan, and Daniel Patrick Moynihan. 1963. *Ethnicity, Theory and Experience*. Cambridge, MA: Harvard University Press.

Goode, Tawara D., M. Claire Dunne, and Suzanne M. Bronheim. 2006. *The Evidence Base for Cultural and Linguistic Competency in Health Care*. The Commonwealth Fund, October. www.commonwealthfund.org/Content/Publications/Fund-Reports/2006/Oct/The-Evidence-Base-for-Cultural-and-Linguistic-Competency-in-Health-Care.aspx.

Gooden, Susan T., and Blue Wooldridge. 2007. Integrating social equity into the core of the human resource management course. *Journal of Public Affairs Education* 13(1): 59–77.

Hajer, Maarten A., and Hendrik Wagenaar. 2003. *Deliberative Policy Analysis: Understanding Governance in a Network Society*. Cambridge, UK: Cambridge University Press.

Hewins-Maroney, Barbara, and Ethel Williams. 2007. Teaching diversity in public administration: A missing component? *Journal of Public Affairs Education* 13(1): 29–40.

Johnson, Richard Greggory, and Mario A. Rivera. 2007. Refocusing graduate public affairs education: A need for diversity competencies in human resource management. *Journal of Public Affairs Education* 13(1): 15–27.

Katz, Jacob. 1980. *From Prejudice to Destruction: Anti-Semitism, 1700–1933.* Cambridge, MA: Harvard University Press.

Kellar, Elizabeth. 2005. Wanted: Language and cultural competence. *Public Management* 87(1): 6–9.

Krislov, Samuel. 1974. *Representative Bureaucracy.* Englewood, NJ: Prentice-Hall.

Lavizzo-Mourey, Risa, and Elizabeth R. Mackenzie. 1996. Cultural competence: Essential measurements of quality for managed care organizations. *Annals of Internal Medicine* 124(10): 919–921.

Lonner, Thomas D. 2007. Encouraging more culturally and linguistically competent practices in mainstream health care organizations: A survival guide for change agents. Monograph, Organizational Development and Capacity in Cultural Competence series, July. San Francisco: CompassPoint Nonprofit Services. www.compasspoint.org/sites/default/files/docs/research/494_lonnerfull.pdf.

Mayeno, Laurin Y. 2007. Multicultural organizational development: A resource for health equity. Monograph, Organizational Development and Capacity in Cultural Competence series, July. San Francisco: CompassPoint Nonprofit Services. www.compasspoint.org/sites/default/files/docs/research/495_mayenofull.pdf.

McCarthy, Cameron. 1991. Multicultural approaches to racial inequality in the United States. *Oxford Review of Education* 17(3): 301–317.

Meier, Kenneth John, and Lloyd G. Nigro. 1976. Representative bureaucracy and policy preferences. *Public Administration Review* 36 (July/August): 458–469.

Mills, Charles W. 1998. *Blackness Visible: Essays on Philosophy and Race.* Ithaca, NY: Cornell University Press.

Morcol, Goktug. 2002. *A New Mind for Policy Analysis: Toward a Post-Newtonian and Postpositivist Epistemology and Methodology.* Westport, CT: Praeger.

Moreno, Eduardo Araya. 2007. Competency-based educational models for electronic governance: Implications for inclusion and responsiveness in the public service. *Journal of Public Affairs Education* 13(1): 79–86.

National Center for Culture Competence. 2008. Checklist to facilitate the development of culturally and linguistically competent primary health care policies and structures. Excerpt from Policy Brief 1—Rationale for cultural competence in primary health care. Washington, DC. http://nccc.georgetown.edu/documents/Policy%20Brief%201%20Checklist.pdf.

Omi, Michael, and Howard Winant. 1986. *Racial Formation in the United States: From the 1960s to the 1980s.* New York: Routledge & Kegan Paul.

Riccucci, Norma. 2002. *Managing Diversity in the Public Sector Workforces.* Boulder, CO: Westview Press.

Rice, Mitchell F. 2007. Promoting cultural competency in public administration and public service delivery: Utilizing self-assessment tools and performance measures. *Journal of Public Affairs Education* 13(1): 41–57.

———. 2008. A primer for developing a public agency service ethos of cultural competency in public services programming and public services delivery. *Journal of Public Affairs Education* 14(1): 21–38.

Rivera, Mario A., and James D. Ward. 2008. Employment equity and institutional commitments to diversity: Disciplinary perspectives from public administration and public affairs education. *Journal of Public Affairs Education* 14(1): 9–20.

Satterwhite, Frank J. Omowale, and Shiree Teng. 2007. Culturally based capacity building: An approach to working in communities of color for social change. Monograph, Organizational Development and Capacity in Cultural Competence series, July. San Francisco: CompassPoint Nonprofit Services. www.compasspoint.org/sites/default/files/docs/research/496_satterwhitefull.pdf.

State of Minnesota v. Hauser. 2009. No. JV-09–068, Fifth District, May 15.

Steinberg, Stephen. 2007. *Race Relations: A Critique.* Stanford, CA: Stanford University Press.

Taylor, Charles. 1993. *Reconciling the Solitudes: Essays on Canadian Federalism and Nationalism,* ed. Guy Laforest. Montreal: McGill-Queen's University Press.

———. 1994. The politics of recognition. In *Multiculturalism: Examining the Politics of Recognition*, ed. Amy Gutmann, 25–74. Princeton, NJ: Princeton University Press.

Tully, James. 1995. *Strange Multiplicity: Constitutionalism in an Age of Diversity*. New York: Cambridge University Press.

U.S. Department of Health and Human Services. 2001. National standards for culturally and linguistically appropriate services in health care: Executive summary. OPHS, Office of Minority Health, March. Washington, DC. www.omhrc.gov/assets/pdf/checked/executive.pdf.

Walzer, Michael. 1997. *On Toleration*. New Haven, CT: Yale University Press.

Wasserstrom, Richard. 1980. *On Racism and Sexism in Philosophy and Social Issues*. Notre Dame, IN: University of Notre Dame Press.

White, Harvey L., and Mitchell F. Rice. 2005. The multiple dimensions of diversity and culture. In *Diversity and Public Administration: Theory, Issues, and Perspectives*, ed. Mitchell F. Rice. Armonk, NY: M.E. Sharpe.

Winant, Howard. 2001. *The World Is a Ghetto: Race and Democracy Since World War II*. New York: Basic Books.

Wu, Elle, and Martin Martinez. 2006. *Taking Cultural Competency from Theory to Action*. The Commonwealth Fund, October 18. www.commonwealthfund.org/Content/Publications/Fund-Reports/2006/Oct/Taking-Cultural-Competency-from-Theory-to-Action.aspx.

Wyatt-Nichol, Heather, and Kwame Badu Antwi-Boasiako. 2008. Diversity across the curriculum: Perceptions and practices. *Journal of Public Affairs Education* 14(1): 79–90.

Young, Iris Marion. 1998. Unruly categories: A critique of Nancy Frazer's dual systems theory. In *Theorizing Multiculturalism: A Guide to the Current Debate*, ed. Cynthia Willett, 50–67. Malden, MA: Blackwell.

An Assessment of the State of Cultural Competency in Public Administration

SUSAN T. GOODEN AND
KRISTEN A. NORMAN-MAJOR

Cultural competency is an important consideration in public administration and has been for some time. In the field of public administration, Mitchell Rice, Margo Bailey, and Audrey Mathews have been cultural competency pioneers. Their scholarship laid the important foundation for much of the attention cultural competency receives in public administration today, including many of the chapters contained in this edited volume. In essence, they expanded the reach of public administration beyond diversity and representative bureaucracy to emphasize also the need for cultural competency skill building within the field.

As stated in the introduction of this book, cultural competency is a fundamental characteristic of good government. Kurtz and Schrank (2007) note that measuring government is important so that we can be "sure we know how good a government is" (542). Similarly, we conclude this book by offering an assessment of cultural competency in U.S. government at all levels and identifying important remaining questions for academics and practitioners in public administration to consider. In sum, cultural competency in public administration is on the right track but needs to significantly pick up the pace.

ON THE RIGHT TRACK . . .

Cultural competency in public administration is on the right track in at least three important ways: cultural competency is valued within public administration; cultural competency is an important consideration in our Master of Public Administration accreditation process; and certain areas within public administration, particularly those involved in "life or death" public services, are leading the way.

The Value of Public Administration

Fortunately, academics and practitioners alike largely understand justifying the need for and importance of cultural competency in public administration. Cultural competency is valued within public administration. In its most basic sense, it means that public administrators serve a broad array of individuals with varying cultural norms, backgrounds, and orientations. In order to serve these individuals most effectively, public administrators need to provide culturally appropriate services. As Rice and Mathews convey in their chapter: "It appears that organizations that have effectively used the framework and lenses of cultural competency to manage the demographic changes of clients with their organizations have improved the quality and delivery of programs and services to constituents" (page 20). The value of having 911 operators available to communicate with individuals in Spanish is broadly understood. It is the implementation of the cultural competency value that becomes more contentious. Like most questions of public administration, the devil remains in the details.

The implementation of cultural competency can range from simple translation of documents or the provision of a translator in government offices to more complex matters such as adaptations for disabled individuals or incorporation of various cultural norms into public health services. Administrators must determine what the needs of their varying constituencies are and how much can be done to meet these needs in a culturally competent manner. Cultural competency is affected by the availability of resources, whether they are related to money, time, skills and attitudes of employees, the available knowledge base of cultural differences, or public support. Public administrators must decide "how much is enough" as well as what is reasonable to provide. Often these calculations do not coincide, and difficult decisions must be made about who will be served and how well.

The need to make these calculations illustrates the fact that an important challenge remains in developing performance measures for cultural competency. What is the priority of cultural competency training relative to other fiscal needs? How extensive should such client services be? What exactly does the phrase "Yes, services are available to all our clients" really mean? In particular, what do we mean by "available"? How are tensions between cultural competency and other public administration values, especially efficiency, resolved? Are there clear winners and losers over time, suggesting an entrenched (but understated) cultural hierarchy? The breadth and magnitude of offering culturally competent services vary widely. This points to a need to develop and communicate cultural competency guidelines in the administration and delivery of public services.

Within public sector agencies, the pivotal implementation of cultural competency as a high-priority value is best advanced by clear leadership from the top. To what extent do agency heads demonstrate their commitment to cultural competency? Organizations that value cultural competency reflect that in their human resources and budgetary priorities. Such organizations provide evidence of the importance of cultural competency in job descriptions, position qualifications, the hiring process, and performance appraisals. For example, does the agency recognize and reward innovative practices that result in broader and more effective services to a diverse population? It is important to assess similar questions from a budgetary perspective. Examining the budgets of organizations that value cultural competency should provide evidence of its importance. Some examples include professional development allocations to promote ongoing employee training in cultural competency and an assessment of cultural competency in the subcontracts awarded to provide services. Does the examination of an agency's budget reflect cultural competency as a high, medium, or low priority, and how is such an assessment determined?

Additionally, as Peffer cautions us in Chapter 3, cultural competency is not just an optional, altruistic undertaking. The lack of cultural competency can result in real harm for which public agencies can be held legally accountable. Agencies that neglect to give serious consideration to cultural competency concerns may choose to do so at their own peril. The legal context of the delivery of culturally competent public services needs to be carefully reviewed and understood by public administrators.

Cultural competency is clearly a value of public administration. However, the strength and magnitude of this value within public administration are not clearly understood, nor routinely assessed. Public sector organizations necessarily embrace an array of values; however, adequately advancing cultural competency as a strong public agency value requires leadership, significant human resources and budgetary investments, legal compliance, and routine evaluative assessment.

AN IMPORTANT CONSIDERATION IN THE GRADUATE CURRICULUM

Cultural competency emphasis in the public sector is clearly tied to the degree to which public administration programs educate future public servants. The accrediting body for graduate programs in public administration and public affairs, the National Association of Schools of Public Affairs and Administration (NASPAA), is a key actor, as it sets graduate educational standards that are acknowledged and valued by public administration programs and practitioners. Graduates from NASPAA-accredited MPA/MPP programs have a recognized credential that includes specific education and training in core competencies. Rubaii and Calarusse discuss three generations of NASPAA standards and the evolving role of diversity and cultural competency in each. As they note: "Under the standards adopted in 2009, a set of 'universal required competencies' has been articulated that encompasses five broad domains, one of which directly addresses cultural competence. In each of these domains, programs must adopt a set of required competencies related to the program mission and public service values" (page 234).

The inclusion of cultural competency in MPA/MPP accreditation standards elevates it to a level of importance and attention in the graduate curriculum that most likely would not otherwise exist. Like the value of cultural competency within public administration, the implementation of cultural competency education within the curriculum also raises important questions. To what extent do faculty in public administration programs have expertise in cultural competency? How is this assessed? How is cultural competency education structured and delivered? Is it concentrated in one course or is it a smaller area of focus across multiple required courses?

In order for public administrators to be able to assess the budgetary, legal, programmatic, and evaluative aspects of cultural competency in public services, considerations of cultural competence must become second nature to them in their jobs. This suggests it must be interwoven into all aspects of their education and training as public servants. Getting to this point requires that public affairs programs at all levels incorporate cultural competency skills and knowledge into courses across the curriculum and not leave the topic to select courses or electives. While several programs appear to be working toward this end, there is still much to do.

LIFE OR DEATH" PUBLIC SERVICES LEADING THE WAY

The administration of public services spans an enormous spectrum: library services, mail delivery, education, unemployment services, housing, public safety, transportation services, and tax collection, to name a few. Add to this the multiple levels of government—federal, state, and local—and the complexity of public service becomes a challenge not well understood by academics, managers, street-level bureaucrats, and individual clients alike. The value of cultural competency in public sector agencies is not evenly distributed, even in agencies that offer similar types of services. In general, public sector agencies that are involved in the delivery of public safety or "life or death" services give a higher priority to cultural competency. It is vitally important for public safety officials, such as first responders, emergency services providers, firefighters, law enforcement officers, and 911 operators to work quickly and effectively across cultures. The delivery of culturally competent public safety services facilitates more favorable client outcomes, more effective interpersonal communication, and increased service satisfaction from clients. Additionally, it decreases the likelihood of tort liability for failing to provide adequate services or appropriate treatment.

Although cultural competency is heavily stressed in public safety agencies, the magnitude of emphasis varies. For example, to what extent is cultural competency a requirement for licensure? Are educational curricular materials, including operations manuals and policies, Eurocentric or multicultural in orientation? To what extent are visual pictures or symbols used to assist with communication? To what extent is cultural competency institutionalized within the agency? Developing and applying such standards is important to ensuring the implementation of cultural competency in the delivery of public services. These types of standards should be institutionalized across a wide range of public sector functions, not just those providing emergency or public safety services.

. . . BUT NEEDING TO PICK UP THE PACE

Despite these encouraging trends, in at least as many ways, cultural competency in public administration is not quite keeping pace. Cultural competency in public administration falls short in comparison with other public-focused disciplines such as social work and public health, and our cultural competency focus in race, ethnicity, and gender has not kept pace with the current-day complexities of race and ethnicity. Areas of cultural competency such as sexual orientation and ability status occupy second-class status; and cultural competency education, training, and practice operate in a fragmented context, with minimal accountability.

Cultural Competency in Public Administration is Falling Short

In comparison to other public-focused disciplines, namely public health and social work, public administration falls short. Many of the chapters in this volume include examples from health or social service agencies. As Berry-James writes: "Cultural competency policies and programs that address disparities in health and health care are unique in that a *national standard* has been developed for health and health care to promote cultural competency care, suggest organizational mandates, and recommend organizational infrastructure" (page 183). She appropriately challenges public sector professionals at large to develop an approach to conduct assessments of cultural competency.

Regardless of whether the focus is on accreditation standards or agency practice, literature searches routinely result in articles with a focus on health-care delivery or social work. What can the field of public administration learn from these other disciplines? How can their experiences be used to strengthen our educational curriculum, practitioner training, and the overall value and emphasis given to cultural competency across our field?

Need to Broaden Cultural Competency Focus Areas

Many of the scholarly and research studies with a focus on cultural competency in public administration consider race, ethnicity, and/or gender. These remain important primary considerations of cultural competency research. However, the challenge is to advance our work to better align with the current (and anticipated future) complexities in each of these areas. In Chapter 6, Burnier challenges public administrators to think critically about gender competence: "A gender competent public administrator, then, must focus on the gender power relations that are produced and reproduced in the organization both internally and externally, with the aim of discovering who, if anyone, is being advantaged or disadvantaged by them and in what ways" (page 89).

Considerably more work remains in developing cultural competency in public administrators to work more effectively with Native Americans and tribal governments. The First Americans are often last in public sector cultural competency discussions and considerations. Compared with other minority groups, American Indians typically represent a much smaller percentage of the client population. Population size, however, does not negate public service responsibilities. Public administrators have the responsibility to deliver culturally competent public services to the public at large, including small cultural groups. This responsibility includes understanding the fundamentals of tribal sovereignty—that is, acknowledging federally recognized tribes as sovereign nations, not under state jurisdiction. Further, pan-ethnic labels, such as *Latino* or *Hispanic*, commonly used in the United States fail to capture important cultural differences within these communities. A one-size-fits-all approach in serving minority communities is not feasible, responsible, or efficient.

Sexual Orientation and Ability Status Occupy Second-Class Status

There is a dearth of research and cultural competency practices in delivering services to Lesbian, Gay, Bisexual, Transgendered (LGBT) communities and to individuals who are disabled. Keeping in mind the need for public administrators to serve multiple publics, these are two groups that receive considerably less attention in cultural competency research. Sexual orientation is not afforded the same legal status as race and gender. Policies differ considerably by state in terms of the recognition of same-sex marriage, civil unions, and same-sex partnerships. These raise important considerations of direct relevance to public administrators in all states, not just those that have more liberal policies. If a same-sex couple who are legally married in Massachusetts travel with their child to Alabama (a state that does not recognize same-sex marriages) and the child is seriously injured in an automobile accident, who makes decisions regarding this child's care (Koppelman 2005)? Public sector street-level bureaucrats will confront situations that require them to exercise appropriate cultural competency and sensitivity in their decision-making process.

Fragmented Context with Minimal Accountability

The current context of cultural competency in public administration is largely characterized by "pockets" of cultural competency. Although such efforts are useful and illustrative, our challenge as public administrators is to advance from being pocket providers of culturally competent services to universal providers of such services. There is a need to replace fragmentation with the systematic provision of cultural competent services. With all the competing demands on agency time and services, this shift is unlikely to occur without clear changes in expectations and accountability. Implementing a collective public sector cultural competency context will likely include legal rulings, executive-level leadership, and accountability measures that assess agency hiring practices, as well as the implementation of services. Although all these motivators are helpful, they can never replace the day-to-day commitment of street-level bureaucrats to operate in a culturally aware, sensitive, and competent manner.

Cultural competency is a core characteristic of good government. Without it, our ability to deliver equitable, effective, and efficient services is woefully incomplete. The result is a tier-based provision of public services, ranging from extremely accessible services for those who are in dominant cultural groups to nonaccessible services for those who are not. Importantly, these disadvantages are cumulative: the more "minority" cultural attributes one has, the less likely one is to access the full range of governmental services. As Mintzberg correctly observes: "Societies get the public services they expect" (1996, 83). Our society should fully expect the provision of culturally competent public services for all of our people. And, as public administrators, we are particularly well suited to advance this aspect of good government. It is time to pick up the pace.

REFERENCES

Koppelman, Andrew. 2005. Interstate recognition of same-sex marriages and civil unions: A handbook for judges. *University of Pennsylvania Law Review* 153: 2143–2194.

Kurtz, Marcus, and Andrew Schrank. 2007. Growth and governance: Models, measures, and mechanisms. *Journal of Politics* 69(2): 538–554.

Mintzberg, Henry. 1996. Managing government, governing management. *Harvard Business Review* (May/June).

About the Editors and Contributors

Abraham David Benavides is an associate professor in the Department of Public Administration at the University of North Texas and serves as assistant chair. He has made national presentations on a number of subjects, including local government, human resources, diversity issues, Hispanic city managers, and ethics. He has published in *State and Local Government Review, Journal of Public Affairs Education, Journal of Spanish Language Media, Journal of Public Management and Social Policy*, and *Public Personnel Management*. Dr. Benavides is on the national council for the American Society for Public Administration as a civil service commissioner for the City of Denton.

RaJade M. Berry-James is an associate professor and director of graduate programs in the School of Public and International Affairs at North Carolina State University. Her teaching and research interests revolve around social equity, program evaluation, and research methods. She earned an MPA from Kean University and PhD in public administration from Rutgers University-Newark. She received the Donald S. Stone Service Award from the American Society for Public Administration and a Certificate of Special Congressional Recognition for Outstanding Public Service to the Community from the Hon. Betty Sutton, U.S. House of Representatives (OH), for her work in cultural competence.

James Francisco Bonilla is an associate professor of conflict studies in the Hamline University School of Business. He is the founding director of the Hamline University Race, Gender & Beyond Program, a multicultural teaching faculty development program. His current research interests include diversity in outdoor and environmental organizations and assisting organizations in becoming more racially and culturally diverse. He brings to this work a quarter century's experience educating for cultural diversity.

Samuel L. Brown is an associate professor at the University of Baltimore. His current research interests are in the area of health policy and health services research. He has published in a wide range of health policy journals, including *Health Care Financing Review, Health Finance, Journal of Health and Social Policy*, and *Journal* *of Management and Social Policy.* He holds a PhD from the University of Maryland Baltimore County.

DeLysa Burnier is a professor of political science at Ohio University, where she teaches public administration and American politics. She writes about gender and public administration, interpretive policy analysis, and teaching pedagogy. She has published in many journals, including *Public Administration Review*, *Administrative Theory & Praxis*, and *Journal of Public Affairs Education.* She received her PhD from the University of Illinois at Urbana-Champaign. She is a faculty associate at the George Voinovich School of Leadership and Public Affairs and is currently director of graduate studies in political science.

Crystal Calarusse is the chief accreditation officer of the National Association of Schools of Public Affairs and Administration (NASPAA) and has responsibility for academic quality and development. She directs accreditation efforts with the Commission on Peer Review and Accreditation, a specialized accrediting body dedicated to quality assurance in professional graduate education in public administration and policy. Ms. Calarusse received her master's of public policy degree from the University of Maryland, College Park.

Parthenia Dinora is the director of research, evaluation, and program development at the Partnership for People with Disabilities at Virginia Commonwealth University. The Partnership is Virginia's University Center of Excellence in Developmental Disabilities funded by the Administration on Developmental Disabilities. Dr. Dinora has worked in the disability field for more than fifteen years, both in direct service positions and conducting multiple research and evaluation studies on disability supports and services. Her main areas of interest are self-direction in disability policy and building person-centered and family-centered disability support systems.

Frances L. Edwards is the deputy director of Mineta Transportation Institute's National Transportation Security Center of Excellence, and a professor and director of the master of public administration program at San Jose State University. She has been a director of emergency services in California for twenty-two years. Her publications include "Effective Disaster Response in Cross Border Events" in the *Journal of Contingency and Crisis Management*; two books on terrorism in the NATO Science Series; a chapter in ICMA's "Green Book on Emergency Management" (*Emergency Management: Principles and Practice for Local Government*, 2nd ed., ed. William L. Waugh Jr. and Kathleen Tierney); six monographs for MTI; chapters in professional books; and more than thirty articles.

Mark French is an openly gay elementary school principal in Minnesota who has advocated on behalf of GLBT students, families, and staff members for over twenty years. He has presented at local, state, and national conferences and has contributed to magazines, websites, and textbooks. He is completing his doctoral degree in leadership, studying the experiences of gay elementary school teachers.

Susan T. Gooden is a professor and director of graduate programs in the L. Douglas Wilder School of Government and Public Affairs and executive director of the Grace E. Harris Leadership Institute at Virginia Commonwealth University. She has published numerous scholarly articles, book chapters, and technical reports on social equity, welfare policy, and postsecondary education. She has conducted several research studies for MDRC and for other national research organizations. She teaches courses in public policy and administration, social equity and public policy analysis, research methods, and social welfare policy. She is a fellow of the National Academy of Public Administration. A native of Martinsville, Virginia, she received an AS in natural science from Patrick Henry Community College, a BA in English from Virginia Tech, and an MA in political science from Virginia Tech. She received her PhD from the Maxwell School of Citizenship and Public Affairs at Syracuse University.

Chima Imoh is the president and founder of Knowledge Economics for Africa, a nonprofit organization that attracts human resources and foreign investments into Africa. He is also the publisher of *The Jobs* magazine. He consults and manages training activities in private and nonprofit sectors, and regularly consults as joint venture facilitator for firms contemplating investments abroad. Prior to these activities, he had been on the academic staff of the engineering faculty of the University of Science and Technology, Port Harcourt, Nigeria. He was later employed by the federal government of Nigeria from 1984 to 1996. Imoh holds a master's in International Management and is a doctoral candidate in Public Policy and Administration.

Richard Greggory Johnson III, Phi Beta Kappa, is an associate professor in the public administration program at the University of San Francisco. Dr. Johnson has published five books, including *A Twenty-First Century Approach to Teaching Social Justice: Educating for Both Advocacy and Action*. He has also published many peer-reviewed journal articles. His research centers on social justice and human rights in public administration and policy, targeting issues of race, gender, sexual orientation, and social class. Dr. Johnson holds a doctorate in public administration and policy from Golden Gate University, an MS from DePaul University, and an MA from Georgetown University.

Glenda Kodaseet is a graduate student in the University of New Mexico's School of Public Administration. As a member of the Kiowa Tribe of Oklahoma, her indigenous perspectives contribute to and emphasize the role that cultural competency plays in learning environments.

Carrie D. La Tour is a graduate student at New Mexico State University (NMSU) pursuing a master's degree in public administration with a specialization in the implementation of cultural competency in federal and state policy. Her undergraduate degree is in anthropology. She is currently an instructor for the Government Department at NMSU, where she teaches classes in globalization and international political issues and is also an instructor for the New Mexico certified public managers program.

Allen N. Lewis is an associate professor at the University of Pittsburgh Department of Rehabilitation Science and Technology, School of Health and Rehabilitation Sciences in Pittsburgh. He has conducted many refereed and invited presentations regionally, nationally, and internationally. He has authored or co-authored numerous publications (refereed articles, book chapters, abstracts, proceedings, encyclopedia entries, and technical reports). He has been a principal investigator on federal grants totaling more than $3 million. Dr. Lewis has guest edited several special issues of rehabilitation journals and serves on the editorial board for the Journal of Vocational Rehabilitation and International Scholarly Research Network Journal, Rehabilitation, and is an ad hoc reviewer for the Journals of Black Psychology, Adolescent and Family Health, and Spinal Cord Medicine. Dr. Lewis has had a longstanding commitment to working in the public health and disability arena for twenty-nine years: six years as a direct service clinician; five years as a state-level program manager and administrator; seven years as a state agency and academic center research manager; and eleven years as an academic researcher, administrator, and professor.

Pamela H. Lewis was a doctoral fellow in the Department of Rehabilitation Counseling at Virginia Commonwealth University. Dr. Lewis's primary research interests are in health disparity/equity; organizational behavior and change; performance improvement and evaluation.

Leah Ann Lindeman is a research assistant and is pursuing her Master's of Art in Teaching in the School of Education at Hamline University. She brings to her work six years of experience as an organizer for health-care workers, including Tibetan, Somali, Filipino, and Latino immigrants in the San Francisco and Twin Cities area.

Audrey L. Mathews is a professor emerita of public administration at California State University, San Bernardino, and has thirty-plus years experience with local and state governments as a professor, budget director, planning commissioner, workforce investment board member, and consultant. She is a National Academy of Public Administration Fellow and wrote and edited *The Sum of the Differences: Diversity and Public Organizations* and its accompanying reader. She has published numerous articles about public finance and personnel management, economic redevelopment, organizational behavior, diversity management, and race and ethnic studies.

Lorenda A. Naylor is an assistant professor in the College of Public Affairs at the University of Baltimore. She earned a PhD in public administration from American University, an MPA degree from Kansas State University, and an MPH degree from the University of Kansas. Her research interests include social equity, maternal and child health, and public administration education.

Kristen A. Norman-Major is an associate professor, chair, and director of Public Administration programs in the School of Business at Hamline University. She earned her MPA from the University of Minnesota and a PhD in political science from Vanderbilt University. Her research focuses on social policy, particularly related to children and families. Her teaching and research emphasize issues of diversity, social equity, and cultural competency in public administration, and she is particularly interested in the pedagogy of bringing these issues to the classroom as an integral part of public administration education.

Shelly L. Peffer is an assistant professor of public administration at Long Island University, Brooklyn, where she teaches public administration and law in the graduate program. She holds a PhD from the Maxine Goodman-Levine College of Urban Studies at Cleveland State University and a JD from Cleveland Marshall at Cleveland State University. Her research interests include public administration, law and administrative theory.

Diane-Michele Prindeville is an associate professor in public administration at New Mexico State University and academic director of the New Mexico Certified Public Manager Program. She has a background in rural community development and municipal management. Dr. Prindeville combines research, teaching, and public service activities as a way of engaging students and making her academic work useful to her community. She has published in *Political Research Quarterly*, *Women and Politics*, *Journal of Latino-Latin American Studies*, *Gender & Society*, and *Social Science Journal*. Her interests include tribal politics and administration, women's leadership, and LGBT issues in public service.

Norma M. Riccucci is an award-winning author and professor of public administration at Rutgers University, Newark.

Mitchell F. Rice is a professor of political science at Texas A&M University. He is former director of the Race and Ethnic Studies Institute at Texas A&M University (1997–2004) and a Fellow of the National Academy of Public Administration, Washington, DC. He is the author or coauthor of *Diversity and Public Administration*, 2nd ed. (2010); *Public Policy and the Black Hospital* (1994); *Blacks and American Government* (1991); *Health Care Issues in Black America* (1987); and *Contemporary Public Policy Perspectives and Black Americans* (1984). Dr. Rice's twenty-five book chapters and more than 100 articles and other writings (focusing on race and ethnicity, public policy, social policy, health policy, cultural competency, and diversity) have appeared in numerous professional and scholarly journals.

Mario Rivera is Regents' Professor of Public Administration, University of New Mexico. Widely published in areas related to public ethics, especially concerning diversity and racial justice in higher education and public administration, he has been a mentor and advocate for students and faculty of color for thirty years. Dr. Rivera's advocacy work has aimed to strengthen affirmative efforts at inclusion in relation to disability, sexual orientation, and other constitutive aspects of personal identity. Former editor of the *Journal of Public Affairs Education*, he is currently senior editor of *The Innovation Journal: The Public Sector Innovation Journal* (La Revue de l'innovation).

Nadia Rubaii is an associate professor of public administration in the College of Community and Public Affairs at Binghamton University, State University of New

York. She has published, taught, and consulted with public and nonprofit organizations and professional associations on issues of diversity for more than twenty years. Her particular interests are language and cultural diversity of minority and immigrant populations in the workplace and in communities. Dr. Rubaii has been active in the National Association of Schools of Public Affairs and Administration, having chaired the Diversity Committee, the Commission on Peer Review and Accreditation, and the Task Force of Education and Training for the competency-based standards adopted in 2009, and she will assume the position of president of NASPAA in the fall of 2011.

Wallace Swan has a master's in public administration from the Humphrey Institute in Minneapolis, Minnesota, and a master's and a doctorate in public administration from Nova Southeastern University in Ft. Lauderdale, Florida. He has worked in city, county, and state government; taught as a community faculty member at Metro State University, adjunct assistant professor in political science at the University of St. Thomas, and adjunct instructor teaching public finance; and served as director of a doctoral program learning cluster at Nova Southeastern University. He is currently an adjunct professor at Hamline University in the graduate public administration program, teaching public fiscal management, and a contributing faculty member at Walden University, teaching a course called Ethics and Justice in the MPA program. He has published numerous books, chapters, articles, and professional papers.

Naomi Rae Taylor is a doctoral student and a lecturer in Hamline University's School of Education, and an associate with the Center for Excellence in Urban Teaching. Her research areas include multicultural education in P–16 curriculum, service learning, critical urban education, gender equity, critical race pedagogy, and social justice education. Naomi is a certified Qualified Administrator for the Intercultural Developmental Inventory (IDI) as an instrument to measure intercultural competency.

Felecia D. Williams is an associate professor of political science in the History/Political Science Department at Virginia Union University. Her research interests include internationalization of college and university campuses, disparity issues, and issues affecting urban populations. She teaches courses in American government, research methods, comparative politics, urban and metropolitan politics, and public administration. Prior to her current academic appointment, she taught as an adjunct at the University of Richmond, Virginia State University, and Piedmont Virginia Community College, where she was selected as a Virginia Council for International Education faculty delegate to the United Kingdom. She earned her PhD from Virginia Commonwealth University and her MPA from the University of Virginia.

Heather Wyatt-Nichol is an assistant professor in the College of Public Affairs at the University of Baltimore. She earned a PhD in public policy and administration from Virginia Commonwealth University and an MPA degree from Old Dominion University. She has published book chapters and articles on a variety of topics in public administration and feminist journals. Her research interests include diversity management, ethics, family-friendly workplace policies, organizational behavior, and social equity.

Index

CPSIA information can be obtained
at www.ICGtesting.com
Printed in the USA
/04n2035210417
/FS

9 780765 626776